NOT FOR KING OR COUNTRY

Edward Cecil-Smith, the Communist Party of Canada, and the Spanish Civil War

Not for King or Country tells the story of Edward Cecil-Smith, a dynamic propagandist for the Communist Party of Canada during the Great Depression. Born to missionary parents in China in 1903, Cecil-Smith came to Toronto in 1919, where he joined the Canadian militia and lived a happy life ensconced in the Protestant missionary community. He became increasingly interested in radical politics during the 1920s, eventually joining the Communist Party in 1931. Worried by the growing strength of fascism around the world, particularly in China, Germany, Italy, and Spain, Cecil-Smith quietly departed Canada in early 1937 and became among the first volunteers to fight for the Republic in the Spanish Civil War. Cecil-Smith was motivated to fight not out of any sense of traditional patriotism ("for king or country") but rather by the conviction that the onward march of fascism had to be stopped and Spain was where the line had to be drawn.

Not for King or Country is the first biography of a Canadian commander in the Spanish Civil War and the first book to critically analyse the major battles fought in by Canadian and American volunteers. Drawing upon declassified RCMP files, records held in Russian state archives, audio recordings of the volunteers, a detailed survey of maps and battle records, and the Communist Party press, *Not for King or Country* breaks down the battles and the Party's activities in a way that will be accessible to interested readers and scholars alike.

TYLER WENTZELL is an independent scholar based in Toronto. He is a Canadian infantry officer and a graduate of the Royal Military College of Canada and the University of Toronto Faculty of Law. This is his first book.

Not for King or Country

Edward Cecil-Smith, the Communist Party of Canada, and the Spanish Civil War

TYLER WENTZELL

UNIVERSITY OF TORONTO PRESS
Toronto Buffalo London

Toronto Buffalo London
utorontopress.com
Printed in Canada

ISBN 978-1-4875-0379-6 (cloth)
ISBN 978-1-4875-2288-9 (paper)
ISBN 978-1-4875-1879-0 (EPUB)
ISBN 978-1-4875-1878-3 (PDF)

Library and Archives Canada Cataloguing in Publication

Title: Not for King or country : Edward Cecil-Smith, the Communist Party of Canada, and the Spanish Civil War / Tyler Wentzell.
Names: Wentzell, Tyler, 1983– author.
Description: Includes bibliographical references and index.
Identifiers: Canadiana 2019019166X | ISBN 9781487503796 (hardcover) | ISBN 9781487522889 (softcover)
Subjects: LCSH: Cecil-Smith, E. (Edward) | LCSH: Communists – Canada – Biography. | LCSH: Soldiers – Canada – Biography. | LCSH: Soldiers – Spain – Biography. | LCSH: Spain. Ejército Popular de la República. MacKenzie-Papineau Battalion – Biography. | LCSH: Spain – History – Civil War, 1936–1939 – Participation, Canadian. | CSH: Canada – Social life and customs – 1918–1945.
Classification: LCC DP269.47.C2 W46 2019 | DDC 946.081/42092—dc23

University of Toronto Press acknowledges the financial assistance to its publishing program of the Canada Council for the Arts and the Ontario Arts Council, an agency of the Government of Ontario.

Canada Council for the Arts
Conseil des Arts du Canada

ONTARIO ARTS COUNCIL
CONSEIL DES ARTS DE L'ONTARIO
an Ontario government agency
un organisme du gouvernement de l'Ontario

Funded by the Government of Canada
Financé par le gouvernement du Canada
Canada

MIX
Paper from responsible sources
FSC® C016245

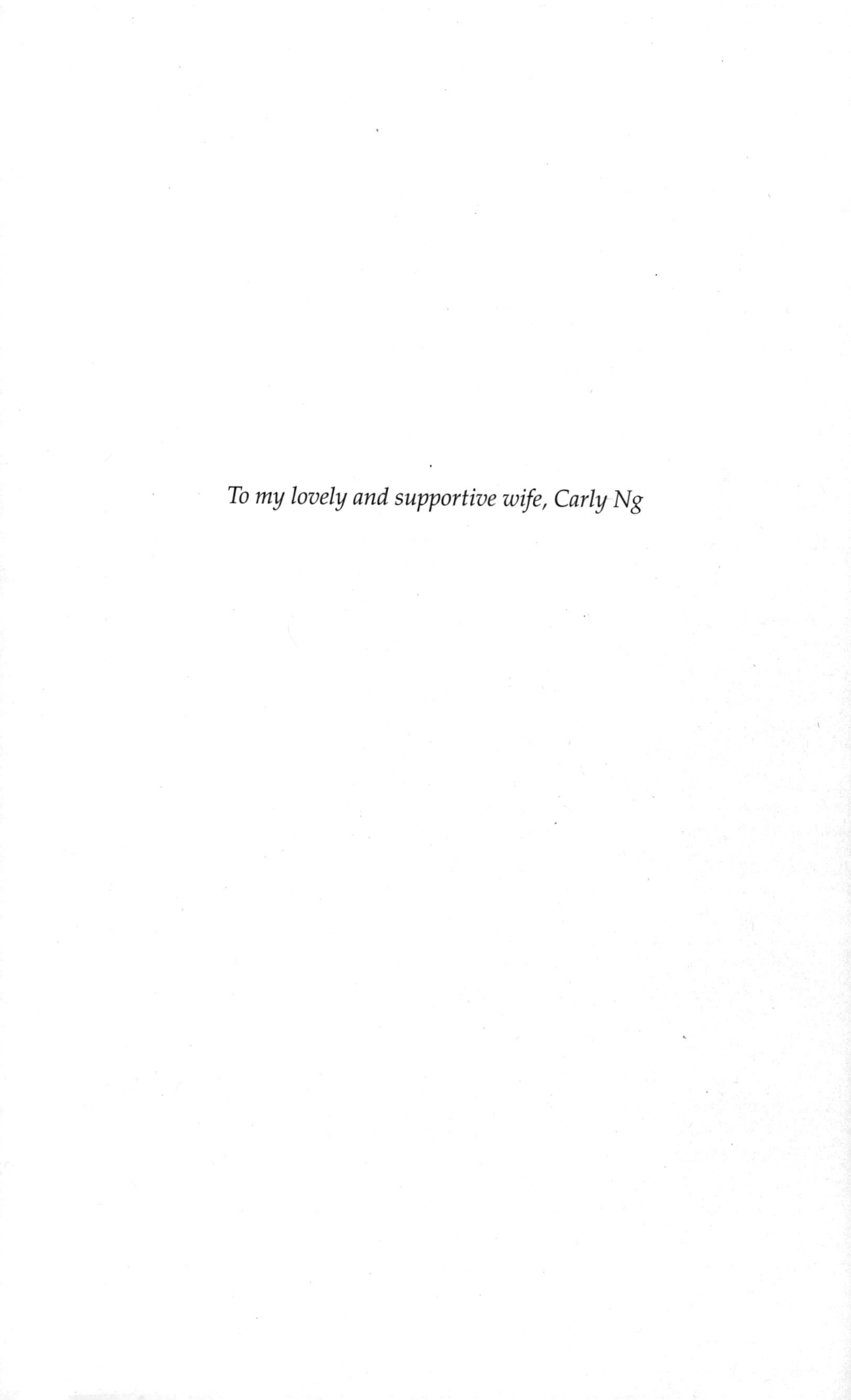

To my lovely and supportive wife, Carly Ng

Contents

Acknowledgments ix

Maps xi

Introduction 3

Part One: A Son of the Empire (1903–1931)

1 An Idyllic Youth 9
2 Radicalization 19

Part Two: A Canadian Communist (1931–1936)

3 Joining the Party 31
4 "Theatre – Our Weapon" 42
5 Art, Propaganda, and the Popular Front 59
6 Defend the Soviet Union! 74

Part Three: A Volunteer for Spain (1936–1938)

7 *"No Pasaran!"* 93
8 *Los Norteamericanos* 108
9 The Fighting Canucks 133
10 The Defence of Teruel 145
11 The Retreats 156
12 Crossing the Ebro 168

Part Four: A Dedicated Anti-Fascist (1938–1942)

13 Coming Home 183
14 A Second Anti-Fascist War 211

Conclusion 227

Notes 231

Bibliography 311

Index 325

Photo section follows page 152

Acknowledgments

The list of people to thank for their help on this project is long and distinguished. I am sure that there will be many people that I fail to include in the following acknowledgements, so let me begin with a blanket thank you. Thank you to the scholars, researchers, writers, friends, and family members who have assisted me every step of the way. Thank you for sharing your research, discussing ideas, and reviewing the manuscript. I am particularly indebted to Len Husband, the editorial staff, and the two anonymous reviewers at the University of Toronto Press. Any errors or omissions in this work are my own.

Thank you to my friends and family who have shared in this endeavour, especially my wife, Carly Ng. You were always so supportive as I shared every odd fact and detail of my research, even though I know I must have been absolutely insufferable. Thank you. Thank you to Andy Belyea, my friend and professor, for his encouragement and extensive editorial assistance. Thank you to Christie Kong, who reviewed the embarrassingly rough first drafts of the manuscript. Thank you to Finnegan Wentzell for always listening.

Thank you to Bill Smith, son of Edward Cecil-Smith, for sharing your memories of your father with me. We rarely saw eye to eye on politics, but I appreciate your perspective and am grateful that it never conflicted with our shared desire to tell your father's story. Thank you to James Reamey of the London Free Press for introducing us.

I could not have written this book without the assistance of the incredible writers and scholars who helped and advised me. I was fortunate to tap into the small but passionate "Mac-Pap family," including Michael Petrou, Myron Momryk, Mark Zuehlke, John Peter Kraljic, Chris Brooks, Ray Hoff, Janette Higgins, and the members of the Mackenzie-Papineau Battalion Facebook group. Thank you for sharing your research and offering your insight. Professors Alan Filewod of Guelph University, Larry Hannant formerly of Camosun College, Greg Kealey of the University of New Brunswick, Yan Li of the University of Waterloo, Dave Macri of Hong Kong University, Ian McKay of McMaster University, Heather Murray of the University of Toronto, Kirk Niergarth of Mount Royal University, Bryan Palmer of Trent University, and Bart Vautour of Dalhousie University all generously shared their time and expertise. Of these, I must especially thank Ian McKay, for his extensive feedback on an early version of the manuscript, and Kirk Niergarth, for his support and making so many introductions. Thank you to William Kaplan for sharing your research on the Canadian Seamen's Union. Thank you to Jack Granatstein for your encouragement and notes on the manuscript. Thank you to Chris Moore for all of your coaching. Thank you to Madame Adrienne Clarkson, Brian Stewart, and Steve Otto for all of your encouragement.

Many thanks are owed to the research staff of a range of public and private institutions. In no particular order, the following individuals were especially helpful: Ian Grant and Alvyn Austin of the Chefoo Schools Association, Caese Levo from the Anglican Diocese of Toronto Archives, Anita Hayes from the Overseas Mission Force, Davorin Cikovic from the CBC Radio Archives, Donna Bernardo-Ceriz from the Ontario Jewish Archives, and Tom Reid of the Thomas Fisher Rare Books Library at the University of Toronto. Thank you to the entire staff at Library and Archives Canada, the Toronto Reference Library, and the Thomas Fisher Rare Books Library for all of your hard work in making research like this possible.

Lastly, I must thank the mentors who gave me the encouragement I needed to start this project in the first place. Doug Delaney, of the Royal Military College of Canada, has encouraged me to research and write since I was a second-year cadet. He was the first person to suggest to me that there was a book worth writing about Cecil-Smith, and, moreover, that I was actually capable of writing it. Jim Phillips, of the University of Toronto, has been a wonderful mentor to me since the first year of law school. This book was supposed to be a paragraph for a paper I wrote for you in second year. I may have overdone it ... I must also thank Kevin Murphy, of Sackville High School. I have not seen you in years, but should we meet again or a copy of this book cross your desk, I want you to know that your skill and passion as a history teacher has had a lasting impact on me.

Maps

Map 1 China in the early twentieth century, showing key locations of Cecil-Smith and his family, the route of the 1934–35 Long March, and the approximate location of Norman Bethune's death.

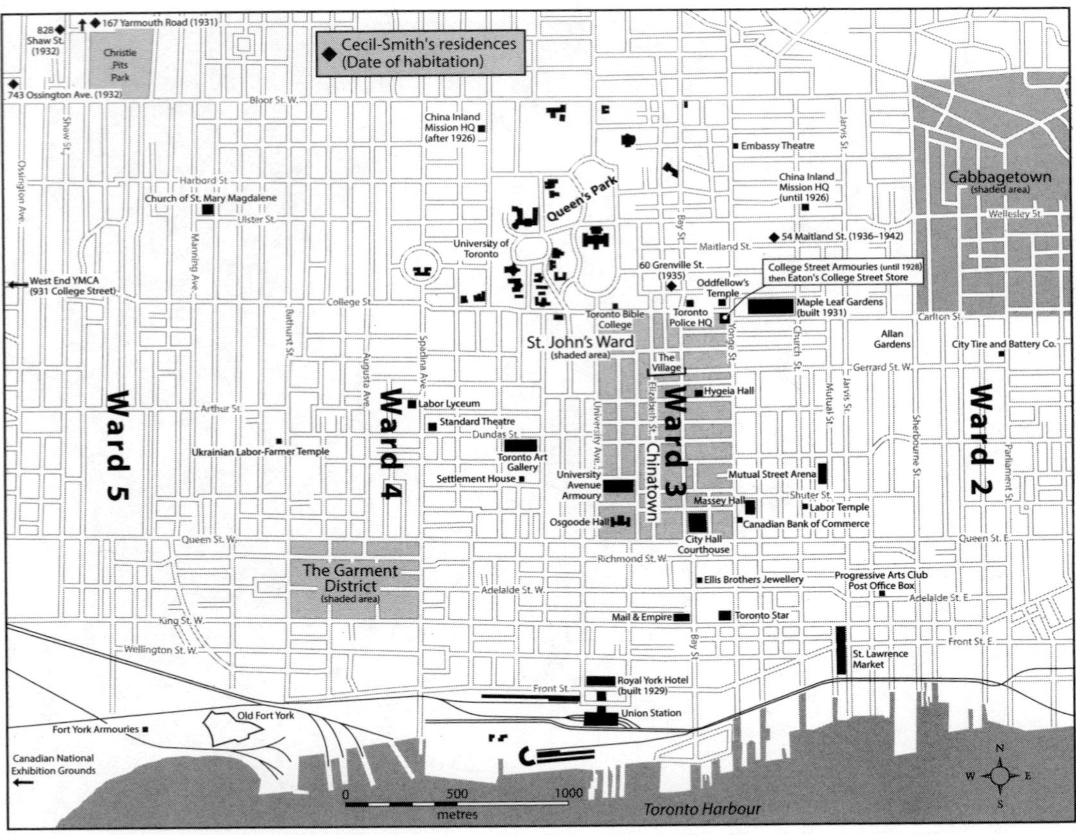

Map 2 Toronto in the 1920s and 1930s, with Cecil-Smith's places of residence.

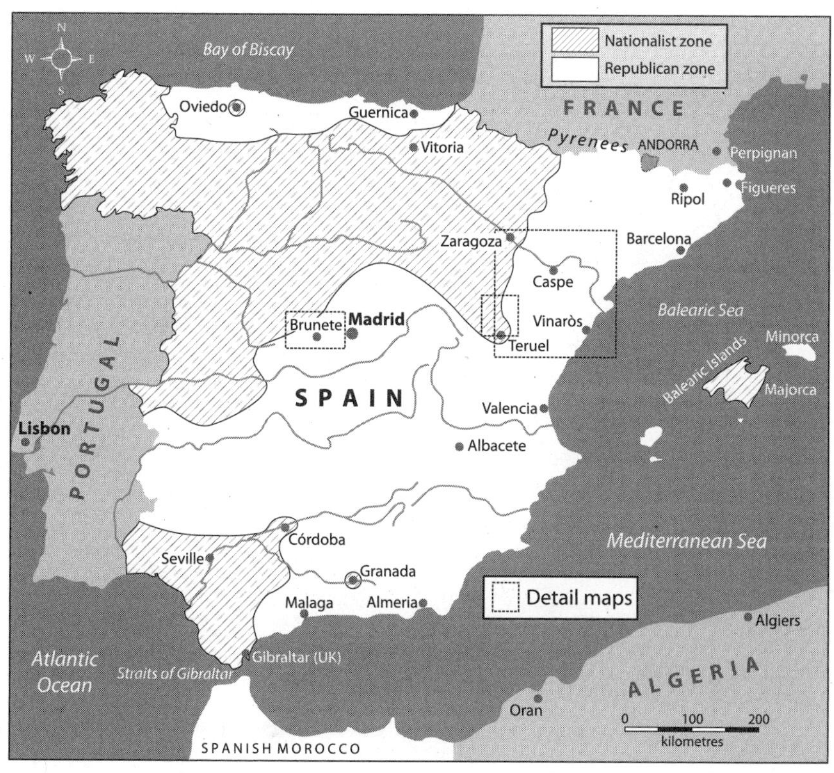

Map 3 Spain, July 1936.

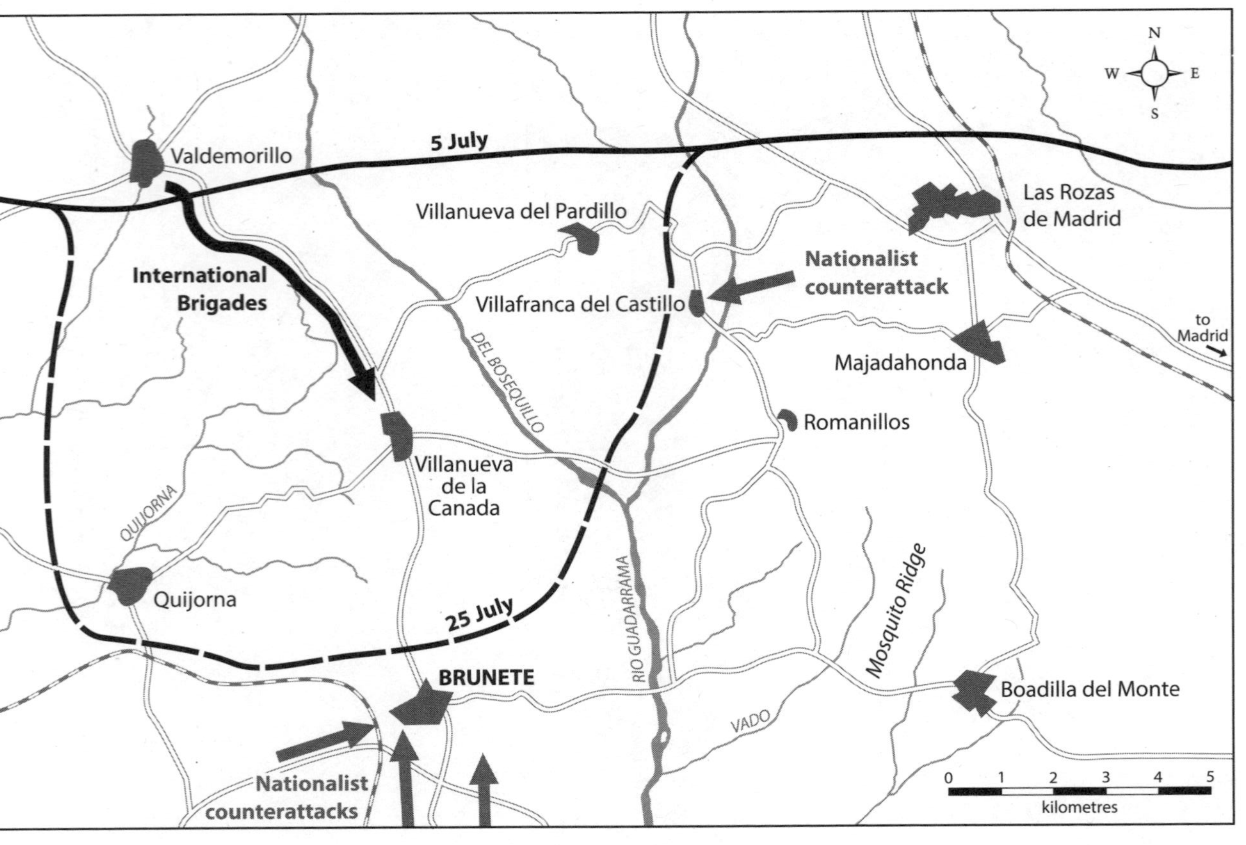

Map 4 Battle of Brunete, detail, July 1937.

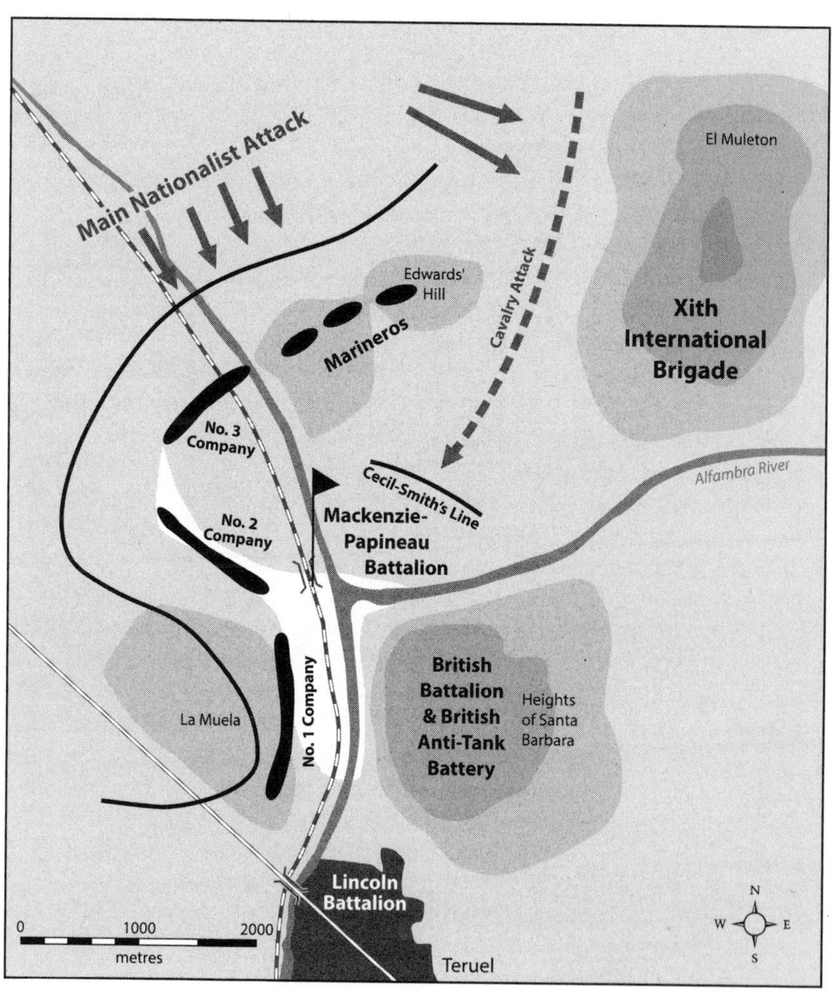

Map 5 Defence of Teruel, detail, January 1938.

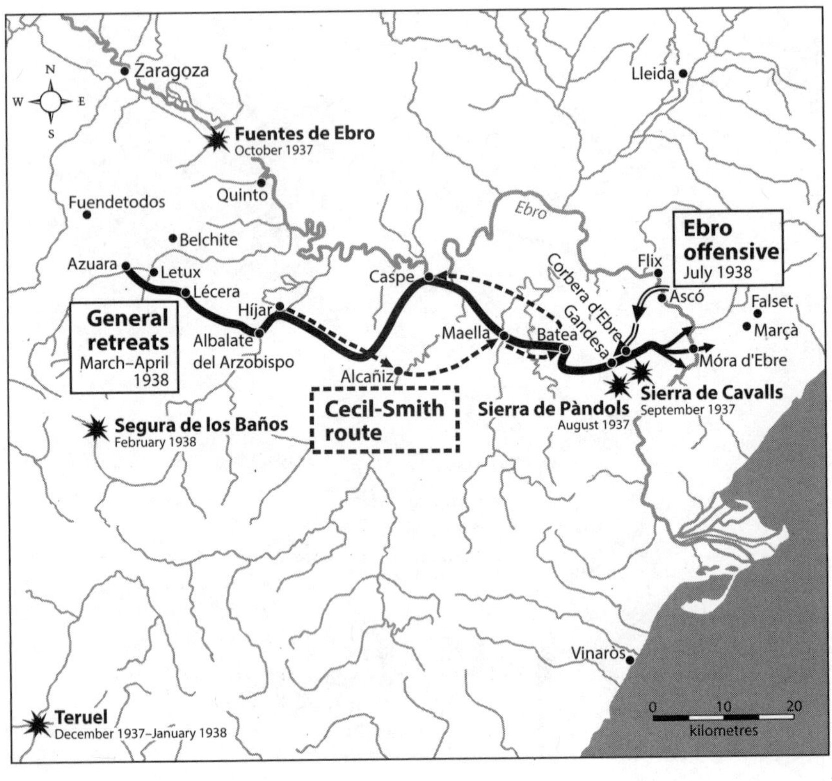

Map 6 The Retreats and Ebro Offensive detail, March–September 1938.

NOT FOR KING OR COUNTRY

Edward Cecil-Smith, the Communist Party of Canada, and the Spanish Civil War

Introduction

On 4 February 1939, Edward Cecil-Smith stood on a balcony overlooking a welcoming crowd in Toronto's Union Station. When he had last been in this building, two years earlier, he had boarded a train to New York, leaving quietly and without fanfare so as to avoid the attention of the police. It had been the first step in a journey to the battlefields of Spain. Now, a veteran of that conflict, he stood before his fellow volunteers and more than 10,000 well-wishers who had gathered to greet them. He did not wear the uniform of a returning soldier but rather the poorly fitting civilian clothes of a Spanish soldier who had been killed in the war, a gift from the Republican government. The crowds cheered and the band played patriotic songs. Cecil-Smith addressed the gathering, telling them that "Spain is not licked," that the Republic of Spain, for which the volunteers had fought, would still triumph over the fascists. He warned his fellow volunteers not to expect any assistance from the Canadian government. Instead, they could expect assistance from the divine, for they had provided a great service to humanity. And he cautioned his audience that a wider war in Europe was coming.[1]

This book is a biography of Cecil-Smith, but my interest was not originally in the man himself. This study grew from a simple question: why did Canadian volunteers fight in Spain? Why did nearly 1,700 Canadians, among perhaps 45,000 non-Spaniards, leave their homes to fight in a war in which their country was not a party? The traditional refrain of "for king and country" was clearly an inadequate explanation. As commander of the Mackenzie-Papineau Battalion, the nominally Canadian unit within the International Brigades, Cecil-Smith seemed like an appropriate case study, a good place to start my investigation. I learned, however, that he was not the archetypical volunteer, either in comparison to the common assumptions about the volunteers or the data compiled by historian Michael Petrou.[2]

Cecil-Smith was not a drifter. He was not unemployed. He was not unattached. He was not an adventurer. He was an educated, thoughtful, employed, bookish, married man who described himself as a pacifist. Upon learning that Cecil-Smith was fighting in Spain, one colleague wrote that it seemed no more incongruous than "a debutante in a dainty light evening gown playing tag with a ferocious tiger."[3] So why did he go? The answer is neither short nor pithy. Cecil-Smith was drawn to the Republican cause for a number of reasons.

Cecil-Smith saw great injustices in Canadian society in the late 1920s and throughout the 1930s. Born to a missionary family in China in 1903, he came to Canada in 1919 and began his political career as a fairly standard representative of Toronto's white, Anglo-Saxon Protestant middle class. Yet he came to believe that capitalism was an inherently evil system and turned to communism, made manifest in the Soviet Union and championed in Canada by the Communist Party of Canada, as the solution to the social and economic problems facing Canadians in the interwar period. He was a leading light in many of the party's major front organizations: the Progressive Arts Club, the Canadian Labor Defense League,* and the Friends of the Soviet Union. He wrote, directed, and acted in a play, *Eight Men Speak*, which was banned after one performance, and wrote for and edited party newspapers and magazines, including the *Worker*, the *Daily Clarion*, the *Labor Defender*, *Soviet Russia Today*, and *Masses*. Although he was never a member of the party's inner circles, he was a prolific writer and organizer for the party.

When the Spanish Civil War erupted in the summer of 1936, Cecil-Smith was drawn to the Republican cause. As a practical matter, he had served in the militia in Canada and Shanghai, and felt that he could make a meaningful contribution to the war effort. He also saw what was happening in Spain as part of a worldwide conflict between ideologies. In Spain, a fascist uprising was destroying a democratically elected government. That uprising was heavily supported by Nazi Germany and Fascist Italy. However, it would be a mistake to view Cecil-Smith's actions as being strictly in the cause of democracy. He yearned for revolution and the imposition of the dictatorship of the proletariat, and such hopes flamed his desire to fight fascism. Spain provided him with the battlefield where he could do so.

Considering the breadth of Cecil-Smith's activity – from commanding a battalion in Spain to playing a leading role in nearly every party front organization of the interwar years – his absence from existing scholarship seems unusual. He is mentioned in various histories of the Spanish Civil War, but

---

* Contrary to current practice in Canadian English, "labour" was, at the time, often spelled without a "u." I use the current spelling in the narrative but preserve the spelling used in contemporary quotations and in the names of periodicals or organizations. Similarly, although the word "defence" was generally spelled with a "c" in Canada, the Canadian Labor Defense League consistently spelled the word with an "s."

not in any particularly depth. He is also mentioned in the histories of the radical theatre, but mostly for his writings and not for his actions or background. His closest brush with fame in the secondary literature is a brief mention of his return from Spain in Pierre Berton's *The Great Depression*.[4]

There are a few possible explanations for Cecil-Smith's absence from the historical record. First, he was argumentative and not always good at following orders, which meant that he was never admitted to the party's pantheon of heroes and thus was rendered more or less invisible. Second, he never told his own story. He gave interviews, wrote articles, and drafted the beginnings of a history of the Mackenzie-Papineau Battalion, in which he consistently singled out the courage of individuals under his command. He rarely provided details of his own exploits. Third, the history of Canadians in the Spanish Civil War is deeply grounded in oral history, specifically in a series of Canadian Broadcasting Corporation interviews conducted in the 1960s. Cecil-Smith was already dead when these interviews were conducted. Consequently, his story has been largely left out of what little has been written about the Canadians in Spain. Fourth, it is easy to forget about lost causes: the revolution that Cecil-Smith desired never transpired, and the Republic lost the civil war.

What has been written about Cecil-Smith is often confusing or misleading. Take, for instance, the seemingly simple issue of his military service before the Spanish Civil War. Arthur Landis, the author of *The Abraham Lincoln Brigade*, wrote at one point that Cecil-Smith had been a member of the Princess Patricia's Canadian Light Infantry (PPCLI), a Permanent Force infantry regiment, and at another that he had been a "regimental officer of engineers."[5] Both statements are incorrect. Victor Hoar, the first Canadian writer on the subject of Canadians in the Spanish Civil War, wrote that a contemporaneous document, *The Book of the XVth Brigade*, incorrectly claimed that Cecil-Smith was a member of the PPCLI.[6] This statement is perplexing, given that that volume correctly stated that Cecil-Smith had served with the Royal Canadian Engineers.[7] More recently, Mark Zuehlke wrote that Cecil-Smith had been an officer in the Canadian Army, which is also not correct: Cecil-Smith had been a senior non-commissioned officer.[8]

There is also a recurring claim that Cecil-Smith fought somewhere in South America in the years leading up to the Spanish Civil War. Tim Buck, the general secretary of the Communist Party of Canada, recalled that Cecil-Smith had been involved as a guerrilla in South America, where he had gained considerable experience in "the military side of revolt" and "off the cuff" warfare.[9] This claim has been cited with authority, despite a lack of any other substantiating evidence. The *Canadian Encyclopedia*, for instance, states that Cecil-Smith was "a former adventurer in South America."[10] However, these supposed adventures likely did not happen.

They are not mentioned in Cecil-Smith's own writings, contemporary records, or his various service files. He never spoke of such adventures to his son, not even as much as a vacation in Latin America.[11] Nonetheless, it is impossible to prove definitively that they did not happen. Should evidence to the contrary become available, it would no doubt reveal a fascinating chapter in both Cecil-Smith's life and likely the broader relationship between Canada and Latin America in the 1920s and 1930s.

This book is the first biographical treatment of Cecil-Smith. It will principally follow his life chronologically, with slight deviations along the way to accommodate the variety of his political activities. It begins with a description of his unusual childhood as the son of missionary parents in the heart of southwestern China and his move to Toronto in 1919 at the age of seventeen. By 1931, he was a card-carrying member of the Communist Party of Canada. Party politics between 1934 and 1936 – the transition years from the militant Third Period (1928–1934/35)* and the more inclusive Popular Front (1935–39) – were complicated and require a deviation from the chronology. These years have been split into thematically driven chapters – chapters 4, 5, and 6. Chapter 7 returns to the chronology, with Cecil-Smith's decision to volunteer in Spain.

Cecil-Smith was both a man of his times and someone quite extraordinary. He elicits mixed reactions. Some see him as a hero; others a villain. Some see him as a dupe; others as a passionate freethinker. In my opinion, he does not fall into a tidy category – I do not think many of us do. It is important to approach the subject with some political agnosticism and a detached historical sensibility. Although it is important not to forget what we know about the Cold War, the Second World War, the gulags, and the Soviet Union under Joseph Stalin, it is also important to frame these histories in richer terms. Cecil-Smith did not have the benefit of such hindsight. The entrenchment of global capitalism and democracy today seems more or less to have rendered fascism, anarchism, and communism, in various forms, as failed experiments or dead-end ideas. But, in the interwar years, these ideas were debated as viable solutions to the social, economic, political, and even cultural crises of the day. Cecil-Smith had imperfect information and believed the stories of success coming out of the Soviet Union. He believed that the USSR had found the solution to the struggles afflicting the working class during the Great Depression. To understand his motivation, we need to try to look at the world as he would have seen it at the time.

---

* The First Period had begun with the creation of a communist homeland, the Soviet Union, in 1917. The Second Period was the capitalist world's efforts to stabilize itself. The Third Period was the period during which Moscow believed that capitalism would finally collapse.

PART ONE

A Son of the Empire (1903–1931)

Chapter One

An Idyllic Youth

Edward Paul Cecil-Smith was born into a family of faith, conviction, and fearlessness in China on 10 March 1903.[1] He was the third child of two particularly scholarly and daring missionaries: George Cecil-Smith and Ida White Roberts. Young Edward went to Chefoo School, a British-style boarding school in China, and there learned about the glories of the British Empire. After a brief stint in Shanghai, he came to Toronto in 1919 with his sister to begin a new life. They were welcomed by an active missionary community and the Chefoo alumni in the city. He got a job at the Canadian Bank of Commerce, joined and succeeded in the Canadian militia, and married Lilian Gouge, the secretary at the missionary organization's office. These hardly seemed like the formative years of a political radical.

Cecil-Smith's parents came from different backgrounds but found a common calling in the missionary movement. Ida came from a working-class family. She was born in Australia, but her parents returned to their native England with her when she was two. George came from a family of merchants in Bristol; they were well off, owning a large estate called Dolphin Lodge and a tea plantation in India.[2] George and Ida were not acquainted with each other when they responded to a China Inland Mission's recruiting drive in the late 1880s for missionaries to expand into China's vast interior. Ida arrived in China in 1890, and George arrived the following year.[3] They met in that country, marrying in 1892 in Chongqing, the gateway to the Yangtze River, and travelling south overland to Guizhou province.* Nearly

* Note that, for simplicity, the modern *pinyin* transliteration of proper nouns will be used instead of the Wade-Giles system that was used at the time. For example, "Guizhou" is the *pinyin* transliteration but was transliterated as "Kweichow" in the Wade-Giles system when the Cecil-Smiths lived there.

twice the size of New Brunswick, Guizhou was home to about four million inhabitants spread throughout seventy-three walled cities and uncounted towns and villages.[4] With the exception of the occasional sabbatical year, Guizhou would be their home for the next fifty years.

George and Ida lived in Anping, an outstation of Anshun.[5] Like the other missionaries of the China Inland Mission, they wore Chinese dress, and George grew a queue, the distinctive "pigtail" worn by Chinese men during the Qing Dynasty.[6] They lived in a standard Chinese house without windows. Light entered only "through the paper covering of the lattice-work door."[7] George and Ida held religious services in the guest room, where the dirt floor was muddy enough that they could not kneel in prayer when it rained. They preached mostly to the Han Chinese who lived in the town but also ministered to at least one Miao family, which travelled sixteen kilometres by foot to services every Sunday.[8]

Ida described working with one especially memorable convert in Anping. He was a local doctor and apothecary who closed his shop on the Sabbath. Most converts only attended Sunday services, but this particular man found one session of worship per week to be inadequate. He also visited the missionaries each morning and evening to participate in their prayers. Ida challenged the convert to further demonstrate his faith by doing away with idols in his home and tea shop. She was especially concerned with the image of a Buddhist figure hanging on his shop wall and advised him to destroy it. The convert burned the image, earning him Ida's respect but also "heavy and subtle prosecutions [*sic*]" from the other villagers.[9]

Ida spoke of the destruction of such idols with great pride, but Han Chinese and Miao reaction to such acts illustrate the tension that existed between the missionaries and the locals. In the missionaries' efforts to save souls, they were also destroying the extant culture. A small shrine, for instance, was a common element in most Chinese homes. It was a place to pay homage to the gods of their faith and their ancestors. Buddhists had images of the Buddha and various bodhisattvas around their homes. Such items were as much an element of their culture – their art and heritage – as their religion. For George and Ida, they were simply forbidden idols that stood between potential converts and salvation.

Perhaps this conflict was part of the reason George and Ida only had ten converts after ten years of preaching. While many prospective converts seemed to enjoy attending the services, few were willing to fully abandon their old ways and convert to Christianity.[10] Many were suspicious of the missionaries and their efforts, sometimes to the point of violence. In 1898, for example, the first outstation built in the Guizhou countryside among the Miao met with disaster. The locals burned the mission house and murdered the first Miao convert, Ban Xeo Xiao, and the missionary, W.S. Fleming.[11]

Such tensions came to a head during the 1900 Boxer Rebellion, a violent uprising against foreign interference in China. The "Boxers" were members of the Righteous and Harmonious Fists, a religious sect that practised martial arts and claimed that they could not be harmed by guns, cannons, or knives. The Boxers sought to purge China of foreign influence. In the summer of 1900, they attacked foreign business people, missionaries, and Chinese Christian converts. The violence was most acute north of the Yangtze River, but Guizhou did not escape the bedlam.

At the time of the uprising, Ida was in Guiyang with her five-year-old son, Sydney.[12] George and many of the men from the mission were touring the countryside. Ida feared for her life: there was little hope of rescue or escape if the Boxers came for her. She recalled Elder Chen, the first Chinese Christian convert in Guizhou province, coming to her after having made arrangements for the safety of his own family, and telling her,

> "Now you and I will die together if the LORD so wills."
>
> I remonstrated saying he had better go as death could not benefit me and I must wait for my husband. He replied, "Can I hide? My face is my 'sign board' (*chao pai*). For twenty years I have been known throughout this city as a preacher of the Gospel; can I now be hid? No, no, not any more than you, and we will die or live together."[13]

Ida was captured by a mob soon afterwards. They dragged her to the top of the city walls and attempted to throw her to her death.[14] Somehow, she survived the fall without any serious injury. She escaped and reunited with George upon his return to Guiyang.

The empress dowager seized on the tumult and ordered that all foreigners in China were to be killed. Had the acting governor of Guizhou province followed this order, it seems unlikely that George, Ida, or Sydney would have survived. They were simply too far from the sea to escape, and too isolated to hide for any length of time. Fortunately, the acting governor of Guizhou refused to follow the order, fearing repercussions from the foreign powers if he harmed the missionaries. Instead, he provided escorts to the foreigners as they fled to the coast.[15] Ida and Sydney left Guizhou in August with most of the other missionaries. George followed shortly thereafter.[16]

More than two hundred missionaries and thousands of Chinese Christian converts were killed during the Boxer Rebellion.[17] Ida narrowly escaped death, and George likely endured similar trials during the uprising. After such an experience, a missionary might be forgiven for considering an early retirement. Missionaries faced great personal risk, and surely the mass xenophobic reaction must have caused them to question their efforts. The Cecil-Smiths, however, were undeterred. They returned to Guizhou province in 1901 with Sydney and newborn daughter Frances to carry on with their missionary work in the provincial towns. George and Ida both became increasingly involved in long expeditions to the outstations to preach to the Miao. George led one expedition to "a place among the mountains where no foreigner had ever been," where he preached to a crowd of fifty people, "most of whom had not before heard the Gospel."[18] Ida accompanied him on many of these expeditions and soon led them herself.[19]

In addition to their seemingly fearless missionary work, George and Ida were also scholarly people. George was a frequent contributor to the *Chinese Recorder*, a magazine for English-speaking missionaries in China. He wrote about everything from the role of music in worship to the proper use of Chinese characters.[20] Ida wrote pamphlets, spoke at conferences about women's issues, and transliterated Chinese texts to help missionaries learn the language.[21] And although they were, at heart, intellectuals who loved a rousing scholarly debate, they varied their communication to suit their audiences. When speaking to the Miao and Han Chinese people, who were generally illiterate and lacked formal education as British missionaries would recognize it, George and Ida used simple tools to communicate their points and tried to grab their audience's attention.

The couple were creative in their communication techniques. Like the other missionaries of the China Inland Mission, they used a "wordless book" when preaching. The book consisted of a panel of four blocks of colour to illustrate God's plan: "black for sin; red for Jesus' sacrifice; white for sanctification; and gold for heaven," a tool that corresponded nicely to an existing Chinese depiction of cosmology.[22] They told modified parables, stories that resonated with the local culture, put on simple plays, and even organized a science fair – "an exhibition of scientific apparatus, curios, mineral products, maps, pictures, students' work, etc." – to attract the attention of potential converts.[23] The couple did whatever was necessary to communicate their points to their audience, an approach, we shall see, adopted by young Edward Cecil-Smith in his future propaganda efforts.

Edward was born at the mission station in Guiyang, Guizhou province, in 1903. Presumably Ida took some rest while pregnant, but she was quick to return to work once Edward, their third and final child, was born. The children were raised largely by Chinese nannies, and Sydney, Frances, and Edward spoke Mandarin before they spoke English. Edward's first word was "rabbit," spoken in Mandarin.[24] They wore Chinese dress, and the boys grew queues like George, customs considered vital to integrating with the locals but perceived by the European population to be detrimental to their development as Britons. To ensure a more European education for the missionary children, the China Inland Mission established the Chefoo School.

Edward was sent to Chefoo at the age of five. He was given a haircut – he lost his queue and grew his hair out to a more conventional European style. When he cried at the prospect of leaving for school, his parents scolded him and told that this was "un-British" conduct.[25] Fortunately, George and Ida must have thought, Chefoo was precisely the place to deal with such a defect. Through education, sport, and ceremony, the institution was designed to ensure that the missionary children would receive a "proper" education.

Edward came to love his time at Chefoo. The seaside town, now known as Yantai, on the Shandong Peninsula had a mild climate and miles of white sand beaches; the setting was much more pleasant than the rocky hills of Guizhou province.[26] The children learned Shakespeare, Latin, and mathematics to the British public school standard and were evaluated with the Oxford exams. Edward particularly enjoyed his studies of British history. He recalled that he had been taught that the British peoples and their institutions had "contributed quite a bit towards establishing democracy in the world." Britons, he learned, had played an essential role in maintaining freedom around the world, including defeating "that terrible monster Napoleon" and combating piracy on the high seas.[27] It was an idealized version of British history, but it was appealing to the boy. Edward even learned a little about Britain's history with Spain, that distant and exotic land, in the context of the Peninsular Campaign during the Napoleonic Wars.[28]

Just as importantly as academics, Chefoo also taught the children about the glories of British culture and institutions. Edward played cricket, soccer, and tennis. He ate puddings for dessert on special occasions like Queen Victoria's birthday. The headmaster led the children in prayer every morning, and the two church services every Sunday were conducted according to English prayer services.[29] The teachers were full members of the China Inland Mission, just as concerned with developing the soul as the mind. Despite never having set foot in Britain,

Edward emerged from the experience feeling as British as if he had been raised in George's hometown of Bristol.[30]

Although the school must have seemed like an oasis to Edward, it was not entirely isolated from events in the outside world. The year 1911 was especially dramatic. An outbreak of bubonic plague on the Shandong Peninsula required the children to stay at home for an extended winter break. In October, Sun Yat-sen overthrew the decaying Qing Dynasty and installed a republic. The Chefooites* viewed this change very positively. Sun was, after all, a Christian. One student remarked in a letter that "this revolution sends a ray of hope down on China's broadening future."[31] Edward was only eight years old at the time and probably had little interest in Chinese politics. It seems unlikely that he would have fully grasped the gravity of the revolution, but he must have had an inkling. Emboldened by the regime change, the Chinese servants at Chefoo demanded that their salaries be doubled. When the headmaster refused, the students had to do their own chores.[32]

Edward left Chefoo in the summer of 1917, at the age of fourteen. He went to Shanghai, the centre of Western commerce in China, and got his first job as a clerk at the Shanghai Dock and Engineering Company.[33] Given his young age, it was likely some form of apprenticeship. He also began his unique military career in Shanghai, joining the Shanghai Volunteer Corps.[34]

The Shanghai Volunteer Corps was an unusual organization. It was not a Chinese military unit; rather, it was controlled by the Shanghai Municipal Council, a completely non-Chinese organization that administered the international settlements.[35] The corps was commanded by a seconded British army officer and composed of sub-units made up of volunteers from the different communities of foreigners. The British settlers, for instance, contributed a rifle company to the defence of the international settlements in Shanghai. This undertaking was no small matter when Edward arrived in 1917; the First World War was raging, with no end in sight. In the event of an uprising by the Chinese people, the foreigners could not expect reinforcements in a timely fashion.

Edward would have normally been too young to join the Shanghai Volunteer Corps. However, against the backdrop of the First World War, the militia seems to have seen fit to take on just about anyone deemed competent and trustworthy.[36] Edward already knew

---

* Students and alumni of Chefoo referred to themselves as "Chefooites" at the time. They later adopted the title of "Chefusian."

military drill and how to take care of a uniform from his time at Chefoo. He was well suited to take part in corps parades through the streets of Shanghai, and would have learned how to fire a Lee Enfield rifle, the standard weapon across the British Empire.[37] It seems unlikely that he would have received much training in tactics, but he enjoyed the discipline, camaraderie, and the sense of connection with his community. Later, he must have found the International Brigades in Spain to be oddly reminiscent of this unusual multinational force.[38]

Edward later told his family that the seeds of his communist ideals were planted in Shanghai.[39] The situation in China made little sense to him. Foreigners treated the Chinese poorly. A contemporary observer recalled a beautiful park with a telling bilingual sign on its iron gates: "Chinese and dogs not allowed."[40] Edward remembered the police and the army chasing absconding "debtors," who were really escaped slaves. As a member of the Shanghai Volunteer Corps, he may have even been involved in such a chase. Nearly as distressing was the frequent sight of police officers beating rickshaw coolies whenever there was a disagreement over fares with a foreign customer. He recalled that the policeman "almost invariably hits indiscriminately with his three foot club at the coolie or at the rickshaw. Wheels, tops, shafts and skulls, he cracks all with fine abandon and indiscrimination."[41] The government was corrupt, and the glaring disparity between the rich and the poor was enough to shake anyone's belief in the status quo. The inequities of the city offended even the young Cecil-Smith's sense of morality. Fortunately, he did not stay very long.

Edward left Shanghai for Toronto in 1919. The China Inland Mission had created the Toronto Bible College to educate and train laypeople for missionary work. His sister, Frances, had been admitted as a student. Edward, only sixteen at the time, accompanied her and their mother to Toronto. The family left by way of Hong Kong with eighteen other missionaries and arrived in Vancouver aboard the *Empress of Asia* on 30 June 1919.[42] They took the train east, passing through Winnipeg, the site of the recent Winnipeg General Strike. After six weeks of political ferment, the strike had culminated in a violent clash between the strikers and the North-West Mounted Police.[43] Thirty strikers were wounded and one was killed. The strikers blamed the heavy-handed actions of the Mounties; the Mounties blamed the "dangerous reds." Canada, it seemed, might not be entirely isolated from the pressures that had led to revolution in China.

Edward, Frances, and Ida arrived in Toronto in early July 1919. George joined them in June 1920.[44] There is no record of their early impressions, but it seems likely that they adjusted to life in Toronto fairly easily. Edward and Frances had spent the bulk of their youth living in communal housing among missionaries and their families at Chefoo School. Now they were on the other side of the world, certainly, but they found themselves in similar living arrangements. They were staying among a sizeable contingent of missionaries, including at least sixteen graduates of the Chefoo School and their families, at the mission's North American headquarters.[45] Although records show that Frances studied at the nearby Toronto Bible College, Edward's activities, and those of his parents, are unknown. His RCMP file states that he attended Trinity College at the University of Toronto, but the university has no record of this.

After less than a year of living together in Toronto as a family, George and Ida left for a missionary-recruiting drive in England in May 1921 and then returned to China.[46] Frances continued her studies at the Toronto Bible College, and Edward, at the age of nineteen, enlisted in the Canadian Engineers as a sapper.* He had enjoyed his time learning military-style drill in Chefoo and training with the Shanghai Volunteer Corps, and so the more challenging aspects of being a military engineer looked especially interesting to him.

Edward paraded at the College Street Armouries, not far from the China Inland Mission headquarters, on his evenings and weekends. Theoretically, the sappers were trained in a variety of battlefield tasks in addition to basic soldier skills. The engineers were called on to construct obstacles, bridges, and roads, and to demolish those of the enemy. Cecil-Smith was fortunate enough to attend advanced training at the Canadian School of Engineering in Halifax, where he learned how to operate the searchlights at the Halifax Citadel and how to construct trenches, defensive works, and basic obstacles.[47] He also received training in explosive demolitions. He recalled years later that he came close to accidentally injuring a senior officer when a charge exploded too early.[48]

Most of Edward's training in Toronto was rudimentary. The engineer companies were so small that proper technical training was virtually impossible. The companies were meant to include more than a hundred soldiers but rarely comprised more than a dozen or so. Groups

* Cecil-Smith's International Brigade file says he joined the Canadian militia in 1921, while his Second World War service file says he joined in 1922. At the time, Toronto was home to two companies of Non-Permanent Active Militia engineer companies: the 2nd and the 8th. It is not known which of these companies he joined.

of soldiers that size cannot properly construct an entire bridge, for instance, and, even if they could, only the Royal Military College of Canada in Kingston, Ontario, had any bridges with which to train. The College Street Armouries had little equipment or space with which they could conduct training and instead used models and diagrams of engineering equipment. They "war gamed" tactical problems using maps and hosted guest speakers with relevant experience either as civilian engineers or as veterans of the Great War.

Edward enjoyed his time in the militia, but his primary social circle through the 1920s involved his fellow Chefooites. There were fifty-two alumni in Toronto by 1925,[49] and Edward and Frances grew increasingly close with them. The boarding rooms at the mission headquarters provided a "clubhouse" setting where the alumni socialized in their spare time. They organized regular outings together, such as dinners in Chinatown, where they no doubt surprised the staff by placing their orders in Mandarin.[50] Edward became long-time friends with many of the alumni but grew especially close to his childhood friend David Hogg.[51] They shared a common love of literature and the arts, classical music, and, later, debating working-class issues.[52] Edward also met his future wife at the mission's headquarters. Lilian Gouge was the secretary, so they must have run into each other frequently.[53] The two had a lot in common. She was inquisitive, well read, and full of energy. Although she came from a working-class family and had not attended a fancy boarding school like Chefoo, she was an autodidact who enjoyed music, arts, theatre, and literature and never backed down from a good debate.[54]

When the boarding rooms at the China Inland Mission were shut down in 1925, the sixteen Chefooites who had been living there found joint accommodations where they could.[55] Three of the young women shared an apartment together, as did three of the young men. Three others moved into Knox College. Frances (who would return to Guizhou province as a missionary in early 1926)[56] rented a flat with fellow Chefooites Marian and Isabel Taylor. Edward, Jack Brock, Dede Coulthard, and Stan Olsen moved into the West End Young Men's Christian Association at 931 College Street.[57] Edward did not just live with Brock, Coulthard, and Olsen – all four of them worked together as clerks at the Canadian Bank of Commerce.[58]

The China Inland Mission headquarters had provided the Chefooites with a natural space for their social gatherings. Although the mission opened its new offices on the University of Toronto campus in 1927, the loss of their "clubhouse" appears to have spurred the Chefooites on to create a formal alumni association, and they also created a National Executive Committee in Toronto to organize their activities. Edward was elected the group's first president and later the North American director of the Publications Committee.[59] Little of what this committee may have produced remains, but a few letters published in the *Chefoo Magazine,* the normally tame and conservative Chefooite alumni magazine, have survived.

Edward's entries in *Chefoo Magazine* provide the first written evidence of how much he enjoyed provocative public debate. In 1926, a fellow Chefooite on the Publications Committee, writing under the pseudonym "Sir Galahad," challenged the very nature of the religious education on offer to students at Chefoo. He questioned the teachers: "We know you will tell them they need God – you told us – but will you tell them why? – you never told us. Not hinting, suggesting or quibbling, we ask for them, but the truth, the whole truth, which alone can make them free. You believe in a final reckoning, you say. Will we be held responsible for what we never knew, or will you be held responsible for what you never told?"[60] Sir Galahad's challenge to Chefoo was considered sensational and led to a chain of letters to the editor, with one reader demanding an apology.[61] On behalf of the entire Toronto Publications Committee, Edward wrote to the editor and expressed its solidarity with Sir Galahad.[62] The letter's content, Edward explained, had been discussed and supported by the entire committee before submission to the magazine (and in all likelihood, Sir Galahad was actually Edward's friend and fellow committee member David Hogg).[63] The Chefooites in Toronto, it would seem, not only did not frown on such "radical" thoughts but actually invited such polemical conversations.

By early 1926, Edward did not have any family remaining in Toronto, as his parents and sister had returned to Guizhou province. There is no indication that he ever saw any of them again. But he had made a happy life for himself in Toronto. Lilian and Edward married on 9 October 1927 at St. Michael and All Angels Anglican Church, north of Christie Pits Park.[64] According to their family, the two moved to their first home, on Toronto's Centre Island, shortly after their wedding. They joined the Queen City Yacht Club on Algonquin Island and sailed on Hogg's boat.[65] They went to art galleries and the theatre, and they read and debated with each other and with friends in restaurants and coffee shops. On the face of it, they lived an ideal life. British institutions and British values had provided Edward and his loved ones with everything they needed in life: community, a home, employment, leisure time, and civil liberties. Underneath the surface, however, he was starting to feel less certain about their infallibility. The seed of critical thinking that had invited him to start questioning religious education was beginning to grow.

Chapter Two

Radicalization

Edward Cecil-Smith was educated in the glories of the British Empire, well-integrated with like-minded Torontonians, a banker at the Canadian Bank of Commerce, a member of Canada's Non-Permanent Active Militia, and a married man. He did well in the militia in Toronto. He embraced the discipline of military service and rose quickly through the ranks. By 1928, at only twenty-five years of age, he was a sergeant major, the senior non-commissioned officer of his engineer company.[1] He was also appointed the sergeant major of the Infantry School in Toronto.[2] This was an especially high honour. The Infantry Schools were established to allow the Permanent Force, the full-time soldiers, to train the infantry regiments of the Non-Permanent Active Militia. The role of sergeant major at the school would normally be filled by a Permanent Force infantry sergeant – an experienced, full-time infantry non-commissioned officer – not a Non-Permanent Active Militia engineer sergeant. His appointment to this position indicates that Cecil-Smith was a particularly competent soldier and disciplinarian.

At roughly the same time, Cecil-Smith lost his job at the Canadian Bank of Commerce. He found other work to make ends meet, including driving a truck for the T. Eaton Company and working in a lumber mill.[3] He later found a job as a machinist for the Acme Motor and Gear Company.[4] There, he had his first exposure to unions and joined the International Association of Machinists and the American Federation of Labor.[5] At Acme, he may have encountered fellow machinist Tim Buck, a labour organizer and future leader of the Communist Party of Canada. Cecil-Smith was becoming increasingly interested in politics and joined the Labor Party of Ontario, a socialist but not revolutionary political party.[6] He began to discuss his political ideas in coffee shops and attended political rallies to learn about new and different ideas, many of which challenged his old way of thinking.[7] Cecil-Smith enjoyed attending these meetings, first in a personal capacity and soon in his role as a journalist.

Cecil-Smith began his career in journalism in 1929. He had always enjoyed writing and had served as the North American director of the Chefooites' Publications Committee, although there is scant record of his writings in that role.[8] David Hogg, Cecil-Smith's old friend, had already worked as a journalist for several years and perhaps helped Cecil-Smith find a job in the field.[9] Cecil-Smith was working as a jewellery salesman at Ellis Brothers in early 1929, but by the summer he was a police reporter for the *Mail and Empire*.[10] He would work as either a writer or editor for the rest of his life.

Cecil-Smith's colleagues at the *Mail and Empire* remembered him for his intellect and argumentative nature. One reporter recalled him as "a marathon conversationalist" whose "talk was frequently in gusty vernacular, but in unguarded moments he would lapse into the language of culture."[11] Another recalled that

> he argued for the love of argument often ... He held that orange crates were the best bookcases, because they threw into more prominence the value of the books themselves.
>
> Feet spread out, eyes twinkling behind thick glasses, he would lean back in one of the old office swivel chairs after the last edition was put away and fence with words against ten or twelve reporters and editors, ready to sit until daybreak to back up his point.[12]

Cecil-Smith loved to argue. Sometimes it was personal – he had a fiery temper – but it was just as often an intellectual exercise. As for his language, he preferred to come across as a "working-class bloke" instead of a petit-bourgeoisie intellectual. He grew increasingly embarrassed by anything that signalled his connection to wealth or privilege.

One of his favourite points of debate was the Great War. The former sergeant major of the Infantry School had left the militia in 1928, not long after he had lost his job at the bank. He had swung from being pro-military to, as one colleague recalled, a "pugnacious pacifist."[13] Another reporter described him as a "violent pacifist."[14] These examples provide a strong illustration of the ambiguous nature of the term "pacifist." It is clear that Cecil-Smith was not against violence per se: he had served in the militia in Shanghai and Toronto, and would eventually fight in Spain and volunteer for military service in the Second World War. He was not against war, but he was against unjust wars.

Cecil-Smith did not see the Great War as a just war or a glorious undertaking. That cataclysm, he came to believe, was one of the "ridiculous wars engineered by the military clique."[15] Capitalists got rich off such wars, while the working class fought and died in them. Such wars were followed by what he saw as a predictable and recurring pattern: after a brief period of prosperity, crippling debt and mass unemployment set in. The rich stayed rich, and the workers were worse off than ever. Cecil-Smith believed that the veterans of the Great War, no matter how brave, were a "bunch of saps" or "dupes" for allowing themselves to be so played.[16] A journalist who knew Cecil-Smith in these years recalled that he once said, "You'd never catch me shouldering a gun."[17] Another recalled him saying that, if he had to go to war, "'I'm going as a batman [a personal assistant] to a chaplain. Strictly non-combatant stuff for me."[18]

When he was not badgering his co-workers, Cecil-Smith was out on his beat as a police reporter. He covered the court decisions, criminal investigations, and incidents where it was anticipated that the police would play a role. One of his first stories was covering the clash between two mortal enemies: the Toronto police and the Communist Party of Canada (CPC). The party was preparing to celebrate International Red Day on 1 August 1929, and the Toronto police was intent on preventing these celebrations.

International Red Day was a peace rally, but also a celebration of solidarity with Soviet Russia, the anticipated victim of a future imperialist war. The crowds sang revolutionary songs like "The Red Flag," "The Red Army March," and "The Internationale." "The Internationale" and "The Red Flag" were nineteenth-century songs, but in the twentieth century they were most deeply associated with the Soviet Union. "The Internationale" was the Soviet anthem, and its language is provocative enough to quote:

> Arise, ye prisoners of starvation,
> Arise, ye wretched of the earth.
> For justice thunders condemnation,
> A better world's in birth.
> No more tradition's chains shall bind us,
> Arise, ye slaves no more in thrall,
> The earth shall rise on new foundations,
> We have been not, we shall be all.

The chorus continues:

> 'Tis the final conflict,
> Let each stand in his place,
> The international society
> Shall be the human race.[19]

Party members called each other "comrade" and displayed revolutionary symbols like the red star and the hammer and sickle. The party had conducted these rallies every year since 1925, but in 1929, in Toronto, there was a "new sheriff in town" charged with trying to contain them.

Dennis Draper had been appointed Toronto's new chief constable. A former brigadier in the Canadian Expeditionary Force during the Great War, he was known as a strict disciplinarian and a fervent anti-communist, characteristics that seemed to make him appealing to the city fathers, despite his not having any previous experience in policing. As a reporter who covered Draper for several decades recalled, "To Draper, the fight against crime was as simple as finding the enemy on the battlefield."[20] In July 1929, he forbade the CPC leadership from holding their annual International Red Day meeting.[21] The party did not heed the warning, and Cecil-Smith was on hand to report on the ensuing events for the *Mail and Empire*.[22] Draper, knowing where his enemy would be, did not miss the opportunity.

Some 10,000 people gathered in Queen's Park for International Red Day. Some were members of the CPC, others were sympathetic to its cause, and still others simply stopped by to watch the show – a police ban on the events would surely lead to an event worth taking in. A roster of prominent speakers were to address the crowd from the bandstand: Jack MacDonald, the soon to be ousted general secretary of the party; Tim Buck, his successor and leading light of the CPC until 1962; A.E. Smith, the leader of the Canadian Labor Defense League; and Lily Himmelfarb, a Young Communist League leader nicknamed "Red Lily." However, in Cecil-Smith's words, "any speeches came from Toronto's police force and were orders to keep pedestering."[23]

Himmelfarb and Buck approached the bandstand to begin their speeches at 7:30 p.m. The police stopped them but were generally non-violent in their efforts, except when Tim Buck was struck while being escorted out of the park: "He was walking between two uniformed policemen when a detective struck him in the face, splitting his lip so badly that blood ran from his mouth."[24] The police then moved to disperse the crowd. Motorcycles rode over the curb, and the mounted unit came into the park "through the scattering crowd."[25] Tongue in cheek, Cecil-Smith called the bedlam an exhibition of "horses, motorcycles and communist riding." Himmelfarb "stood and yelled and booed, some of her remarks jarring to the tender ears of a constable who was nearby. He rushed over, 'who yelled that?' he demanded. Then he looked at her about five feet in height and told her in a fatherly manner to keep moving."[26]

Cecil-Smith was uncritical of the police in this instance. He simply wrote that the police "did their duty," and "on the whole, they seemed to enjoy it ... Most of them were good natured in their commands to the milling crowds."[27] But a demonstration a few days later stretched his interpretation of what constituted the duty of the police. A follow-up protest on 13 August was met with greater police violence. This time, Cecil-Smith's narrative was less sympathetic: "Batons and Feet Used Freely as City Police Rout Reds. Communists and Curious Spectators Suffer as Draper's Men Charge Queen's Park Crowd with Horses, Motorcycle and Wooden Clubs. No questions were asked ... Blood was shed."[28]

Cecil-Smith provided a graphic, blow-by-blow account of the arrest of Jack MacDonald. Standing four feet from MacDonald, he watched him plead with the police: "I haven't even said a word, boys, please."[29] A police officer punched him in the mouth when he tried to say more. MacDonald made a run for it but was intercepted by a plainclothes officer who kicked him nine times before he fell again. "For God's sake, don't kick me. For God's sake, don't!" MacDonald shouted. "He ducked his head as two fists landed on the back of his neck. Another kick straightened him." MacDonald struggled free one more time, making it as far as the 48th Highlanders of Canada memorial to the Great War at the north end of the park, where he was tackled one final time. Oscar Ryan – a former member of the CPC's Central Executive Committee, a Young Communist League organizer, and future friend of Cecil-Smith's – was also supposed to speak but seems to have escaped the violence.[30]

Leaving the scene of MacDonald's arrest, Cecil-Smith returned to the chaos in the centre of the park. He recounted, "Horsemen swept through the fleeing groups. As far as the eye could reach men and women were running, with motorcycles and horses close behind him ... In all directions, as the reporter walked back down through the park, the grounds resembled a scene from a motion picture spectacle. Men and women cowered behind trees and bushes as horses and motorcycle officers charged down on them. Horsemen paused for no one."[31] Cecil-Smith took note of Detective Sergeant William Nursey, a member of Draper's Red Squad, a group specially tasked with monitoring and disrupting the CPC and similar organizations, as the detective interviewed a suspected "red." This would not be Cecil-Smith and Nursey's last encounter.

After the bedlam died down, Cecil-Smith went to the "brown house," the police headquarters at Bay and College Street, to learn about police preparations for the day. While he waited to interview Dennis Draper, Cecil-Smith chatted with a police officer. The officer, whom Cecil-Smith later described as "an illiterate gunman in uniform ... who could hardly spell his name correctly," asked him, "'Why the hell do you bastards keep riding the police? Why don't you get wise to yourselves? Don't you realize that if you don't beat the living jesus out of these reds, they'll take old man [Joseph E.] Atkinson's paper [the *Toronto Star*] away from him one of these days? Look what they did in Roosia [*sic*]. Where would you be then? It ain't only the banks these guys is after, it's the papers too.'"[32] Cecil-Smith came to believe that the reds taking away the banks and the papers alike was not the worst thing that could happen to Canadian society.

Cecil-Smith interviewed Draper later that evening. The chief constable denied that anyone had been injured in the altercation and claimed that the police had acted with due restraint. When Cecil-Smith questioned him specifically about the treatment of Jack MacDonald, Draper shot back, "Are you defending MacDonald?" Surely, Draper said, someone who stayed at a public demonstration after being told to move along was "acting unwisely" and got what he deserved.[33] Draper admonished the press coverage of the event. He told Cecil-Smith that the press must ignore the communists and not cover their demonstrations or the police treatment thereof. Draper advised him not to publish what "one of them [a party member] says about being kicked." He continued, "I am proud to say that ninety-nine percent of the people of Toronto are the finest people on earth, but we must not allow these foreigners to rule."[34] Such sentiments were echoed in the *Globe*'s coverage of the same event. That paper praised the police's "victory" over the CPC in preventing their "firebrand oratory," noting that "the brazen defiance of Canadian tradition shown by the instigators of the meeting could but result in the exercise of police authority."[35]

When the dust settled after the Battles of Queen's Park, there were many broken bones and bruised egos, and six actual arrests. Stewart Smith (the son of A.E. Smith, and a recent graduate of the Communist International's prestigious Lenin School in Moscow), Meyer Klig, and four others were arrested at the rally.[36] Down at the stockyards, near old Fort York, Emily Weir was arrested for distributing "communistic literature" to factory workers.[37] The police laid charges for these actions through the catch-all offences of "vagrancy" and "obstructing police."

Cecil-Smith witnessed Meyer Klig's unnecessarily violent arrest at Queen's Park, which led to him having further doubts about the police, the justice system, and the society they represented. Klig was arrested because he did not leave the rally when ordered to do so. He had been protesting peacefully and did not fight with the police or resist arrest. Regardless, following his arrest, Klig was dragged inside the provincial Parliament Buildings, struck in the face several times, and suffered a ruptured eardrum. He stood trial, and his case concluded the same way that many of them did at the time: as one historian puts it, "the presiding magistrate invariably ruled in favour of the officer and sentenced the accused to the maximum penalty," a state of affairs that further infuriated Cecil-Smith.[38] Klig was sentenced to sixty days hard labour.[39]

Charges of this kind were heard in the police courts, part of Cecil-Smith's beat as the police reporter for the *Mail and Empire.* The police court heard low-level offences and was presided over by a magistrate instead of a judge. Cecil-Smith was disgusted by what he saw in these courts. He felt that Magistrate Robert Browne regularly trampled on the rights of British subjects, showing no respect for the freedoms of association, expression, or political belief traditionally espoused by the common law. People were arrested for striking, organizing labour, public speaking, demonstrating, and distributing literature. Immigrants had few rights and regularly faced deportation for little more than the crime of being unemployed, an all too frequent occurrence following the stock market crash in October 1929.[40] These same immigrants could find themselves before the magistrate simply for performing theatre in their native tongue.[41]

Cecil-Smith also encountered a source of hope in these courtrooms. He met Oscar Ryan, the director of publicity for the Canadian Labor Defense League (CLDL) and editor of its magazine, the *Canadian Labor Defender.*[42] Cecil-Smith and Ryan would have encountered each other frequently. Getting to talk, they would have learned that they had much in common. They were both voracious readers. Both loved poetry, theatre, cinema, and visual arts. They were also both exceptionally stubborn and up for a debate. In Ryan, Cecil-Smith found someone he could verbally spar with, and, agree or disagree, nothing was personal and there were no hard feelings. The two became fast friends and stayed that way into old age.[43] Ryan was also an important organizer for the Young Communist League, an advocate for the Soviet Union and its policies, and a CPC stalwart. Ryan taught Cecil-Smith about the party and the league, and pointed him toward various books and pamphlets on communism. Ryan surely spoke about what he perceived to be the successes achieved by the Soviet Union, such as the purported eradication of crime by improving social conditions.[44] Cecil-Smith was intrigued by this ideology and Ryan's organizations.

The Canadian Labor Defense League was a legal aid and civil rights organization. It hired barristers, notably labour lawyer J.L. Cohen, to defend members of the working class who could not otherwise afford them. It assisted workers facing eviction or deportation, and charges arising from labour organizing, demonstrating, and distributing literature.[45] The league, for instance, paid for the defence of those arrested at the Battles of Queen's Park. It did commendable work, from the perspective of access to justice: from January 1929 to February 1930, the league handled eighty-eight such cases in the police and county courts of Toronto, many of which would have been covered by Cecil-Smith.[46]

The CLDL was also a front for the Communist Party of Canada. The organization was run by party member A.E. Smith and affiliated with the International Red Aid, an organization in Moscow, to provide for the legal defence of Communist political prisoners. On the sixteenth anniversary of the Soviet Union, in 1933, an advertisement by the Toronto section of the league in *Soviet Russia Today* declared, "Warmest proletarian greetings to the toilers of the Soviet Union, to the Canadian Section of the FSU [Friends of the Soviet Union] and to the powerful Soviet Section of the International Red Aid on the occasion of the sixteenth anniversary. We pledge our solidarity with the toilers of the Soviet Union. We pledge our readiness to defend their great achievements by mobilising the masses for the struggle against Terror, Political Reaction, and Fascism in Canada."[47] The league's detractors saw the organization as a diabolical Bolshevik organization intent on disrupting Canadian society in order to set the conditions for revolution. Its supporters saw an altruistic humanitarian organization seeking to relieve suffering and injustice.[48] Cecil-Smith gravitated toward the latter interpretation. He joined the league in 1930.[49] It was his gateway into the Communist Party of Canada.

The transition from a supporter of the CLDL to a member of the Communist Party of Canada was not an entirely smooth one for Cecil-Smith. For him, a key point of contention with the party was that it was formally atheistic. Party members spoke ill of religion and the clergy; after all, Marx had described religion as "the opiate of the masses." Oscar Ryan had publicly stated that he was in favour of teaching evolution to children (scandalous at the time), opining that religion was "one of the bulwarks of the capitalist state, which must be destroyed," and refusing to swear on the Bible in court.[50] But Cecil-Smith was a religious man. He had received a religious education at Chefoo, was married in a church, later cited scripture in explaining why he volunteered to fight in Spain (and even regularly attended church while there), and had his son baptized in 1942.[51] How did he reconcile these seemingly divergent belief systems?

Cecil-Smith did not see communism as mutually exclusive of Christianity. In fact, his Christian values led him to the revolutionary ideology. Through the Canadian Labor Defense League, Cecil-Smith encountered A.E. Smith, the head of the league and a former Methodist minister who eased this transition. Smith had turned his back on the church as an institution, but he had personally reconciled communism with Christianity by adopting the tenets of the social gospel, a Protestant movement that "rested on the premise that Christianity was a social religion, concerned, when the misunderstandings of the ages was stripped away, with the quality of human relations on this earth ... It was a call for men to find the meaning of their lives in seeking to realize the Kingdom of God in the very fabric of society."[52] Smith taught that entrance into the Kingdom of God did not entail individual salvation but serving others in this life.[53]

The theological journey of Smith and Cecil-Smith led them to communism.[54] As Smith later wrote, "I saw that Jesus was a Communist. I linked his life with the old prophets, the great preachers of the Old Testament, who were early Communists. Of course they were not scientific but they stood for the principles of communism. They practiced common ownership, and they believed in the Communist maxims: 'From each according to his ability, to each according to his need,' and, 'He who will not work, neither shall he eat.'"[55] These ideas resonated with Cecil-Smith. Even later in life, after he had stopped going to church, he frequently cited two particular bible verses: "And all who believed were together and held all things in common" (Acts 2: 44) and "It is easier for a camel to go through the eye of a needle, than for a rich man to enter into the Kingdom of God" (Mark 10: 25).[56] For Cecil-Smith, then, Christianity and communism were not discordant at all. He came to see communism as the best ideology available to address the ills of society, and the Communist Party of Canada as the best organization from which to champion it. His convictions would become further entrenched as a consequence of the fallout from the economic crisis of the 1930s.

The Great Depression began with the crash of the New York stock market in October 1929. About one-third of Canadians were soon out of work. So began a decade of darkness that would further foment Cecil-Smith's disillusionment with the economic and political structures that he already viewed with suspicion. In June 1931, 40,500 of Toronto's 242,000 wage earners were unemployed, and by January 1932, 10 per cent of Toronto's population was drawing some kind of relief.[57] "Today," Cecil-Smith wrote in 1932, "every worker knows something of unemployment. Either he, his friends, or neighbours are facing actual starvation through it."[58]

Edward and Lilian were severely affected by the Depression. Although Cecil-Smith was employed by the CPC full-time throughout the 1930s, such work did not pay very well and the couple had to constantly move to keep a roof over their heads. There is no record of an address for them for 1930, one appears in 1931, two more in 1932, and none between 1933 and 1934, all of which suggests a life of transience and uncertainty.[59] During the same period, they must have lived in substandard housing, for by 1935 or 1936 Lilian had contracted tuberculosis, a disease often associated with poor living conditions.[60] They regained some stability only in 1936, when they moved into an apartment on Maitland Drive that they would occupy for six years.[61]

Cecil-Smith's experiences in the early years of the Depression convinced him that capitalism was an inherently flawed ideology. Unemployment could not be solved by an improvement in the economy; improvements to the existing system might *decrease* unemployment, but it could not ever *eliminate it*, because of capitalism's inherently self-serving nature. Cecil-Smith was critical of a capitalist model, in which there would always be some unemployment, not only because of inefficiencies but because of the deliberate, and dehumanizing, tendency to maintain a reserve of unemployed labourers. These labourers were essential to business interests, which needed idle workers to be available for sudden business opportunities – a new plant here or a new mine there.[62] From Cecil-Smith's perspective, some workers were always kept unemployed so that bankers and millionaires could seize opportunities as they wished. Only a centralized economy could ensure full employment and address desperately needed social support such as housing security, sanitation, and health care. Such problems, Cecil-Smith reasoned, would be achieved only by putting the workers in charge, by imposing the dictatorship of the proletariat.

PART TWO

A Canadian Communist (1931–1936)

Chapter Three

Joining the Party

Cecil-Smith worked for both the *Mail and Empire* and the *Toronto Star* during his brief years as a mainstream journalist in the late 1920s and early 1930s.[1] Politically, the *Star* seems as if it would have been a better fit for Cecil-Smith. As he became increasingly left wing, the *Mail and Empire* would have been a difficult place for him to continue to work. That paper was English Canada's premier conservative daily newspaper, while the *Star*, sometimes derisively nicknamed the *Red Star* or the *King Street Pravda*, was more liberal.[2] Although Cecil-Smith's politics were probably a better fit at the *Star*, he still ran into trouble at that paper. As the Communist paper the *Worker* later recorded, "when Toronto news reporters were seriously discussing unionization, he [Cecil-Smith] was one of a number of the most active who were suddenly thrown out from the capitalist papers and found themselves blacklisted. Newspapermen are still talking about a union, but not quite so openly."[3] Cecil-Smith stopped working for the *Star* and the *Mail and Empire* sometime in 1930 or 1931. He did not work for the mainstream press again until 1936.

At roughly the same time that he lost his job as a mainstream reporter, he began working on a new project with Oscar Ryan, publicity director of the Canadian Labor Defense League and editor of its magazine, the *Canadian Labor Defender*. Cecil-Smith and Ryan began to organize an informal gathering of artists – painters, writers, poets, actors, and sculptors – who were interested in issues facing the working class.[4] Ryan wrote that there was a real need for such an organization. The Finnish and Ukrainian communities in Canada, he noted, had a strong workers' culture, but they confined themselves to their own nationalities. They produced plays, folk dance performances, and concerts depicting working-class issues in their own halls.[5] But where were the artists that represented the working class at large?

Dramatic events were unfolding that deeply affected the working class, events that would surely be ignored by mainstream artists. For instance, Ryan pointed to recent events in Estevan, Saskatchewan, where the party's labour union, the Workers' Unity League, had organized a miners' strike. The strike had culminated in a violent confrontation with the RCMP, described by some as an attack on a peaceful assembly and by others as an escalation of force against riotous strikers. Three miners were killed; their tombstones would be emblazoned with a red star and the inscription "Lest We Forget. Murdered in Estevan, Sep. 29, 1931 by RCMP."[6] What organization would commemorate the events at Estevan? Who would produce an art work to remind future generations of the workers' struggle?[7] Ryan felt that no such organization existed but that the need for such a group was greater than ever.

The informal group of artists and intellectuals that banded together through Ryan and Cecil-Smith eventually grew into the Progressive Arts Club. The club was conceived as a venue for members of the middle-class literati and intelligentsia to come together and discuss working-class issues and enjoy art.[8] Edward Cecil-Smith had long been fascinated with the power of language and symbolism, and his wife, Lilian Gouge, had a strong interest in community theatre, so their interest in the arts club was not surprising.[9] Their friend David Hogg, a lover of art, the theatre, and classical music, was also an early member.

Important to an understanding the evolution of the club is the fact that the Communist Party of Canada had traditionally scorned intellectualism. This orientation created a difficult environment for Edward and Lilian. Peter Hunter, a graduate of the Communist International's political training at the Lenin School who later was involved in organizing Canadian volunteers for the Spanish Civil War, recalled that intellectualism was often a good way to get in trouble in the party. He recalled that the intellectual Cecil-Smith was a rarity in the CPC; he liked to read and to debate ideas.[10] By contrast, Hunter was more inclined to follow the party doctrine as it was taught to him; he was less likely to get in trouble this way.[11] There was also a stigma attached to speaking like an intellectual; Cecil-Smith had a British accent and was embarrassed by his polished manner of speech.[12] As someone who knew him at the *Mail and Empire* later remarked, Cecil-Smith forced himself to speak in vernacular but his natural tendency was to speak as the British public school lad that he had been.[13]

Members of the Progressive Arts Club met at each other's homes in the evening and on the weekend until they were able to rent space in Settlement House, near the Toronto Art Gallery (now the Art Gallery of Ontario).[14] While the club sometimes met as a whole, it fostered smaller groups – the Workers' Theatre[15] and the Writers' Group (the latter chaired by Cecil-Smith) – that also held meetings at Settlement House.[16] The Writers' Group produced propaganda materials, including scripts for the Workers' Theatre.

The Progressive Arts Club attracted a broad variety of left-leaning artists and students. William Krehm was a student at the University of Toronto who had joined the party's arch-rival, the Trotskyist Communist League of America (Opposition). Krehm would ordinarily be shouted down at any party gatherings, but he felt completely welcome at the meetings of the Progressive Arts Club.[17] Three other university students became particularly important within the organization: Myrtle Eugenia Watts, Dorothy Livesay, and Stanley Ryerson. Watts (better known as "Jim" or sometimes "Jean") was a particularly rare member of the CPC: openly bisexual and from a moderately wealthy family.[18] Livesay was a poet and journalist who twice won of the Governor General's Award for poetry and was later made an officer of the Order of Canada. Ryerson was a talented historian recently returned from the Sorbonne and resuming his studies at the University of Toronto. Connected to the Toronto establishment through his grandfather Egerton Ryerson, he hardly seemed a natural fit for the Communist Party of Canada, but he would become a key leader in the party and Canada's pre-eminent Marxist historian.[19]

The forum was pleasant for Cecil-Smith. He enjoyed the work and the conversations, which laid the groundwork for the Progressive Arts Club to become more directly engaged in working toward specific sociopolitical goals. One event in particular urged this process along and served as a catalyst for Cecil-Smith to engage in more explicit political writing: the arrest and trial of the leadership of the Communist Party of Canada.

Long-standing tensions between the government and the CPC reached a boiling point in 1931, culminating in a national police operation that arrested much of its leadership. On 11 August 1931, Tim Buck, the party's general secretary and a close friend of Oscar Ryan, was arrested at his office in Toronto.[20] Malcolm Bruce, the editor of the party's newspaper, the *Worker*, was arrested in Calgary. The party's organizational secretary, Sam Carr (a Ukrainian-Canadian graduate of the Lenin School), was arrested in Vancouver.[21] The police did not find Tom Ewen (the general secretary of the Workers' Unity League) in Toronto, but he turned himself in a few days later. Leaders of affiliated cultural groups were arrested, as well: Tom Hill (the leader of the Finnish Organization of Canada) and Matthew Popovich and John Boychuk (the leaders of the Ukrainian Labor-Farmer Temple Association). Two other people seemed to just be caught up in the raids – Tomo Cacic, a Croatian activist who did not hold a senior leadership position,[22] and Mike Golinsky, a seventeen-year-old member of the Young Communist League, who was soon released.

Tim Buck and the other seven defendants (collectively known as, "the Eight") were charged with seditious conspiracy and breaching section 98 of the Criminal Code, a wartime provision that had not been removed after the armistice.[23] Section 98 outlawed radical groups "whose professed purpose" was to "bring about any governmental, industrial or economic change" by "the use of force or violence."[24] It expressly prohibited promoting such ideas through word or print.[25] The law modified long-standing common law principles that protected freedom of expression and assembly, as well as the presumption of innocence. The law as written was deliberately vague in order to maximize the government's discretionary powers.[26] Fear of revolution, such as that which had overthrown the Russian tsar in 1917, had been brought to a fever pitch in Canada during the 1919 Winnipeg General Strike. Although such fears had waned in the 1920s, they resurfaced during the Great Depression. Section 98 provided a convenient tool to try to contain what the government perceived as growing dissent and unrest.

A great deal rode on the outcome of the trial of the CPC leadership. A finding of guilty against Tim Buck under section 98 would effectively outlaw the party. It would put the onus on the accused to prove that they did *not* have any relationship with the party. Raised and educated in the belief that the British legal tradition was sacrosanct, Cecil-Smith was disgusted with this perversion of justice. Where were their rights to political belief? To association? To assembly? To speech? To be innocent until proven guilty? Such guarantees had all been thrown out the window when they became inconvenient for a government that, from what Cecil-Smith could see, was doing little to improve the plight of the working class during the Depression.

The arrests were meant to frighten people away from the party, but they had the opposite effect on Cecil-Smith. He became more active in the Canadian Labor Defense League and began writing for the *Worker.* The timing of his involvement with the paper was auspicious. Stewart Smith, the party's director of agitation and propaganda, was trying to change the *Worker* "from a screaming leaflet into a broad left-wing newspaper presenting some arguments for our proposals for labour and farmer action."[27] Cecil-Smith's particular skill set developed as a professional journalist was in demand and could be put to good use. He joined the staff of the *Worker* as a newspaperman and assistant editor and went on to play an important role in the party's newspapers for the next eight years.[28] At the same time, he formally joined the Communist Party of Canada, sponsored by Oscar Ryan and Emil Miller, a Young Communist League organizer.[29]

Cecil-Smith's first big story for the *Worker* was covering *Rex v. Buck et al.*, which began on 2 November 1931.[30] It was a good assignment for him: after all, he had covered the courts for the *Toronto Star* and the *Mail and Empire*. He went to the City Hall courthouse to report on the trial with Oscar Ryan.[31] On the first day, neither they, nor the reporters from *Ukrainian Labor News* or *Vapaus*, the Finnish left-wing paper, were permitted inside the courtroom. A police officer in the corridor told them straightforwardly that "we do not recognize your press."[32] Unable to watch the trial, Cecil-Smith and Ryan initially reported on the drama taking place outside the courtroom.[33]

Canadian Labor Defense League supporters tried to organize a protest outside the courthouse. Anticipating such a protest, the police seized copies of the pamphlets and dispersed the crowds before they could reach critical mass. The printers who made the pamphlets were arrested and charged with contempt of court. The police visited the offices of the *Worker* in an effort to determine who ordered the printing of the pamphlets, but no one would admit to it. Cecil-Smith expressed pride in this small act of solidarity among the working class.[34]

On the second day of the trial, Ryan and Cecil-Smith were allowed into the courtroom. They missed the opening statements, but it quickly became apparent that Crown prosecutor Gordon K. Sommerville's case depended on demonstrating two threats posed by the party. First, the Crown intended to show that the party's ideology itself was a threat to the state. Sommerville claimed that the trial was not about "argument, criticism, ideas, speeches, theories ... but the deliberate, long continued, subtle, Moscow controlled plot to overturn, by force of arms, by violence, by bloodshed, our institutions of church and state."[35] As the government saw it, the CPC sought the complete overhaul of the Canadian political and economic system by way of a violent, Bolshevik-style revolution. Second, the Crown would show that the party and its members were agents of a foreign power: the Soviet Union.

The eight defendants denied that they were violent revolutionaries. Hill, Bruce, Ewen, and Buck all testified that they did not personally advocate violence, and the Crown did not introduce any evidence to the contrary. Yes, the Eight explained, they believed in revolution, but the revolution they spoke of was inevitable due to the inherent weaknesses of the capitalist system. Marxist theory *predicted* a revolution. Capitalism was on the wane, and the revolution was inevitable – the party did not have to bring it about.[36] Buck said that the revolution could be armed, or it could be peaceful, depending on the circumstances.[37] The fact that it was armed in Russia did not mean that it necessarily had to be armed in Canada.

The Crown argued that the party was merely a puppet controlled by invisible strings from Moscow. Buck agreed that the party took direction from the Communist International in Moscow (the Comintern), although Ewen argued that the CPC did not receive "direction" from Moscow but merely "guidance."[38] To his detriment, Ewen explained that the party advocated defence of the Soviet Union, "*no matter who the aggressor against the Soviet Union is.*"[39] This was a dangerous remark for the Eight because it implied that their loyalty to the Soviet Union superseded their loyalty to Canada or the British Empire. Sommerville capitalized on the misstep. In his closing address he implored the jury, "Do not forget the question of the allegiance of these men to the Fatherland [the Soviet Union]."[40]

The jury returned their verdict on 13 November after only two hours of deliberation: the Eight were found guilty of seditious conspiracy and violation of section 98.* In an instant, the Communist Party of Canada became illegal. It was now a criminal act to be a member of the party, to possess or distribute its literature, or to attend its meetings. Unlike under any other criminal law, the onus rested on the accused to *disprove* the alleged association, not on the Crown to prove it beyond a reasonable doubt. Even the slightest affiliation with the party could provide sufficient grounds for deportation, and this began generating fears among many immigrant communities, who constituted a large segment of the party's membership.[41]

At another moment in history, the decision in *Rex v. Buck* might have been cause for public outcry. However, in 1931 the fear of communism ran deep. The party's animosity toward religion and threat to established bourgeois civil order aside, an increasing number of Canadians feared foreign-controlled agents who might be seeking to overthrow the government, seize private property, reorganize and further ruin the economy, and otherwise rob Canada of its institutional stability. The idea was terrifying, and, for many, the fact that no act of revolutionary

* The ruling on seditious conspiracy was overturned on appeal before the Ontario Court of Appeal, which held that the charge had not been proved, as no conspiracy had been established.

violence had been undertaken or planned was irrelevant. Interestingly, although there was certainly persecution of the Communist Parties in Great Britain and the United States, neither country actually banned these parties during the 1930s. Only Canada took this exceptional step.

By the time the trial was concluded, the remaining members of the party's central leadership had gone underground. Some would stay there until Prime Minister Mackenzie King repealed section 98 in 1936. For the time being, however, the party had to operate through its fronts: the Canadian Labor Defense League, the Progressive Arts Club, the Workers' Unity League, and the Friends of the Soviet Union. The *Worker* did not shut down, but it immediately carried a proviso: "It will be noticed that this number of 'The Worker' does not bear the caption 'Official Organ of the Communist Party of Canada.' The Worker Publishing Association, an undertaking registered with the authorities, is the sole owner and publisher of 'The Worker.'"[42]

The banning of the Communist Party of Canada did not deter Cecil-Smith. Indeed, the court's decision seemed only to galvanize him. He had been raised in the missionary tradition of advancing one's beliefs at great personal risk. For Cecil-Smith's parents, this meant braving isolation, the elements, the Boxers, and bandits (and, later, the Red Army), to save the souls of the Chinese people. Edward's mother, Ida, stated that, despite these risks, "the best paying thing in the world ... is to be a missionary."[43] Perhaps, then, it was not surprising that her son risked police surveillance, beatings, and imprisonment, not to prepare souls for the afterlife, but to prepare workers for the revolution.[44] Later, the same ethic would lead him to take up arms in the service of Republican Spain.

There is no indication that Edward Cecil-Smith was ever involved in violence or physical preparations for a revolution. He did not advocate violence in his writings, and his RCMP file does not indicate that he was ever suspected of committing, preparing for, or inciting violence in any way. In fact, his writings cautioned that the time for revolution was not yet at hand; the apparatuses of state control in Canada were still too strong and the workers still too disorganized for such acts to make any sense. In a 1934 editorial in the *Worker*, he wrote that "a revolutionary attempt without a revolutionary situation would be suicidal folly, and at the present moment no one in his right mind would pretend that such a situation exists."[45] For the time being, preparing for the revolution meant organizing and educating the masses to be ready to take control when the old order collapsed.

Cecil-Smith believed that there was a moral imperative to prepare for the revolution: "Unless we are really prepared, as a class, to take things over after we have given the push to the toppling structure, and to build a classless system in which profit has no place, we had best crawl back to our flop houses and thank God for our slumgullion and cast off clothes."[46] The workers either had to be prepared to take control, or they had to resign themselves to their current destitution. Only when the time was ripe, and workers were prepared, would Canada be pulled from its squalor, with its people enjoying the favourable conditions that party members believed existed in the Soviet Union, a country, Cecil-Smith argued, where all unemployment had been eliminated.[47] There could be no half-measures. The better prepared the proletariat, Cecil-Smith wrote, "the simpler and less bloody will be the final struggle against capitalism."[48] He maintained that preparing for the revolution required electing representatives of the working class to public office, developing a class consciousness among the workers, and developing a highly trained vanguard to lead them.[49] The workers would face opposition every step of the way, but each of these conflicts were "the preliminary skirmishes which are rehearsals for the revolution."[50]

Cecil-Smith threw his weight behind the goal of developing the class consciousness of the proletariat through the Progressive Arts Club. The forum allowed him to apply his interests in the arts as well as his experience as a journalist. He had worked on a number of periodicals since 1929, but the Progressive Arts Club gave him the opportunity to edit one of his own. The organization launched its own magazine, *Masses,* in April 1932, with Cecil-Smith as the editor-in-chief.

Masses was similar in concept and design to its American equivalent, *New Masses*, which had been in operation since 1926.[51] Despite the outward similarities, *Masses* was a stand-alone publication containing principally original content, with some British and American material. *Masses* ran for only twelve issues but provided a valuable forum for Canadian left-wing artists to share poems, short stories, and plays. Readers could order books on workers' issues, scripts for plays, and left-leaning songbooks. It published articles on how to organize local clubs, art exhibitions, and theatre productions, and included plenty of discussion by Cecil-Smith and others on the importance of workers' culture. Cecil-Smith also appears to have helped illustrate the magazine with distinctive linoleum block cartoons.[52]

The opening editorial of the first edition of *Masses* emphasized the working-class credentials of the staff. They were all workers who were "disgusted with the barren fields of bourgeois culture."[53] They called for sympathetic intellectuals to "climb down from their ivory towers" to help them, but emphasized that the workers would create their own culture, with or without their assistance. They had "a whole battlefield of barbed wire to traverse," but the struggle was right and necessary. Cecil-Smith wrote a companion piece in the *Canadian Labor Defender*, explaining that, "For many years the Canadian working class have continued their struggle without any great aid from intellectuals, artists and writers."[54] *Masses* would change this. The workers, "politicized or not," lived in unique circumstances that provided much fodder for artistic expression. Furthermore, authors and artists are "gradually being forced to take sides in the class conflict."[55] Cecil-Smith wanted to make sure they picked the correct side. These "class collaborators" were essential to the Progressive Arts Club's success. Cecil-Smith's writings indicate that he had not entirely accepted the doctrine of the Third Period – strict working-class solidarity in the face of capitalism's impending collapse – nor was he obedient enough to maintain the facade of acceptance.

Cecil-Smith and Oscar Ryan were eager to recreate in Canada what they perceived to be a vibrant workers' cultural scene in the Soviet Union. Replicating Soviet-style theatre would help the working class shed their preconceived notions of the natural order of society and assist in producing the class consciousness necessary for the revolution. Furthermore, Soviet-style cultural production, they believed, was superior to the "drivel" coming out of Hollywood and the bourgeois theatre scene. Ryan gave a glowing description of the state of the theatre in the Soviet Union:

> The theatre has truly become a popular and far-flung institution in the U.S.S.R. To list only a few outstanding organizations, there are children's theatres, the Tram (a youth theatre), the many trade union theatres, the Red Army theatre organization. Then there are the theatres of the national minorities, among many of whom the idea of a theatre was not even developed before the revolution – the theatres of the Chuvash, Moldavian, Tartar, Tadjik, Uzbek, Bashkir, Marman, Mongolian, and scores of other national minorities. These are true people's theatres in the full sense of the word – theatres which are "national" in form, revolutionary in content ...
>
> The Soviet Theatre is a dynamic theatre; the setting, the acting, the direction, the plays, are blended into technical, artistic and social achievements with which none other can compare. Why? Because the Soviet theatre has the benefit of Marxist interpretation, dialectic handling, that brings the most out of a playwright's script, that brings life and a new social meaning even out of Shakespeare. It interprets, analyzes, teaches.[56]

Cecil-Smith and Ryan wanted to create Canadian plays that would "teach" and unify the Canadian working class. They were inspired by Soviet methods, such as the use of short agitation and propaganda plays ("agitprop") and chants (the back-and-forth repetition of key words and slogans). The Soviet Union provided materials in various languages through the All-Union Society for Cultural Relations with Foreign Countries, known by its Russian initials, VOKS. VOKS had an Anglo-American Division that sent English-language pamphlets, magazines, political writings, and even movies and music to those interested.[57]

Cecil-Smith corresponded with VOKS, but mail between Canada and the Soviet Union was monitored closely by Canadian authorities and therefore unreliable. Intercepted mail would often be seized. For example, in the summer of 1932, customs officials stopped five documents sent to Cecil-Smith from Moscow, including four editions of the provocatively titled monthly magazine *Literature of the World Revolution*, edited and printed in Moscow by the state publishing house.[58] The fifth document was an article in Russian called "The Cultural Revolution of Soviet Russia," described by the translator as "displaying a revolutionary phraseology without being revolutionary in fact."[59] Now that the party was outlawed, it was a criminal offence to possess or distribute such literature. The customs officials notified the RCMP, which launched its first investigation of Cecil-Smith.[60] RCMP Commissioner James Howden MacBrien and Assistant Commissioner of Customs Charles Blair decided to "exclude" these documents: they were seized and not allowed into the country.

Commissioner MacBrien directed the Toronto RCMP detachment to launch an investigation of Cecil-Smith. The Toronto Criminal Investigations Branch assigned its principal detective to the case, Detective Corporal Robert W. Irvine. Irvine purchased a copy of *Masses* and staked out the magazine's post office box. Dressed in plain clothes, he waited for Cecil-Smith and then casually struck up a conversation when he arrived to check his mail. He provided a physical description, the first on record: "Age: about 32 years. Height: about 5-8. Build: fairly stout. Weight: about 150 lbs. Hair: Brown. Complexion: Fair. Eyes: Brown. Nose: Straight. Ginger mustache. Teeth: Little crooked, clean. Wears glasses. Smooth and quiet speaker. Swears a little. Married man." He also noted that Cecil-Smith had previously been a reporter for the *Mail and Empire* but now appeared to be unemployed.[61]

Irvine's report, along with the correspondence between the RCMP's National Headquarters and the Toronto detachment, marks the beginning of Cecil-Smith's extensive RCMP file. It contains a wealth of information about Cecil-Smith's life, cataloguing his whereabouts in general, attendance at party meetings, and some of his writings. Although Cecil-Smith did much of his public work through front organizations – presenting an additional hurdle for a would-be prosecutor – by 1934, the RCMP had more than enough information to build a case against him for violating section 98. They could easily show that he was a member of this illegal organization, possessed its literature, openly promoted it, and attended its meetings. In spite of the opportunity, the RCMP or the political decision-makers showed that they could be selective with such information and did not simply prosecute party members at every available opportunity. In Cecil-Smith's thirty years under close surveillance, he was not charged even once; nor is there any indication that the RCMP seriously considered laying charges against him.

Cecil-Smith held his RCMP pursuers in extremely low regard. His comments in an editorial in the *Worker* are instructive and worth quoting in full:

> Are the mounties thugs? Disregarding the dictionary definition of thug, which will refer you to an East Indian secret society, the word has a very definite meaning in English, and especially on this continent where it is very often used in the newspapers. A thug is an armed bully, hired to defend the ill-gotten spoils of a gangster chief and to beat down the resistance of those who are not willing to be robbed peacefully. He is a plug-ugly who does not hesitate to shoot, to club, and to injure the victims in the interests of his chief. He does not necessarily take a large share of the profits, but on the contrary is sometimes quite poorly paid for the risks he takes. Often, to bolster up his courage for particular deeds, he resorts to drugs.
>
> By such a definition, I think we must at once agree that not only the Mounted Police, but also provincial and city police are thugs.[62]

Cecil-Smith's point of view was largely the product of the strike-breaking roles filled by the police at the time. He had also seen Toronto's Chief Constable Dennis Draper's police terminate peaceful rallies in Queen's Park. He had read about the RCMP's role in ending strikes in places like Estevan, where some of the striking miners had been killed. He viewed the police in general as enforcers of an unjust system, little better than the police he had seen beating rickshaw coolies back in Shanghai.

Chapter Four

"Theatre – Our Weapon"

The Workers' Theatre was conceived as part of the Progressive Arts Club in the summer of 1931. Cecil-Smith saw this type of theatre as an important element of the workers' struggle. It disrupted the cultural hegemony of the capitalists and provided a tool to communicate with, and especially educate, the working class. It could help create the class consciousness that he believed was a prerequisite for the revolution. The Workers' Theatre's motto, "Theatre – Our Weapon," symbolized its agenda. It was not merely providing depictions of the class struggle; rather, it members were active participants in it, as one of their chants suggests:[1]

> Is it possible for our theatre NOT to be a weapon?
> Chorus: NO!
> 1st: Down with the theatre where the bourgeois come to amuse themselves!
> 2nd: Down with the theatre where the idle parasites come to amuse themselves!
> 3rd: Down with the theatre where drunken debauchery dopes the minds of the master and their obedient slaves!
> 4th: Down with the theatre which lulls the indignation of the hungry slaves of capitalism!
> Chorus: DOWN WITH IT!
> 1st: Long live the theatre of revolutionary anger!
> 2nd: The theatre organizing the will of the workers!
> 3rd: The theatre which has inscribed on its Red Banners
> Chorus: REVOLUTION![2]

Cecil-Smith was passionate about promoting the Workers' Theatre. Although he had no personal interest in acting or creative writing, he saw great value in this kind of storytelling. He came from a family of intellectuals; he and his parents happily read, digested, debated, and wrote about the primary texts of their faith. Though their respective audiences sought different answers, parents and son alike employed similar rhetorical and strategic approaches to persuading the masses to "believe." Whereas Cecil-Smith's parents hiked miles into the Chinese countryside, went to where the people were gathered, and told modified parables that they believed would resonate with their audience, the Workers' Theatre would put on simple plays that would resonate with the workers in their halls and on picket lines. Like his parents, Cecil-Smith would help shape the stories and promote activities in service of a higher ideological cause.

Creating the Workers' Theatre was no small feat. The Communist Party of Canada had few people with any real experience in the theatre. Toby Gordon had some training in New York City, which proved to be immensely valuable to the organization. Jim Watts did not have any real training, but she was well educated and approached the endeavour with incredible energy. Oscar Ryan had a natural inclination toward theatre and cinema; he would write film and theatre reviews in the party press for decades, and wrote a few plays and poems of his own. Lilian Gouge, Cecil-Smith's wife, did not write creatively, but she enjoyed acting. Creating a successful Workers' Theatre required attracting people with the right skills, such as Watts's fellow students at the University of Toronto, and developing new skills among the existing members. David Hogg, Cecil-Smith's friend from Chefoo, wrote the inaugural piece on the Workers' Theatre for *Masses* in April 1932. He described the group as "young and crude" but noted that it just needed "a chance at birth. Help is needed, talent, ideas, plays, encouragement, informed constructive criticism."[3]

Most of the Workers' Theatre's first productions were borrowed from scripts printed in working-class magazines from Great Britain or the United States. They were generally agitprops or chants, such as *Labor's Love Lost* from the *American Worker's Theatre Magazine*, or *Meerut*, a mass recitation from England. These productions were relatively simple and cost effective. Mass recitations did not require any costumes or sets, and agitprops generally involved fewer than five actors dressed in black uniforms using small props to distinguish the characters, like a top hat for a capitalist, or a wooden rifle for a soldier. By the summer of 1933, the Workers' Theatre had a repertoire of at least ten plays and chants, including some that had been produced by the Progressive Arts Club's own Writers' Group.

Cecil-Smith chaired the Writers' Group. With the exception of *Eight Men Speak*, which is discussed below, he did not write any plays, poems, or short stories. His role as chair seems principally to have been to harness the creative energy of the writers and ensure that works had sufficient propaganda value before being performed by the Workers' Theatre. Oscar Ryan, often under the pseudonym Maurice Granite, wrote for the Writers Group, including poems, essays, movie reviews, and the mass chant *Unity*, which depicted how capitalists sought to divide and confuse workers confronted with the challenges of the Depression:

> 1st Cap[italist].: Less say 'sall the fault of the Jews.
> 3rd Cap.: And the Indians.
> 2nd Cap.: And of course the Reds.
> 4th Cap.: Not the Jews, Not the Indians – Only the Reds![4]

The chant's message was that the workers' only defence was to unite as a group.

Many of the works produced by the Writers' Group were based on current events. Dorothy Livesay wrote a pantomime for children about Joe Derry, a Young Communist League leader who had been arrested under section 98; Cecil-Smith provided the illustrations when it was printed in *Masses*. Another play, *Eviction*, was about Nick Zynchuk, a young man shot and killed by a police officer during an eviction in Montreal.[5] Livesay wrote a story, "Zynchuk's Funeral," about the same young man's funeral procession, which turned into a protest march of 10,000 people and was met with police violence.[6] Stanley Ryerson wrote *War in the East*, an agitprop about Japan's 1931 invasion of Manchuria. The play featured four symbolic characters – War, Priest (symbolizing religion), Capitalist, and Mikado (Japanese imperialism) – and their interactions.[7] Cecil-Smith likely took a particular interest in Ryerson's writing, given his personal experiences and interest in China.

The Workers' Theatre performed these chants and agitprops wherever it could reach an audience of workers. Toby Gordon recalled that the group performed "in workers' halls, outdoors on trucks or on bandstands in parks."[8] It also provided entertainment at Canadian Labor Defense League and Workers' Unity League rallies, May Day celebrations, and events for Ukrainians, Finnish, and Macedonian cultural groups.[9] To help promote its productions, Cecil-Smith travelled with the Workers' Theatre when it went on tour.[10] He also wrote letters to publications like *Canadian Forum* to promote the group more broadly.

The Workers' Theatre performances at picket lines were particularly notable. In St. Catharines, the troupe came across 165 striking workers at the Canadian Canners Ltd. factory. Seeking to help the strikers, the actors performed their plays for those on the picket lines. The next day, theatre members deliberately returned to participate more directly in the demonstrations. Cecil-Smith was spotted by the RCMP at this second event. He was organizing party members, unemployed workers, and the striking workers themselves.[11] The Workers' Theatre performed works from its repertoire for the crowd, but its members also helped make banners and signs for the workers, pushed a boxcar in front of a gate to keep out "scabs," and eventually got arrested (but were quickly released) by the local police for interfering in the strike.[12] The following autumn, they would perform for strikers during the Stratford Furniture Workers strike in Stratford, Ontario, where the Royal Canadian Regiment was called out to maintain order. Lilian Gouge was at the site of the strike with the Workers' Theatre, but there is no record of her husband being there with her.[13] This smaller-scale activism would set the stage for what would become the most infamous of the Workers' Theatre performances: *Eight Men Speak*, a play based on the trial and imprisonment of the CPC leadership. It would both elicit further suppressive actions against the party and, ironically, engender more public sympathy for it.

On 18 October 1932, the *Globe* carried a distressing story out of Kingston, with the headline "Shots Fired by Guards."[14] The Kingston Penitentiary, home of much of the party's senior leadership, had been the scene of a prisoner strike that turned into a riot. Two hundred soldiers of the Royal Canadian Horse Artillery at the nearby Tête de Pont barracks were called in to stabilize the situation. The party in Toronto knew little beyond the fact that shots had been fired in the prison. Officials claimed that only ten shots had been fired, but locals in Kingston had reported hearing between thirty and a hundred shots, suggesting a serious altercation.[15] Buck and the other imprisoned leaders were not allowed mail, phone calls, or visitors. The Canadian Labor Defense League organized an emergency delegation to go to Kingston and then on to Ottawa to meet with the minister of justice to intercede on behalf of the prisoners. Cecil-Smith, then a member of the league's National Committee, was elected to head the delegation.[16]

Cecil-Smith and the other members of the delegation would try to determine the state of the prisoners in Kingston. Their demands included that prisoners have the right to receive visits from their families, that a public hearing be held into the rights of the political prisoners, and that there be no discrimination against the strikers.[17] Cecil-Smith went to Kingston ahead of the rest of the delegation. He planned to link up with militant unions in order to engineer a protest meeting and to rally the media to raise awareness of the delegation's mission. He was unsuccessful. He sent a telegraph back to the Canadian Labor Defense League headquarters in Toronto: "Cannot trace Union Trades Council say defunct four years have more leads to follow tomorrow. Press gone save one drunk but caught [the Toronto] Star and tipped them off."[18] Without a warrant, a telegraph clerk gave Detective Robert Irvine of the RCMP a copy of the message, which he placed in Cecil-Smith's file.

The rest of the league's delegation arrived in Kingston on 25 October.[19] Lilly Adler, Buck's personal secretary, and James Hicks, a league representative, escorted the wives and children of the Eight.[20] Beckie Buhay, the future chair of the Friends of the Mackenzie-Papineau Battalion, was there in her capacity as the league's national secretary and as the wife of Tom Ewen, one of the prisoners.[21] The group went to the prison. Cecil-Smith's article in *Canadian Labor Defender* described the ominous scene: "Grey Walls of Kingston. Portsmouth Penitentiary. Grey limestone walls stretching from the highroad to the dull-colored lake, silhouetted against a threatening sky. The only joyful thing, the flag of imperialism dancing on its staff over the main gateway, in the wet miserable wind that carried a heavy smudge from a passing lake freighter."[22] The "flag of imperialism" had once meant a great deal to Cecil-Smith. Now it represented what he felt was an increasingly repressive regime, a corruption of the values that he held dear.

As the delegation entered the prison, they were greeted by soldiers from the nearby garrison. The soldiers, "all steel helmeted, all armed with ball-loaded rifles ... all medal-less youngsters from the Kingston artillery garrison. They were here to show that the capitalist dictatorship does not hesitate to use force and violence against striking workers."[23] The guards summoned the senior officer at the prison to meet with the delegation. Brigadier D.M. Ormond, the inspector of penitentiaries dispatched to Kingston to take control and investigate the situation, met them at the front gate.[24]

Ormond had little time for the delegation. Cecil-Smith wrote that Ormond simply said, "You saw my announcement in the press? Time is inopportune ... Too busy to answer telegrams. Go see the minister of justice."[25] The visitors did not see their incarcerated family members or get any new information about their health or well-being.

Having some extra time in Kingston, the delegation wandered about Princess Street and some of the residential neighbourhoods to distribute pamphlets. These documents were "the first worker handbills seen on the streets of Kingston," Cecil-Smith proudly claimed.[26] He recalled, "They read them, these Kingston workers. They have never seen anything like it before, but they stop in the streets and read these leaflets."[27] Not everyone was pleased. The Kingston branch of the Royal Canadian

Legion condemned the leaflets and called for a general ban on the distribution of revolutionary literature, concerned that these documents were "bound to cause considerable trouble."[28] The delegation continued to Ottawa to meet with representatives of the federal government to plead their case.

Cecil-Smith despised the Conservative government and particularly Prime Minister R.B. Bennett. He referred to Bennett simply as "R.B." or "Iron Heel" Bennett, a nickname that came from an August 1932 speech in which Bennett criticized those calling for reform: "What do they offer you in exchange for the present order? Socialism, Communism, dictatorship. They are sowing the seeds of unrest everywhere. Right in this city such propaganda is being carried on and in the little out of the way places as well. And we know that throughout Canada this propaganda is being put forward by organizations from foreign lands that seek to destroy our institutions. And we ask every man and woman in this country to put the iron heel of ruthlessness against a thing of that kind."[29] Cecil-Smith wrote that Bennett only shed "crocodile tears" for the plight of the Canadian working class. He was quick to point out that the prime minister was a millionaire and that the 1927 Directory of Directors showed him to be a director at Calgary Power, Canadian General Electric, and the Royal Bank of Canada. He thought that Bennett cared only for the well-being of big businesses and would say, and do, whatever it took to ensure their success.[30]

The delegation met with Minister of Justice Hugh Guthrie in Ottawa.[31] Guthrie invited his deputy minister, four reporters, and a stenographer to the meeting to ensure that he could not subsequently be misquoted. Guthrie did not trust the delegation. He had been instrumental in the creation of section 98 in the first place, as well as an important driving force in Bennett's campaign against the Communist Party of Canada.[32]

Guthrie listened as Cecil-Smith outlined the league's demands, but he budged little. Guthrie explained that he did not like the word "demand" and that there was nothing wrong with the prison conditions* – conditions described by the *Worker* as "agonizing and unendurable."[33] Furthermore, Guthrie said, the "strike" was just a riot. There could not be normal visits to the prison, from family or anyone else, until

* The riots eventually led to the appointment of Justice Joseph Archambault to examine the state of Canadian prisons. In 1938, after four years of investigating, *The Royal Commission Report on Penal Reform in Canada* (better known as the Archambault Report) concluded that the conditions of the prisons at the times of the riots were, if not "unendurable," certainly improper. The Archambault Report led to a series of reforms that focused prison resources on rehabilitation instead of punishment.

normal discipline was restored. However, he said that he would instruct Ormond to let the prisoners write letters to their families within the next three weeks and to allow them greater reading privileges.[34]

Cecil-Smith returned to Toronto and presented the results of the delegation to a Canadian Labor Defense League public meeting at the Ukrainian Labor-Farmer Temple.[35] RCMP Detective Irvine, who had closely monitored Cecil-Smith's trip to Kingston and Ottawa, and Constable H.J. Stanton, attended.[36] Cecil-Smith described Ormond as lacking in courtesy, "similar to that of other Generals in Toronto," and Guthrie as a "smooth talker." Irvine did not think much of Cecil-Smith's oratory. He recorded that Cecil-Smith "made a poor attempt" to describe the delegation's activities, and that he "is not a very good speaker, he talks very low and is hard to understand." This description was presumably not offered simply for the sake of an insult, but rather was an assessment of Cecil-Smith's leadership potential within the party. Irvine also noted that the audience comprised 850 people, "the majority being foreigners."[37]

The events of October 1932 at Kingston Penitentiary became clearer to the party and the public at large when the Eight were allowed to receive visitors in January 1933. This new knowledge would both confirm their worst fears about trusting the government and inspire Cecil-Smith to orient the Progressive Arts Club toward a specific goal: the release of the Eight. Through Buck's wife, Cecil-Smith learned that the prisoners had held a strike on the afternoon of 17 October and that the strike had escalated into a riot. Guards were taken hostage, the army was called in to calm the situation, and shots were fired. The situation seemed resolved by the end of the day.[38] But on 20 October, it was clear that calm had not been fully restored. The prisoners protested from inside their cells. The army returned and shots were fired into some cells to quiet the prisoners. One prisoner was shot in the shoulder and did not receive medical treatment for twenty-two hours.[39] Tim Buck's cell was shot into seven times.[40]

Buck stood trial during the summer of 1933 on charges of inciting the riot. Cecil-Smith returned to Kingston with Beckie Buhay to observe the trial.[41] Their presence attracted greater police attention than had their previous visits. This time, they were stopped by Kingston police, their vehicle was searched, and their chauffeur was brought in for questioning.[42] Cecil-Smith was again disappointed in the Canadian courts when Buck was found guilty of inciting the riot and the government announced that it would not take any disciplinary action against the guards who had fired on him. These shots, Minister of Justice Guthrie explained in the House of Commons, "were fired for purposes of frightening him [Buck] or stopping him ... not with the idea of injuring him."[43] Whatever the guards' intentions, it would have required an extraordinary feat of marksmanship to fire through Buck's small cell window fifty feet above the ground with confidence that they would not hit him as he stood in the window. The party viewed the incident as a failed attempt at political assassination.

Cecil-Smith had remained active in the Canadian Labor Defense League for several years, but, by the spring of 1932, he was increasingly devoting his time to the Progressive Art Club. He edited and wrote in *Masses*, chaired the Writers' Group, and promoted the Workers' Theatre. These activities, he believed, worked toward the important goal of preparing the working class for the revolution. However, he would soon find that the Progressive Arts Club could be used to meet the more immediate goals of the party and the Canadian Labor Defense League: the repeal of section 98. At their first national convention, during the summer of 1933, the league's membership discussed the riot, the continued imprisonment of party leaders, and the progress of their campaign against section 98 and for the release of the Eight. The membership decided that, although legal challenges to section 98 had to continue, the law could be defeated only by appealing to "the working class courts – the streets."[44]

The convention minutes make no mention of the theatre as a tool in this public relations campaign, but Cecil-Smith and Oscar Ryan believed that the theatre could make a valuable contribution. Together, they put the Workers' Theatre to work as a propaganda tool for the Canadian Labor Defense League's campaign against section 98: they would produce a play to put the government itself on trial.[45] The play would give the Eight, silenced by the state, the opportunity to be heard by the workers. Hence, the title of the play: *Eight Men Speak*.

Cecil-Smith and Ryan's new project was ambitious. The Workers' Theatre normally produced short plays with five actors dressed in black. *Eight Men Speak* grew into a six-act play with sets and a cast of thirty-two actors. Jim Watts was the play's first director but stepped aside when the load became too heavy – it took four people to replace her.[46] It was a gargantuan undertaking, made all the more challenging by the ambitious timeline. Remarkably, the play was written, produced, and performed within two months. Ryan and Cecil-Smith worked together closely, both writing and directing the play, handling public relations and advertising, coordinating the activities of the Progressive Arts Club as a whole, and even performing in the final production.

The writing alone was a challenge. The play was written by four people: Cecil-Smith, Ryan, Mildred Goldberg, and Frank Love. Love appears to have been the primary author of the play, with Goldberg writing the mass chants. Cecil-Smith and Ryan became increasingly involved as time began to run short. Cecil-Smith wrote Act 5, the defence, which Love described as the best scene in the play, and Cecil-Smith and Ryan are presumed to have written the trial scenes in Act 3, given that they had been present for the actual prosecution of Tim Buck.[47] Ryan had written short plays before, but this was Cecil-Smith's first attributed work of creative writing.

Cecil-Smith and Ryan organized all the elements of the Progressive Arts Club to play a role in the production. The artists were brought in to design and produce the sets. Avrom Yanovsky, who illustrated the pages of the party press, created the sets and played the role of Sam Carr.[48] Seamstresses from the needle workers' unions assisted with costumes. They also needed more actors. The play's four directors – Toby Gordon, Cecil Greenwold, Oscar Ryan, and Cecil-Smith – all acted in the play, as did its writers. Watts, the original director, stayed on as an assistant to Oscar Ryan and also acted in the play. Lilian Gouge, Cecil-Smith's wife, acted in the play and also worked as the stage manager.[49] When they needed still more actors to complete the cast, they drew upon the Men's Unemployed Council.

Members of the Workers' Theatre had grown accustomed to regular run-ins with Dennis Draper's Red Squad. The detectives of the Red Squad became regular theatregoers, attending rehearsals and performances. Oscar Ryan later recalled,

> Periodically, the Red Squad would turn up at rehearsal – and the Red Squad were people like Det. Sgt. William Nursey, Det. Dan Mann, Det. Simpson. These were great beefy types, six, seven feet or twenty feet tall – I don't know. They wouldn't always arrest people because they knew as soon as anybody was arrested the Labor Defense League would get its lawyer on the job immediately and get them out on bail, if at all possible. But they would harass. They would bother us. There were very few directors who could conduct a rehearsal with three or four cops, plainclothes detectives, standing there, grinning at you. Standing there with their arms akimbo saying, "Show us, boys!" and knowing, as some of the actors in the cast knew, that they could be deported because they were foreigners.[50]

The Toronto police monitored the Workers' Theatre in general, but *Eight Men Speak* seemed to attract particular attention. The Toronto Board of Police Commissioners carefully reviewed the reports from the Red Squad detectives regarding the play's production. On 1 December 1933, the commission decided that, instead of banning the play before its inaugural performance, officers would attend *Eight Men Speak*, take notes, and ban the play if necessary.[51]

Eight Men Speak was rehearsed at the Ukrainian Labor-Farmer Temple Hall, but would be performed in the Standard Theatre, a venue that the CPC had used in the past. In 1929, in a celebration to mark the fifth anniversary of the death of Lenin, a party rally at that theatre had been dispersed by the Toronto police's Red Squad for refusing to abide by a police prohibition against the use of foreign languages in public halls. When a speaker uttered words in Yiddish, he was arrested and escorted out. A second man spoke Yiddish; he was also arrested. Then the police used tear gas, for the first time in Canada, to drive the crowd out of the theatre. Detective Sergeant Nursey had been on hand that cold January evening in 1929.[52] He was again at the Standard Theatre for the first performance of *Eight Men Speak*, this time quietly taking notes.

Eight Men Speak debuted to a full house on 4 December 1933. The audience gathered for what has been called a "party rally in theatrical disguise."[53] The play opens with a garden party where female representatives of the bourgeoisie, played by Jim Watts and Lilian Gouge, chat with Cecil-Smith's character, the prison warden, and other members of their class. Watts's character is the prison warden's wife. Gouge's character, described as a "sleek English adventuress," flirts openly with the husbands at the party, with Cecil-Smith's character "entangled in her snares." Their conversations lampoon the prison system and their detachment from the working class. When Gouge's character learns that the Eight had been "making speeches and organizing Soviets," she exclaims "How frightful! Why weren't they shot?" Cecil-Smith, described as "every inch a military man," replies, "Oh, this is a democratic country, Mrs. Berkeley, so we gave them five years."[54]

Eight Men Speak goes on to mock the Canadian criminal justice system, depicting the trial of the Eight for violating section 98, and of Buck for inciting the inmates to riot, as farcical. Judges are shown to be blindly deferential to police testimony, which is itself characterized as biased against the working class. Decisions are rendered by a jury of literal puppets. Along the way, the play highlights state violence against workers, such as the RCMP's shooting of striking miners in Estevan. The ghosts of the three dead workers introduce themselves and explain that they were killed: "Because we organized!"[55] The ghosts of two other martyrs appear next: "I am Peter Grabowski, unemployed transient, shot in the back at Hornepayne, because the tabernacle of property had been desecrated"; then "I am Nick Zynchuk, killed by a police bullet in the back, killed at an eviction in Montreal, killed to intimidate the unemployed in Montreal."[56] Thomas Jones, a prisoner in the cell next to Tim Buck's, then takes the stand to tell the story of the shooting. Tim Buck appears in a window, and guards fire five shots at him. The stage goes black after the fifth gunshot.[57] Buck, although still alive, is symbolically placed in the pantheon of martyrs.

The Eight speak out against such persecution in their mass chant in Act 4. They implore the workers of different backgrounds and circumstances to fight back – against the system and all that it represents – and to not to allow themselves to be cowed by self-serving capitalists.

The play transitions to the "Workers' Court" in Act 5, the act written by Cecil-Smith. Guard X – whose name mocks the anonymity that the state affords its henchman – the guard who shot into Tim Buck's cell, is now on trial before the Workers' Judge, played by Ryan. The audience plays the role of the jury. Toby Gordon plays the prosecutor, a lawyer from the Canadian Labor Defense League. Cecil-Smith's character – Mr. Capitalism, of the law firm Capitalism, Capitalism, and Exploitation – defends Guard X for the charge of shooting at Buck in his cell. Wearing a bald cap and padding around his waist, to parody the well-fed capitalist, Cecil-Smith's character implores Ryan to disregard the testimony of criminals against Guard X. Instead, Ryan should believe the testimony of Guard X's character witnesses, who testifies that Guard X would "not do such an un-British and un-Christian thing as this."[58] Besides, Cecil-Smith argued, this trial is about something much more important than Guard X's guilt or innocence.

Cecil-Smith's character insists that the Workers' Judge quash the indictment, lest society itself be overturned. Cecil-Smith gives an impassioned plea:

> This whole procedure is resulting in a wave of unrest among the laboring classes ... As a result, the unity which should exist between employer and workman, in these days of tribulation (*great display of sorrow*) when we should all pull together – this spirit of team play ... without which the glorious British Commonwealth of Nations could not have been built – this spirit of self-sacrifice which enables us to send so many thousands of the best flower of Canadian manhood to give up their lives on the fields of Flanders for our sakes (*here he shows signs of breaking into tears*) – these glorious things are now seriously endangered ... If this sort of thing goes on, we shall no longer be able to govern as we have been used. We shall no longer be able to send gunboats to Anyox, or tanks to Stratford, to help our friends, the mine owners and manufacturers.[59]

The parody continues as Cecil-Smith examines his witnesses: a prison guard who formerly served in the British Army, a priest, and

Mr. Dufrie, the minister of justice (a very thinly veiled parody of Hugh Guthrie, the actual minister). Their testimony speaks little to the actual shooting but rather parodies their use of religion and state hegemony to keep the capitalists in power.

The trial culminates with the closing submissions of Cecil-Smith's Mr. Capitalism and Toby Gordon's Canadian Labor Defense League character. Cecil-Smith has by this time abandoned any attempt to prove that Guard X did not shoot at Tim Buck and instead focuses on the devastating consequences to society if Guard X is held accountable for his actions:

> This sort of thing must be as long as we value the age old traditions of the British people. Never must we allow dissension to be sown among us. We must always preserve the blind faith with which we have taught the man in the street to regard our institutions – our state – our prison system – our banks – our Empire ...
>
> Therefore I say again that on no account can we permit this charge against Guard X to be proven. If this court finds Mr. X guilty, it will be doing serious harm to the beliefs which we have cultivated through church and school; and which our press has been maintaining for the past century.
>
> Why, I tell you, this is a terrible thing that you are doing. Exposing the prison system, and the methods in which we have to use the police and troops.
>
> Don't you understand?
>
> *(He goes over to Guard X and places his hand on the prisoner's shoulder.)*
>
> Look at this poor man. Remember that he has a wife and eight children. Buck was only a prisoner – and a worker at that. It isn't as if he was anybody of importance. It's much more important that we keep the Canadian working class quiet at this time.
>
> Surely we have enough trouble with strikes and hunger and unemployed demonstrations without dragging this thing into it.
>
> I implore you all, not to let this thing go any further, I can absolutely promise that we will devise new ways of keeping the workers quiet in the future – if we possibly can.[60]

After a brief rebuttal by Toby Gordon, Oscar Ryan asks if Guard X has anything to say for himself. Guard X's defence is an indictment of capitalism. He frantically responds:

> What if I did shoot at Buck? You can't do anything to me and let *him* get away (*pointing at Capitalism, who also is visibly wilting*). He's in this just as

> deep as I am. All my life, I've listened to him and his friends, and if you don't like Buck being shot at, you've got to take it out of him, too ...
>
> How am I any different from the police, or the militia? We all do the same job. And he's the guy (*pointing to Capitalism*) who uses us all. Ever since I was a kid in school, I've been told that he was always right. At church I was taught to obey my masters, and that's what I do. They pay me and I deliver the goods. The newspapers and the radio tell me that these reds are a menace to civilization, so one or two less of them wouldn't be so bad.

At this point, the crowd of workers, clearly agitated, moves menacingly toward Guard X and Mr. Capitalism. Guard X grabs Cecil-Smith's character by the arm, advising "Let's get out of here." They gather their things and move to flee. Oscar Ryan raps his gavel and rises to his feet: "Stop! Fellow citizens of the Jury. You have heard the evidence in this case. You must now decide whether the accused, Guard X and his master, Capitalism, are guilty of this charge, or not guilty. What is your verdict?" Guard X and Mr. Capitalism cower in fear. The crowd of workers point at them and exclaim as one: "GUILTY!"[61] The curtain drops.

At the moment the curtain went down, the orchestra began playing "God Save the King," as was required by law at the time. The audience booed and jeered. Frank Love later recalled that the audience, playing the role of the jury, was booing the antics of Guard X and Mr. Capitalism and were merely continuing to boo as the anthem began to play.[62] The *Toronto Star* reported events differently. The *Star* reporter wrote that the audience loudly booed and jeered the anthem but began cheering when the band struck up "The Internationale."[63] Such conduct was considered sensational and unpatriotic, reinforcing the commonly held view that the party was a den of dangerous foreigners.

Eight Men Speak was not well reviewed by the critics. Toby Gordon, a leading actress, a director, and Oscar Ryan's companion and later wife, put it succinctly: "It was a bad play."[64] The *Varsity*, the student newspaper at the University of Toronto, described it as, "surprisingly good and surprisingly bad." It lacked a sense of connected action to provide any kind of continuity through the six acts, the scenery was "meagre," and most of the acting "incongruous." Although the working men were depicted somewhat realistically, Guard X was portrayed as "dope fiendish," and the "bourgeois parts were burlesqued beyond credibility." These caricatures were unnecessary and distracted from the play, as "surely even the proletariat are familiar with human beings as they are even if they take the form of exploiters or parasites!"[65]

In spite of these shortcoming, the play was a bold attempt to expand the capabilities of the Workers' Theatre, to tell stories on stage that might not otherwise be told, and to present new theatrical styles to Toronto audiences. A *Varsity* editorial noted that the play was valuable, as it introduced students, the "so-called bourgeoisie," to something new. Although the play was "an atrocious sample of Soviet art," the editorial asked, "Let the Communists speak out of their experiences and let us hear their interpretations of the times through which we are passing. They are bound to be fraught with meaning."[66] Good play or bad, the infusion of revolutionary themes and Soviet-style theatre struck the editor as an important addition to the Toronto theatre scene.

The CPC viewed the single showing of *Eight Men Speak* as a success and believed that further productions were viable. The *Worker* announced on 30 December that the play would return to the stage by popular demand.[67] Stewart Smith recalled that the Workers' Theatre had planned to tour the show across the country.[68] However, the play would not be performed again. Detective Sergeant Nursey had attended the first showing and submitted his report to the Toronto Police Board, which in turn passed it on to the provincial attorney general, William Herbert Price. The play attracted negative attention at the federal level as well. The RCMP included news of the play in its weekly bulletins, and Price passed Nursey's notes all the way to Prime Minister Bennett himself. The prime minister's secretary responded on his behalf in a letter to R.C. Matthews, the senior cabinet member from a Toronto riding: "Mr. Bennett has read the file and thinks that appropriate action should be taken through the Attorney General of the Province to protect society against these attacks."[69] The prime minister of Canada himself had directed that a theatrical production be banned from the stage.

The play was banned via a regulatory bluff. On 11 January, Isadore Axler, the manager of the Standard Theatre, was called in to Queen's Park for a meeting with the inspector of theatres. The matter was put to the manager in simple terms: if you put on the play, you will lose your licence. The manager cancelled the scheduled second performance.

Cecil-Smith was incensed by Axler's decision to cancel the play. He criticized Axler, whom he described as a member of a "Jewish socialist organization." Cecil-Smith believed that the manager should have shown solidarity with the working class and risked his licence. He saw Axler's decision as an example of "how the 'socialist' theatre owners line up against the working class when the pinch comes."[70]

Cecil-Smith, Oscar Ryan, and Frank Love went to Queen's Park the following Monday to argue for their right to perform *Eight Men Speak*.[71] They hoped to meet with Premier George Stewart Henry or the attorney general, but instead met only with W.A. Orr, an official with the Treasury Department. Orr told the delegation that the government had exercised its authority at the request of the Toronto Police Board, a request the board had every right to make.[72] Yet J.R.L. Starr of the Toronto Police Board denied that such a request had been made. Regardless, Cecil-Smith believed that the order had come right from Ottawa, from Prime Minister Bennett.[73] His assessment was correct, but it is unclear where he got his information or whether it simply reflected his predisposition again Bennett, as the prime minister's involvement was not part of the public record at the time.

The banning of *Eight Men Speak* made more headlines than the performance itself. The *Toronto Star* noted that the Toronto Police Board had failed to "keep within the law," and that it was going beyond its powers in order to persecute the Progressive Arts Club.[74] In doing so, the *Star* was presenting the club as a sympathetic character in the unfolding drama.

The Canadian Labor Defense League and the Progressive Arts Club held a public meeting at Hygeia Hall in Toronto on 17 January 1933 to discuss both the ban on *Eight Men Speak* and the progress of the campaign against section 98. The meeting was attended by 1,500 people, the same-sized audience who had seen *Eight Men Speak*. Red Squad detectives Nursey and Mann attended and took notes.[75]

Cecil-Smith spoke on behalf of the Progressive Arts Club. He explained the state of the ban and that he and a delegation had a meeting with Premier Henry in two days to demand that he lift the ban on the play. Canada, he explained, was the only "not avowedly Fascist" country in the world that banned workers' plays.[76] He noted that such interference did not occur even in imperial Japan.[77] He was hopeful that he could secure permission to perform the play during the International Theatre Campaign planned in March in solidarity with Moscow's International Union of Revolutionary Theatre. The *Varsity* wrote that Cecil-Smith's comments "revealed some startling information as a direct cause of the action of the authorities, information so startling in fact, that the publication of it would have left *The Varsity* open to a libel suit."[78] Cecil-Smith claimed that the "startling revelations" were merely that the federal government was fearful of opening an investigation of the shooting at the prison because of what it might reveal. He noted that guards shooting at a prisoner in their cell constituted attempted murder. The attorney general had a clear responsibility to investigate "or be in grave dereliction of his duty."[79]

Max Kaplansky represented the Student League of the University of Toronto at the meeting. The *Varsity* student reporter recorded that Kaplansky expressed solidarity with the Workers' Theatre, saying, "We represent a part of the students which realize that the students have common interests with the working-class, especially as many of us will face unemployment when we leave the University. It is for this reason that we protest against this oppression."[80] During intermission break in the meeting, the Workers' Theatre performed Mildred Goldberg's chant from Act 4 of the play in defiance of the ban. The Red Squad detectives looked on but made no attempt to stop the performance or subsequently revoke Hygeia Hall's theatre licence.[81]

A.E. Smith spoke as the representative of the Canadian Labor Defense League. He had visited Russia earlier in 1933 and had found Russian prisons to be much more humane than those in Canada. Upon his return, he threw himself with greater vigour into improving Canada's prison conditions and repealing section 98.[82] Smith told the audience about his visit to Prime Minister Bennett in November with a petition for the repeal of section 98 bearing 450,000 signatures. Smith applauded *Eight Men Speak* for its truthfulness in the face of oppression.[83] He explained, "Authorities objected to the play for the same reason that an ugly man objects to a mirror which shows him as he is."[84] Whether the government was prepared to accept responsibility or not, Smith claimed that the depiction of the incidents in the play was completely truthful. He was later charged with sedition for the contents of his speech, tried, and found not guilty.

The meeting concluded with a resolution to be sent to the attorney general against the suppression of the theatre. The resolution was printed in *Masses* as "Resolution on the Freedom of the Stage in Canada."[85] It called for rescinding the ban, establishing full freedom of the theatre, and granting full freedom to the Progressive Arts Club to operate in Ontario and throughout Canada. An oddly specific element of the resolution called for George Dickson-Kenwin, a Shakespearean actor in Toronto, to end his criticisms of the Workers' Theatre movement. The resolution, as printed in *Masses*, was left blank at the bottom so supportive individuals and organizations could clip it, sign it, and mail it to their members of Parliament.[86] The attendees passed a second resolution to protest the persecution of Ludwig Renn (who would later serve with the International Brigades in Spain) and other German Communists. The resolution would eventually be sent to Adolf Hitler's government.[87]

Cecil-Smith and Ryan continued to lobby, unsuccessfully, for the opportunity to perform *Eight Men Speak*. They tried to have it performed in other cities, but without success. The Winnipeg Workers' Theatre attempted to stage the play in May 1934. When the group refused to provide Winnipeg police with the script for review before the performance, Ontario authorities helpfully furnished the police with a copy.[88]

The police then shut down the city's Walker Theatre on the evening of the play's only attempted performance.

If the play could not be performed, perhaps the script could be shared more widely. The Progressive Arts Club printed the script as a pamphlet later in May and sold copies through *Masses* and workers' bookshops. Cecil-Smith wrote in the foreword that "every effort must be strained to break the system of censorship, which is only another of the signs of the rapid fascization of the Canadian government in preparation of war." Cancelling licences was a common tactic of "capitalist lawyers and lobbyists," but it could not defeat the working class itself. In Tokyo, he knew, 40,000 workers had organized themselves to support their own theatres. In acting with such solidarity, these theatres became impervious to government censorship. Cecil-Smith hoped that the same thing could be achieved in Canada.[89] His goal was not realized. In July, *Eight Men Speak* was banned from being posted through the mail.[90] It was not publically performed again until 1982.[91]

In spite of being a "bad play" that, in the 1930s, was only ever seen by 1,500 people, *Eight Men Speak* was surprisingly effective in achieving its goals. The play was meant to raise awareness of the Eight in prison and the injustice of section 98. It communicated its messages to an audience of 1,500, but the controversy surrounding the banning worked to spread those messages much more widely than the Workers' Theatre could have hoped. Coupled with what some viewed as the attempted political assassination of Tim Buck and the sedition trial of A.E. Smith, the government appeared heavy handed. It seemed that the public perception of the CPC was changing, although this did not translate into any particular success at the ballot box.

Despite remaining an illegal organization, the party was growing in popularity. From its lowest point in 1930, with a membership of merely 1,300, it grew to 3,000 by 1933 and 5,500 by 1935.[92] This seems incredible, given that the party was legal in 1930, but illegal in 1933 and 1935. In the same timeframe, the Canadian Labor Defense League had grown from 10,000 to 25,000 members.[93] Perhaps because of this increase in popularity, the federal government appeared to be losing its appetite for persecuting the party. The Eight were slowly released from prison, despite not having completed their sentences. In July 1934, Sam Carr and Matthew Popovich were released. Later that month, Malcolm Bruce, John Boychuk, and Tom Hill were released. Tom Ewen was released soon afterwards. Tomo Cacic had already been deported.[94] Only Tim Buck remained in prison.

Chapter Five

Art, Propaganda, and the Popular Front

The Progressive Arts Club gained notoriety following the banning of *Eight Men Speak*. It survived the ban and undertook new initiatives. It claimed to have succeeded in inspiring similar organizations across Canada, raising awareness for the Communist Party of Canada and providing a valuable front organization while the party remained illegal and underground. Cecil-Smith did much of his most interesting writing as the CPC transitioned from the militant "class-versus-class" doctrine of the Third Period to a more inclusive Popular Front strategy in 1934–35, first in *Masses* and then in the pages of the *Worker*.

Cecil-Smith was the closest thing the party had to a cultural theorist.[1] *Masses* provided him with an effective outlet to express some of his opinions on the relationship between art and communism. The connection was highlighted on the front page of the first issue of *Masses*, which stated that the Progressive Arts Club "rejects the theory that art can have nothing in common with politics, that art functions only by and for art. It asserts that all art, whether by the conscious will of the jingo intellectual, or by the self-styled aloofness of the ivory tower recluse, is under capitalism (as in preceding societies), the art of the ruling class. Art is propaganda, or more precisely, a vehicle of propaganda."[2] While some artists associated with the Progressive Arts Club, such as Jim Watts and Toby Gordon, sought to improve the aesthetics of their cultural production – with better sets, better writing, better acting, and so on – Cecil-Smith and Oscar Ryan were more interested in the political potential that art offered. They were the political commissars of the theatre, ensuring it was wielded as a weapon for the party.

Cecil-Smith was an advocate for the role of art in revolutionary politics. He argued that art both reflects and reinscribes social, psychological, and ideological thinking, our mindset, and he doubted that anyone could adopt a truly revolutionary mindset while immersed in reactionary or bourgeois art. For him, revolution would not come about just as the result of economic factors; it would require a cultural shift: "Neither Marx nor the leading Marxists have ever ignored the part played by revolutionary culture in the dialectic process of history. Neither have they considered the arts themselves to be outside the realm of dialectics." The party's ignoring culture was "certainly not Marxian. That there exists a body of such opinion, not altogether confined to the rank and file, in the working class movement of Canada, is certainly not a healthy sign."[3] Clearly, Cecil-Smith was frustrated by the CPC's disregard for the role of cultural factors in preparing for and bringing about the revolution. The US Communist Party had been very successful in appealing to artists and making use of their skills to promote their cause.[4] The Canadian party, he believed, had to make similar efforts in order to develop and promote revolutionary culture if the revolution were to be successful.

Cecil-Smith engaged in a debate with T. Richardson about the nature of "pure art" in the pages of *Masses*.[5] Richardson asserted that art and propaganda are different ideas. A painting could be a very good invocation of socialist principles but still be a very bad painting (e.g., ugly and defective in the technical application of colours, form, and brush strokes) and therefore very bad art. Art should not be dismissed simply because it did not meet a socialist purpose. "The artist," Richardson wrote, "is a friend of socialism, but he must be free to create."[6] Cecil-Smith countered that art "is the message of humanity to humanity." As a human endeavour, it is always imbued with societal values, of either the "ruling class" (the capitalists) or the "new ruling class" (the workers). Otherwise, art is sterile and unintelligible, nothing more than a demonstration of technical skill. The implication is that there is no such thing as pure art apart from propaganda; art must necessarily be propaganda, whether the artist realizes it or not.

Cecil-Smith addressed the dichotomy of art and propaganda when he responded to critics of *Eight Men Speak*. In his article "Propaganda and Art," he wrote that the theatre "establishment" was critical of the play but that such criticisms could be dismissed outright: "Those who have a vestige of pride left in their hearts for traditional British drama ... will care nothing about how this play was produced, or how it was acted. They will regard it as an insult to the British Empire."[7] On the other hand, he thought, politically engaged critics – such as the readers of the University of Toronto's *Varsity* and the Young Communist League's *Young Worker* – would focus on the utility of the play: "those who have a vestige of revolution in their hearts, will care nothing about how this play was produced, or how it was acted. They will regard it as a weapon of class struggle."[8] It did not matter whether the play was objectively good or bad; what mattered was whether it advanced the workers' cause.

Cecil-Smith's article acknowledged the validity of bourgeois culture. He quoted two of the Soviet Union's most lauded cultural theorists, Nikolai Bukharin and Anatoly Lunacharsky, to make the point that art's value was that it could promote political consciousness and spur people to action. Bourgeois art was legitimate art: as an expression of the culture of the dominant class, it merited acknowledgement, even though it had a negative influence on the world. Moreover, it was more mature and more sophisticated than the relatively new field of revolutionary art. Bourgeois artists had more experience and more technical skills in writing plays, designing sets, composing music, and developing print publications whose composition both visually and intellectually appealed to a wider audience. Ideally, the Workers' Theatre and similar organizations could learn and benefit from the experiences and skills of the bourgeoisie. They could, and should, he thought, develop their own art "from the point where the bourgeoisie had left off" by co-opting the mechanics of their art for revolutionary purposes.[9] Cecil-Smith's experience with newspapers had taught him that this was possible; he had learned his craft in the employ of the "capitalist dailies" and had gone on to apply these skills in the service of the party.

Cecil-Smith's acceptance of a role for bourgeois art and artists hardly seems like a radical proposition, but the proposal was problematic for the party for two key reasons. First, he invoked the writings of Nikolai Bukharin. Bukharin had once been an influential member of Stalin's inner circle and the leader of the Comintern from 1926 to 1929, but he then fell from power and was executed following one of Stalin's show trials in 1938. Publicly agreeing with Bukharin in the 1930s was risky business: it was either very bold or very stupid of Cecil-Smith to do so. American Jay Lovestone, for instance, had been expelled from the US Communist Party in 1929 for his support of Bukharin. Second, Cecil-Smith's opinions were at odds with the party's general anti-intellectual attitude and the "class-versus-class" strategy of the Third Period.

A reviewer in the *Worker* criticized the complexity of Cecil-Smith's article, calling it "involved" and suggesting that "a worker on reading E. Cecil-Smith's effort would not grasp the central points at issue."[10] (The reviewer did not seem to think much of the average worker's intelligence.) Stanley Ryerson, on the other hand, disagreed with Cecil-Smith's entire interpretation. In the next issue of *Masses*, Ryerson called Cecil-Smith's points "simply bunk," "merely wrong," and, "just a mistake." He criticized Cecil-Smith for adopting the bourgeois definition of propaganda – "the spreading of subversive, untrue ideas" – and accused him of being overly charitable toward the bourgeoisie. Bourgeois and proletarian art could not exist "side by side," and it was wrong to view bourgeois art as a legitimate expression of class feelings. This idea "abandon[s] the fundamental positions of Marxism and ... mislead[s] everybody."[11]

The comments by Ryerson and the *Worker*'s reviewer are a telling demonstration of the anti-intellectual attitude prevailing in the party. The reviewer had not criticized Cecil-Smith's clarity of thought or writing but contended that his ideas were simply too complicated for a worker to understand. Ryerson was an intellectual himself – he had studied at Upper Canada College, the University of Toronto, and the Sorbonne – but had shown himself to be sufficiently doctrinaire to be valuable to the party's central leadership. Ryerson had once been a junior member of Cecil-Smith's Writers' Group but was now on an upward trajectory that would bring him to the party's innermost circles. His position was an apt reflection of party doctrine during the Third Period.

Cecil-Smith responded to Ryerson's editorial in the same issue, a benefit of editing the magazine. Ryerson's argument, he pointed out, was overly sectarian and stifled creativity. The Workers' Theatre movement could not develop and grow if it could not even acknowledge the bourgeois theatre. This sectarian attitude had already affected its productions. Artists and writers were unsure of the doctrinally acceptable limits of their art. One very good writer and critic for the Progressive Arts Club, Cecil-Smith wrote, "has practically quit writing altogether, because he has come under this influence and believes that the little he knows about the class struggle is 'utterly insufficient.'"[12] Cecil-Smith concluded that the subject was an important one that required further debate.[13]

Cecil-Smith's writings and actions had showed sympathy for both the bourgeoisie and the petite bourgeoisie (which included small business owners, journalists, artists, professors, and even, to some degree, university students). This was contrary to the party's doctrine at the time: during the Third Period, it viewed both of these groups as the enemy of the working class. According to Marx, the petite bourgeoisie had a vested interest in maintaining the capitalist state; its collapse would be the end of their relative dominance over the working class. Cecil-Smith did not entirely disagree – he referred to the petite bourgeoisie as "the backbone of any fascist movement" – but he did not believe that every member of the class was necessarily an enemy.[14] In his view, bourgeois art could be co-opted, and some members of the petite bourgeoisie could be enticed to become allies to the workers' cause without necessarily rejecting their class. He himself was a journalist, after all, and was quick to point out that Marx had also been one.[15]

Cecil-Smith and Oscar Ryan engaged with the students at the University of Toronto in order to persuade them that they had an important role to play in the revolution. At the time, such institutions were not working class in the slightest. In Canada in 1930, only an estimated 3 per cent of university-aged students attended university – such an education was reserved for the well-off.[16] Cecil-Smith disagreed with party orthodoxy and wanted to actively recruit students for the Progressive Arts Club. During the tense period surrounding the banning of *Eight Men Speak*, he regularly approached the *Varsity*, the university's student newspaper, and engaged with the Student League, an on-campus organization that had firmly fallen under the control of the CPC in the course of 1932–33, thanks to Jim Watts and the increasingly doctrinaire Stanley Ryerson.[17] Ryan, through years of working as a Young Communist League organizer, also saw the value of having youthful and energetic people in the club.

Cecil-Smith also tried to spread his influence through *Canadian Forum*, a liberal, but hardly radical, arts magazine. It was composed and read by Canadian professors, intellectuals, and artists from coast to coast. He thought that they could become valuable allies and were an audience worth courting. In one article in the magazine, he promoted the Workers' Theatre as "the new Canadian dramatic movement in very truth. A drama rooted in the lives and struggles of the toilers of Canada's shops, mines, farms, and slave-camps. Plays written in the heat of life by the same workers. Mass recitations and plays presented by worker-actors who understand what they are doing because they can live the very parts they take."[18] Cecil-Smith downplayed the party's role in the Progressive Arts Club in his writings for *Canadian Forum*, instead presenting the Workers' Theatre as part of a movement independent from, and bigger than, the party. He claimed that there were hundreds of such artistic organizations across the country trying to reveal the truth about working-class realities.

The Progressive Arts Club appeared healthy in the months following the ban on *Eight Men Speak*. It announced that it was taking steps to establish a Workers' Symphony Orchestra, and the Workers' Theatre established a training school to improve the quality of its performances.[19] The Workers' Theatre continued to stage performances and even hosted a week-long theatre festival in Toronto to parallel the third International Theatre Campaign produced by Moscow's International Union of Revolutionary Theatre. Cecil-Smith had hoped that *Eight Men Speak* would be performed as part of the festival, but he could not get a theatre to agree to put its licence at risk by allowing it to be performed.

Cecil-Smith promoted the theatre festival in the *Worker*, explaining that the Workers' Theatre and events like the festival were more important than ever: "The four years just past have seen an ever deepening world crisis which has shaken capitalist civilization to its roots, making more and more obvious the decay which had set in years ago. This decay is just as clear in bourgeois art and culture as in any other phase of life and particularly clear in the capitalist theatre." The workers needed to continue to produce their own theatre to tell their own stories. The "oppressors" knew the power of workers' theatres: "Revolutionary playwrights and actors have been murdered and imprisoned by reactionary elements and government in Germany, China, Japan and elsewhere. Their plays have been banned in nearly every country of the capitalist world, including Canada."[20] Cecil-Smith invited speakers as well as music, dance, and drama groups to take part in the festival.[21]

The RCMP and presumably members of Dennis Draper's Red Squad attended the theatre festival and kept careful notes. The RCMP noted that 3,500 people attended one of the events at Massey Hall – 2,000 more than saw *Eight Men Speak*. Cecil-Smith spoke at the event, telling the tale of *Eight Men Speak* and the sedition trial of A.E. Smith. Prime Minister Bennett, Cecil-Smith explained to his audience, "had a hand in" these events.[22] The RCMP observer noted that Cecil-Smith did not say exactly what Bennett had a hand in, no doubt a subtle countermeasure Cecil-Smith had adopted following the sedition trial. Cecil-Smith explained that censorship was continuing – the police had forced the staff at Massey Hall to cancel the performance of one of the dance troupes that night – and that "the Workers Theatre is the best weapon of the revolutionary class, ... part and parcel of the revolutionary party, and intended to carry on their work."[23] The March–April edition of *Masses* lauded the festival as a success.

As a magazine, *Masses* appeared to be successful. It claimed to have a greater readership than *Canadian Forum*, but, nevertheless, the March–April 1934 issue was its last. The *Worker* announced in June that publication of *Masses* had been suspended only temporarily. The editorial board had decided that, in spite of the magazine's success, "parallel growth has not been shown artistically and politically."[24] The editorial board planned to broaden its base of support among the trade unions and attract more intellectuals and artists. The next issue was planned for the fall, but *Masses* was never revived. It is unclear what real efforts were made to reactivate the publication, or what discussions were held behind closed doors regarding the required political and artistic growth. Given Cecil-Smith's argumentative nature, it seems likely that these conversations would have been heated. Cecil-Smith had lost a platform that allowed him to write with relative freedom. His subsequent writings for the *Worker* would be more closely monitored and fully vetted by the party's leadership.

Cecil-Smith had written for the *Worker* since 1931, but articles did not begin to include his name until June 1934. Following the dissolution of *Masses*, he was listed as a "special correspondent" for the *Worker*. He covered a recruiting drive for the Workers' Unity League organized by Meyer Klig, the same man whom he had seen beaten and arrested at the Battle of Queen's Park.[25] Cecil-Smith also covered the labour tensions that almost led to a strike by Toronto's police officers and, elsewhere, the party's efforts to prevent the Christmas-time eviction of eleven families.[26] Each piece relayed a factual accounting, to be sure, but also contained overt critiques of the political struggle underlying the events. For instance, regarding the evictions, Cecil-Smith was quick to juxtapose the "Christian charity" of the municipal government at Christmas with the Canadian Labor Defense League's desire to assist the workers regardless of the season. As for the police strike, Cecil-Smith asked, "Will this mean that those active in pressing these demands will be trailed by other police? Does this mean that the 'Red Squad' will be brought to work on the cases of activities in the Toronto Police Association? This seems to be the clear intimation of these statements in the opinion of more than one labor leader."[27] Behind the scenes, Cecil-Smith managed the *Worker*'s twenty or so paid correspondents operating across the country and was responsible for bringing in new features to increase the newspaper's popularity.[28]

Cecil-Smith had begun his political journey with the Ontario Labor Party but, by the 1930s, had firmly thrown his lot in with the Communist Party of Canada. These were not the only political parties that sought to alleviate the plight of Canada's working class during the Great Depression. Canada had a great variety of parties with "farmer," "worker," "labour," and "socialist" in their names during the 1930s, many of whom united under the banner of the Co-operative Commonwealth Federation (CCF) in 1933. Some were moderate labour-socialists, while others were more revolutionary in character.[29] At the same time, the pressure of the Depression forced "mainstream" political parties to examine the viability of policies that were once the exclusive domain of labour-socialist parties. American president Franklin Delano Roosevelt proposed a "New Deal" for the American people in 1933, a series of significant social programs to alleviate the suffering of the Depression years. In 1935, with a federal election looming, Prime Minister Bennett began proposing similar programs, which garnered him some support from the CCF.

Cecil-Smith and the party press were highly critical of the CCF and the pseudo–labour-socialist policies being promoted by Bennett's government. The proposals did not go far enough, as they saw it, and were imposed merely to quell the revolutionary spirit that was growing among the working class. One party commentator wrote that the industrialists were "leopards [who] cannot change their spots"; only a program like the Soviet five-year plans, designed by workers for workers, had any chance of success.[30] CPC commentators deemed the social democrats of the CCF to be "social fascists" and traitors to the working class. *Socialism and the CCF*, a CPC pamphlet by G. Pierce (actually Stewart Smith), stated that "a fundamental community of ideas exist[s] between the Fascism of Hitler and the social-fascism of the C.C.F."[31] Cecil-Smith made similar criticisms of the CCF leadership in the *Worker.* He considered the CCF leadership to be opportunistic, duplicitous, and naive.

Cecil-Smith believed that the timing of the CCF's appearance in the political arena in 1933 was all-too convenient. The CCF appeared "just at the time when the Communist party was outlawed."[32] The CCF capitalized on the success of the CPC in the "leftward shift of thousands of workers, farmers, intellectuals and others," and then offered them "something 'just as good' and at the same time nice and 'Canadian,'" – a reference to the Communists' association with Moscow.[33] But the CCF platform, Cecil-Smith argued, was not "just as good." The new party sought "nothing more or less than the reorganization of capitalism," a completely inadequate solution to the crises of the day.[34]

Cecil-Smith believed that incremental reform could not achieve the socio-economic changes that Canada required to break free from capitalist demagoguery. Capitalists currently held all of the power, and they would not relinquish this power willingly; indeed, they would readily employ state violence to ensure their continued hegemony:

> A gunboat is the answer to Anyox miners asking for conditions more nearly human; three dead and dozens wounded is the answer to miners in Estevan protesting against the coal barons; tanks and troops are the answer to Stratford furniture workers when they organize; mass arrest in Rouyn, and so forth; can we honestly believe, if these are the individual answers from the various bosses, that they will answer more severely when they are attacked all together? No, we cannot believe it.[35]

For Cecil-Smith, only the imposition of the dictatorship of the proletariat, through revolution, could bring about meaningful change.[36] The CCF's proposed method of bringing about incremental reform, he believed, was doomed to fail when the capitalists fought back, as they clearly had shown they would. Furthermore, he argued, the CCF's approach to reform was dangerous to the working class insofar as it offered a panacea and eroded their desire for revolution. To further his point, Cecil-Smith invoked Marx's depiction of Louis-Napoléon Bonaparte's "reactionary" seizure of power in France following the 1848 revolution:

> Marx wrote, "The revolutionary point of the socialist demands of the proletariat was blunted, and these demands were given a democratic gloss. Conversely, in the case of the democratic demands of the petty bourgeois, the purely political form was affected and they were made to seem as socialist as possible. That was the origin of social democracy."
>
> Could this have been more clearly stated if it had been written in 1934 about the Farmer-Labor-Socialist platform and theories of the CCF?[37]

Cecil-Smith directed the readers to Pierce's *Socialism and the CCF*, which described the desire for parliamentary reform as a "capitalist deception."[38]

Cecil-Smith was a vocal critic of the CCF. He attended their meetings, read their magazines, and wrote about them extensively in an effort to discredit them. He was particularly critical of the CCF's stance on A.E. Smith's sedition trial. When some members of the CCF came out in support of A.E. Smith, a known member of the CPC, and free speech, the Ontario CCF moved to purge its membership of such sympathizers. Graham Spry, the CCF lieutenant for Ontario, suspended the Ontario CCF's Provincial Council and undertook a widespread reorganization of the provincial party's structure to remove or marginalize dissenters.[39] Cecil-Smith asked, "Is this the action of a working class party, or of the third party of Capitalism?"[40] He wondered how a party claiming to represent workers' interests could turn its back on such a flagrant act of oppression.

Cecil-Smith considered Spry to be especially duplicitous. Spry owned the CCF newspaper, the *New Commonwealth*, and was the leader of the League for Social Reconstruction, an organization popular among leftist intellectuals. How could such a person discipline members of his own party for taking a stand on a freedom of expression issue like the sedition trial of A.E. Smith? Cecil-Smith read Spry's writings and was quick to point out any inconsistencies in his ideas. For instance, in January 1935, Cecil-Smith noted that Spry had denounced the Communist Party as "the last left-wing element in Canada that ... makes impossible the unity of the people against the financial and capitalist minority,"[41] but he had also instructed CCF members to not work with the Communist Party of Canada in the upcoming election. It appeared, Cecil-Smith pointed out, that Spry himself was the barrier to cooperation. Two months later, Cecil-Smith criticized Spry for a *New Commonwealth* editorial in which he claimed that the CCF had always been in favour of non-contributory social insurance. Cecil-Smith wrote that Spry's claim was false, and that his requests to Spry for evidence had gone unanswered.[42]

Cecil-Smith was also critical of the national leader of the CCF, J.S. Woodsworth. A Methodist minister, Woodsworth was a progressive social-gospeller who rejected communism largely because of its connection to violent revolution. Socialism, Woodsworth believed, would be achieved by incremental reforms through the existing system of government, not by revolution. Cecil-Smith disagreed and found frequent opportunities to attack and discredit Woodsworth. When the CCF leader visited China and Japan in 1934, Cecil-Smith wrote four articles criticizing virtually every public statement Woodsworth made about the trip. Cecil-Smith specifically painted Woodsworth as the enemy of democracy, the working class, and national minorities.[43] He accused the CCF leader of slandering the Chinese Communist Party and its work among Chinese peasants. Woodsworth refused to give an interview to Oscar Ryan on the subject, leading Ryan to write, "CCF Leader Refuses to Back Down on Chinese 'Red' Banditry Falsehoods."[44]

In January 1935, Cecil-Smith attended a public meeting led by Woodsworth at Massey Hall, where the CCF leader spoke about his support for Bennett's proposed reforms. Cecil-Smith quoted Woodsworth as saying, "I must compliment the Prime Minister ... Hitherto the capitalist system has been sacrosanct. Now that he has denounced many of the perils of the capitalist system and said that it should be judged on its merits, we can examine it and find that it is not functioning and cannot function. Further than that, Bennett has done a service by telling us that big business and the system has to be regulated. I think Mr. Bennett deserves credit for hitting a few thundering blows at the theory of laissez faire."[45] Cecil-Smith wrote that "thousands left disappointed" by Woodsworth's endorsement of Bennett and his "fascist proposals."[46] Cecil-Smith criticized Woodsworth for his naivety, titling his article "CCF Leader Gives Help to R.B.'s Dope."[47]

~

By 1934, the very survival of communism was threatened by the global rise of fascism, which caused Cecil-Smith great concern about the future of the revolution. He described fascism as "both the open dictatorship by force, imposed by capitalists, when the farce of bourgeois democracy is seen through and the danger of proletarian revolution is imminent, and also the ideological preparation and demagogy that leads directly to it."[48] In Germany, Adolph Hitler had been appointed chancellor in January 1933, after which the Nazi Party won nearly half of the seats in the Reichstag. Between his appointment as chancellor and the election, Hitler used the excuse of the Reichstag fire, the unexplained destruction of the German parliament, to scapegoat and destroy the German Communist Party, the largest and most successful Communist Party outside of the Soviet Union.

Fascist politics thrived elsewhere as well. In Italy, Benito Mussolini's Fascist Party was firmly entrenched and was growing increasingly aggressive, as evidenced by Italy's invasion of Abyssinia in 1935. Imperial Japan waged war in China, against China's Communist and Nationalist territories alike. Cecil-Smith also noted the growing influence of fascist ideology in Hollywood films.[49] Even in Canada, support for fascism was growing. Fascist leader Adrien Arcand enjoyed growing popularity in Quebec, and "Swastika Clubs" sprang up across the country.[50] In August 1933, a baseball tournament turned violent at Toronto's Christie Pits Park when anti-Semitic fascist supporters and a Jewish baseball team came to blows. Cecil-Smith may have been present for the Christie Pits Riot, or would at least have felt personally connected to the event – his latest address was less than five minutes away from the park.[51]

In the face of rising fascism, Cecil-Smith and others sensed that they needed to form a broader coalition of allies, and one step toward that occurred after Tim Buck was finally released from prison on 24 November 1934.[52] His welcome-home celebration was organized for 2 December at Maple Leaf Gardens, the largest venue in Toronto. Some 17,000 people attended, and 8,000 more stood outside in the cold in a show of support. This was a staggering crowd, given that the party was still outlawed and that attending such a rally could be considered a criminal act. The Progressive Arts Club decorated the stadium with forty-foot-long portraits of Stalin and Lenin and covered the stage with red carnations and roses and a giant wreath with long red taffeta streamers. Ukrainian and Finnish dancers and musicians provided entertainment until the guest of honour made his grand entrance: "Thirty-four men in white trousers and gym shorts from the Workers' Sporting Association carried Tim Buck shoulder high to the platform amid a storm of cheers. Behind came 14 young women in wine-colored knitted suits walking with military precision."[53] It was a show worthy of Moscow's Red Square.

Buck was defiant toward the government. The party was still illegal, he said, but would not stay underground. He challenged the authorities to arrest him again. Buck exclaimed to cheers that his arrest was supposed to be a deathblow to the party, but "a few more death blows like that and we'll be on the threshold of socialism!"[54] As at the performance of *Eight Men Speak,* the crowd cheered for the playing of "The Internationale" and booed during "God Save the King."[55]

Cecil-Smith was in attendance, reporting for the *Worker.* His article on the rally quoted parts of Buck's speech at length, in which Buck articulated a shift in the party's policy: "We Communists believe that it is possible in Canada, without forgetting our doctrinal differences, for all trade unions and for all parties of the working class and progressive middle class parties to join in the fight against reaction and to build a strong united front for this fight."[56] The fight was the most important thing the working class would ever undertake: it would have to forge a united front against "fascism and imperial war," as well as a "popular front" with the bourgeoisie and the petite bourgeoisie, which it had previously spurned.[57] The CCF was no longer the enemy but a potential ally that had to be courted; the real enemy was "monopoly capitalists" and fascists.

Buck's speech at Maple Leaf Garden marked the Communist Party of Canada's shift away from the militant class-versus-class doctrine of the Third Period. A few years earlier, at the onset of the Depression, capitalism appeared to be on the wane. Now, fascism was growing in strength, and there was a legitimate fear that communism might not survive at all. Buck was not the only Communist leader to reach this conclusion. Georgi Dimitrov, a Bulgarian Communist who had been arrested in Germany for alleged involvement in the Reichstag fire, was now the general secretary of the Comintern's Executive Committee. He had watched the Nazis dismantle the German Communist Party, an action that was possible in large part because the various parties on the left had been divided in the 1933 German election. If they had stood in solidarity, they might have defeated the Nazis at the polls. At the Comintern's Seventh World Congress in the summer of 1935, Dimitrov announced the Comintern's policy of creating a "Popular Front against Fascism."[58] The Comintern officially placed the goal of defeating fascism above all else.[59] Buck recalled that the resolution "stated perfectly what I had been groping for when I came out of Kingston Penitentiary."[60] The party held that the Popular Front did not signal the end of a movement toward world revolution, just its postponement.[61]

The first test of the Popular Front in Canada came during the 1935 federal election. Some CPC members, including Tim Buck, Tom Ewen, and A.E. Smith, ran for office, but in large part the party supported CCF candidates. The CPC did not win any seats, while the CCF won seven. Bennett's Conservatives were soundly beaten by Mackenzie King's Liberals. The Conservatives had been elected in 1930 with a majority government, winning 135 of 245 possible seats; in 1935, they were reduced to just 39 seats. The Liberals had been elected with a solid majority of 173 seats, nearly twice as many as they had won in the 1930 election. The Social Credit Party won 17 seats, and the Reconstruction Party held a single seat. The CPC had high hopes for this new government, first because it seemed more likely to pursue social reform policies, and second because it would be less likely to persecute the party. The Liberals had promised to repeal section 98 due to its infringement on fundamental civil liberties.

Just weeks after the election, the RCMP observed Cecil-Smith teaching at a "Communist School." Twenty-two students, all members of the party, had gathered at City Tire & Battery Co. near Cabbagetown, Toronto's Anglo-Saxon slum, to learn about the Marxist texts and the party's plan for infiltrating the CCF.[62] Cecil-Smith read and explained the first fifteen pages of Karl Marx and Friedrich Engels's 1848 book, *The Communist Manifesto*.[63] He stopped after each paragraph, explaining the significance of each, much like the Bible studies with which he had grown up. The first fifteen pages of *The Communist Manifesto* cover Marx's interpretation of world history, specifically through the lens of the relationship between the bourgeoisie and the proletariat, and the exploitation that this relationship induces. Marx and Engels sought a classless society free of this exploitation. "The theory of Communism," they wrote, "may be summed up in a single sentence: Abolition of private property."[64] Cecil-Smith recommended that all of the students get their own copies of *The Communist Manifesto*, Joseph Stalin's *The Foundations of Leninism*, and Lenin's *Left Wing Communism* and *State and Revolution*.[65]

Cecil-Smith reminded the students that they had all been instructed to provide the party with their place of employment and a list of co-workers that they trusted. All party members, he explained, were required to work to form a union at their place of employment. They were also required to "quietly flood" the ranks of the CCF. Those already known to be party members were not supposed to join the CCF, presumably because they would be easily detected and it would reveal the party's infiltration strategy. Cecil-Smith explained that the CCF was "to be looked after by the inside method."[66] This directive is interesting, as it suggests that the party, having supported the CCF in the election, now sought to clandestinely infiltrate it. In this arrangement, the CCF was the "host" and the CPC the "parasite," but it was important that the host not perceive itself to be infected. The much-derided Trotskyists similarly tried to infiltrate socialist organizations around the world in order to expand their influence, a tactic dubbed the French Turn.

In addition to teaching at the "Communist School," Cecil-Smith continued to write for the *Worker.* By the winter of 1935–36, he was the newspaper's editor for Toronto "and district."[67] This gave him the opportunity to visit Ottawa to report on the debates in the House of Commons. He also interviewed members of Parliament, including CCF leader J.S. Woodsworth.[68] Cecil-Smith's description of his interaction with Woodsworth was polite and professional. He did not criticize him or his policies, which seems at odds with his public denunciations of Woodsworth as an enemy of the working class just months earlier, and his direction to party members to "look after" the CCF by the "inside method." His restraint is a reminder that Cecil-Smith, although often publically argumentative, was writing for the CPC's newspaper: he had an editor-in-chief who would ensure that his writings shifted along with the party's policies, and so they were not necessarily a reflection of his personal beliefs. Furthermore, the public face of the party as expressed in the *Worker* was not necessarily in line with its more clandestine activities.

Cecil-Smith and Woodsworth discussed the composition of the newly elected House of Commons, particularly the role of the CCF and the Social Credit Party. Although Woodsworth philosophically disagreed with Social Credit, he was confident that together they could bring about positive change for the working class. He commented that, "as Socialists we don't believe that the government can possibly solve any basic problem under capitalism. The contradictions in the system will prevent it."[69] However, he believed that joint action with Social Credit could force concessions from the Liberal government that could improve the lot of the people and "add to the contradictions" in the system that would "hasten the onset" of socialism. Woodsworth presented socialism as an inevitability, but one that would be achieved through incremental reform in Parliament, not through revolution. The two also discussed the CCF's position on section 98. Woodsworth affirmed his commitment to repealing that provision. Prime Minister King had promised to repeal it, Woodsworth said, but had since adopted a "do nothing" attitude. Woodsworth pledged that "we shall remind them of it and if they refuse to introduce it, we shall do so ourselves."[70]

Such CCF intervention was not necessary. In the summer of 1936, the King government repealed section 98. Police surveillance continued, and the charge of vagrancy was liberally applied to limit party activities such as soap-box speaking, rallies, and distribution of literature, but it was no longer a crime to simply be a member of the party. The party celebrated the repeal but did not change much about how it did business.[71] It continued to do much of its public-facing work through front organizations, which attracted a broad following in the spirit of the Popular Front, while maintaining many of the clandestine networks and security countermeasures it had necessarily put in place during its years of illegality. These networks would be particularly important and useful in facilitating the party's activities during the Spanish Civil War.

Chapter Six

Defend the Soviet Union!

In the depths of the Great Depression, Cecil-Smith believed that the British and Canadian ways of life were broken. Rampant unemployment and homelessness and poor living and unsafe working conditions were compounded by restrictions on freedom of assembly, association, and political belief. The "system" was not working. Parliament, the church, the courts, the very institutions that Cecil-Smith had been raised to hold in the highest esteem, now seemed to be tools of oppression that did not do enough to remedy the plight of the working class. The Soviet Union, on the other hand, seemed to have created a utopia for working men and women. While Canada was economically stagnant, the Soviet Union seemed to surge forward with each successive Five-Year Plan. Cecil-Smith was a vocal advocate for the Soviet Union and its policies until at least 1941.[1]

Canadians expressed considerable interest in knowing "the truth" about Soviet Russia. *Canadian Forum* remarked that, "apart from the weather and the depression, no subject creates more lively discussion among great masses of people in all countries than that of the creation of a planned socialist state in the Soviet Union."[2] But getting information out of the Soviet Union was no small feat. J.S. Woodsworth remarked in the House of Commons that he was surprised at the degree of censorship in Canada. While he received a weekly newspaper from the Soviet Union after his visit in 1931, many others had had their subscriptions "excluded" by the censor.[3] Similarly, Cecil-Smith had documents from the Soviet Union excluded by the censor. Many Canadians were therefore dependent on the reports coming from those who had visited the Soviet Union.

Many visitors described well-stocked hospitals, thriving cultural centres, and productive farms. Frederick Griffin, a visiting *Toronto Star* reporter, described Russia as a paradise: "It is new. It is vivid. It is stupendous."[4] The Soviet Union, as he described it, had ensured employment and happiness for its people. Exploitation, "in the Communist sense of the word," had been eliminated, and Griffin seemed convinced that even greater days lay ahead.[5] But many such visitors received heavily filtered information through the guides employed by the state-run tourist agency, *Intourist*, and the state-produced English-language daily, the *Moscow Daily News*.[6] Other visitors offered different depictions of the state of affairs in the Soviet Union. Politically conservative visitors, such as the future Ontario premier George Drew, reported unqualified destitution and squalor.[7] With such conflicting descriptions, many did not know what to believe.

Cecil-Smith and his contemporaries saw the reports by the likes of George Drew and the Canadian government's attempts to censor Soviet materials as deliberate attempts to hide the Soviet Union's successes from the working class. Such strategies were part of a propaganda war fought between the working class and the "millionaire bankers and industrialists." When representatives of the capitalist class visited Russia, they returned claiming to have seen starving people and closed factories. When workers visited Russia, they saw happy and healthy workers. The millionaires, Cecil-Smith claimed, were lying to Canadian workers at every turn, trying to convince them that the Soviet system was a failure and certainly not worth pursuing. "Who should Canadian workers believe?" Cecil-Smith asked, although the question was a rhetorical one.[8]

The Communist Party of Canada positioned itself to be a key provider to Canadians of information regarding the Soviet Union. The success of the USSR was, after all, a strong selling point for the party's ideology. The CPC newspapers – the *Worker* and its successor, the *Daily Clarion* – carried considerably more coverage than "the capitalist dailies" of events in the Soviet Union. The party newspapers covered developments in Soviet economics and politics, like the progress of Stalin's Five-Year Plans or the adoption, in 1936, of the Soviet Constitution. The party papers also covered lighter fare, including description of the exploits of Soviet athletes and scientists, or interviews with recently returned visitors to the Soviet Union. They carried advertisements for cultural events in Toronto ranging from performances by Russian folk dancers to the screening of Russian films such as *Chapaev* and *Battleship Potemkin*.

Cecil-Smith had never been to the Soviet Union, yet he wrote editorials on the subject garnered from second-hand information. For instance, he wrote an editorial in the *Worker* in November 1934 explaining how Soviet democracy was superior to its Westminster equivalent. He wrote that Soviet citizens lived in "the freest form of society yet evolved," democracy brought "to a height to which no capitalist country, no matter how democratic it calls itself, would dare to even conceive of."[9] Soviet democracy involved electing fellow workers to local councils based on places of employment, like factories or collective farms. Anyone over the age of eighteen, he explained, could run for office or vote. This was different from the Canadian system, which excluded immigrants and non-property-owning workers from voting or running for office. Cecil-Smith had personally encountered the shortcomings of the Canadian electoral system in December 1932, when he attempted to run as a candidate for the Board of Education in Ward 2, only to find that he could neither vote in that election nor run for office, as a result of not being properly registered on the voters list.[10] Most likely, he was not on the list because he had no fixed address at the time: although he had two known addresses in 1932, he had none in 1933.[11] Moving this often was likely the result of evictions either due to financial trouble or landlords taking issue with his politics. In either event, his living arrangements prevented him from participating in the Canadian democratic system. Parliamentary democracy, he argued, was nothing more than "an organ of the ruling class ... which they use for the suppression and to legalize the exploitation of millions of toilers in factory or farm."[12]

In addition to his editorials, Cecil-Smith interviewed "witnesses" who had recently returned from the Soviet Union. In January 1935, he interviewed two members of a recently returned workers' delegation – Thomas Rossett, a longshoreman, and Peter Munro, a Vancouver streetcar driver – before they delivered speeches at Toronto's Oddfellows Hall. Rossett told Cecil-Smith that he had been impressed by the quality of the Soviet docks in Leningrad. The equipment was new and modern, and the workers had clubhouses paid for with their union dues. Munro told Cecil-Smith that he was extremely impressed by the working conditions of the streetcar drivers in Moscow. They worked seven hours a day with a break for lunch, and had holidays, sick leave, and free medical care, as well as a pension after twenty-five years of service or upon reaching fifty-five years of age. The car barns had recreation rooms, classrooms, and a restaurant. Vancouver drivers were paid more than their Moscow comrades, Munro said, but otherwise he thought that the working conditions in Moscow were superior.[13]

Cecil-Smith was a member of the Friends of the Soviet Union. The advocacy and awareness group had existed since 1927 but had been relatively dormant until 1932.[14] He joined the organization in 1932 and was a member of its national executive council.[15] He was also a member of the editorial committee of, and a frequent contributor to, its magazine,

Soviet Russia Today. As *Masses* was for the Progressive Arts Club, *Soviet Russia Today* was the Friends' primary mechanism for outreach. The magazine helped the organization advance its three stated goals: to spread accurate information concerning the Soviet Union, to counteract the "lies and slanders of its enemies," and to "mobilize all elements who were sympathetic to the Soviet Union for the struggle against the war preparations of the imperialists."[16] Cecil-Smith edited the magazine and wrote one article per issue from its inaugural September 1933 issue until late 1935. This was no small feat, considering he was still active with the Canadian Labor Defense League and the Progressive Arts Club, was writing for and editing the *Worker*, and also was writing for and editing *Masses* until its last issue in March–April 1934. It is clear that Cecil-Smith was devoting himself full time to work for the party.

The first edition of *Soviet Russia Today* came out in August 1933. It was illustrated, mostly with photographs instead of the distinctive linoleum block drawings in *Masses*, *Canadian Labor Defender*, and the *Worker*, and sixteen pages in length. Cecil-Smith wrote an editorial on war plans against the Soviet Union by Canada, Great Britain, the United States, and Japan, but the first edition focused mostly on working conditions and industrialization in the Soviet Union.[17] The magazine carried first-hand accounts of conditions in that country, such as a letter from a collective farmer in Siberia and another from a Canadian who had recently moved to the Soviet Union to begin a new life.[18] They reported that they enjoyed job security, safe working conditions, short hours, and plenty of food, although the Canadian writer said she missed such small luxuries as rayon stockings and polo shirts. However, given the rate of industrialization in the Soviet Union, she wrote, she was confident that she would have her shirts and stockings soon enough.[19] The first edition also included accounts from the Friends of the Soviet Union's workers' delegation to Russia.[20] J. Francis White, a member of the editorial board of both *Soviet Russia Today* and *Canadian Forum*, tidily summarized the tone of *Soviet Russia Today*'s comparisons between Canada and the Soviet Union:

> In the last four years there has been a world crisis in the capitalist countries. International trade has been more than cut in half, unemployment is mounting year after year, wages have been cut, the store-houses are filled with produce but the workers have not enough money to buy the goods that they have manufactured.
>
> When we turn to the Soviet Union, we find a tremendous contrast as compared to the depression which is becoming more and more severe in the capitalist countries. In the Soviet Union there is no unemployment,

> there is a job for everyone who is willing to work. Hours of labor have been reduced, and wages are steadily rising. Hundreds of thousands of new houses and apartments have been built for the workers, besides club-houses, sports stadiums, amusement parks, rest homes, hospitals and theatres. Illiteracy is being abolished. Social services – accident and old age insurance, children's nurseries, medical and dental services – are being improved each year.[21]

White had also written a six-part essay on his own experiences as part of the workers delegation to the Soviet Union for *Canadian Forum*, although his descriptions in that publication were much less effusive than in *Soviet Russia Today*.[22]

The pages of *Soviet Russia Today* asserted that the Soviet Union was a utopia in every way. Prisons were humane and focused on rehabilitation instead of punishment, and crime rates were falling everywhere as the social problems causing criminal behaviour were reduced or eliminated.[23] The magazine explained the system of paid vacation enjoyed by all Soviet workers, equality among black and white citizens, and the cultural freedoms enjoyed by the different ethnic minority groups around the country.[24] The arts were said to flourish. Individual artists and theatre groups were free from the restraints of government censorship or of self-censoring, which in other countries might be necessary to ensure the economic success of their productions: they were free to create.[25] Multiculturalism was embraced, employment was 100 per cent, people had enough to eat, and children received excellent free education and played sports. Even Soviet museums and children's toys were said to be superior to their Canadian equivalents.[26]

In addition to telling positive stories about the Soviet Union, *Soviet Russia Today* provided the Friends of the Soviet Union with a forum to attack detractors. When a visitor to the Soviet Union described it as a grey, lifeless, decaying society where alcoholism and political persecution were rampant, Cecil-Smith was quick to attack the critic. For instance, when Humphrey Mitchell – a trade unionist and member of the CCF – reported seeing starvation in Russia, Cecil-Smith branded him "a vicious hater of the Soviet Union."[27] When a *Mail and Empire* reporter published accounts of widespread famine in Ukraine – which, of course, we now know to be accurate[28] – Cecil-Smith wrote that he was clearly lying. He claimed that it was impossible for the writer to have seen these things, as the roads in Ukraine were impassable in the spring.[29] Such accounts, Cecil-Smith said, were meant to deceive and distract the working class.[30] The capitalists did not want the workers to realize that there were solutions to the problems they faced.

One of these problems was the issue of socialized health care and its relationship with sanitary housing. Readers of *Soviet Russia Today* were told that the Soviet Union had established a system of socialized health care and had heavily invested in improving the quality of housing. Socialized health care was decades away in Canada, and housing in many of Canada's large cities was of poor quality. A 1934 study by the Ontario lieutenant governor, Dr. Herbert A. Bruce, examined the state of housing in Toronto's slums, specifically St. John's Ward and Cabbagetown. The homes of the unemployed and the working poor were described as cold, damp, overcrowded, and vermin infested.[31] Beyond providing deplorable living conditions, this kind of housing made people sick. Tuberculosis was common. The ill and their families became public charges. The Bruce Report concluded that these slums should be razed to the ground and replaced with public spaces. *Soviet Russia Today* juxtaposed the Canadian state of affairs with the Soviet solution to the problem. Articles by Canadian doctors such as Frederick Banting, co-discoverer of insulin, praised the Soviet medical system.[32]

The most famous advocate of Soviet health care was Norman Bethune, a thoracic surgeon at the Hôpital du Sacré-Cœur in Montreal, who would become famous for his exploits in Spain and China. Bethune himself was a survivor of tuberculosis, and was struck by the inequity of the disease, which hurt the poor more than the rich. Bethune wrote that "there is a rich man's tuberculosis and a poor man's tuberculosis ... The rich man recovers and the poor man dies ... We, as a people, can get rid of tuberculosis, when once we make up our minds it is worthwhile to spend enough money to do so."[33] Bethune visited the Soviet Union to attend the International Physiological Congress in Moscow in the summer of 1935 and was inspired by what he saw. Upon returning to Montreal, he publicly endorsed the Soviet system of health care. He found that the Soviet system put sufficient emphasis on improving social and housing conditions, which reduced the risk of tuberculosis in the first place. He spoke at a Friends of the Soviet Union meeting in Montreal in October 1935, advocated for health care reform, and secretly joined the still illegal Communist Party of Canada in November.[34] As noted earlier, at some point during 1935–36, Lilian Gouge, Cecil-Smith's wife, had caught tuberculosis. The couple went to Montreal so that Gouge could be treated by Bethune; the surgery was a success and she survived.[35] In the course of the treatment, the three learned that they had much in common: they all had a strong interest in the arts, as well as working-class issues, communism, and the Soviet Union. Gouge and Bethune formed an especially strong bond.

Cecil-Smith and the editorial staff at *Soviet Russia Today* sought to reach a broad audience, people who might not gravitate toward the Communist Party of Canada but might be otherwise convinced to support the Soviet Union. Before the transition to the Popular Front, the 1933 pamphlet "What Is the Friends of the Soviet Union?" explained that the group sought to form a coalition of "the widest numbers of workers, farmers and all liberal elements, regardless of political affiliation."[36] The pamphlet claimed that the group was not a CPC front; rather, it was formed by members of other parties and welcomed people of any political stripe. Cecil-Smith likewise minimized the connection of the organization and *Soviet Russia Today* to the party. He noted in an editorial that the magazine staff included members of the CCF, the Socialist Party, the Labor Party, and the Independent Labor Party. He conveniently excluded any mention of the Communist Party of Canada, even though he and co-editor William Sydney were well-known party members.[37] Unlike his writings in the *Worker*, Cecil-Smith's *Soviet Russia Today* editorials avoided Marxist language and refrained from criticizing the CCF. The Friends' goal was to build a broad base of support that could resist what they perceived to be war preparations against the Soviet Union.[38]

The goal of building support for the Soviet Union included lobbying Prime Minister Bennett's Conservative government to drop its trade embargoes. Canada had imposed specific trade embargoes on the Soviet Union in 1931 in response to allegations that Soviet suppliers were deliberately attacking Canadian businesses by undercutting their lumber, wheat, and fur prices, although *Soviet Russia Today* claimed that low Russian prices were simply the result of superior Soviet farming and manufacturing processes.[39] Britain and the United States had imposed similar embargoes but had resumed normal trade by November 1933. The Friends of the Soviet Union wanted Canada to drop its embargoes as well, and decided to make the matter an election issue in 1935.[40] *Soviet Russia Today* carried articles about the different positions of the Liberals, Conservatives, and CCF regarding the resumption of trade with the Soviet Union, and encouraged its readers to lobby their candidates.[41]

Cecil-Smith considered the continuing embargoes on the Soviet Union to be an example of how Canada's big businesses were unduly influencing foreign policy:

> Down in Nova Scotia and Ontario and elsewhere, there are steel mills standing idle or nearly so. These could be put to work turning out many thousands of tons of steel rails.

> Canada also has very large supplies of aluminum and nickel, two metals which the Russian industries need very badly and which, as yet, cannot be produced by Soviet mines in sufficient quantities ...
>
> Farmers of Canada find their farms overstocked with high-grade dairy and beef cattle, with horses, with thoroughbred swine and sheep. Vast tracts of land in the Soviet Union are today without sufficient of these animals ...
>
> Why then is it impossible for us to exchange these valuable things with the products of the Soviet Union which we cannot and do not produce in Canada? Simply because sufficient pressure has not been brought to bear on the federal government by those of us who desire such trade.
>
> We can, and we must, force the government to raise the embargo on Soviet products, so that the work of the Russian workers and farmers in accompanying their second Five-Year Plan may be lightened, and also, that we ourselves in Canada need not starve in such large numbers.[42]

Cecil-Smith argued that the embargo was detrimental to the working class in two ways. First, it generally weakened the home of socialism. Soviet citizens would have to work longer and harder to establish true socialism, although they would not be stopped. Second, the Soviet Union was a gigantic potential marketplace for Canadian goods such as steel, wheat, lumber, and manufactured goods. Canada, he argued, could sell upwards of $100 million worth of goods to the Soviet Union every year, giving jobs to thousands of presently unemployed Canadian workers.[43]

Ultimately, however, the embargo did not become a major election issue. Prime Minister Bennett's government maintained the embargoes throughout its mandate, although it did examine potential barter arrangements.[44] Following their election in 1935, Mackenzie King's Liberals announced that they would examine dropping the embargoes. Canada resumed normal trade with the Soviet Union in September 1937.

Cecil-Smith feared that growing tensions in Europe would result in an imperialist war against the Soviet Union in the near future. Unlike many of his contemporaries, he also had a strong interest in events in the Far East. He never returned to his native China, but he read newspapers and missionary magazines on the subject and corresponded regularly with his mother, father, and sister in Guizhou province – his brother, Sydney, had moved to Darjeeling in India to oversee the family's tea plantation.[45] Based on the available information, Cecil-Smith believed that a wider war in Asia was even more likely than in Europe. Japan had invaded Manchuria, China's northeastern-most territory, and established the puppet state of Manchukuo in 1932. Japan invaded Inner Mongolia, territory along the Soviet Union's southern flank, the next year. Russia's loss to Japan in the Russo-Japanese War of 1904–5 was still a relatively fresh memory, and there was renewed concern that the two powers might again go to war.[46] Meanwhile, China was being torn apart by an internal struggle between the ruling Nationalists and the Chinese Communist Party.

Cecil-Smith held the Nationalists in extremely low regard. He called them "the butcher government of Nanking," which he claimed had killed "one and a quarter million" Chinese people between 1927 and 1933.[47] Some of these deaths were the result of incompetent governance, while others were due to rampant corruption by government officials and the wholesale slaughter of peasants who stood in their way. Cecil-Smith likely remembered the warlord soldiers of the Guizhou Army from his childhood; they were so notorious for their addiction to opium that they were known as "two gun soldiers," carrying both their rifles and their opium pipes wherever they went.[48] The Nationalists and their warlords, Cecil-Smith believed, were the enemies of the Chinese people. The Chinese Communist Party and its Red Army, on the other hand, would be their saviours.

The Nationalists had pursued a series of extermination campaigns against the Red Army during the early 1930s. Although the Red Army had been expelled from the cities and were operating in the countryside as "bandits," Cecil-Smith believed that they were growing in strength because of their military shrewdness and the moral correctness of their cause. In an editorial in late 1933, he wrote that he was certain that the Red Army would emerge from the struggle victorious.[49] That army, he asserted, was working to improve the lot of the Chinese people. It had established soviets around China to put the peasants in control. The effect was that the army was able to seize and hold ground that the peasants would not soon give up to the Nationalists. The Red Army, he wrote, "truly seem[s] to be becoming invincible."[50]

Cecil-Smith and his parents had very different points of view on the conflict in China. He wrote that his father was "certainly no lover of the Communists. He sometimes writes to me and tells me how horrible they are."[51] George Cecil-Smith, Edward's father, was by that time the superintendent for all the China Inland Mission missionaries in Guizhou province, responsible for the missionaries and the mission houses. He preferred the steady hand of the province's governor, Zhou Xizheng, and was dismayed when Zhou was killed when the warlord armies in Yunnan province invaded to enforce Nationalist rule.[52] The installed Nationalist governor and his successors were unable to maintain stability in the province – road construction halted and banditry skyrocketed. Some of these bandits were common criminals, but others were elements of the Red Army. Missionaries were targeted for ransom.

George saw this disorder first-hand while travelling to Sinan[53] to acquire property to re-establish a mission house. The Yunnanese soldiers were billeted in homes along the main roads, conducting patrols and "anti-bandit" operations to subdue the Red Army and secure the area. Pressing on, George was captured by bandits and "convicted" in a sham court "as a Christian, deceiving the people; as an Englishman, an enemy of the Chinese race; as an Imperialist injuring the Chinese."[54] He was held for sixteen days before a German missionary was able to negotiate his release.[55] This was George's most dramatic, but not last, encounter with the Red Army. In 1933, while returning travelling overland from Chongqing to Guiyang, George heard rumours of "General Mao's defeated soldiers holding the road" outside of Zunyi.[56] George soon encountered a band of Red Army soldiers. The soldiers robbed him and his party, "but the leader on learning that we were missionaries ordered that our loads should be restored to us."[57] The travellers encountered two more such roadblocks before they safely arrived in Guiyang; George recalled "how thankful we were to see Kweiyang [Guiyang] the following day!"[58] In 1934–35, a large portion of the Red Army rested in Guizhou for four months during what has become known as the Long March.

In the autumn of 1934, the Nationalists launched an extermination campaign to rid southern China of the Red Army, once and for all. The Nationalists had attempted to encircle the force's base area in the Jiangxi Soviet, but the army had escaped and marched west into Guizhou province. George was in Guiding at the time, where he narrowly avoided capture, but some of his missionaries were taken by the Red Army.[59] China Inland Mission missionaries Alfred and Rose Bosshardt were seized on the roads; Arnolis and Rhoda Hayman, along with their two children, were captured near Jiuzhouzhen. Canadian missionary Grace Emblem of the West China Mission was captured near Jiuzhouzhen. George left the safety of Guiding to try to find them. He found Rhoda Haymen, Rose Bosshardt, and the children, who had been released by the Red Army, and he made arrangements for them to escape to the safety of the coast.[60] The Red Army later released Emblem, but Alfred Bosshardt and Arnolis Hayman remained prisoners and accompanied the troops for much of the Long March.

George's objections to the Chinese Communists were both practical and ideological. These "bandits" caused disorder in his adopted home.

He had been kidnapped twice, and he lived in constant fear that this wife, Ida, his daughter, Frances, or the other missionaries under his charge might suffer the same fate. Moreover, their "godless" philosophy undercut his life's work of saving souls. The words of Alfred Bosshardt, written after the experience of the Long March, are telling:

> Many reports have referred to our captors as "bandits" or "robbers" because of their methods of working, but the truth is that the leaders are convinced Communists, disciples of Marx and Lenin, and do what they do from principle. They are in touch with other bands by wireless and work with [the] U.S.S.R.[,] referring to Russia as their "Mother." Let us recognise this Red menace to civilisation, the home, and the Church as from the devil, and resist this force by wielding the Sword of the Spirit and using the shield of faith. The war is in the heavenlies. Let us pray for the harassed multitudes who are like sheep without a shepherd, and do all in our power to give them the Word of God before they believe a lie. The comrades are taught to aim at world revolution and their consciences are so lulled to sleep by the teaching they receive that virtue appears to them as weakness and vice becomes a duty. Communism is all the religion they want.[61]

The connection between the Chinese Communist Party and the Soviet Union was not a mere conspiracy theory, although it was often exaggerated. The Comintern in Moscow assigned Otto Braun, a German adviser, to the Chinese Communist Party's Red Army, and he accompanied them during the Long March. Meanwhile, Manfred Stern (born Moishe Stern), another German Communist assigned by the Comintern, worked as a military adviser in Shanghai. Later known by the *nom de guerre* Emilio Kleber, Stern would become the first commander of an International Brigade in the Spanish Civil War.[62]

Despite George's disapproval of the Communist ideology and the Red Army's actions in Guizhou province, his son Edward held that that army did much good and advanced the cause of the peasants. In Guizhou, the Red Army seized grain from wealthy farmers and sold it to the poorer peasants for less than its usual cost. The Red Army recruited government soldiers, offering more pay, and, "more than that, they actually pay what they promise."[63] In territories occupied by the Red Army, Edward Cecil-Smith wrote, peasants unionized, there were no workers under the age of fourteen, employees aged sixteen to eighteen worked shorter hours, peasants worked eight-hour days, and any grievances could be brought before a special labour court.[64] He highlighted stories of mercy and kindness by the Red Army, and he was not the only missionary child who felt this way.

Edward Cecil-Smith's life, and his views on the Communist Party of China, mirrored those of clergyman, missionary, and political activist James G. Endicott. Born in China to missionary parents, Endicott came to Canada and fought in the Canadian Expeditionary Force during the Great War. He returned to China as a missionary, living variously in China and Canada with his wife, Mary. Although he did not join the Communist Party in either country, he became one of the Chinese party's strongest advocates. While serving as a missionary in Chongqing in the early 1930s, he proselytized and taught English to Communist prisoners. His biographer recalls one event as Endicott and his family departed the prison one day:

> As the Endicotts were on their way out the gate, their six-year-old son, Norman, whispered, "Aren't the prisoners coming out too?"
>
> "No," was the reply. His eyes grew wide with wonder and he began to ask questions about Communists and about what they were trying to do in China. The question came up again at dinnertime and showed he had been doing some thinking on his own. "Do Communists try to help the poor people?" he asked.
>
> "Yes," answered his parents.
>
> "Well, isn't that what Christians try to do?"
>
> "Yes, certainly," was the reply.
>
> "Then why are the Communists in jail and you aren't?"
>
> It was not an easy question to answer. The standard reply about the Communist believing in violence sounded hollow, especially in the Chinese setting. "Out of the mouths of babes and sucklings hast thou ordained strength," the Psalmist once suggested. "Wise men are sometimes foolish," Jim reflected to Mary afterwards. "Is this a case where the young and innocent know better?"[65]

Endicott's Christian values, like Cecil-Smith's, attracted him to communism.[66]

Cecil-Smith remained interested in the plight of the Chinese people, both in China and in Canada. In June 1935, he spoke at the Moss Park Chapter of the Canadian Labor Defense League. An RCMP observer noted that Cecil-Smith's talk was on "the history of the Soviet-Red Movement, the strifes, the bloodshed ... and charged the C.L.D.L that it was up to them to help China."[67] In addition to sending aid to the Red Chinese, Cecil-Smith told the crowd that they should also help the Chinese immigrant community in Canada. Cecil-Smith, through the missionary community and the Chefoo alumni, knew all too well that the Chinese immigrant community was often persecuted. He recommended that the Moss Park Chapter take a leadership role in supporting Chinese immigrants and immediately help establish a Chinese branch of the Labor Defense League.[68]

Cecil-Smith's writings show that the fear of another world war weighed heavily on his mind. He was apprehensive about a coming war in both Europe and Asia. He desired peace, but he was not a true pacifist. He believed that the Great War had been an imperialist war, and therefore an unjust war. Any war against the Soviet Union would similarly be unjust, but he clearly did not have an issue with war as a political tool, in some cases. When the Nationalists threatened Republican Spain, he took up arms. When Germany invaded Poland, he volunteered again. Cecil-Smith did not reject the use of force but rather sought to steer a broad base toward understanding what he saw as the peaceful characteristics of the Soviet Union.

Cecil-Smith's first article in *Soviet Russia Today*, "Canadian Capitalists Foster Intervention," laid out his perception of the international situation.[69] He saw that several regions of the world were on the brink of war. Japan was poised to strike at Soviet Siberia, and a war between the United States and Japan also seemed likely. There was also a very real risk, he claimed, of a war between the United States and Great Britain. A war between the United States and Japan, or the United States and Great Britain, he postulated, would be very damaging to Canadian interests. Consequently, he claimed, Prime Minister Bennett was trying to engineer military intervention against the Soviet Union, which would preclude war among the capitalist powers. An Anglo-American war against the Soviet Union would be the least destructive to Canadian interests, and Canadian bankers and industrialists (like Bennett himself) could get even richer in the process.[70] In this formulation, Canada was not just pandering to American and British interests in their aggression against the Soviet Union – it was one of the ringleaders.

The CPC received directions from Moscow in May 1934 to create a Canadian branch of the World Congress Against War and Fascism, a movement with reasonably broad support but controlled by the Comintern.[71] A youth congress for prospective members of the proposed organization was held in Toronto in August with 300 representatives. All but three of them (whom Cecil-Smith denounced as Trotskyists) voted in favour of a resolution to pursue the goals of preventing war and fighting the spread of fascism.[72] The resolution also included a strong endorsement of the perceived role of the Soviet Union in pursuing these goals:

> The danger of war results from the attempt, on the part of the bankers and industrialists, to insure larger profits at home and abroad, particularly through the new redivision of world markets and sources of raw materials. Since in the Soviet Union there are neither bankers nor industrialists, there is absent all interest in aggressive war preparations. Therefore, the Soviet Union purses a positive and vigorous peace policy and alone among all governments proposes total disarmament. Serious struggle against war involves the support of this peace policy.[73]

The youth congress was followed by the first congress of the Canadian League Against War and Fascism. In anticipation of the latter, a writer described as an "initiating member" reminded readers of the key role of the Soviet Union in the success of the peace movement:

> True peace lovers ... must discern and understand the powerful force of peace which emanates from the Soviet Republic, the strength of [the] Red Army is, unlike that of other armies of the world, a safeguard for peaceful construction and not hellish destruction of life and property ... To many persons, politically inexperienced, such a slogan [Defend the Soviet Union!] seems of no immediate concern and of slight importance. To class-conscious workers, and to those more familiar with political intricacies, there seemed to be no doubt at all as to the vital importance of identifying the movement for world peace with Soviet defence. To stress the importance of Soviet Russia's role towards preserving and maintaining world peace would be a great service not only to the Soviet Union but to all who earnestly wish to escape another war ... We must remember that it was with the cry of peace, of ending the senseless slaughter of the last World War, that the U.S.S.R. was born.[74]

Supporting the Soviet Union, the organizers argued, was the best mechanism through which the workers of the world could ensure peace.[75]

Cecil-Smith was strongly in favour of the establishment of the Canadian chapter of the League Against War and Fascism. His editorials regularly highlighted fascist aggression, especially by Japan, and the arms race by the imperial powers. "No longer can there be any doubt as to the cause of all this activity," he wrote. "The various imperialist powers are getting ready to throw themselves at each other's throat."[76] Bankers and industrialists stood to make a lot of money out of this war, he explained. The working class had to organize to prevent another war in which the millionaires would get richer and the working class would simply be cannon fodder. He added that, since the Soviet Union had neither bankers nor industrialists, it was the only true ally of the working class in maintaining world peace.[77]

A related point that received considerable attention in the pages of *Soviet Russia Today* was the idea that the Soviet Union and its Red Army was a force for peace in the world. The Red Army was celebrated and presented as a fundamentally different organization from the "bourgeois" armies of capitalist states. An article by William Sydney, "Defenders of the Interests of the Toilers of the World," described "capitalist armies" as manifestations of the societies that they served: "On the one hand [such an army] is composed of a large number of conscripted or recruited soldiers from among the workers and peasants, and on the other hand there is a smaller number of officers, recruited from among the ruling capitalist class."[78] The soldiers, he explained, are kept separate from the political and working life of the country, which enables an officer, "a member of the class that exploits him in civilian life," to use him as a tool of exploitation against his own class. The author further insisted that every soldier in the Red Army had been trained to understand his role as a protector of all workers everywhere. The Red Army, Sydney explained, was as concerned with the well-being of a Canadian worker as a Russian worker. It was therefore the duty of every worker to support the Soviet Union and to "build a more solid ring of supporters and sympathizers around the Soviet Union, ready to defend it today and tomorrow."[79]

Cecil-Smith attended the first congress of the league as the Progressive Arts Club representative. The three-day congress covered a number of subjects. Defeating fascism, after all, required displacing an idea. Many of the delegates argued that such a defeat could be achieved only by improving the lot of the working class generally. Perhaps not surprisingly, given that he was representing an arts group, Cecil-Smith was quoted in the congress report as saying that "the intellectual suffers as much as the worker under capitalism and artists and writers must prostitute their art in order to earn a living."[80]

RCMP detective Robert Irvine attended the opening ceremonies of the congress, and one of his informants attended the daily sessions. Although Irvine was "unimpressed" by the organization, his supervisors told him that he was underestimating the league. The RCMP National Headquarters considered the organization's broad appeal as "one of the most outstanding things accomplished in the Party's history."[81]

The Canadian League Against War and Fascism was successful in bringing together a wide variety of organizations in Toronto.[82] The first congress in Toronto attracted 261 delegates representing 211 different organizations. It soon had the support of individuals and groups otherwise reluctant to associate with the CPC, including *Toronto Star* columnist and Methodist minister Salem Bland, Toronto rabbi Maurice Eisendrath, Kenneth Woodsworth (J.S. Woodsworth's nephew), the Women's International League for Peace and Freedom, and the Fellowship for a Christian Social Order.[83] Although the CCF initially declined to join the organization, its leaders still viewing the Canadian League Against War and Fascism as a mere Communist front, within six months CCFers Graham Spry and Sam Lawrence, the latter a sitting member of Ontario's Provincial Parliament, would attend the league's congress, and there were open signs of cooperation between the CCF and the league.[84] The composition of the league's national leadership similarly indicated broad support. The national council was led by A.A. MacLeod, who, like Cecil-Smith, was both a Communist and a devout Christian. The league's vice-chair, secretary, and treasurer, however, were not members of the Communist Party of Canada. They were active members of the Socialist Party of Canada, an organization with which the CPC had cut ties after denouncing it as Trotskyist.[85] Despite this strained relationship, the CPC, the Socialist Party of Canada, trade unions, and ex-servicemen organizations found a common cause through the Canadian League Against War and Fascism.

The pages of the *Worker* and *Soviet Russia Today* show that the CPC believed that the working class faced threats from every direction. The Soviet Union was threatened by the Western powers and Japan on its southern flank. The Chinese Communists were under threat from the Nationalists and the Japanese. The German Communist Party had been exterminated by the Nazis, and there were fears that something similar could happen in France and Spain. Spain had otherwise been absent from the pages of the *Worker,* but the saga of a 1934 miners' strike in Asturias attracted much attention. Cecil-Smith had no way of knowing it, but the unfolding events in Spain would come to define this phase of his life.

While, in 1931, fascism was entrenched in Italy and growing rapidly in Germany, the declaration of the Second Spanish Republic provided a welcome bit of hope in a dismal time. The republic moved to strip the traditional power brokers – the monarchy, the landowners, the army, and the clergy – of their influence and establish a more egalitarian society. But the backlash was fierce. The republic's first coalition government was defeated in the 1933 election by the Confederation of Autonomous Right-wing Groups (known by its Spanish acronym, CEDA), a Catholic party that had emerged in large part due to the anticlerical policies of the republican government.[86] CEDA aggressively moved to undo the earlier reforms.[87] In response, the Communist Party of Spain and various anarchist groups called for a general strike. The new government violently put down these strikes, notably when the army, under Francisco Franco, crushed the Asturian miners' strike in October 1934.[88]

The strike and its suppression was a prelude to civil war. The *Worker* reprinted a document, "DIRECT from the COMINTERN," in October 1934, addressing the Spanish situation:

> To all members of the Socialist International! To the Toilers of all lands! The fascist-monarchist reaction in Spain has hurried all the armed strength of the army, the navy and the aviation flotillas against the workers and peasants who, under the working class alliance accomplished through the fighting unity between Communists and Socialists have sealed this alliance with their bloodshed on the fields of battle, a battle which is still going on.
>
> A victory for the fascist-monarchist reaction in Spain would – after the seizure of power from fascism in Germany and Austria – means not only immeasurable torture for the workers and peasants of Spain, but would signify a heavy blow for the international proletariat.[89]

The Comintern called upon the workers of the world to pursue "mass action" in support of Spain. In just a few years, it would ask for much more.

PART THREE

A Volunteer for Spain (1936–1938)

Chapter Seven

"No Pasaran!"

Cecil-Smith did not seem to be a likely candidate to fight in a war. Although he had trained as a solider in his youth, by the late 1920s he was considered to be a "violent pacifist" who preferred to focus his energies on intellectual pursuits.[1] He considered the soldiers of the Great War to have been pawns in a game played by the capitalist class. But he did not feel the same way about the Spanish Civil War. He viewed the defence of the Spanish Republic to be a just war. He was inspired by the image of international volunteers and workers' militias shouting "*No Pasaran*!"(They shall not pass!) from the barricades as they defended the Republic against fascist aggression. He took up the cause, not out of a traditional sense of defending king or country, but for values that transcended national boundaries.

Sometime in 1936, Edward Cecil-Smith and Lilian Gouge moved to a new apartment in Toronto's Ward 2.[2] This apartment was special to them. After years of precarious housing, bouncing from one home to another, sometimes for just months at a time, they finally found a clean, dry apartment that they could afford. This would be their home for the next six years.

Just as important as the apartment itself, Cecil-Smith and Gouge liked the neighbourhood. They had met one another at the nearby China Inland Mission headquarters, since moved onto the University of Toronto campus. Then, in 1932, although he lived in Toronto's west end, Cecil-Smith had tried to stand for election as Ward 2's representative on the Toronto Board of Education.[3] Cecil-Smith and Gouge also liked the neighbourhood because it was within easy walking distance of where they spent their leisure time: the Village, a bohemian stretch of Gerrard Street between Chestnut and Bay Streets that was filled with artists and artisans as well as coffee shops and tea rooms.[4] It was an ideal place to meet with their friends and have long discussions about the latest book they were reading or an exhibit they had seen at an art gallery.

By the summer of 1934, Gouge and Cecil-Smith had lost the Progressive Arts Club as their preferred forum for conversation regarding politics and culture. The organization had been dissolved, a casualty of the CPC's move toward the Popular Front, so Gouge and Cecil-Smith became increasingly involved in Toronto's other leftist cultural circles. They attended discussion groups in the Village's coffee shops, Russian cultural events hosted by the Friends of the Soviet Union, art exhibitions at the Toronto Art Gallery, and plays by Myrtle Eugenia Watts (who now tended to go by Jean instead of Jim) and Toby Gordon's Theatre of Action, the successor to the Workers' Theatre. Running in these circles almost certainly brought them in contact with Paraskeva Clark, a Russian artist whose work was on display at the Toronto Art Gallery, and Pegi Nicol MacLeod, the art editor of *Canadian Forum.* These connections brought them again in touch with Norman Bethune.[5] Bethune visited Toronto several times during the summer of 1936, and Gouge visited him at least once in Montreal (it is unclear if Cecil-Smith accompanied her). Gouge recalled attending a party at Bethune's apartment where the guests were invited to dip their hands in gold paint and press them against the wall.[6]

Meanwhile, Cecil-Smith continued to work for the party's newspaper, the *Worker*, which published three times a week, and joined the editorial committee of its replacement, the *Daily Clarion.*[7] The *Worker* carried a title and a history that invoked the class-against-class spirit of the Third Period. Like the Workers' Unity League and the Progressive Arts Club, the transition to the Popular Front meant that it had to go. The *Daily Clarion*'s name did not carry the same political baggage, and its language would be less communistic. A daily newspaper, it would carry a blend of news, sports, comics, and sections for women and children that could compete with the "capitalist dailies" – like the *Toronto Star* and the *Globe and Mail* (the recent consolidation of the *Globe* and the *Mail and Empire*) – in order to reach a broad audience and help support the Popular Front. At the same time, it would provide advertising space for the CPC and its fronts, give the party's perspective in news stories and editorials, and ensure that international events of relevance to the party were given sufficient coverage. Cecil-Smith, as a former journalist for "capitalist dailies," was likely of considerable assistance to the editor-in-chief, Lenin School graduate Leslie Morris, as they made this transition. The first edition was published on May Day 1936.

Like the *Worker,* the *Daily Clarion* would carry significant news coverage of events in Spain, where the conflict between the left and the right was playing out in stark terms. The right-wing victory in the 1933 election, followed by the suppression of the 1934 Asturian miners' strike, had been deeply troubling for party members and supporters, particularly when viewed against the backdrop of Hitler's coming to power in Germany. However, the introduction of a Popular Front coalition in Spain seemed a cause for optimism. The Popular Front coalition united leftists of all kinds; it included the Communist Party of Spain, but they were small in number and their principal contribution to the Popular Front was the name itself.[8] The right-wing Catholic CEDA had similarly built alliances with Carlists, monarchists, the Falange, and other conservative groups, calling themselves the National Front (the Nationalists). In February 1936, the Popular Front (the Republicans) defeated the Nationalists at the polls and formed a new government.

The tensions between the Nationalists and the Republicans – between the right and the left – only grew worse following the election. Peasants in the countryside rioted against the landowners. The landowners fled to the cities. The Nationalists abandoned moderation, organizing terror squads and diverting assets to assist a military conspiracy under the leadership of General Emilio Mola.[9] The front page of the May Day inaugural edition of the *Daily Clarion* showed a photo of several agitated soldiers and their horses, providing one example of the ongoing conflict between the Republicans and Nationalists. The caption read, "A bomb hurled among the soldiers during the celebration of the anniversary of the founding of the Spanish republic. Communists were blamed. But it was proven that the fascists did it, trying to provoke splits in the People's front. Several soldiers were killed in this explosion. In the immediate centre can be seen one of the riderless horses, whose rider was killed."[10] It was just one incident among many as tensions between the progressive Republican government and its supporters came into conflict with Spain's traditional power brokers.

Concurrent with his full-time duties at the *Daily Clarion*, Cecil-Smith was elected president of the Communist Party of Canada's local committee for Ward 2.[11] In this capacity, he was responsible to the Toronto Committee for recruiting, organizing meetings and study groups, and supporting broader party activities. One of his first responsibilities as Ward 2 president would have been rallying local support for the May Day festivities. His committee members marched in the parade as it passed through their ward on its way from East York to Maple Leaf Gardens.

May Day parades were an annual tradition, but the 1936 parade was special. The first edition of the *Daily Clarion* was printed and widely distributed during the celebration, and, although the CPC was still illegal (section 98 would be repealed later that summer), the party would openly march in the parade. More importantly, this parade would be the first to be jointly organized by the Co-operative Commonwealth Federation and the Communist Party of Canada, and it was the largest May Day parade Toronto had ever seen, with more than 25,000 marchers.[12] The joint parade was a tremendous act of solidarity, a victory for the Popular Front ideal, but the victory was quickly soured by the reaction of the Ontario CCF's leadership. The Ontario CCF ejected three prominent members and four regional organizations from its ranks for their involvement in the parade.[13] The message from Graham Spry and the Ontario CCF was clear: do not collaborate with the CPC.

Sometime later that summer, Cecil-Smith lost his job at the *Daily Clarion.* The reason is unclear. He was, in his own words, dismissed from the staff for "developing an uncomradely attitude towards another comrade."[14] What was the nature of this conflict? Did Cecil-Smith's argumentative nature get the better of him? Did he pick a fight with the wrong person, such as the paper's influential editor-in-chief Leslie Morris or the party's director of agitation and propaganda, Stewart Smith? And what did they argue about? Was it a personal, editorial, or ideological matter? There are no other records of these events, and so we can only guess. Whatever Cecil-Smith's transgression, it was not so bad as to merit his expulsion from the CPC. He remained a member of the party and the president of the Ward 2 Committee.

Losing his job at the *Daily Clarion* would have been a terrible blow to Cecil-Smith's ego and livelihood. He and his wife had just moved into a new apartment, and the fear of eviction and returning to a precarious housing arrangement must have been daunting. Employment prospects during the Depression were poor in general, and few newspapers were likely to hire someone like Cecil-Smith, given his history of labour organizing and work with the Communist Party. Many potential employers would immediately discount him as a troublemaker. Fortunately, he was able to find a job as a correspondent for the *Montreal Star.*[15] He certainly needed this job, but returning to work at a "capitalist daily" after working in the party press for so long must have been a bitter pill to swallow.

~

The Spanish Civil War erupted on 18 July 1936. Cecil-Smith, like most close followers of the news, was well aware of the disorder in Spain and the Nationalist backlash against the reforms of the Republican government, but the rebellion that sparked the war came as a surprise. Emilio Mola directed the plot, organizing a military uprising in all fifty of Spain's provinces and encouraging the soldiers to be "violent in the extreme" to break any organized resistance.[16] On 20 July, the Republicans declared victory over the Nationalist rebels, announcing the next day that they were arming their citizens in a bid to hold on to the capital.[17] The citizens' defence against the uprising provided a terribly romantic image, played up in the pages of the *Daily Clarion* and other sympathetic English dailies like the *Toronto Star*.[18]

By the end of the month, the Nationalists seemed to be growing in strength, largely due to the support of Fascist Italy and Nazi Germany. Mussolini secretly provided a squadron of bombers, but some of them crashed or had to make emergency landings on the way to Morocco, informing the world of Italian involvement.[19] Hitler provided twenty transport planes, which would ferry Francisco Franco and the Army of Africa to the Spanish mainland.[20] Russia later sent more modest contributions of equipment and advisers to assist the Republican government. These contributions elevated the uprising to a proxy war between ideologies.

Meanwhile, the international community sought to starve the conflict by imposing a blockade and sanctions on Spain.[21] In September 1936, several countries established the Non-Intervention Committee to pursue this policy, yet the committee included the very countries that were supporting their proxies in the conflict. There never was a clearer example of foxes guarding the henhouse. Canada was not part of the committee, but it publicly supported that body's position. As Prime Minister Mackenzie King explained in a speech before the League of Nations, "Canada does not propose to be dragged into a war which she has no interest, and over the origin of which she has no responsibility or control through any automatic obligation."[22]

The *Daily Clarion*, in article after article, expressed a very different position. The Canadian people, it argued, *did* have an interest in Spain: the defence of democracy and the defeat of fascism. The caption below a photo of five young Republican women carrying rifles with fixed bayonets declared, "They are the forefront of this fight for democracy."[23] Oscar Ryan, Cecil-Smith's old friend, explained in an editorial that, contrary to what was presented in movies, the Spanish people were not "90 per cent ... aristocracy and the other 10 per cent bull fighters," but rather ordinary people who faced the same dangers as the working class in Canada. A democratically elected government pursuing reforms to better the lives of their working class, he explained, was collapsing under the weight of a coup supported by Nazi Germany: "They've got rifles in their hands. They're protecting us here in Canada against the madness of world fascism. We mustn't fail them. We are their rearguard."[24]

Yet some were not content with simply being the rearguard. When the war was only a month old, some Canadians began clamouring for the opportunity to go to Spain to defend the Republic. Edo Jardas – a Croatian immigrant who had been a member of the CPC since 1929, notably serving as the Workers' Unity League organizer at Anyox – approached Sam Carr about organizing and dispatching a group of southern Slavs to fight in Spain.[25] In Winnipeg, 1,000 unemployed men volunteered to form a battalion. In their petition to Prime Minister Mackenzie King, the Winnipeggers wrote, "Today we are idle men. We do not want history to record that we remained idle when international fascism hammered humanity with blows that struck at the very heart of democracy. We yearn to carry through the worthy mission of helping to defend a world's people from impending destruction."[26] The appetite was there. People wanted to go to Spain; they did not need to be rallied. Finally there was an opportunity to do more than protest – a volunteer in Spain could actually *fight* the fascists.[27] These enthusiasts merely needed an organization with the resources and discipline to organize them and get them to Spain. The party would soon oblige.

CPC leaders A.A. MacLeod and Tim Buck visited Spain early in the conflict to learn more about the nature of the war. They returned separately, bringing back different messages and launching new projects to support the Spanish Republic. MacLeod, the leader of the Canadian League Against War and Fascism, returned to Canada in early October 1936 after having spent two weeks in Madrid, Valencia, and Barcelona. He landed in New York with a small incendiary bomb in his briefcase bearing a German manufacturer's stamp, proof of Nazi involvement in the conflict. The bomb was presumably taken from him by a duly concerned public official. MacLeod emphasized to reporters that what was happening in Spain was not a civil war – it was an invasion by Moors and foreign legionnaires supported by German Nazis and Italian Fascists. Spanish president Manuel Azana had told MacLeod that they desperately needed medical aid; MacLeod therefore intended to rally the Canadian League Against War and Fascism toward filling a ship full of medical supplies and food aid for Spain.[28] Although this goal was not to be realized, MacLeod did play an essential role in establishing the Committee to Aid Spanish Democracy, hosting delegations from Republican Spain on speaking tours in Canada, and organizing what would become Norman Bethune's Servicio Canadiense de Transfussion de Sancre, the Canadian Blood Transfusion Service.[29] Although the CCF leadership had shown itself unwilling to condone cooperation with the CPC as recently as May Day 1936, the cause of Spanish democracy was sufficiently pressing for them to set these misgivings aside.

The Committee to Aid Spanish Democracy was a broad coalition of anti-fascists within which the CPC and the CCF could work together.[30]

The intermingling of the two groups was such that it was not even clear which could truly claim to have created the new organization.[31] Communists A.A. MacLeod and A.E. Smith were on the board. Ben Spence, recently ousted from the CCF for cooperating with the CPC during the 1936 May Day celebrations, was the chairman. *Toronto Star* columnist and Methodist minister Salem Bland was the honorary chairman. Dr. Rose Henderson, a CCFer who had long been active with the Women's International League for Peace and Freedom, was also on the board. Graham Spry, who had ejected Spence and the other CCFers for their collaboration with the Communists, later became a vice-president of the committee.[32] From the party's point of view, it appeared that the Popular-Front might finally come to pass.[33]

By the time Tim Buck returned from his three-month visit to Russia, France, Belgium, and Spain in mid-November, the public was paying a great deal of attention to events in Spain. The CCF and the CPC, working together through the Committee to Aid Spanish Democracy, had jointly hosted representatives of the Republican government in Toronto and Montreal, and had sponsored Bethune's medical mission. Bethune arrived in Spain the week before Buck returned to Canada. Meanwhile, the battle for Madrid was raging. The Nationalists were at the city gates, and foreign volunteers were playing an important role in the city's defence.[34] German, Italian, British, French, and Polish volunteers of the first of the International Brigades arrived in Madrid on 8 November.[35] This International Brigade was all the more interesting to Canadians because it was commanded by an Austrian-born naturalized Canadian who had been a member of the CPC in Toronto for five or six years in the 1920s: Emilio Kleber.[36]

This was an incredible moment for any Canadian interested in Spain. Bethune was running a medical mission there. A Canadian was commanding a brigade of international volunteers in the defence of Madrid. For the first time, it was easy for Canadians to see themselves as playing a role in the defeat of the Nationalists in Spain. Lionel Edwards, later a company commander in the Mackenzie-Papineau Battalion, recalled the effect of the news reports: "It was a tremendous story, the carrying out of the immortal slogan that Madrid would be the grave of fascism."[37] Cecil-Smith was no doubt among the 7,000 people in Toronto who went to the Mutual Street Arena to hear what Buck had seen on his travels in Spain.

The rally in the Mutual Street Arena had many of the usual trappings of a CPC rally. The dais was decorated with the flags of Russia and, in this case, the Spanish Republic. As required by law, the public address system played "God Save the King," albeit weakly; two different bands played four different versions of "The Internationale." Stewart Smith introduced Buck, who regaled the audience with stories of what he had seen and experienced during his three weeks in Spain. On the eighteenth anniversary of the armistice of the Great War, Buck declared that a second world war had already begun. He described the attacks he had observed on the outskirts of Madrid, the presence of German and Italian aircraft and tanks, and his chance to fire a rifle at Nationalists. At the same time, he maintained, untruthfully, that there was not a single Russian rifle in all of Spain.[38]

While the Republicans, Buck stated, were orderly and lawful, the Nationalists were guilty of terrible crimes. He described how men, women, and children were locked in cottages that were set alight "just for fun." In Toledo, sixty people per day were executed by the Nationalists for two weeks. In Badajoz, 2,000 people were murdered with machine guns. The Republic would emerge victorious, of this he was sure, but it needed help. Spain needed friendship, money, and medical support. Donations from the attendees that night raised $1,000, half of which went to support Bethune's medical mission, the other half of which would help finance Buck's run for office to serve on the city's Board of Control.[39] Buck did not mention, publically at least, that Spain also needed volunteers.

Buck later described his experiences in Spain and the decision to send Canadian volunteers to Spain. José Diaz, the chairman of the Communist Party of Spain, called a meeting in Aranjuez, not far from Madrid. It was attended by Diaz; Buck; Dolores Ibrarruri, a Communist Party member sitting in the Spanish Parliament and best known by her nickname, *La Passionaria* (the Passion Flower); and André Marty, a leading figure in the French Communist Party, the Comintern's representative in Spain, and later the commissar of the International Brigades. They discussed the idea of creating units of foreign volunteers to bolster the Spanish Republican Army. Buck had agreed to recruit 250 Canadians, a goal that would be quickly surpassed.[40]

Buck's version of events was certainly true, but it leaves a lot out. He presents the recruiting effort as a friendly gesture toward his Spanish comrades. In reality, this was a worldwide movement organized by the Comintern. Kleber, the commander of the first International Brigade, was not Canadian at all; this was merely a cover story. His real name was Manfred Stern, an agent of Moscow who had advised the Red Army in China (1933–34) and, before that, had run a Soviet spy ring in New York City (1929–32).[41] The Soviet Union would provide Spain with weapons and advisers in limited quantities, and the world's Communist Parties would provide the soldiers. Buck and the other members of the CPC's Central Executive Committee were surely aware that, on 18 September, the Executive Committee of the Comintern had approved the "recruitment of volunteers, having military experience among workers of all countries, with the purpose of sending them to Spain."[42] Stalin publicly called Spain's struggle "the common cause of all advanced and progressive mankind."[43]

One of the Canadians who answered that call was Edward Cecil-Smith. What motivated a Canadian man, married, employed, and in his mid-thirties, to enlist for a war in Spain? Soldiers volunteer to go to war for a host of reasons. Duty to king and country are oft-cited ones, but that clearly was not the case here. Neither the Canadian government, nor King Edward VIII – nor, after the abdication crisis in late 1936, King George V – were calling on anyone to go to Spain. In fact, Britain and Canada erected barriers to prevent their subjects and nationals from fighting there. Britain invoked the 1870 Foreign Enlistment Act in January 1937, and Canada's minister of justice, Ernest Lapointe, announced that Canada was creating a new and improved version of the British statute, still in effect in Canada, such that it would better apply to the circumstances in Spain.[44] Technically speaking, Cecil-Smith was not violating Canadian law at the time of his departure, but it was clear to everyone that king and country were asking that Canadians *not* go to Spain.

Soldiers also sometimes go to war to seek adventure, to get away from their old life, or because they feel compelled to do so by peer pressure. Again, this does not seem to describe Cecil-Smith. He was employed, married, had a good home for the first time in years, and had an active social life in Toronto. He was not a drifter and seemed far too introverted and thoughtful to be merely seeking adventure. He also would not appear to have been under any undue peer pressure to volunteer. He was the only Canadian Chefooite to go to Spain, and Ward 2 did not produce very many volunteers. In fact, in June 1938, Cecil-Smith mentioned in a letter to a friend that he and Jim Raily (born Ivan Ralloff), a Bulgarian Canadian who had joined the party in 1936, were, as far as he knew, the only people from the Ward 2 Committee who had gone to Spain.[45] Cecil-Smith did know two early volunteers for Spain, but both had gone in non-combatant capacities. He knew Bethune, who had left in October 1936, and former Progressive Arts Club member Jean Watts, who left in early 1937 as the *Daily Clarion's* correspondent. None of this paints a picture of someone who was under any particular external pressure to volunteer. Cecil-Smith's desire to go would seem to have come from within.

As a student of history, Cecil-Smith must have sensed that this was a key moment in world events. After the war, he provided both religious and historical justifications for his desire to fight in Spain. Upon returning, he told a crowd that the situation in Spain reminded him of the teaching that one should help the downtrodden and that Jesus Christ would take these actions as done unto him.[46] He also noted that the British people had a long tradition of battling despots, and that the world was a better place for it.[47] Even if his own country was not at war, in his mind it was still right for him to volunteer his services to combat the modern-day Bonapartes manifested in Franco and Hitler. As a practical matter, he also believed that he could make a valuable contribution. He had military experience, with a working knowledge of trench construction, demolitions, and basic soldiering as a senior non-commissioned officer.[48]

Cecil-Smith was less public about the role his politics played in his decision to go to Spain, but it must have been a key element. In Spain, war was being waged between the forces of good and evil. The victor would determine the future of Spain. Would it be a democracy where the Spanish Communist Party might survive, organize, and eventually see the revolution? Or would it be a fascist state, the puppet of Mussolini and Hitler, with the Communist Party eliminated entirely, as it had been in Italy and Germany?[49] For some, the war was about seeing the defeat of fascism and the survival of Spanish democracy for Spanish democracy's sake. Cecil-Smith, however, was not merely an anti-fascist. He remained a dedicated Communist and saw the conflict through that lens. Communism, he believed, was the future. He expressed as much in an editorial he wrote for *New Frontier,* the leftist arts magazine established by Jean Watts, Dorothy Livesay, and Stanley Ryerson.[50]

This editorial, entitled "The Future of Humanity," was written two months after the outbreak of the Spanish Civil War. He wrote in response to an article by Professor E.A. Havelock that appeared in the August issue of *Canadian Forum.*[51] Havelock had stated that communism was dying off, and Cecil-Smith wrote to state that he could not be more wrong. Communism, he wrote, was the only possible future.[52] He asserted that the revolution was coming, although the reallocation of property would be upsetting for the current power brokers: "Hardly cricket, but the class war is a pretty grim affair." As usual, Cecil-Smith avoided language that might suggest he was advocating violence. Instead, he wrote,

> If I may be permitted to add, communists teach that the stronger we organize the labour and popular fronts, the simpler and less bloody will be the final struggle against capitalism. A vastly stronger people's front in

> Spain, six months ago, would have prevented the fascists from ever daring to take up arms against the democracy. Force does not always have to be violent. A sufficient show of force at the right time may even prevent violence altogether.
>
> The past twenty years have given the world proletariat many experiences of victory and defeat from which to learn. Germany, Italy, Austria and Hungary, etc. on the one hand; and on the other the Soviet Union, France, Spain, China and elsewhere.
>
> To conclude. The future of the human race is bound up with the future of communism. If it were possible for the die-hard anti-unity leaders of labour to forever prevent the united front and the people's front, then we must face a dark future indeed, no less than "the common ruin of the contending classes." But fortunately we have ample proof that the common people are learning fast and are forcing their "leaders" towards unity. This can be seen not only in France and Spain, but also in Norway, Britain, and even in Canada.
>
> The future of humanity is communism, the classless, stateless society, in which man will forever cease to use force against man, when exploitation will end and the real history of human development will at last begin.[53]

Communism was the future. It had to be. And it was the future for all of the world's working-class people, including those in Spain. By volunteering for Spain and defeating fascism on the battlefield, Cecil-Smith had an opportunity to further this goal.

Equally motivating must have been the leadership role that the Comintern was playing in Spain. For the first and only time in Cecil-Smith's life, the Comintern was organizing the workers of the world to behave as a class, not as disparate peoples in disparate lands, in the pursuit of a single goal: the preservation of the Spanish Republic. How could he not heed the call? Here he was being presented with a problem to which he could be part of the solution. Bethune, a physician, could lead a medical mission, but Cecil-Smith did not have that skill set. He had been trained as a soldier for many years, and the Comintern itself was asking for such volunteers to go to Spain.

The CPC quickly established a secretive recruiting network to get volunteers to Spain. Committees interviewed and vetted the volunteers (screening out undercover RCMP officers and Trotskyists), arranged for medical inspections, and moved the volunteers from across Canada, safe-house to safe-house, as far as "Toronto Station," from which they would be dispatched to Europe. Paul Phillips and Peter Hunter, who had recently returned from the Lenin School in Moscow, greeted the volunteers in Toronto and assisted them by finding temporary lodgings and getting them some clothes and luggage for the trip.[54] The first five volunteers departed in late December 1936.

Cecil-Smith was not immediately eligible to go to Spain. He was married, and the party wanted volunteers who were single. If a volunteer was killed, the party did not want to be encumbered with the costs of supporting the widow.[55] As a member of the party, Cecil-Smith also needed to apply for permission to go to Spain. A replacement would have to be found to take over his responsibilities for the Ward 2 Committee. Despite these issues, someone in the party made the determination that Cecil-Smith could proceed to Spain.

The next step for a volunteer was an interview by the local committee, which presumably went well enough in Cecil-Smith's case. He also passed a medical inspection, despite the glaucoma that necessitated his wearing thick glasses.[56] Next he quit his job with the *Montreal Star* and was issued his luggage.[57] Given that he lived in Toronto, he was able to stay at home with his wife, whose feelings about the matter are unrecorded, until it was time to go. In February 1937, he would receive train tickets to take him to New York, and from there to France and on to Spain.

He had ample opportunity to read the newspaper reports regarding events in Spain while he waited to depart. The reports varied widely. Instead of objectively presenting the confusing and cruel events of a chaotic civil war, each newspaper seemed to pick a side, presenting either the Nationalists or the Republicans as the heroes or the villains.[58] The press alternately described the events in Spain as either a Red or a White Terror. The Red Terror was the mob violence against the traditional power brokers in Spain, particularly the Catholic Church. More than 6,000 priests and religious Spaniards were murdered in the course of the war.[59] The White Terror described the atrocities committed by the Nationalists, mass killings committed against anyone they viewed to oppose them.

Both sides were responsible for atrocities, but the crimes were hardly congruent. As historian Paul Preston has noted, "If there was a difference in the killings in the two zones it lay in the fact that the Republican atrocities tended to be the work of uncontrollable elements at a time when the forces of order had rebelled, while those committed by the Nationalists were officially condoned by those who claimed to be fighting in the name of Christian civilization."[60] The Nationalists had to bear responsibility for the advent of terror bombing against civilians. With some limited exceptions during the First World War, the use of airpower against civilian targets was a new and horrifying dimension of modern warfare, one carried out by Spanish Nationalist, Nazi German, and Fascist Italian aircraft against Republican cities.

The *Toronto Star* carried two especially distressing headlines on 9 February 1937. The first read "Assert Rebels Shoot 1,000; 300 Women Said Abused."[61] This was yet another example of the White Terror, this time in Azuara, a village in which Cecil-Smith would be fighting in a year's time. The second read "Charge Italians, Nazis Shelled Line of Retreat."[62] This article reported that Nationalist, German, and Italian ships and aircraft had attacked civilians fleeing the town of Malaga. Initial newspaper reports claimed 4,000 civilians had been killed. Later estimates ranged from 5,000 to 15,000. The event was witnessed by Norman Bethune and later described in his pamphlet *The Crime on the Road.*[63] Cecil-Smith found such incidents heart breaking and cowardly: "They [these pilots] are afraid to fly down and machine-gun an army that has machine guns to defend itself, but they do come down to strafe the roads where the women and children and old men are trying to leave the city under fire."[64]

On the morning of 15 February, a cold winter's day, Cecil-Smith said his final farewells to his wife, Lilian Gouge. With some pocket money, train tickets, and a single innocuous briefcase filled with some changes of clothes and a spare pair of eyeglasses, he quietly made his way to Toronto's Union Station.[65] There were no parades, no brass bands, no well-wishers to see him off. He quietly boarded the train with two other volunteers, and they made their way to Niagara Falls. He told the border officials that he was going to New York and on to France for an extended vacation, a common story told by the volunteers, given that the Paris World Fair was beginning in May.[66] In New York, he received a set of third-class tickets for the White Star Lines steamer the *President Roosevelt.* He set sail on 17 February.

Until they boarded the *President Roosevelt,* Cecil-Smith and the other Canadian and American volunteers had moved in small groups, keeping their intentions secret and being careful to avoid attention. But the transatlantic crossing was long, and it would not have required much detective work to figure out who among the passengers were going to Spain. Although they came from all over the United States and Canada, many of them had connections to each other through the CPC and its fronts, as well as any number of industrial and/or labour organizations. Cecil-Smith likely knew several of his fellow Canadian travellers, or at least had a few contacts in common. They would certainly get to know one another on the long journey to Spain.

Among the volunteers on board was Joseph Kelly, a member of the CPC since 1932, and a veteran of the Great War, the Irish Republican

Army, and the 1935 On-to-Ottawa Trek.[67] There were also three future Canadian company commanders on-board: Lionel Edwards, Bill Halliwell, and Alec Miller. Edwards had been a member of the Progressive Arts Club in Calgary before he joined the party in 1934, and he had written an editorial titled "Authorship and Canadiana" for *Masses* in 1932; Cecil-Smith and Edwards likely knew each other, at least through correspondence.[68] Edwards served as an organizer in the On-to-Ottawa Trek and was arrested and charged under section 98 during the Regina Riot.[69] Bill Halliwell, from western Canada, of no known party affiliation, was a veteran of the British Army in the Great War.[70] Alec Miller, from Edmonton, who had been a member of the CPC since 1930, was also a veteran of the Great War.[71]

Robert Kerr, a Scottish Canadian, was also on the ship. Kerr had been an organizer in the Workers' Unity League and had played a role in the On-to-Ottawa Trek.[72] Although he had served in the British Army during the Great War, he was not going to Spain to fight. He was going to work as the CPC's political representative there. He had a silk streamer stitched into his necktie stating as much.[73]

In no time at all, the volunteers would have identified what so many of them had in common. Many of them were members of the Communist Party, whether in Canada or the United States, and they were all anti-fascists. All of them had made the decision to put their life on hold, quietly cross the Atlantic, and don the uniform of the Spanish Republican Army. Once they identified one another, there seemed to be little point in pretending to be strangers. From the shipping lists, seventy-seven future members of the International Brigades can be identified among the *President Roosevelt*'s third-class passengers – fifty-six Americans and twenty-one Canadians. They were comfortable enough to gather together on the deck for a group photo (see the photo section of this book).

When the ship landed in Le Havre, France, the volunteers resumed their secretive movements. They travelled to Paris for processing (where both the CPC and the CPUSA – the Communist Party of the United States of America – maintained offices) and spent a few nights in designated safe-houses in that city. Cecil-Smith, one of the few volunteers who spoke French, must have enjoyed his visit to the City of Lights, knowing that they would soon be in cities shrouded in wartime blackout conditions. Just days later, they boarded trains to the French border town of Perpignan. Earlier volunteers had been able to enter Spain as tourists, but the French government had since closed the border. The volunteers had to enter Spain discretely by way of tried-and-true smuggling routes through the Pyrenees Mountains.

Guides met them at the border and marched them eighteen hours up and over the Pyrenees in the dark of the night, taking care to avoid French border patrols.[74] It was a gruelling hike – as Cecil-Smith later put it, "before they could fight Franco, they had to fight the Pyrenees"[75] – but the view from the mountaintop was stunning.[76] Even in the darkness, the glint from the snow and the starlight in the clear mountain air was beautiful. Cecil-Smith had seen mountains before, first in his childhood home in Guizhou province and then in Canada as he travelled through the Rocky Mountains en route from the West Coast to his new home in Toronto, but this was different. This was Spain. Here he filled his lungs with fresh air and marched on with a sense of purpose. After years of writing, thinking, and organizing with little to show for it, here in Spain he would take up arms and tangibly fight the forces of fascism.

Chapter Eight

Los Norteamericanos

Cecil-Smith had secretly travelled across the Atlantic to take up arms in defence of the Spanish Republic. He had quietly departed Toronto in the company of two comrades, joining a larger group of nearly eighty Canadians and Americans in New York. In France, he passed through a sophisticated network of supporters, encountering more and more like-minded anti-fascists as he went. Arriving at the first secure base in Spain, the massive, cold, humid, and smelly Sant Ferran Castle in Figueres, Cecil-Smith would have laid eyes on volunteers from around the globe, no longer hiding from the authorities.[1] He would have heard a cacophony of languages: Finnish, Hungarian, Ukrainian, Italian, Yiddish, French, German, and more. This was a truly international force, perhaps reminding him a bit of the diverse groups that had made up the Shanghai Volunteer Corps. But here in Spain, they were not fighting to defend the status quo of a corrupt outpost. Their cause was something much greater: to dig the grave of fascism.

From Figueres, Cecil-Smith and the other volunteers made their way by trucks and trains to the headquarters of the International Brigades in Albacete. He reported for duty on 7 March 1937.[2] The volunteers were ushered into the town's bull-fighting arena, where they handed in their passports (for safekeeping, but no doubt also to deter potential deserters), and answered some basic questions to facilitate their sorting.[3] Country of origin? Political affiliation? Languages spoken? Military experience? This information helped the organizers sort the volunteers into the appropriate units and training stream. Some volunteers were needed immediately at the front, while others were needed to run training or to receive it. Language was an essential organizing criterion for sending volunteers to a unit where they could comfortably work.

In many ways, Cecil-Smith was rather different from the other Canadian volunteers. Most volunteers for whom we have data worked with their hands, the top five vocations being miners, lumberjacks, factory workers, drivers, and mechanics.[4] The majority of the volunteers were members of the CPC but from rural Canada's mining and logging communities where the party apparatus was much more egalitarian. Cecil-Smith had not worked with his hands in years and was more accustomed to the strict discipline and hierarchy of the Communist Party of Canada in Toronto. There were few journalists among the Canadians, and few who openly enjoyed intellectual pursuits.[5] Cecil-Smith was also different in that he had previous military experience as a senior non-commissioned officer. Although the Comintern had hoped for volunteers with previous military experience, only about one in eight Canadian volunteers actually had any.[6] Some had combat experience in the Great War, but, unlike Cecil-Smith, few of them had held leadership appointments.

Nonetheless, Cecil-Smith was very average among the Canadian volunteers in terms of his age, party affiliation, and the fact that he had been born outside Canada. The average Canadian volunteer in 1937 was thirty-two years old; Cecil-Smith was thirty-four.[7] Many had experience in labour activism. For instance, an estimated five hundred Canadian volunteers had participated in the 1935 On-to-Ottawa Trek.[8] More than three-quarters of the Canadian volunteers were members of the Communist Party of Canada or the Young Communist League, and 78 per cent of the Canadian volunteers had been born outside Canada.[9] Some groups – specifically, Finns, Hungarians, Ukrainians, Poles, and southern Slavs (self-identified as either Macedonians, Bulgarians, Slovenians, Serbs, or Yugoslavs) – were over-represented relative to their percentage of the Canadian population.[10] The Canadian volunteers were diverse, but united in their politics and their shared immigrant experience.

At the time of Cecil-Smith's arrival, fewer than fifty Canadians were in Spain, but more would soon follow. Given their immigrant background and the use of language as an organizing criterion, the Canadian volunteers could end up almost anywhere in the International Brigades.[11] A Polish Canadian might be sent to the predominantly Polish XIIIth Brigade, or a German Canadian to the XIth.[12] However, the majority of Canadians and Americans, often treated as interchangeable *Norteamericanos,* were funnelled into the XVth Brigade's Lincoln Battalion alongside a large contingent of Cubans and Latin Americans, as well as Irish volunteers who had voted to not serve alongside their British comrades.[13]

The Lincoln Battalion was commanded by Robert Hale Merriman, an American. He was not a member of the CPUSA, although many certainly believed that he was, given that he had arrived in Spain by way of Moscow, where he was studying agricultural economics.[14] Before the war, he had trained as a cadet officer through the Reserve Officer Training Corps.[15] This was rudimentary training compared to the challenges of commanding a battalion in battle, but Merriman was one of the first Americans in Spain and quickly established himself as a courageous, athletic, and energetic leader.

By the time Cecil-Smith arrived in Spain in early March, the Lincoln Battalion had already been in action for a month in the Jarama Valley. They had played an important role in halting Franco's attempt to cut Madrid off from Valencia. Jarama was the first battle for most of the volunteers, including Merriman, and some terrible mistakes were made. Notably, on 27 February, Merriman was ordered to launch an attack against a line of Nationalist trenches. When the promised air, tank, and artillery support failed to materialize, Merriman correctly assessed that launching the attack would be suicidal. The brigade commander thought otherwise and ordered him to launch the attack anyways; if he refused, Merriman would be relieved of his command. Merriman did as he was ordered, and was almost immediately shot in the shoulder.[16] Casualties were terrible. Irish poet Charles Donnelly, a member of the Irish National Congress and commander of the Irish volunteers, was among those killed. His last words were "even the olives are bleeding ..."[17] The Lincoln Battalion had arrived in Jarama with 373 volunteers of all ranks but soon were down to only 80.[18]

The much-weakened state of the battalion meant that newly arrived volunteers had to be sent immediately to the front to hold the line at Jarama. This included some of the *Norteamericanos* with whom Cecil-Smith had travelled to Spain. Canadian Great War veteran Bob Kerr was told that the credentials stitched in his necktie, which were meant to excuse him from frontline duty, would "make a nice souvenir" – he was sent to the front anyways.[19] Bill Halliwell and Joseph Kelly, also veterans of the Great War, were likewise dispatched to the front.[20] Others, like Cecil-Smith (with peacetime service), Lionel Edwards (with no military service), and Alec Miller (a Great War veteran), stayed in Albacete to receive training.[21] The determination of who went to the front and who stayed for further training appeared to be arbitrary, a balancing act of sending personnel with experience to the front immediately while retaining others in the rear for training to ensure that the units continued to develop and improve.

Cecil-Smith, although dismayed that he was not going to the front immediately to do the job for which he had signed up, stayed at the various training bases in and around Albacete to receive basic training.

Although he had been a regimental sergeant major in the Canadian militia, nearly a decade had passed since that time, and Cecil-Smith no doubt benefited from the new training. Volunteer Gerry Delaney, a member of the CPC since 1930 and not of any previous military experience, recalled a standard training day:[22]

> 5:30 am we got out of bed, made the bed, wash, shave, clean barracks and then breakfast;
> 6:30 or 7 a.m. fall in for parade;
> 7:30 to 8:30 a.m., we had rifle instruction, we were taught how to field strip, clean and care for a rifle;
> 8:30 to 11:30 am. Field manoeuvres on section [platoon]* or company scale. We then marched back to the barracks, wash up for lunch.
> 1:30 to 2:30 pm. automatic arms instruction, how to mount and dismount guns, set them up in position and clean and care for them.
> 2:30 to 3:30 pm. Theoretical lecture on any given subject of warfare.
> 3:30 to 5:30 pm. more field drill and manoeuvres.
> 6:00 pm. Supper. Then free time to visit or read or write letters.
> 9:30 pm. Lights out and bed.[23]

Basic weapons training was complicated by a lack of resources and of uniformity of equipment. Cecil-Smith recalled that they had weapons from Canada, the United States, Great Britain, Paraguay, Mexico, Argentina, Portugal, France, Spain, Germany, Sweden, Switzerland, Poland, Czechoslovakia, Italy, Russia, Romania, and Japan.[24] He remembered that the similarity between the different kinds of Mauser revolvers was particularly problematic: the Spanish Mauser took a 7 millimetre bullet, while the German Mauser took a 7.62 millimetre bullet, and the Czech Mauser took a 7.9 millimetre bullet.[25] It was a nightmare for training, maintaining stores of spare parts, and resupplying ammunition in an organized way. Clearly, a soldier could easily make use of the wrong ammunition, causing an irreparable stoppage or even an explosion that would injure his face and/or destroy his weapon.

---

* Note that within the Spanish Republican Army, including the International Brigades, a *peloton* (platoon) was a group of eight to ten soldiers under a *sargento*, and two *pelotons* composed a *seccion* (section) under a teniente (Michael Alpert, *The Republican Army in the Spanish Civil War, 1936–1939* (Cambridge: Cambridge University Press, 2002), 316). This differs from terminology in the Anglo-American tradition, where the terms are the opposite: sections, or squads in the United States, form platoons. To avoid confusion, this text will use terminology more familiar to the English-speaking reader.

Machine guns were an essential part of basic training, as light machine guns provided the bulk of an infantry company and platoon's firepower. Like rifles and pistols, there were a variety of machine guns, but the two most common was the Bren gun, the mainstay of the Canadian and British forces during the Second World War, and the Soviet Degtyaryov. Cecil-Smith recalled that, while the barrel changes on the Bren gun were easier, which allowed the gun to maintain fire longer, the Degtyaryov was easier to take apart and clean, which made it less likely to jam. He also preferred the Degtyaryov's forty-seven-round drum to the Bren gun's thirty-round magazine. He recalled that the two weapons were on par in terms of weight, size, and firepower.[26]

Regardless of the weapon system, the volunteers had little ammunition with which to train – most of it was needed at the front. Weapons handling was practised repeatedly without ammunition, the volunteers using their imagination as their instructors told them how the weapons would behave when loaded with real bullets. Even if a volunteer was fortunate enough to fire enough rounds through a particular weapon to gain confidence that the sights had been appropriately adjusted, the weapons belonged to the Battalion of Instruction and would not be the weapon with which the volunteer would go into battle.[27]

The volunteers performed most of their tactical training with dummy rifles, little more than pieces of wood. The tactics taught would vary from instructor to instructor, each one teaching a given tactic as it was taught to them in his home country. Consequently, there was a great deal of variety. Ronald Liversedge, a Canadian volunteer, member of the CPC (and previously the Communist Party of Great Britain), and a veteran of both the Great War and the On-to-Ottawa Trek, recalled that even something as simple as drill – getting a formed body of troops to march, stop, and change directions in unison – was complicated.[28] Commands were given in both Spanish and English, and volunteers with military experience taught others the way they had been taught in their country of origin. As Liversedge obvserved, "We never throughout the war had a uniform method."[29] The only thing they all had in common was the Republican salute: a raised fist.

Given that Cecil-Smith went on to become the highest-ranking Canadian in the Spanish Civil War, it might be presumed that he had ambitions on an officer appointment from the very beginning. He did not. He had not served as an officer during his time in the militia, and he did not seek to become one in Spain. He later remarked that a commission merely meant "more work, and you had to buy your own clothes."[30] He was much more content to serve as a *soldato* and rise through the ranks on his merit as a non-commissioned officer. Cecil-Smith had little interest in the responsibilities of command, and was also painfully aware of his own shortcomings.

Cecil-Smith was organized, tactically competent, and well read in military matters. But he was not a particularly charismatic person. He was prone to biting sarcasm and mockery, and came across as arrogant and aloof. He liked to argue, debating ideas found in literature, not sit around and affably chat and crack jokes. He made friends, but generally only among intellectuals. Rapport building is an important leadership skill for any military leader, but it was especially important in the largely proletarian International Brigades, where elitism was despised. Commanders had to carefully walk the line between connecting with their soldiers and maintaining enough distance to remain objective. These were not skills at which Cecil-Smith excelled.

Lawrence Cane, an American who later fought in the US Army during the Second World War, served under Cecil-Smith in the Mackenzie-Papineau Battalion. Cane saw his fair share of military leaders in Spain and the Second World War, and so his assessment of Cecil-Smith as a leader bears some weight:

> In his bearing he was aloof and showed little warmth toward the men in his immediate command or in the battalion. He was contemptuous and superior, frequently surly. I know of no one to whom he endeared himself, or anyone who really was his friend.
>
> Yet he had guts and was a competent commander and in the long run that's what he has to be measured by. Officers don't have to engage in popularity contests, and should be gauged by their accomplishments. Smith had to make some mighty tough decisions, and a lot of guys bought it in carrying them out, but that's what combat command is like.
>
> So the guys didn't like him, but what has that got to do with the achievements of the Mac Paps under his command?[31]

This assessment may seem somewhat harsh, but it likely is accurate. As a leader, Cecil-Smith was not loved. He did not inspire those under his command. But he was tactically competent, respected, not unduly influenced by any political ambitions he might have had within the party, and, perhaps most importantly, he was among the few who were willing to take on the burden of command, however grudgingly. The *Norteamericanos* suffered from a lack of soldiers willing to undergo officer training and accept their commission.[32] When called upon to serve as an officer, Cecil-Smith reluctantly accepted the responsibility. By about early April, he was moved from the basic training establishments to Pozorubio, home to the Officer Training School and the Non-Commissioned Officer School.

Robert Merriman, released from the hospital after being treated for his wounds in the 27 February attack, was assigned as the commander of the Pozorubio camp just as Cecil-Smith entered it.[33] Merriman's shoulder was still encased in heavy builders plaster while it healed (lighter medical plaster was at a premium in Spain due to the Non-Intervention Committee's blockade), but he was well suited to the task of establishing leadership training in this secretive, austere tent city hidden in a pine forest. His recent combat experience, training in the United States, and knowledge of the Russian language from his time in Moscow were important assets. His ability to speak Russian allowed him to better work with and translate for the Red Army advisers, who played an important role in Pozorubio.

Officially, these Red Army soldiers were all volunteers who had decided to go to Spain in an unofficial capacity, not as serving members of the Red Army. This, of course, was a fiction that fooled no one.[34] Some of the Red Army "volunteers" – such as pilots, tankers, and artillery crews – served directly in combat. Others were engineering or communications specialists, and many others were required simply to work as translators. These personnel were important, but their numbers were small: the number of Russians in Spain at any time was likely never greater than 3,000, and only about 200 or so were available to work as instructors and advisers.[35] Consequently, although they were vital to its functioning, it should not be imagined that Pozorubio was teeming with Red Army instructors. Merriman makes frequent reference to these advisers in his diary, referring to them in code to protect this poorly kept secret. He refers to Russians as "Mexicans," "men from the old country," "others of his kind," or even "dedushka," the Russian word for grandpa.[36] Russians and Russian equipment were frequently referred to as Mexican, likely because Mexico was the only other country that was publicly supporting the Spanish Republic.

Cecil-Smith was consistently impressed by the Red Army advisers he encountered in Pozorubio. He recalled that, "they all seemed to be an excellent type of soldier and officer, not to mention gentlemen."[37] And he learned a lot from them, later noting some differences between Russian tactics and those in which he had been trained in Canada. In offensive operations, the Red Army advisers emphasized the importance of puncturing the enemy's defensive line along a narrow front. Sufficient reserves had to be held back such that they could be rushed through the breach once the opening was established. The breakthrough, not the attack on the enemy lines, was where victory was achieved.[38] This meant beginning the attack with a detailed plan, focusing resources on a narrow frontage, and attacking the enemy where they were weakest.

In defensive operations, the advisers emphasized the importance of establishing an elastic defensive line. Cecil-Smith's training in Canada had focused on the importance of erecting ironclad, rigid lines of defence that could not be broken. The Soviet system accepted that a determined enemy could breach any line eventually. Commanders should instead create depth in their positions, maintain reserves to deal with breaches, and be able to absorb an enemy attack. This was not a passive act of giving up ground, but an active one of luring the enemy into successive traps. Platoons and companies withdrew from their positions at pre-selected breaking points along the line, using prepared routes and supported by fire. The enemy, perceiving these openings as success, would exploit the opportunity and push their reserves forward. The advancing enemy would soon find themselves surrounded by supporting obstacles and prepared positions for units in depth.[39] Thus, the destruction of the enemy took place behind the forward line of troops.

Cecil-Smith quickly transitioned from student to instructor at Pozorubio. He was fulfilling officer functions as early as April, although he was not himself commissioned as an officer until June.[40] Merriman mentions Cecil-Smith in his diary on two occasions at the end of April and again at the beginning of May as working with Walter Garland, an African-American member of the CPUSA with previous military experience in the US Army, who had recently healed from his own wounds at Jarama.[41] Cecil-Smith and Garland led officer candidates through tactical problems.[42]

Although Cecil-Smith did not yet have combat experience like Garland or Merriman, he drew upon his training in the Canadian militia and his extensive reading in military history. The exercises he and Garland ran were relatively straightforward. They would gather the officer candidates around a blackboard or a map model, laying out a piece of terrain and a hypothetical scenario such as leading a company in the advance, conducting a raid against a fortified position, crossing a river, or defending a piece of terrain. Candidates would present their plan, showing that they understood how they wanted the operation to unfold, how they would articulate their plan to their subordinate commanders, how they would employ their key weapon systems, and how they would evacuate their wounded and resupply their soldiers with food, water, and ammunition. It was a lot like the table-top exercises Cecil-Smith would have been involved in with the militia in Toronto.

The scenarios became more complicated if Nationalist tanks were introduced. The infantry companies in the International Brigades had very limited firepower with which to fight tanks. They did not have personal anti-tank weapons, such as the American bazooka or the British Projector, Infantry, Anti-Tank (PIAT), both developed in 1942. There were some armour-piercing bullets (which required a great deal of luck to be effective) and an anti-tank hand grenade (which required the soldier to be perilously close to the tank).[43] Commanders had to plan well in advance for defence against tanks; they were taught to use prepared positions with snipers who could fire at the tanks' vision ports, and to throw bottles of flammable liquid or grenades at the tanks when they were within range.[44] These tactics were of limited value when defending from unprepared positions. By the summer of 1937, the XVth Brigade had a limited complement of Soviet-made 45 millimetre anti-tank guns, but there were never enough, and they were only occasionally given to the companies or battalions.[45] Cecil-Smith recalled that this limited anti-tank capability was "obviously deficient" for modern warfare.[46]

As Cecil-Smith worked in the training establishment, the Lincoln Battalion remained on the line at Jarama, and more and more *Norteamericanos* arrived in Albacete. The new arrivals stayed in the nearby town of Madrigueras. Some went to the Lincolns as reinforcements, but by the end of April there were enough volunteers left in Madrigueras to justify the creation of new battalion. Merriman noted in his diary that Cecil-Smith was being considered to take command of a company in this new battalion.[47] Later that month, Merriman met with the recently arrived Serbian-American volunteer Mirko Markowicz to discuss the creation of the new battalion and the selection of its officers.[48] Merriman had no love for Markowicz, who had made advances toward his wife, but he had decided to set aside these differences and to put the war effort first.[49]

Markowicz had been a prominent leader within the Communist Party of Yugoslavia, but had fled to Moscow after the party was banned. He studied at the Communist University of the National Minorities of the West in Moscow, served as an officer in the Red Army, and then went to the United States, where he led the CPUSA's Serbian section.[50] He had arrived in Spain from Moscow a month earlier and was generally discouraged by the state of discipline within the International Brigades. He described the prevailing attitude: "We're volunteers. If we want to accept orders and discipline, it's ok. But if we do not like an order, we don't have to carry it out. We have the right to decide what to obey and what to reject."[51] He hoped to replicate in the new *Norteamericano* battalion the discipline he had come to expect in the Red Army – an army that was not nearly as egalitarian as many of the volunteers believed.[52]

Merriman, Markowicz, and Cecil-Smith were all of the same mind regarding discipline within the International Brigades. At the end of the war, Cecil-Smith recalled that "many of them [the Canadian volunteers] have not entirely got over the belief that leaders will appear when needed and at other times are not necessary."[53] As a group, they refused to accept "permanent authority." All three men were viewed as strict disciplinarians, but Merriman complimented his demands with a great deal of personal charisma. Neither Markowicz nor Cecil-Smith had magnetic personalities, and consequently had mixed reputations among the volunteers. They were competent but unloved, with reputations as strict disciplinarians and aloof leaders.[54]

Markowicz and Merriman discussed three names for potential leaders in the new battalion: American Walter Garland and Canadians Bill Halliwell and Cecil-Smith.[55] All three had done well as instructors and in their training. Garland, whom Cecil-Smith had worked with extensively in Pozorubio, and Halliwell, whom Cecil-Smith had sailed with on the *President Roosevelt*, were immediately taken on as company commanders in the new battalion. Cecil-Smith was not, and he continued to work in the training system. However, he would soon join the new battalion when Halliwell was transferred to the Lincoln Battalion in June.[56] Cecil-Smith was commissioned, promoted to *teniente,* and brought in to replace Halliwell on 4 June 1937.[57] He joined the new battalion, named after George Washington, at Tarazona de la Mancha.

Training in Albacete, Pozorubio, Madrigueras, and Tarazona de la Mancha did not occur in isolation from the events of the civil war. Albacete was bombed by Nationalist aircraft on occasion.[58] Volunteers were routinely plucked from their training to reinforce units in the field, and Merriman's diaries mention a number of events that required staff and students alike to mount honour guards for funerals or to provide an armed guard for ammunition or new weapons.[59] When there was unrest, the international volunteers were called upon to secure government facilities. One such episode, which involved Cecil-Smith, occurred during the unrest in Catalonia in May 1937.

Cecil-Smith and the majority of the international volunteers had passed through Catalonia when they had arrived in Spain. These border crossings, however, were not under the firm control of the Republican government, but a complicated, dual power arrangement that emerged following the Nationalist uprising. An alliance of anarchist and labour groups supported by the *Partido Obrero de Unificacion Marxista* (the

POUM) had seized de facto control of the region, but it had left the regional government, the *Generalitat*, intact for limited purposes. This arrangement was unsatisfactory for the Republican government, which sought to consolidate its control over Catalonia and the border, centralize command of all anti-fascist military forces in the Republic, and satisfy the increasingly influential Soviet advisers who sought the stamp out the POUM, which had a historical association with Leon Trotsky.[60] Tensions reached a boiling point in May 1937, when the Republican government moved to seize control of the Barcelona telephone exchange, after which barricade fighting broke out in opposition – as eloquently described by George Orwell in *Homage to Catalonia*.[61] The Republican government suppressed the uprising through mass arrests (including a single Canadian, former Progressive Arts Club member William Krehm) and executions in the months to come.[62]

Before the Republican government had regained control of Catalonia, there was considerable fear that similar uprisings might occur elsewhere in the Republic. Cecil-Smith and others were pulled out of the training schools and tasked with providing additional security for the Albacete governor.[63] As with training, weapons for internal security tasks were inadequate. Cecil-Smith was issued an 1871 French *chassepot* as his personal weapon. As he acerbically recalled, this gun "was considered to be quite a weapon in the Franco-Prussian War" but was not exactly state of the art or even in good working order by 1937.[64] Finding ammunition for the antique was also a challenge – Cecil-Smith only had three bullets. He counted himself lucky that he did not need to fire them as he stood guard in front of the governor's mansion: in the end, there was no uprising in Albacete.[65]

In addition to training and performing guard duties, Cecil-Smith also busied himself with political work. He was a member of a small group of Canadians in and around Albacete who lobbied for a company or a battalion under a Canadian name. Other groups had battalions or even brigades bearing the names of their national heroes. The Germans had the Thaelmann Brigade. The Americans had the Lincoln Battalion, and later the Washington Battalion and John Brown Battery. The Irish had the Connolly Column, a platoon that initially formed part of the British Battalion but fought with the Lincoln Battalion at Jarama and beyond. Cecil-Smith and other Canadians thought that a company or unit should bear a Canadian name in recognition of their contribution to the war effort. This would give the volunteers a special *esprit de corps* and provide a valuable rallying symbol for supporting efforts on the home front.

Joseph Kelly, an Irish Canadian who had returned from fighting with the Lincolns in Jarama, called a meeting of the Canadians at the camp in Madrigueras in late April. He wanted to discuss the feasibility of forming a Canadian company within one of the battalions of *Norteamericanos*. There was only one battalion at the time, the Lincoln Battalion, but a second was in the making. CPC members Cecil-Smith, Bob Kerr (also returned from combat in Jarama and now representing the CPC in Spain), Edo Jardas (a Croatian Canadian recently healed from his wounds at Jarama, where he had served with the Dimitrov Battalion), and two recent arrivals – François Poirier and Harry Rushton – were also in attendance.[66] The group decided that a Canadian company should be created and named in honour of William Lyon Mackenzie and Louis-Joseph Papineau, the leaders of the rebellions in Upper and Lower Canada in 1837–38. Kerr was elected to approach the XVth Brigade Headquarters with the idea. The brigade's leadership said they would take the suggestion "under advisement."[67]

The Canadians in Spain wrote to Prime Minister Mackenzie King in late May, at which point Markowicz's battalion had been established and there were rumours that a third *Norteamericano* battalion would be formed. The writers of the letter invoked the names of Papineau and Mackenzie, the latter being King's own grandfather and namesake:

> We feel we are upholding those principles of democracy that our forefathers fought for in 1837. If fascism wins here, it will mean an onslaught upon the remaining democracies of Europe. France, Britain, Belgium, and Czechoslovakia are marked down as the next victims of bestial, aggressive fascism.
>
> We ask that the Dominion government assist the Loyalist government of Spain, in the League of Nations, by facilitating the purchase of food and water materials by the Loyalist government in Canada. We ask that measures be taken to prevent the rebels from receiving any aid or comfort from Canadian sources. We call upon the Canadian people to support our Bethune medical unit.

The seemingly Popular Front group concluded, "We implore you from the depths of our hearts to do everything possible to help Spanish democracy. In so doing you are serving your own interests. We are here for the duration, until fascism is defeated. We, Liberals, CCFers, Communists, and Democrats from Quebec to British Columbia, Catholics and Protestants, call upon all Canadians who cherish peace and democracy to heed our call, to act, to save humanity from fascist barbarism." The letter, signed by Bob Kerr, Larry Ryan, Cecil-Smith, Harry Rushton, Edo Jardas, Walter Dent, Douglas Stewart, and François Poirier, was sent to Mackenzie King and other potential supporters.[68]

In Canada, the letter was ignored by the prime minister but widely promoted by an organization calling itself the Friends of the

Mackenzie-Papineau Battalion. The Friends announced its establishment and intention to act as an information bureau and support organization for the volunteers.[69] It was soon organizing fundraising events, advertising in the pages of the *Daily Clarion,* gathering together care packages to send to the volunteers, and organizing rallies with guest speakers from Spain. The organization fulfilled a public role, but also a clandestine one. Tim Buck recalled that it provided the public face for the recruiting apparatus, running rallies, designating "recruiting sergeants," organizing medical inspections, and sending the volunteers on to the main recruiters in Toronto. The organization was mostly able to raise sufficient funds to send volunteers to Spain. Buck expressly denied that any money ever came from Moscow, although he admitted that the Friends had received some money from the CPUSA in New York.[70] The Friends always publically denied any connection between itself and the recruiting effort.[71]

Home-front support for the Canadian volunteers in Spain transcended political membership. For example, the letterhead of the Friends of the Mackenzie-Papineau Battalion would later carry the names of forty-two sponsors. There were Communists among them, certainly, but most were not: Albert Einstein, H.G. Wells, Ernest Hemingway, Upton Sinclair, city mayors, aldermen, members of Parliament, priests, rabbis, and professors seemed eager to lend their name to the cause. J.B. Salsberg, a long-time CPC leader, noted that no cause in the party's history ever attracted such broad support.[72] Donations were plentiful; people who would not give a dime to the party were eager to put together a care package for a volunteer in Spain. The CPC cleverly put itself in a leadership position, directing and harnessing this widespread support and energy.

A few key points regarding this leadership role are worth noting. First, although many Canadians in Spain likely desired a unit bearing a Canadian name, the Canadians known to have lobbied for it were all members of the CPC. All six known participants in the first meeting to discuss the matter were members of the party, as were all eight signatories of the open letter. Bob Kerr was the official representative of the party in Spain. Douglas Stewart had been at the Lenin School when the Spanish Civil War broke out and had arrived in Spain by way of Moscow.[73] Additionally, the names used suggest some effort at misdirection. Walter Dent, for instance, had been a leader in the CCF Youth Movement until his expulsion for unknown reasons in May 1936, after which he joined the Young Communist League (YCL) and the party.[74] Including Dent's name would seem to substantiate the claim of CCF participation, even though only eight members of the CCF have been identified among the Canadian volunteers.[75] Similarly, François Poirier was a member of the CPC, but his French name would seem to lend some credence to the claim that the group spoke for Quebec democrats.[76] This messaging overstated the strength and pervasiveness of the Popular Front.

Second, the Friends of the Mackenzie-Papineau Battalion had deep ties with the CPC. It announced its creation the day after receiving the letter from the volunteers in Spain, a remarkably short period of time if it had had no forewarning. Tim Buck stated that "we," meaning the CPC, set up the organization.[77] Although many non-Communists participated in the Friends, even in national leadership roles (for example, the long-time director Beatrice Colle), most of the national board members were also prominent CPC leaders, including Stewart Smith, Sam Carr, Leslie Morris, and Colle's successor, Beckie Buhay.[78] Paul Phillips, a YCL leader, sat on the board of the Friends and also quietly managed the recruiting effort, assisted by Peter Hunter, recently returned from the Lenin School in Moscow.[79] The Friends initially used Bob Kerr, the CPC's representative in Spain, as its principal liaison. When he planned to leave Spain, the Friends sent a formal representative of its own – Jack Taylor (real name Muni Erlick), a member of the party's Central Executive Committee – to Spain from December 1937 until July 1938.[80]

Third, there was the choice of the name for the organization: the "Friends of the Mackenzie-Papineau Battalion." The names Mackenzie and Papineau were presented as if they had been selected by the Canadians due to their place in the pantheon of Canadian folk heroes, as if they were as well known to Canadians as Washington or Lincoln were to Americans. On the contrary, despite the centennial of the Upper and Lower Canada Rebellions, neither Mackenzie nor Papineau were widely perceived as romantic revolutionary figures in mainstream Canadian culture. Indeed, Cecil-Smith later noted that they were completely unknown to most Canadians until after the battalion was formed.[81] Mackenzie and Papineau were symbols that the CPC used in its increasingly Canadianized Popular Front propaganda; in a 1935 editorial, Cecil-Smith himself had invoked them as tragic revolutionary figures.[82] Stanley Ryerson penned an entire book on his interpretation of the role of the rebellions in Canadian history. In his *1837: The Birth of Canadian Democracy*, which was published during the centenary of the rebellions, he stated, "Just as, in 1837, it was they, the working people, 'yeomen and mechanics,' who formed the back-bone of the movement led by Mackenzie and Papineau, so once again, today, the Canadian working class is proving to be the best and truest defender of liberty, sending the best of her sons to defend Democracy with their life's blood, on the battle-fields of Spain."[83] Ryerson drew a straight line from Mackenzie and Papineau's struggle, to the fight against the fascists in Spain and the monopoly capitalists in Canada.[84] As Tim Buck recalled, "we chose the name *quite deliberately*."[85]

Finally, the simple fact was that no battalion existed when the Friends of the Mackenzie-Papineau Battalion was formed. In late May 1937, the XVth Brigade headquarters had taken the idea of creating a Canadian company "under advisement." There was no Canadian battalion, nor was there any certainty that such a battalion would be created. Furthermore, it is clear from the Friends' materials that the group was not using the term "Mackenzie-Papineau Battalion" as a nickname for Canadian volunteers in Spain, but rather as the name of an actual battalion attached to the "Lincoln (American) Brigade."[86] Years later, Tim Buck still insisted that the battalion was at full strength by the beginning of May and had earned a solid reputation in combat by July 1937.[87] Such statements were demonstrably false, but the idea of a Canadian battalion was immensely more valuable than the idea of disparate volunteers.

It was serendipitous that a battalion within the XVth Brigade would receive the name Mackenzie-Papineau, but this was far from a sure thing until the end of June. The XVth Brigade's newsletter refers to the new battalion as the William Henry Battalion, and Robert Merriman, its first commander, notes the selection of Mackenzie-Papineau as the battalion's name in his diary only at the very end of June. A.A. MacLeod, in Spain after his visit to the League of Nations in Geneva to protest the bombing of Guernica, likely played a role in convincing the XVth Brigade of the importance to Canadians of such a gesture. He famously gave a rousing speech to the *Norteamericano* volunteers, explaining the historical significance of the names to Canadian and American volunteers alike. The name of the new battalion was formally announced on Canada's national holiday, Dominion Day, 1 July 1937.[88]

~

Teniente Cecil-Smith joined Markowicz's Washington Battalion in early June 1937.[89] By then, this second *Norteamericano* battalion was billeted in Tarazona de la Mancha, not far from its previous base in Madrigueras but, Markowicz hoped, far enough away from the ready supply of alcohol and the hard-drinking French volunteers that the *Norteamericanos* could focus on training. Living arrangements were comfortable, much better than Cecil-Smith's quarters in Pozorubio. Instead of tents, the volunteers in Tarazona lived in converted houses, ate good, albeit repetitive, food that always seemed to include chickpeas fried in olive oil, and appreciated the simple joy of functioning indoor plumbing. The battalion reached a strength of four hundred volunteers and started collective training at the battalion level.[90] Cecil-Smith took command of No. 2 Company, his first command appointment, and worked to quickly familiarize himself with the organization.

The Washington Battalion had both Canadians and Americans in leadership positions. Markowicz was the battalion commander. No. 1 Company was commanded by Hans Amlie, an American and the brother of Thomas Amlie, a serving Congressman and member of the Wisconsin Progressive Party. Amlie had served in both the US Army and the Marine Corps during the Great War and in peacetime. He came to Spain by way of the Socialist Party of America's highly unsuccessful attempt to organize volunteers for Spain independent of the Comintern.[91] Cecil-Smith took command of No. 2 Company. No. 3 Company was commanded by Edo Jardas, a Croatian Canadian. Walter Garland, with whom Cecil-Smith had worked at Pozorubio, commanded the Washington's Machine Gun Company.[92]

The command team of a company in the International Brigades was different than that of a modern Western military company. It consisted of the company commander, a second in command (normally an *alfarez*, similar to a second lieutenant), and a commissar (normally of the same rank as the commander). Although commissars are often referred to as political officers, their duties were much broader than that description would suggest. They were viewed as a check and balance on a commander's otherwise unbridled authority. The commander and the commissar had to co-sign written orders as well as requests for military supplies.[93] A handbook produced in October 1936 explained that commissars were responsible for the soldiers' welfare, including inspecting weapons and equipment, assisting the commander in his duties, and establishing a "discussion room" and stimulating political discourse.[94] The commissars also performed counselling and morale duties within the unit, similar to a chaplain; performed propaganda duties against the enemy; and assisted with matters involving the locals. In battle, the commissars were expected to go wherever they were most needed, which could often be a dangerous proposition.[95]

Commissars were not an exclusive invention of the International Brigades; they had existed in the Spanish Republican Army since the beginning of the civil war.[96] Membership in a Communist Party was not a requirement for such a role, although the Spanish Communist Party saw the position as one of influence and quickly moved to dominate it.[97] The commissars in the International Brigades were largely members of their respective country's Communist Party, and their role in political education seemed to be more pronounced than in fully Spanish units. Commissars screened for Trotskyists and led political education activities. The latter responsibility was viewed to be important, as the foreign volunteers would eventually go home and had to be sufficiently well educated politically to perform their work in Spain and their home countries alike.[98]

Morris Henry Wickman, an African-American leader in the CPUSA in Philadelphia, served as Cecil-Smith's company commissar.[99] Wickman was responsible to Cecil-Smith, but he was also beholden to the battalion commissar, David Mates, who similarly had a joint responsibility to Markowicz and the XVth Brigade Commissar, Steve Nelson, and so on.[100] Despite this convoluted structure, which Cecil-Smith would come to loathe, he and Wickman got along well. Cecil-Smith had himself been considered for a commissar's position at Pozorubio, and the two men were the same age and likely had much to talk about.[101] Wickman was a sailor and a longshoreman who served as the secretary of the International Labor Defense (the equivalent of the Canadian Labor Defense League) and had travelled in the Soviet Union.[102] Like Cecil-Smith, he was untested in combat.

The second in command of a company in the International Brigades also fulfilled roles that a modern observer would associate with the senior non-commissioned officer in a company: the company sergeant major. These tasks included maintaining discipline and a high level of skill at arms within the company. Cecil-Smith's second in command was David "Andy" Anderson. Anderson was mostly well suited for this job. Twenty-five-years-old, he had spent eight years in the British Army in the Gordon Highlanders, including two years on the Northwest Frontier. Anderson had much more military experience than most of the soldiers in the Washingtons, including Cecil-Smith and Wickman. But he also had a lengthy record of bad behaviour, including a string of merit-based promotions and discipline-related demotions – the Gordons had promoted him to lance corporal six times and to corporal twice.[103] He appears to have been demoted at least once during his time with the International Brigades, as well.[104] Anderson was more of an adventurer than a political revolutionary, but he respected the party members within the International Brigades. He recalled, "When things got very, very hard, there was always a member of the Communist Party [who] came to the fore and tried to explain things. They were always the ones that gave the lead and took the risks."[105]

Cecil-Smith led a unique command team that likely could not have existed anywhere but the International Brigades. A Canadian commander, born in China and speaking with an English accent, a Scottish second in command who had served on the Northwest Frontier, and an African-American commissar from Philadelphia at a time when

African-American officers were virtually unheard of in the British, American, or Canadian military. Cecil-Smith was eager to go into battle with them. He would not have to wait long.

On 11 June, just five days after he commissioned and arrived at the battalion, Cecil-Smith was preparing to lead his company in a night exercise. That training was cancelled when Markowicz received orders for the Washingtons to depart Tarazona and move to the Jarama Valley. Twelve trucks arrived to take them to the front. The battalion quickly loaded its limited personal equipment onboard and departed at 3:08 a.m.[106] Merriman, his commissar, American Joseph Dallet, and the other *Norteamericanos* staying behind (those who would make up what would become the Mackenzie-Papineau Battalion) were on hand to wish them luck. Dallet noted in a letter home that he was very impressed by how efficiently the Washingtons had departed; the new battalion would seek to match or exceed this example set by their comrades.[107]

Although the Washington's departure went smoothly, little else did. The trucks and volunteers did not carry enough rations or fuel for the trip, and poor planning by staff officers meant that none was awaiting them along their route. The soldiers went without, and the drivers stole fuel from the locals.[108] The battalion received 250 rifles, but only 6 heavy machine guns and 2 light machine guns,[109] a paltry amount of firepower that suggested that Cecil-Smith's company likely arrived at the front with only rifles. Such shortcomings were all too common in the International Brigades. There was never enough equipment, and despite the experience of Soviet advisers and the dedication and spirit of the volunteers, the International Brigades lacked experienced staff officers to plan and non-commissioned officers to execute on critical details. But after months in the training system, Cecil-Smith was eager to join the XVth Brigade and to see combat.

The Washington Battalion became the sixth infantry battalion in the XVth Brigade. The brigade included a headquarters, supporting arms such as a Machine Gun Company, and five infantry battalions that had been in Jarama since February. Most of the *Norteamericanos* were already in the Lincoln Battalion. The British volunteers had a battalion that never took on a name that stuck. Spanish soldiers were sprinkled throughout the XVth Brigade, but they formed the bulk of the *Voluntario 24* (the 24th Volunteers or simply the 24th Battalion). The Dimitrov Battalion (named after Comintern leader Georgi Dimitrov) contained a mix of Czechoslovakian, Croatian, German, Hungarian, and Austrian volunteers. The Sixth of February Battalion, named after the 1934 riots in Paris that had led to the creation of several anti-fascist groups, gave a home to the Franco-Belgian volunteers.

The XVth Brigade was commanded by Vladimir Copic, a Croatian Communist. Copic had been drafted into the Imperial Austro-Hungarian Army during the Great War and had been captured by the Imperial Russian Army. He spent much of the war in prisoner of war camps, where he learned about communism, an ideology he believed could play a role in liberating his native Croatia. Copic became a founding member of the Communist Party of Yugoslavia (CPY) but, like Markowicz, had to flee the country after the CPY was banned and he stood trial. He attended the Lenin School, after which he became the Comintern's representative with the Communist Party of Czechoslovakia. He became the XVth Brigade's commander shortly after arriving in Spain in February 1937, and he had ordered the ill-fated attack on 27 February that Merriman had protested.[110] Markowicz and Copic, being members of the CPY and the Yugoslav diaspora in Moscow, were likely connected in a number of ways.

On 16 June, five days after departing Tarazona, the Washingtons relieved the Dimitrov Battalion. The Dimitrovs were in a second line position in Morata, not manning trenches in front of the Nationalists. If something happened, the Washingtons would be called upon to assist. But nothing happened. The soldiers simply waited in their tents for thirteen days. An occasional errant artillery round landed nearby, but the most "action" they got came on 22 June, when a torrential rainstorm washed away their tents and much of their personal equipment.[111] Occasionally the battalion prepared to counter a Nationalist offensive, but nothing ever came of it. Finally, on 30 June, after not firing a shot in the Jarama Valley, the unit was given orders to depart for Torreldones, 150 kilometres away.

The Washingtons loaded into their trucks and departed for Torreldones. From there, they marched twenty-three kilometres, carrying about fifty pounds of fighting equipment: their rifle, 200 rounds of ammunition, a canteen, a blanket, one or two hand grenades, a gas mask, a rucksack, a steel helmet, and a pick and shovel.[112] The weight and the heat were too much for some of the soldiers, many of whom left their packs and blankets behind in order to lighten their load.[113] The rest of the XVth Brigade, relieved of their positions in Jarama, trickled into the waiting area over the next two days. Then, at 9 p.m. on 4 July, the Washingtons moved to a position near Valdemarillo. They reached their destination at 2 a.m. and finally received orders and a cognac ration – "liquid courage."[114] They learned that they were already in their attack position for the Brunete Offensive.

Cecil-Smith and the other soldiers of the XVth Brigade knew almost nothing about the Brunete Offensive until just before it was launched.

Strict secrecy had been maintained to ensure the element of surprise. Up to this point, the Republicans had been on the defensive, reacting to Franco's assaults on the outskirts of Madrid and in the Jarama Valley. By the summer of 1937, Nationalist forces were entrenched on three sides of Madrid – the frontline all too closely resembled a set of jaws closing around the capital. To make matters worse, the Nationalists had seized Bilbao in the north. The loss of that city was a blow to the Republic, and it also meant that the Nationalist forces once required in the north were free to focus on sacking Madrid. The Republicans needed to strike a blow against Franco, and soon. The Brunete Offensive was meant to put the Nationalists back on their heels and seize the initiative.

The Republican plan was to drive into the Nationalist salient and seize the Heights of Romanillos. This would threaten the Nationalist interior lines, forcing Franco's forces to either withdraw or reallocate men that would otherwise be used in his continued offensive against Madrid. The Republicans devoted 50,000 soldiers, 136 pieces of artillery, 128 tanks, and 150 aircraft to the operation.[115] It was the largest Republican offensive up to that point, and it stood to change the course of the war.

The XVth Brigade's mission was to drive southeast towards the Heights of Romanillos and capture and hold Mosquito Ridge. Copic organized the XVth Brigade into two regiments. The First Regiment – the 6th of February, Dimitrov, and 24th Battalions – was commanded by *Mayor* Gabriel Fort, a French Socialist who had served in the French Army during the Great War.[116] The Second Regiment – the British, Lincoln, and Washington Battalions – was commanded by British *Mayor* Jock Cunningham, a Scotsman with experience in the British Argyle and Sutherland Highlanders, including leading a mutiny in Jamaica for which he spent six years in prison, and later a miner and member of the Communist Party of Great Britain.[117] The British Anti-Tank Battery, fighting in its first battle, was under the command of Jarama veteran Malcolm Dunbar. Like Merriman, Dunbar was not a member of the Communist Party. He was, as historian Richard Baxell has noted, "a middle-class, Cambridge-educated, homosexual aesthete, ... [who] could hardly have been a less typical volunteer."[118]

In the early morning, the XVth Brigade advanced south along the Valdemorillo-Brunete Road. They would follow behind a Spanish brigade tasked with seizing the town of Villanueva de la Canada, the primary Nationalist strong point along the axis of advance. With Villanueva de la Canada taken, they would continue the advance toward Mosquito Ridge. Copic arranged his brigade with the First Regiment forward left, to the east of the road, and the Second Regiment (which included Cecil-Smith in the Washingtons) forward right, to the west.[119] The British Anti-Tank Battery advanced down the road.[120]

Events did not unfold according to plan. The Spanish brigade ahead of the XVth Brigade failed to seize Villanueva de la Canada. Some accounts say it was because they mistook fleeing civilians as retreating Nationalist forces and bypassed the town to maintain momentum.[121] Other accounts say that their attack was repulsed, and the brigade simply continued with their advance.[122] In either event, it fell to the XVth Brigade to dislodge the Nationalists from the village. Copic ordered the British and Lincoln Battalions to seize the town, but the Nationalist forces were well prepared.[123] They had constructed pillboxes and fortified fighting positions in the existing buildings, including a hardened machine gun nest in a church steeple. Due to poor coordination, the assaulting infantry battalions did not receive any artillery support, or even supporting fire from the XVth Brigade's own Anti-Tank Battery, possibly deemed too valuable to lose.[124] A smattering of Republican tanks provided some fire support, but they did not accompany the assaulting infantry, and the first attack was repelled.[125]

Copic next tried to encircle the town. The First Regiment pushed to the east. Its Dimitrov Battalion moved first and took a position to the east of the town to block the road to Romanillos.[126] The 6th of February Battalion and the 24th Battalion took positions to the northeast and cut the road to Villanuevo del Pardillo.[127] *Mayor* Fort, the regimental commander, lost an eye early in the battle and the commander of the Dimitrov Battalion, Hungarian volunteer Chapiev (born Miklos Szalway), took command of the First Regiment.[128]

The Second Regiment moved to the west of the town. The Lincoln Battalion, under the command of Oliver Law, an African-American CPUSA member who was likely the first African American to command an integrated unit of both black and white soldiers in combat,[129] maintained its position in the north while the British Battalion moved around the western edge of the town to block the road to Brunete in the south. The Washingtons, who had been following behind the Lincoln Battalion on the road, attacked into the town from roughly the northwest, between the Lincolns and the British Battalion.[130] They assaulted down the hill toward the town, moving through a cornfield that provided cover neither from fire nor observation.[131] Not surprisingly, then, the Washingtons took casualties immediately.

Cecil-Smith's No. 2 Company was one of the assaulting companies from the Washington Battalion. Anderson, his second in command, remembered that Cecil-Smith was cool under fire and quickly earned the respect of his soldiers. He recalled, "All the men were lying flat on their faces, there was Ed, kneeling up – kneeling, mind you – making observations. I'm telling you, when a man can do that, it shows he's all right."[132] Even as soldiers around him fell to their wounds, Cecil-Smith had exposed himself to fire in order to maintain his situational awareness and direct his company more effectively.

Cecil-Smith, armed with a Mauser pistol, picked up the rifle of a fallen comrade. He recalled, "I don't know what I intended to do with the rifle because an officer has no time to fire a weapon while directing an attack." But picking up the rifle saved his life. Five minutes later, he was shot by an exploding bullet. The Nationalist bullet hit his rifle, destroying it and sending shards of metal into his left hand, wrist, and knee.[133] Cecil-Smith would have been shot in the stomach had he not been carrying the rifle. He recalled that moment as being "his closest shave."[134]

Cecil-Smith stayed in the fight despite the injury. He hobbled along, manoeuvring his soldiers, using what cover he could find, to get them closer and closer to the town. The assault made it as far as a ditch on the edge of town, where elements of the battalion were pinned down for the rest of the day.[135] Cecil-Smith and his company were in a precarious position, running low on ammunition and out of water while they baked in the hot Spanish sun, and unable to evacuate their wounded.[136]

Copic pressed the XVth Brigade to further encircle the town. The First Regiment blocked the eastward approaches. The Second Regiment's Lincoln and British Battalions blocked the routes exiting the town to the south and west.[137] The Washingtons remained in their ditch in the northwest, blocking nothing in particular. When the Lincolns were ordered to assault the town from the south later that day, and were again repulsed, the Washingtons had to take over the Lincoln positions along the Quijorna Road. The movement exposed part of the Washingtons to fire as they moved in an open field.[138]

That night, Nationalist forces tried to leave the town hiding among fleeing civilians.[139] The British Battalion skirmished with these Nationalists, following up their engagement with an assault on the town along the Brunete Road. Seemingly without any coordination, the Dimitrovs launched an attack from the other side of the town, and two battalions of Spanish Republican soldiers passed directly through the Washingtons' position.[140] An attack of this fashion, without detailed control measures, would be highly likely to lead to casualties from friendly fire, yet none are mentioned in the accounts of the volunteers. The town was taken by midnight, but Cecil-Smith was not evacuated until the next morning.[141] He had shrapnel in his wrist for months afterwards.

After Cecil-Smith's evacuation, the XVth Brigade fought for two more weeks in the Brunete Offensive. By the end of it, they had been eroded down to only 600 soldiers fit for duty, fewer than a fifth of the brigade's original strength.[142] Copic himself had been wounded by shrapnel. The British Battalion began with 380 volunteers and ended with 50.[143] The *Norteamericanos* in the Lincoln and Washington Battalions had done little better. For instance, all of the company commanders in the Washington Battalion had been wounded. Hans Amlie was wounded in the hip; he was temporarily paralysed from the waist down but would recover.[144] Edo Jardas lost a leg. Walter Garland was wounded and returned to the United States for propaganda duties. As for Cecil-Smith's No. 2 Company, Wickman, his commissar, had been killed in an air raid, and Anderson, his second in command, was wounded and evacuated a few days after Cecil-Smith. Anderson and Cecil-Smith reunited at the aid station, where Cecil-Smith would tease "Andy" good-naturedly about getting evacuated for a relatively minor wound – a cut to the face from shrapnel, "only the size of a dime."[145] The Lincolns had suffered similarly, so the two battalions had to be merged together in order to function. With Oliver Law, the Lincoln commander, killed, Markowicz briefly commanded the merged battalion, but it was to be his last battle. He refused an order to lead an attack that he viewed as suicidal; he was relieved of his command and sent back to the United States.[146] The Washington Battalion would never be reconstituted.

The Brunete Offensive was a failure. The casualties were terrible, and the operation did not achieve its objectives. The Republicans did advance as far as Mosquito Ridge in the Heights of Romanillos, but it could not be held. The Nationalists pushed them back. Although the lines stabilized and the Republicans held some of the ground they had taken, the gains were meagre, given the price they had paid. The Republicans had not forced a grand salient to threaten Franco's internal lines of communications. The failure of the operation was a tremendous blow to the morale of the volunteers in the International Brigades; victory over fascism no longer seemed quite so certain.[147]

While the volunteers fought on the battlefields of Spain, the CPC pursued a propaganda campaign in Canada to raise support for them and the Spanish Republic. The assertion that the Mackenzie-Papineau Battalion had been formed in Spain was part of this campaign, as was Norman Bethune's blood transfusion service and his return to Canada on a speaking tour shortly thereafter. Although the Committee to Aid Spanish Democracy, a joint CCF/CPC effort, oversaw Bethune's mission, the

CPC seemed to reap the benefits when Bethune returned to Canada. In Toronto, Bethune appeared with Stewart Smith, by then a Toronto alderman for Ward 5, and was feted in a parade on 14 June attended by 2,000 people.[148] It was a misleading "victory parade" for Spain, given that the Republicans' only success up to that point was in surviving the Nationalist onslaught.

Bethune was an outstanding spokesman for the Republican cause. He was a charismatic speaker, and he arrived in Canada with a striking documentary, *Heart of Spain,* to demonstrate his organization's activities in Spain. The humanitarian nature of his work left him virtually unassailable by critics of the military-recruiting effort, and it helped that Bethune was not yet publicly known to be a member of the CPC. Consistent with Buck's characterization of the conflict in Spain as the beginning of a second world war, Bethune framed the war as a symptom of a much broader conflict. He told the *Toronto Star*, "What hardly anybody seems to realize ... is that the world war has started already. It started even before the trouble broke out in Spain. It began in 1931 in Manchuria. The Fascists won that time. Then it got going again in Abyssinia, and the Fascists won again. Now it's coming out more clearly in to the open. It ought to be plain to democratic countries what we're up against now, for the conflict is a straight fight between fascism and democracy."[149] While in Toronto, Bethune had a conversation along the same lines with Cecil-Smith's wife, Lilian Gouge.[150]

Bethune's return to Canada is relatively well documented. He was a public figure, a celebrity, and his public actions were recorded in either the press or the surveillance records of the RCMP. He came to Toronto, where he spent much of his time among leftist artists, including Paraskeva Clark, with whom he had a well-documented affair, and attended shows put on by Jean Watts (who did not return from Spain until February 1938) and Toby Gordon's Theatre of Action.[151] Gouge and "Beth" (as Bethune was known to his friends) formed a close friendship during these visits. She recalled that Bethune had told her about his experiences in Spain and his close calls with death. Bethune expressed an interest in pursuing adventures somewhere other than Spain. Gouge had an idea: she told Bethune that he should go to China.[152]

Gouge believed that Bethune could make a true difference in the worldwide revolution by helping in China. The Chinese Communist Party was fighting a war against fascism manifested in both the Japanese invaders and the Nationalist government. She believed that, unlike the Spanish Communists within the Republic, the Chinese Communists would likely win their struggle. She agreed with the conclusions of American journalist Edgar Snow, who wrote in *Red Star over China* that,

> The movement for social revolution in China might suffer defeats, might temporarily retreat, might for a time seem to languish, might make wide changes in tactics to fit immediate necessities and aims, might even for a period be submerged, be forced underground, but it would not only continue to mature; in one mutation or another it would eventually win, simply because (as this book proves, if it proves anything) the basic conditions which had given it birth carried within themselves the dynamic necessity for its triumph.[153]

Gouge told Bethune that the Chinese Communists could use his assistance, and he might be able to play an important role in establishing a home for communism outside the Soviet Union. The conflict he had left behind in Spain was just one battlefield in a worldwide war between communism and fascism. Bethune could apply his trade for the same ideals in China.[154]

The idea of going to China was not unique to Gouge. Bethune likely heard the suggestion from others, as well, as it was clearly on the minds of other volunteers in Spain. Canadian volunteer Lionel Edwards said that he planned on going to China after he returned from Spain because he could carry on the same fight and he "was a tough man to kill."[155] Another Canadian volunteer, upon returning to Canada, told the *Toronto Star* that he prayed to recover from a gunshot to his spine so that he might go to fight in China.[156] After the volunteers to Spain were demobilized in 1939, the RCMP recorded that the CPC had begun recruiting volunteers to go fight in China, although it does not appear that anything ever came of it.[157] So while Gouge's suggestion was likely a contributing factor in Bethune's decision to go, she cannot be credited as the sole source of the idea.

Bethune liked the proposal and soon after made his decision to follow through. While many may have thought about it, the only Canadians who actually went to serve in China were Bethune and nurse Jean Ewen, the daughter of Tom Ewen.[158] Accompanied by an American surgeon, Bethune and Ewen departed in January 1939 and eventually worked with Mao Zedong's Eighth Route Army.[159] It is clear that Bethune sent several letter to Gouge during his time in China, although only one such letter survives.

Chapter Nine

The Fighting Canucks

Edward Cecil-Smith spent the summer of 1937 convalescing and training members of the International Brigades in and around Albacete.[1] He wanted to return to the front, specifically to serve in the newly created, nominally Canadian Mackenzie-Papineau Battalion for which he had advocated. He was with the Washington Battalion when the Mackenzie-Papineau Battalion was formed, and still recovering from his wounds when it fought in its first battle in October. He then joined the junior battalion as a reinforcement, briefly serving as a company commander before he was moved into battalion headquarters. He proved his worth and would soon be the first Canadian commanding officer of "the fighting Canucks."[2]

Following the Brunete Offensive, Cecil-Smith was evacuated to Hospital 15 in Madrid.[3] Bob Kerr came from Albacete to visit him and the other Canadians and Americans, bringing with him packages of coveted cigarettes from home. Ted Allan (born Alan Herman), a CPC reporter from Montreal and commissar to Bethune's Canadian Blood Transfusion Service, had remained in Spain after Bethune's return to Canada. As the medical mission's office was just a few blocks from Hospital 15, he joined Kerr in distributing gifts from the Friends of the Mackenzie-Papineau Battalion. Cecil-Smith, Walter Garland, and the other *Norteamericanos* in the hospital were pleased to receive the visitors and the gifts.[4]

Cecil-Smith was released from the hospital in August 1937. His knee wound healed quickly, but his wrist, presumably requiring surgery, was not fully healed until October.[5] Similar to Robert Merriman's situation following Jarama, Cecil-Smith was wounded badly enough that he could not return to the front line but not so badly that he could not work and be productive. He returned to Albacete to work in the training system until he had fully healed. He again trained officers at

Pozorubio and assisted with the training of the Mackenzie-Papineau Battalion at Tarazona de la Mancha.[6] Merriman, the first commander of the Mac-Paps, would likely have been pleased to involve Cecil-Smith, given their previous working relationship at Pozorubio and his recent experience in establishing and fighting with the Washington Battalion.

The Mackenzie-Papineau Battalion, taking its name on Dominion Day 1937, had the benefit of a lengthier training period than any other battalion in the XVth Brigade.[7] It did not, however, have the advantage of having one commander throughout its training. Merriman was promoted to XVth Brigade chief of staff in August, presumably a tense arrangement given his history with brigade commander Vladimir Copic. Merriman's successor, Rollin Dart, a former pilot in the US Army Air Corps, departed soon afterwards to join the brigade headquarters as a staff officer.[8] Dart's adjutant, a twenty-three-year-old American, Robert Thompson, who was a Jarama veteran and leader in the Young Communist League, took over the Mac-Paps.[9]

While the Mac-Paps trained, the rest of the 35th Division (consisting of the XVth and XIth Brigades) fought in the Aragon. The division commander, General Walter (born Karol Swierczewski), was a veteran of the Russian Civil War, graduate of the Frunze Military Academy in Moscow, and serving member of the Red Army general staff.[10] He had been tasked with retaking the city of Zaragoza, the regional capital that had been held by the Nationalists since the early days of the rebellion. Copic and the XVth Brigade had been assigned operations to chip away at Nationalist control of the region, fighting in Quinto in August and Belchite in September.

The Mac-Paps joined the XVth Brigade following the attack on Belchite, replacing the 6th of February and Dimitrov Battalions. The XVth Brigade was now a predominantly English-language brigade consisting of the Lincoln, British, Mackenzie-Papineau, and 24th Battalions. After the fighting in Belchite, the XVth Brigade went to the quiet Huesca front, where nothing of note happened, after which they resumed the push toward Zaragoza.[11] The XVth Brigade was given the assignment of attacking and seizing Fuentes de Ebro, one of the last obstacles on the path to Zaragoza.[12]

The plan for the attack on Fuentes de Ebro saw the XVth Brigade taking the town from the Nationalists in a single action on 12 October. At noon, Republican aircraft would bomb the Nationalist positions. The International Tank Regiment would then lead the assault. Soldiers from the brigade's 24th Battalion and the Spanish 120th Brigade would ride into battle atop forty-eight newly arrived Soviet BT-5 and T-26 tanks (some crewed by Red Army soldiers, and one commanded by a Canadian Lenin School graduate, William Kardash).[13] The three English-speaking battalions would follow close behind. The Mac-Paps were on the left, the Lincolns in the middle, and the British Battalion on the far right of the assault. The Canadian battalion was fresh and at full strength. The Lincolns were nearly at full strength. The British Battalion, on the other hand, was able to field only 150 volunteers that day.[14]

The plan was workable, but the execution was poor. Instead of layered effects from air attack, artillery, tank-mounted infantry, and dismounted infantry close behind them, there were too many lulls in the fight, giving the Nationalists time to recover. The Mac-Paps, Lincolns, and British Battalion advanced through no-man's-land against an unsuppressed enemy with predictable results, reminiscent of the Lincoln's assault on 27 February. Lawrence Cane, a survivor of the battle, described it succinctly: "We got the shit kicked out of us."[15]

The Mac-Paps sustained significant casualties in their first fight. These included sixteen dead, sixty-three wounded, and four missing, mostly during the first hour.[16] Casualties were especially bad among the leadership. On the left flank, Bill Neure, a German-American mechanic from New York, US Communist Party (CPUSA) member, and commander of No. 1 Company, was wounded in the assault and died the next day.[17] Joe Dallet, the battalion commissar, was killed while encouraging the troops on the left flank. "Call-a-Meeting" Joe Dougher, a CPUSA section organizer and Great War veteran of the US Navy with four years of service in the US Army, was wounded while commanding No. 3 Company.[18] Isadore (Izzie) Schrenzel, a blacksmith, longshoreman, CPUSA member, and commander of No. 2 Company, survived the assault but was killed by a Nationalist sniper the next day.[19] Machine Gun Company Commander Niilo Makela, a Finnish-Canadian miner, lumber worker, journalist, and member of the Communist Party of Canada since 1932, was the only company commander left standing. [20]

The Mac-Paps needed reinforcements in order to hold what little ground they had gained. Cecil-Smith was among the fifty-one reinforcements sent to the XVth Brigade from the Battalion of Instruction.[21] This was hardly enough to make up for the losses of even the Mackenzie-Papineau Battalion, but it was a start. The reinforcements moved into the line on 20 October and found the position to be extremely disorganized.[22] Bill Boyak, a Ukrainian-Canadian member of both the CPC and the Young Communist League, recalled that the soldiers on the line did not know the password, the location of enemy troops, or the locations of their own patrols. In the confusion, a Mac-Pap guard nearly opened fire on one of its own outposts.[23] Cecil-Smith took over Neure's No. 1 Company on the left flank and set about reorganizing the position.[24]

He spent only a brief period of time with the company on the line because Thompson, the battalion commander, had taken ill with fever.[25] Given that Cecil-Smith and Thompson had both been instructors together at Pozorubio, Thompson likely knew that Cecil-Smith was a capable leader.[26] Thompson and his adjutant, Harry Schoenberg, brought Cecil-Smith into battalion headquarters.[27] He was initially supposed to act as an additional adjutant for the battalion commander, but he was effectively in command of the battalion for the final few days on the line and commanded the battalion's withdrawal.[28]

After having fought so hard for so little ground, the XVth Brigade was relieved by the Spanish 143rd Brigade. The 143rd brought only 210 soldiers to defend the eight-kilometre frontage, an obviously inadequate force, but they would not be overrun. Five members of the Nationalist forces met with five members of the 143rd Brigade in no-man's-land, after which the Spanish soldiers moved freely about their trenches. It seemed that some kind of truce had been reached – the Spanish soldiers on this part of the line had little desire to fight one another.[29] Cecil-Smith led the Mac-Paps off the line, just three days after he and the other reinforcements had arrived. Most of the Mac-Paps surely must have been asking they had fought for. Fuentes de Ebro stayed in Nationalist hands, as did Zaragoza.

The XVth Brigade had a brief stay in Quinto before proceeding back to the billets around Albacete. The Mac-Paps returned to their billets in Tarazona in which they had lived during their training and where the Washington Battalion had lived before them. Thompson was still in command, but Cecil-Smith, as the assistant to a sick man, took on many of his duties.[30] Cecil-Smith formally took command of the Mac-Paps sometime in late November, the first and only Canadian to command a battalion in Spain.[31]

As discussed above, Cecil-Smith had not wanted to be an officer in the first place and was certainly not eager to be a battalion commander. The responsibilities of battalion command, he found, were much more pressing than commanding a company. He was not a particularly charismatic man, and he was not as "working class" as most of the Canadian volunteers. It was difficult for him and his men to relate to one another, a matter exacerbated by the larger numbers of troops in a battalion. In a company, Cecil-Smith could have gotten to know his soldiers a bit better by sheer proximity. It was lonely at the top, and the only person Cecil-Smith ever described as his friend in the entire unit was Makela.[32] Cecil-Smith also likely felt completely unprepared to lead a battalion.

Indeed, Cecil-Smith confided to Maurice Constant, a former militia officer in Canada, that he knew he was better suited to lead a company than a battalion.[33] This is hardly surprising. His training at Pozorubio focused on company-level operations. Ideally, he would get some experience in commanding a company while receiving some mentorship by a skilled battalion commander, after which he would take command of a battalion. But he had been wounded on the first day of the Brunete Offensive, and had served as a company commander only for a day or two at Fuentes de Ebro before he was brought into the battalion headquarters. Neither Markowicz nor Thompson were experienced as battalion commanders, and they were unlikely to provide much in the way of mentorship. Cecil-Smith took command of the Mac-Paps with much to learn about commanding a company, let alone a battalion.

He first had to learn the basics about how a battalion functioned. The Mackenzie-Papineau Battalion consisted of a battalion headquarters, three rifle companies, and one machine gun company. Cecil-Smith was familiar with the functioning of a rifle company, but battalion operations, the running of a battalion headquarters staff, and the employment of battalion support weapons would have been new to him. The battalion had a reasonably large staff that included runners (to pass messages to other units), observers (who liaised with flanking units), a signals *teniente* with a *sargento* and eleven soldiers with radios and heliographs, armourers to maintain and repair the weapons, cartographers, a doctor with some medics, and a kitchen staff.[34] For support weapons, the battalion had a machine gun company, which used four or five Maxim guns, plus an assortment of special weapon systems including light mortars and sniper rifles.

Cecil-Smith's learning was aided by the presence of a Red Army adviser.[35] Like many of the other battalion commanders in the International Brigades, Cecil-Smith had a junior officer from the Red Army assigned to him. The advisers worked closely with the battalion commanders – they normally shared their living space in the field – and assisted with training and operations. Cecil-Smith spoke highly of these advisers. He wrote that they were easy to work with, since they all spoke Spanish or English. They were professional, intelligent, and "extremely brave men, though not so foolhardy as some of our Canadian officers were inclined to be."[36] The advisers worked closely with the operators of support weapons – such as the machine gunners, mortar crews, and snipers – and provided mentorship to the battalion and company commanders.[37]

Cecil-Smith provided an example meant to illustrate the inquisitive nature of the advisers, drawing on his experience with "Steve," but that equally demonstrates their role as mentors:

> Take Steve as an example. He used to prowl around the lines day and night helping the boys with emergency repairs which had to be made

> under fire. He always carried a black loose-leaf notebook, which he filled with sketches and notations. Nearly every night he would drag it out and talk about what he had seen.
>
> "Why have you got number five machine gun on the north side of hill 685," he might ask. This called for a reference to a large scale map and the latest reports from the machine gun company and the infantry company in that sector. You would have to show Steve the field of fire from this gun, how it crossed that of other guns from your own and neighboring units, and its tasks both in defence and attack.
>
> He would listen carefully, making notes. Perhaps he would be convinced and put his book away with a nod. Or he might say: "But the sergeant didn't know all that." Or, "Wouldn't it be better to move it 20 metres further up the hill?" Then nothing would satisfy him but that you, he and the machine gun commander must go and look over his proposed position. Sometimes he was right, sometimes wrong. In either case he kept on his toes and kept you on yours.[38]

Unfortunately, Cecil-Smith would have had the assistance of an adviser only very briefly; most had been withdrawn by the summer of 1937 and, with few exceptions, all were gone by the end of the year.[39] This meant that Cecil-Smith would have been exposed to them on operations only during the Brunete Offensive and at Fuentes de Ebro. His anecdote about "Steve" likely comes from holding the line at Fuentes de Ebro. Not long afterwards, Steve and most of the other advisers departed Spain and left Cecil-Smith and his peers to their own devices.[40]

With or without an adviser, even an experienced military officer would have struggled to comprehend the human complexities of an organization like the Mackenzie-Papineau Battalion. Bill Beeching, a volunteer himself and author of *Canadian Volunteers in Spain,* provided the following description: "[The battalion] soon assumed something of the character of the Canadian mosaic: there was a section [platoon] composed almost entirely of Ukrainian-Canadians in Company Two; Finnish-Canadians from Fort William and Port Arthur were the majority in the Machine Gun Company; and Company Three had a section [platoon] made up predominantly of loggers from British Columbia."[41] An anonymous editorialist in the *Volunteer for Liberty,* the brigade's newsletter, observed that Ukrainian and Finnish Canadians were an integral part of the battalion. The "Ukes" had "swell songs and choruses" and could fight even better than they could sing. He praised the Finns as "'the eighth wonder of the world. Although you can't say for what EXactly, they have so many remarkable things to their credit. Size for one thing, discipline for another, and above all their love of Maxims. Dearer than a wife, dearer even than an American cigarette, is the Maxim [gun] to the Finn."[42] But descriptions like this, often repeated for their colour, ignored other ways in which the battalion was marked by diversity.

Despite Bob Kerr's efforts to direct Canadian volunteers in Albacete to the Mac-Paps to make it increasingly Canadian, the battalion comprised much more than Canadians from a variety of immigrant backgrounds. It had begun as a mix of American and Canadian volunteers, and it would remain that way throughout the war. Moreover, like all units within the International Brigades, it contained an ever-growing proportion of Spaniards. The International Brigades had taken a large number of Spaniards into their ranks following the casualties of the summer and fall offensives. The numbers for the Mac-Paps are unknown, but by December 1937, 57 per cent of the members of the International Brigades were Spanish.[43]

The leadership of the Mackenzie-Papineau Battalion was, as it would be throughout the war, a mix of Canadians, Americans, and Spaniards. Excepting when he was sidelined with injuries, Cecil-Smith commanded the battalion from November 1937 until it returned to Canada in early 1939. Harry Schoenberg was Cecil-Smith's adjutant until the end of the war. Although he was a member of the CPUSA, he had joined that party just a month before leaving for Spain, suggesting that he was hardly a party stalwart, but rather someone who saw membership as a means of getting to Spain. More valuable to Cecil-Smith than Schoenberg's politics was the fact that he was an able staff officer with six years of experience in the 71st Regiment of the New York National Guard.[44] Ivan John Nahanchuk, a Ukrainian American from New York and also a veteran of Fuentes de Ebro, commanded No. 1 Company. He was not a member of the CPUSA but did join the Communist Party of Spain.[45] Ricardo Diaz, a Spanish veteran of the militias from the earliest days of the civil war and with the Mac-Paps since Fuentes de Ebro, commanded No. 2 Company, the Spanish company. Another Spaniard, Ramon Gonzalez, commanded No. 3 Company.[46] Saul Wellman, a member of the CPUSA in Detroit, had been the battalion commissar since Joseph Dallet was killed at Fuentes de Ebro.[47] Niilo Makela, the commander of the Machine Gun Company at Fuentes de Ebro, retained his position. Makela and Cecil-Smith were the only Canadians in senior leadership positions in the battalion.

By the beginning of December, the Mackenzie-Papineau Battalion had taken on reinforcements and grown to 506 soldiers, the largest unit in the brigade.[48] Cecil-Smith set about training his men, something he was well suited for, given his work in the Albacete training camps and in the Canadian militia. He focused on core skill sets (moving, fighting, and communicating) and ensured that the training was challenging and progressive. New soldiers had to learn the individual skills of a soldier, then they had to learn to fight as part of progressively larger groups. Cecil-Smith tried to impose the training and discipline required in a professional army. Tim Buck recalled that Cecil-Smith "emphasized the importance of discipline and training ... They [the Mac-Paps] actually went through much of the routine of basic drill that is used in the regular armies."[49] Cecil-Smith worked to overcome the individualistic nature of the volunteers and to develop teams within the battalion. Soldiers had to stick with their sections, platoons, and companies, and not just move about the battlefield as an uncoordinated mass of individuals.[50] This sounds simple enough, but it proved to be a challenge in an organization full of "rank and filers" – that is, volunteers who rejected the idea of permanent authority.

Despite Cecil-Smith's best efforts, the daily reports for the Mac-Paps show that imposing discipline was a constant struggle. Every day, a few soldiers were arrested for drunkenness, insubordination, or disobeying orders. On 9 November, Cecil-Smith had to personally arrest a soldier for failing to obey orders.[51] General Walter, a professional soldier and commander of the 35th Division, recalled that he was particularly disappointed in the Mac-Paps and British Battalion following an inspection in December. He noted, "It is difficult to convey in words the state of weapons and how dirty, especially the rifles. The bores of their barrels were not much different from a seventeenth century musket barrel found at Belchite."[52] This was not simply a criticism of the equipment. Walter was criticizing the poor discipline among the volunteers, who should have held the cleanliness of their weapons as a high priority. "Rank and fileism" resulted in poor discipline in all things.[53]

After a month in command of the battalion, Cecil-Smith received orders from Copic to move the Mac-Paps back to Albacete and on to an unknown destination. In late December, the Mac-Paps boarded trucks for Albacete and then trains, moving through Caspe and Alcaniz, two towns they would return to later that winter. Finally they reached their interim destination: the village of Mas de las Matas.[54] As with the Brunete Offensive, their tasks and objectives were closely guarded secrets until immediately before the operation.

During this time, Cecil-Smith continued to train the battalion. He had completed enough platoon- and company-level training that they could finally conduct some training at the battalion level. On 24 December, Cecil-Smith took the three rifle companies out on their first mock battalion operation, which lasted for four hours, while the Machine Gun Company received training on constructing machine gun positions from the XVth Brigade's fortification unit.[55] It was Cecil-Smith's first time manoeuvring a battalion. The companies continued on with their own training in the afternoon, made all the more difficult by the cold mountain air. The temperature in the mountains at that time of year was normally around –20 degrees Celsius, cold enough that the water coolant in the Maxim guns would freeze if not diluted with a little cognac.[56] Many of the Canadians had endured worse conditions in Canada, but they had had better clothing there. The Spanish Republican uniforms and thin blanket that each solider received were hardly sufficient for the conditions.

On Christmas Day, the Mac-Paps learned from the locals that the Republican Army had seized Teruel, less than a hundred kilometres away. The attack was launched to spoil Franco's planned attack on Madrid, and it achieved that aim.[57] It was also a great propaganda coup. Like Zaragoza, Teruel had been a Nationalist stronghold since the beginning of the war, so its capture by the Republicans was highly symbolic. Moreover, the prevailing forces had been exclusively Spanish soldiers.[58] The *Daily Clarion* described Teruel as "the City of Victory," and the battle as "a military epic" or "Franco's Waterloo."[59] The fact that the city had been seized by the Republican Army on its own, unaided by the International Brigades, was particularly encouraging. The *Daily Clarion* claimed that the victory was evidence that the Republicans had built the unified army they needed, and that this "People's Army" had such high morale that they were unstoppable.[60] Teruel's capture seemed to herald a change in the course of the war.

The Mac-Paps celebrated both the victory and Christmas. The battalion banner appeared for the first time: a red flag bearing the clenched fist of the Republican salute, superimposed over a red star and a green maple leaf. The text exclaimed "Fascism Shall Be Destroyed." The Mac-Paps held a soccer tournament, had a chicken dinner, and hosted a "fiesta" for the children in the village of Mas de las Matas.[61] Some volunteers even cobbled together a Santa Claus suit.[62] Clever soldiers scrounged alcohol (probably including the cognac meant for the Maxim guns) to add to the festivities. Care packages from the Friends of the Mackenzie-Papineau Battalion were distributed, including cigarettes, some chocolates, and boots. Cecil-Smith granted a "Christmas amnesty" to the five soldiers in detention, although three more were arrested almost immediately afterwards. A fourth soldier, the officer of the day assured Cecil-Smith, would be arrested as soon as they found him.[63] At one point, the festive atmosphere reached such a tenor that the battalion, either at Copic or Cecil-Smith's direction, was ordered on a forced march in the frigid night air, "the idea being that this was perhaps the best and only way to sober them up."[64]

The Communist Party of Canada, despite its eagerness to conduct propaganda activity, was surprisingly detached from the exploits of the Canadian volunteers in Spain. The party had sent Progressive Arts Club alumnus Jean Watts to Spain as a reporter for the *Daily Clarion* and had sent Bob Kerr to Albacete to act as its formal representative. In spite of these contact points, the party and the Friends of the Mackenzie-Papineau Battalion did not have much more information about events in Spain than did members of the general public. Thus, information about Cecil-Smith and the Mackenzie-Papineau Battalion was generally late, incomplete, and often incorrect or misleading.

Jean Watts wrote extensively for the *Daily Clarion*, but she rarely covered the activities of the International Brigades. She spent most of her time in Madrid or with Bethune's medical unit.[65] She did travel to Albacete in October, where she interviewed Cecil-Smith and filed a story about Brunete, three months after it had occurred.[66] Likely frustrated by the practical restrictions on her ability to move about the country to properly tell the stories in which she was interested, and eager to play a more direct role in the conflict, she joined the International Brigades herself later that month as a driver and a mechanic.[67] This left the party without a reporter. Watts returned to Canada early in 1938.[68]

As the party's full-time representative in Albacete, Bob Kerr would have had the duty to pass on information that would have been useful for drumming up support on the home front. Kerr, supported by a small staff, should have been intimately familiar with events involving the Mackenzie-Papineau Battalion and passed it back to Canada. So why was so little news making its way back to Canada? It is unclear if the problem was that Kerr was not getting the information, or if his limited access to the transatlantic cable (which he was expected to "share" with his more influential American counterparts) prevented him from passing on the news to the party.[69]

Yet another source of information was Ted Allan. He had wanted to go to Spain to work as the *Daily Clarion*'s reporter, but Leslie Morris had sent Jean Watts instead.[70] Choosing to go to Spain regardless, he volunteered for the International Brigades, although he ended up principally working with Bethune. He wrote several articles about his experiences in Spain for the *Daily Clarion* following his return to Canada in the summer of 1937; by that time, of course, the information was months out of date.[71] For example, in December 1937, the *Daily Clarion* printed Allan's article about his visit with Cecil-Smith at Madrid's Hospital 15 following his wounds at Brunete, five months after it happened.[72]

An example of this disconnect was the reporting on Cecil-Smith's involvement activities at Brunete. Allan and Watts mentioned his injuries in the *Daily Clarion* months after they happened, even though the mainstream press in Canada reported it much earlier. A 10 July 1937 article in the *Toronto Star* stated that Cecil-Smith had been wounded while serving as "an officer in the Canadian Mackenzie-Papineau Battalion."[73] Another article published the same day said that he had been wounded while he was in command of one of the Mac-Paps' three rifle companies, showing that the author was referencing an actual unit and not just a nickname for all Canadians in Spain.[74] The article did not mention the Washington Battalion. Similarly, an article earlier that month in the *Ottawa Citizen* claimed that Canadians Bill Halliwell, Edo Jardas, and Edward Cecil-Smith were all company commanders in the Mackenzie-Papineau Battalion.[75] In reality, *none* of the three were in the Mac-Paps at that time, but rather were serving in the Lincoln and Washington Battalions. Although the Mackenzie-Papineau Battalion did exist at this point, it had not yet taken to the field, and it had only one Canadian officer: Niilo Makela.[76] Given that Cecil-Smith was not quoted in these articles, and their publication coincided with CPC representative Bob Kerr's visit to Madrid to visit injured volunteers, including Cecil-Smith, it seems likely that Kerr fed this incorrect information to reporters in Madrid, painting a picture of an established Mackenzie-Papineau Battalion that had already gone into battle and was commanded principally by Canadian officers.

A second example was the fact that Cecil-Smith's appointment as the first commander of the Mackenzie-Papineau Battalion was announced not by the *Daily Clarion*, but by the *New York Times*. On 7 January 1938, the New York paper printed an interview with Hans Amlie, with whom Cecil-Smith had served in the Washington Battalion. Recently returned from Spain due to a head wound sustained at Belchite, Amlie told the *Times* about his experiences and mentioned that Cecil-Smith had recently been appointed as the commander of the Mackenzie-Papineau Battalion. The story was quickly picked up in Canada and led to articles in the *Daily Telegraph*, the *Globe and Mail*, and the *Toronto Star*.[77] A *Daily Clarion* headline from 8 January 1938 proclaimed that its "Former Editor Heads MacPaps."[78] The article did not mention that the *Clarion* had fired Cecil-Smith, and actually claimed that he had "quietly resigned" from the staff when he left for Spain in February 1937.

While in Spain, Cecil-Smith could conceivably have assisted the *Daily Clarion* in tandem with his military responsibilities, but he seemed to have no interest in doing so. He had initially been active in political matters in Spain, lobbying for what would become the Mackenzie-Papineau Battalion, and writing an article for the *Clarion* where he had called on Canadians to "strengthen [the] rearguard of

[the] fight for democracy."[79] But that was the only article he wrote for the party press while he was in Spain, and, after joining the Washington Battalion in June 1937, he seemed to lose all interest in the politics and propaganda. Nonetheless, the *Daily Clarion* tried to keep up appearances by reprinting Cecil-Smith's letters to friends and thank-you letters to supporters as if he were reporting from the front, but the tone of the letters show that none of them were meant for wide distribution.[80] In one letter to the Friends of the Mackenzie-Papineau Battalion, he admitted that, "in spite of my best intentions I have to admit that I'm a lousy correspondent."[81]

Cecil-Smith found his military duties to be all consuming and saw the propaganda and political intrusions as increasingly annoying. Lawrence Cane, a member of the CPUSA, recalled that Cecil-Smith was "not a politico," meaning that he saw himself principally as a military commander. He had earned his position by military merit, not through his political activity.[82] Cecil-Smith wanted to focus on winning the war against fascism. He saw much of the propaganda work and political education by the commissars to be an unnecessary distraction from training. He was not oblivious to the importance of propaganda – he had dedicated himself to educating the revolutionary vanguard in Canada – but to win in Spain he needed disciplined soldiers who were proficient in fire and manoeuvre. He was chastised by the commissars for this attitude, described as a lack of interest in "the political life of the battalion."[83] It did not help his relationship with the commissars that Cecil-Smith knew the writings of Marx and Lenin as well as they did and was always pleased to engage in a rousing debate.

Like the Communist Party of Canada, the RCMP was dependent on newspaper reports to gather information about what was going on in Spain. The force monitored the mainstream newspapers as well as the *Daily Clarion*. Detectives diligently clipped each mention of Cecil-Smith in the newspapers and added it to his growing file. They had tracked Cecil-Smith fairly closely since 1932, but they had not noticed that he had vanished in February 1937. They first realized he was in Spain through the Croatian-language newsletter, *Slobodna Misao*, in May 1937.[84] The RCMP found out he was a company commander in July 1937 through a Canadian Press article, and that he was the commander of the Mackenzie-Papineau Battalion following the newspaper coverage in January 1938.[85] With few informers and no undercover agents in the party, the RCMP remained completely dependent on public information about events in Spain.[86]

Chapter Ten

The Defence of Teruel

The Christmas celebrations of the Republic's capture of Teruel had been premature. The city, which had been reduced to rubble in the fighting, was still contested; Franco began counter-attacks against the city as early as 29 December, and the Republicans would not fully hold the city until 8 January.[1] Cecil-Smith received his orders from XVth Brigade commander Vladimir Copic on 31 December, two days after the first counter-attacks, to move to support the fight in Teruel. The XVth Brigade would leave their billets in the village of Mas de la Matas immediately and occupy a secondary defensive line around Argente, forty kilometres north of Teruel.[2] Their task was to prevent the Nationalists from isolating Teruel by severing the Teruel–Rudilla highway. The operation in Teruel itself would continue in the hands of Spanish soldiers, for now, with the International Brigades focused on keeping the Nationalist forces from cutting the city off.

From their positions high in the mountains, the Mac-Paps could see Nationalist trucks and artillery and the occasional skirmish between the Nationalists and the Republican forces to the west.[3] Cecil-Smith sent out night patrols to gather information, but the Mac-Paps saw little combat at Argente. Their time on this line was remembered primarily for the penetrating cold (the region was known to be the coldest in Spain), malnutrition, and vermin. The Canadian volunteers did not have the boots, coats, and gloves they needed to fight and live in the mountains. Lice were rampant, and the ranks of the Mac-Paps were ravaged by an illness known simply as Teruel Fever.[4] The only bright spot was the arrival of new weapons from Czechoslovakia. The Mac-Paps received a generous shipment of brand new Mauser pistols and Bren guns.[5]

By 14 January, it appeared that Teruel would fall to Nationalist counter-attacks without the intervention of the International Brigades. The Spanish defenders had been mauled badly in the attack and had defended against vigorous counter-attacks for more than two weeks. The 35th Division, consisting of the XVth and the XIth International Brigades, was brought forward to relieve the beleaguered Spanish Republican soldiers. They occupied a line running roughly north to south, facing the Nationalist forces immediately to the west of the city. The XVth Brigade was assigned to what Copic called the "post of honour" – the city itself and the approaches from the north and west.[6] The predominantly German XIth Brigade, better known as the Thaelmann Brigade after the imprisoned leader of the German Communist Party, moved north to a high feature known as *El Muleton* (the Giant Mule). In between the two brigades, a group of *Marineros* (Spanish naval infantry),[*] occupied three chalk hills blocking the approaches to the Alfambra River valley.

Copic arranged the XVth Brigade with the Mac-Paps' forward and to the right, closest to the *Marineros*, the Lincolns in the city of Teruel, and the British and Spanish in depth. The Mac-Paps' section of the line stretched from the three hills to *La Muela* (the molar), another high feature on the northern edge of Teruel.[7] Behind the Lincolns and Mac-Paps, on the heights of Santa Barbara in a cemetery, the British Battalion, the British Anti-Tank Battery, and the brigade's Machine Gun Company provided the XVth Brigade's depth.[8] The 24th Battalion were not given a position; they were likely retained to act as a reserve and to assist with the demanding task of resupplying the forward troops and assisting with the evacuation of the wounded.

Cecil-Smith and the Mac-Paps were assigned a large and difficult piece of terrain to defend. The 650 soldiers had to defend nearly two kilometres of line, a matter further complicated by the undulating terrain. Hills, rivers, and valleys all provided the enemy with plenty of cover to hide their movement from both observation and fire. Cecil-Smith saw little choice but to string his companies out in a long, thin line without any positions in depth. Cecil-Smith would retain a few machine guns in reserve that could be moved to the front along predetermined routes, thus creating a sort of depth and giving him some flexibility to deal with unforeseen circumstances. Lionel Edwards, a machine gun team commander, referred to this system as "mobile machine gun posts," an innovation that was considered to be quite progressive at the time and that he credited to Cecil-Smith.[9]

* The *Marineros* have generally been referred to as a brigade. However, it was far too small an element to be a full-up brigade. Most likely it was a battalion of *Marineros* or an extremely depleted brigade.

Niilo Makela commanded No. 1 Company on the battalion's left. His company had to climb a twenty-one-metre ridge to reach their positions on *La Muela,* the hill on which the Mac-Paps' anchored their left flank.[10] With a cliff to their rear, such a position posed considerable difficulties for resupply and casualty evacuation but had the benefit of allowing many Nationalist artillery rounds to fall harmlessly behind them. The predominantly Spanish No. 2 Company held the centre of the position, and Ricardo Diaz, commanding No. 3 Company, secured the right flank.[11]

The Mac-Paps arrived on the line with no knowledge of the enemy or the terrain. On the left flank, in front of Makela's No. 1 Company, the soldiers were appalled to discover Nationalist trenches just over fifty metres in front of them.[12] A particularly brazen Nationalist soldier tried to raise the Nationalist flag on an improvised flagpole only a hundred metres from the Mac-Pap trenches.[13] Cecil-Smith needed more particulars on the enemy's location and disposition. He immediately ordered aggressive patrolling to gather this information.

Cecil-Smith went out on several of these patrols himself. On one such patrol, he and Makela were discovered and engaged by machine gun fire; they fortunately escaped unscathed.[14] The next patrol was not as lucky. Marcus Aurelius Haldane, a famously tough First Nations logger from Kamloops, British Columbia, was seriously wounded by machine gun fire.[15] Cecil-Smith carried Haldane back to friendly lines under fire – the soldier survived.[16] Further patrolling allowed Makela to find the Nationalist machine guns, hidden on the second floor of some houses forward of his position. Makela led a night patrol that destroyed the positions with hand grenades thrown through the windows.[17]

These patrols gathered information and kept the enemy on their toes, but their actions proved to be of little use. The Nationalists were massing for an enormous offensive against the Republican line. Franco was intent on retaking Teruel. The Nationalist plan was to attack immediately to the north of Teruel, seizing *El Muleton,* and then pushing to the heights of Santa Barbara, to the northeast of the city, before finally taking Mount Mansueto to the east.[18] With the city cut-off from reinforcements, the remaining defenders would surrender and the Nationalists could avoid the messy business of fighting in Teruel itself. The Thaelmann Brigade on *El Muleton,* the *Marineros,* and No. 3 Company on the Mac-Paps' right flank stood in their way.

The main Nationalist offensive came on 17 January. Cecil-Smith and the Mac-Paps knew an attack was coming. Lionel Edwards, with a machine gun crew on the right flank, recalled hearing the rumble of vehicle engines in the distance. He watched as Nationalist reconnaissance planes marked the Mac-Pap positions with rings of smoke overhead.[19]

The Nationalists first struck the Thaelmann Brigade on *El Muleton* and then the *Marineros* and the Mac-Paps in No. 3 Company on the right flank. The British Anti-Tank Battery provided overhead fire and the volunteers held firm. The assaulting Nationalist infantry ground to a halt, but their cavalry made an attempt to burst into the Mac-Paps' rear. Two squadrons of Nationalist cavalry exploited a gap they found between the *Marineros'* hill positions and the western slope of *El Muleton.*[20] Supported by a creeping barrage, the charging cavalry breached the front line and emerged behind the Mac-Paps.[21] The cavalry were then out of observation from their artillery spotters and could no longer be supported by the Nationalist artillery. The cavalry was vulnerable, but Cecil-Smith's position did not have any depth. He had to employ his mobile machine gun posts along with every spare soldier to counter the charge. The mobile machine gun posts, his staff of clerks and cartographers, and himself in command quickly exited the command post to fight off the cavalry.

The charging Nationalists, although no doubt a fearsome sight, were abruptly halted by Cecil-Smith's improvised defence. The horsemen that survived tried to flee but were killed by No. 3 Company.[22] Cecil-Smith was praised for his quick reaction to the cavalry charge, as well as his "serenity" in the face of danger.[23] The cavalry charge marked the end of the Nationalist offensive on 17 January. That night, under the cover of darkness and the lights of a rare aurora borealis, the Mac-Paps had a chance to evacuate their casualties and redistribute ammunition.[24] Cecil-Smith integrated reinforcements from the XVth Brigade into the position, including machine guns from the Lincoln Battalion and the XVth Brigade's Machine Gun Company.

On 18 January, the Nationalists focused their efforts on the German volunteers on *El Muleton*. The Thaelmann Brigade was subjected to air attack and a fearsome barrage of artillery. Lawrence Cane, who would land with the first wave of American soldiers on D-Day, recalled later that the Teruel bombardment was the fiercest he had ever seen.[25] Fortunately, the Mac-Paps were largely unaffected by the barrage. Cecil-Smith even had time to write a few thank-you letters to well-wishers in Canada, explaining that the soldiers appreciated the donations of chocolates, cigarettes, and boots.[26] He expressed grudging admiration for the skill of the Nationalist gunners as they pounded the Thaelmanns to his right: "Believe me their artillery hit with accuracy and consistency which was almost beautiful in its timing – except when it was directed at our own trenches."[27]

After hours of bombardment, the Nationalists assaulted *El Muleton*. By nightfall, the Germans had retreated, and *El Muleton* was firmly in Nationalist hands. The Mac-Paps were left in a compromised position. The Nationalists had already identified the river valley as a potential weakness in the Mac-Paps' line, and now they held a high feature from which artillery spotters could direct fire and Nationalist commanders could gather valuable information about the Mac-Paps' position.[28]

On 19 January, the Nationalists continued their attack against the XVth Brigade's right flank: the *Marineros* and the Mac-Paps' No. 3 Company. The *Marineros* were hit the hardest. They fought valiantly and held firm all morning, but panic set in later that afternoon. They retreated, leaving the entrance to the Alfambra River valley exposed. Diaz, the Spanish officer commanding No. 3 Company, took an incredible risk. He left his position, presumably leaving Lionel Edwards in charge, and attempted to rally the fleeing *Marineros*.[29] Cecil-Smith applauded Diaz's bravery and leadership, describing him as "unsurpassed" for personal bravery and determination.[30] Meanwhile, Edwards took thirty soldiers and four machine guns from No. 3 Company to seize one of the *Marineros'* three hills in an effort to secure the Mac-Paps' right flank.[31] This hill became known as Edwards' Hill, or sometimes Suicide Hill, as these soldiers fought desperately to prevent the Nationalists from rolling up the XVth Brigade's flank.

The defence of Teruel would depend on the grit of the individual soldiers and the commanders' ability to reinforce and resupply the right flank. Cecil-Smith sent Harry Schoenberg, his adjutant, and Saul Wellman, his commissar, forward to assist No. 3 Company. Wellman later recalled,

> When we reached the 3rd company position and found the company commander, we didn't need a report. The end was not yet in sight and the nightmare would last for another two days. Lionel Edwards, [now] the company commander, and I talked but I can assure you I wasn't making political speeches. He needed help! Help to carry ammunition forward. Help to bring the wounded out. Help to deepen a machine gun pit. Help to clean or wipe a jammed machine gun. Help to find food or water. So, that's what Harry and I did. We carried out the wounded, dug pits, brought food and water, fixed jammed machine guns, and, as our numbers dwindled, we fixed them and fired them. As the fury of the artillery attack increased, our weapons became more unreliable.
>
> That afternoon I sent a message to battalion headquarters that said something like: "Send someone up here who knows more about things than I do!" Organizing picket lines or going to demonstrations hardly

> prepared me for this. I was exhausted and overwhelmed. Comrades were dying all around me. We were holding but for how long? Later I asked Nilo Makela ... about the message. He said "Yes, we got it, but you knew as much as any of us did."[32]

Cecil-Smith re-allocated a platoon from Makela's No. 1 Company on the left flank to shore up the right, and demanded reinforcements from Copic.[33]

Copic sent reinforcements to bolster the Mac-Paps' right flank. The British Battalion, positioned in a depth position atop the Heights of Santa Barbara, dispatched company after company. First they sent their No. 3 Company. No. 4 Company went next, but was heavily shelled en route.[34] No. 1 Company received even heavier fire on their way to front line; they were badly mauled before they even reached the valley floor.[35] No. 2 Company, the machine gunners, provided fire support from atop the heights. Meanwhile, Diaz successfully rallied some of the fleeing *Marineros*. The *Marineros* and British volunteers bolstered the right flank, but they were defending from unprepared ground. With the exception of an abandoned blockhouse, there were no buildings or trenches from which to fight. They defended from whatever depression they could carve out of the frozen earth.

While the Nationalists focused on the Mac-Paps' right flank, the centre and left of their position was relatively quiet. Makela's No. 1 Company on *El Muela* was down to two platoons, the third having been dispatched to assist the right flank. In the middle, No. 2 Company had taken some casualties from artillery fire, including the death of their commander and adjutant. The soldiers of No. 2 Company – mostly young, inexperienced Spanish conscripts – feared that they had been cut off. About forty of them decided that they stood a better chance of surviving if they defected. They abandoned their positions and ran across no-man's-land towards the Nationalists.[36] Makela's soldiers fired at them as they fled.[37] The No. 2 Company commissar left the front to personally report these events to Cecil-Smith. There was now a dangerous gap in the front lines. Cecil-Smith threw everything he had at it – the same paymasters, armourers, clerks, and cartographers from his headquarters who had stopped the cavalry charge days earlier.

On the right flank, the remaining soldiers from No. 3 Company struggled to hold their hill. Edwards recalled, "The fascists blasted hell out of us with heavy artillery and in between barrages sent their troops over to attack. But their men were too scared to get anywhere. We could see them sneaking up with their officers threatening them with revolvers. We let them get in to short range and murder[ed] them."[38] No. 3

Company needed more reinforcements. Edwards sent a runner back to Cecil-Smith's headquarters to make the request, but Cecil-Smith had no one left. If he withdrew anyone else from Makela's No. 1 Company, the Nationalists could seize *El Muela* and dominate the entire position with fire. No. 2 Company was reduced to a collection of armourers and paymasters. Cecil-Smith sent the last soldier he had available to No. 3 Company's aid, an unlucky clerk. The clerk never made it to Edwards' Hill. He either ran away or was killed en route.[39]

No. 3 Company held on to its position through 19 and 20 January. On the night of 20 January, Cecil-Smith ordered Edwards and what remained of No. 3 Company to withdraw.[40] They had fought valiantly. Cecil-Smith later glowed with pride at the courage of these soldiers: "[They] never gave way. They fought like demons. They repulsed attack after attack."[41] But their position was untenable. All of their machine guns were destroyed, and there was clearly no hope of reinforcements. Edwards and the remaining soldiers withdrew to a position to the rear of the hill, ready to fire on pursuing Nationalists.[42] Fortunately, just as the Mac-Paps' defence was about to break, the Nationalist offensive had also run out of steam.

The British Battalion and the Mac-Paps now had the time they needed to evacuate their wounded, bring in reinforcements, and resupply ammunition, water, and rations. General Juan Modesto, commander of the 5th Army Corps, visited them at the front and honoured the Mac-Paps with a unit citation.[43] Wellman received a personal citation; Diaz was promoted to *capitan*; Lionel Edwards was commissioned as a *teniente*. Cecil-Smith was promoted to *mayor*, the highest-ranking Canadian in the Spanish Republican Army.[44]

The badly bloodied XVth Brigade was relieved of its duties on the line on 3 February. They had retained Teruel, "the City of Victory," but the battle was not without its cost. The British Battalion was reduced to about two-thirds of its original strength, similar to the Mac-Paps' casualties.[45] Cecil-Smith reported that of the 650 Mac-Paps that went into battle on 31 December, only 200 remained alive and uninjured.[46]

The Mac-Paps had forty-eight hours rest in an assembly area away from the front. Cecil-Smith reorganized the battalion, incorporated reinforcements, and assigned new command appointments. He made Makela his adjutant. Jack Thomas, who formerly commanded the Machine Gun Company, was put in charge of No. 1 Company.[47] Alec Miller, a Canadian in the Lincolns who had recently recovered from a gunshot wound to the head at Quinto, joined the Mac-Paps as the commander of No. 2 Company.[48] Ricardo Diaz commanded No. 3 Company.[49] The troops had enough time to get some sleep, change their socks, clean and repair their weapons, and little else. Cecil-Smith learned that another Nationalist offensive was anticipated.

The XVth Brigade was tasked with a *golpe de mano* (a surprise attack – literally, "strike with the fist") to disrupt the Nationalist preparations.[50] The XVth Brigade quickly moved nearly a hundred kilometres through the mountains by rail, truck, and foot to the town of Segura de Los Baños, north of their earlier position in Argente. The Mac-Paps' brief stay was dramatic enough to be noteworthy.

They were the first to arrive in Segura de Los Baños after a gruelling march. Cecil-Smith reported to the XVth Brigade headquarters and requested the appropriate billets for his soldiers. He was told that billets were not yet available. The volunteers patiently waited outside in the snow while the brigade staff made arrangements – they had been through worse. The Lincolns and British Battalion arrived shortly afterwards and were immediately assigned their billets. Cecil-Smith again returned to the headquarters and insisted that his soldiers similarly get their billets for the night. None were provided.

After Cecil-Smith's ineffective requests for lodgings, one of the volunteers took it upon himself to make the inquiry. Butch Goldstein, a Russian-American member of the CPUSA and a notorious "rank and filer," was the next Mac-Pap into the XVth Brigade Headquarters.[51] Butch had little time for rank or protocol. He approached twenty-six-year-old Dave Doran, a member of the CPUSA since 1930 and brigade commissar since Steve Nelson was wounded at Belchite.[52] In doing so, Butch had jumped several levels of his chain of command. He demanded billets and rations for the troops, and an argument ensued. It culminated with Goldstein telling Doran to "go fuck himself," a remark that got him thrown into a cell.[53] In punishing Goldstein, Doran had given him exactly what he wanted: a place inside to sleep. The other Mac-Paps received their billets later that night.

~

The line between the Nationalists and the Republicans was poorly defined around Segura de Los Baños. Instead of a line of trenches, the Nationalists had a series of unconnected hill fortifications. Copic's plan for the *golpe de mano* was to seize a series of Nationalist positions and create their own defensible position, strong enough that the Nationalists would divert resources from their offensive in order to get rid of it. The battalions would deploy from Segura de Los Baños and attack their objectives independently. The Mac-Paps' mission was an especially important element of the plan. Their objective, Atalaya, lay between Segura de Los Baños and the other battalion objectives. Their attack would precede the others; the whole operation depended on the Mac-Paps' success.

The attack on Atalaya was Cecil-Smith's first offensive operation as a battalion commander, and the Mac-Paps' first action at night. There was no time for reconnaissance or rehearsals. Cecil-Smith had to rely on hand-drawn maps from locals to prepare his plan.[54] The Mac-Paps left their patrol base at Segura de Los Baños in the evening of 16 February. The night was illuminated by a nearly full moon, which made the march easier but also increased the risk of being spotted by the Nationalists. Assisted by a local guide, Cecil-Smith led the battalion through five kilometres of mountainous terrain. The boots the troops had received in their Christmas care packages from the Friends of the Mackenzie-Papineau Battalion, he wrote in a thank-you letter, "were a godsend. Mountains can play heck with shoes."[55]

Cecil-Smith halted the battalion far enough away from Atalaya that they could not be seen or heard by the defenders. He moved forward for his initial reconnaissance of the objective. He found a hill adjacent to Atalaya, clear of Nationalist soldiers, from which he could see most of the position. He could make out a double ring of barbed wire encircling Atalaya, and many of the trenches and dugouts. This vantage point would double as his firebase. Makela brought up the Maxim guns to support the assault.[56]

With the firebase established, the rifle companies lined up for the attack. Diaz led the advance guard.[57] Soldiers with wire cutters snuck forward to snip the barbed wire (Butch Goldstein was one of them). With the battalion in position, Cecil-Smith radioed Copic to advise that he was about to launch the attack. Frank Rogers, soon the battalion commissar, recorded, "the Canadians opened fire all together, which woke up the men who were asleep on the hill. It must have sounded to the enemy as if the end of the world had come, because according to their information, not a single Loyalist was supposed to be within a four mile distance."[58] The assaulting companies rushed from their position hidden among the rocks toward the barbed wire fences surrounding the Nationalist positions. Only twenty minutes after opening fire, Cecil-Smith sent his second transmission of the night to Copic: the hill was seized. By dawn the Mac-Pap flag was waving over the hill.[59]

The attack on Atalaya had been a great success. The Mac-Paps had seized the fort and captured thirty-four soldiers, two machine guns, and a trench mortar while taking minimal casualties themselves.[60] They had achieved surprise and took advantage of it in a textbook attack.

Makela called it "the most daring and the bravest act I ever saw any group of men do."[61]

The XVth Brigade's other attacks that morning did not go as well. The Lincolns attacked in daylight and the Nationalists, having heard the noise from the Mac-Pap attack, were ready. The Mac-Paps watched the Lincolns attack their objective at nearby Pedigrossa. They had to fight for every inch. Instead of twenty minutes, the attack lasted almost two hours and resulted in several casualties.[62] The British Battalion successfully seized their hill later that day. The *Marineros* had been assigned another hill fort nearby, but their attack did not materialize at all. The Mac-Paps assumed that the *Marineros* had gotten lost.[63]

The Mac-Paps prepared Atalaya against the anticipated Nationalist counterattack. They repaired the barbed wire and dug new trenches. In order to move quickly, they had not carried any defensive stores with them, so they had to improvise with what was on hand at Atalaya. Beyond some tools and barbed wire, the Mac-Paps were pleased to find other Nationalist supplies at the fort. Atalaya was well stocked with fresh food, and the troops "liberated" a feast of roast beef, potatoes, and some cognac.[64] This was a welcome change from the rice and fried chickpeas of which they were tiring. And a hot meal following a successful attack was always good for morale.

As they prepared their positions, the Mac-Paps received a visitor from home. Copic, inspecting the new positions and making his plan for subsequent attacks, came forward and brought Jack Taylor with him.[65] Taylor, an organizer in Vancouver during the On-to-Ottawa Trek and member of the CPC's Central Executive Committee, had arrived in Spain on 24 December to fill two jobs.[66] First, he was the civilian representative of the Friends of the Mackenzie-Papineau Battalion. Unlike Bob Kerr, Taylor was not in uniform and he did not officially represent the CPC in Spain. Second, he was there to act as a reporter for the *Daily Clarion*, a position that had been vacant since Jean Watts had joined the International Brigades in October. Taylor delivered shoes and warm clothes from the Friends of the Mackenzie-Papineau Battalion.[67] Cecil-Smith and his staff were able to properly host Taylor, feeding him some of the "liberated" food as well as some canned tongue that Saul Wellman had been saving for a special occasion.[68]

Taylor informed Cecil-Smith that his appointment as commander of the Mac-Paps had been "big news" back in Canada.[69] Cecil-Smith had not seen a copy of the *Daily Clarion* in months. He chuckled at the coverage, commenting, "such is the road to fame, I guess."[70] Soon, Cecil-Smith's likeness would be a common element of the *Daily Clarion*'s reporting on the war, as well as the promotional materials for the

Friends of the Mac-Paps. For instance, a rally at Massey Hall in Toronto to celebrate the one-year anniversary of the XVth Brigade featured ten-foot-tall posters bearing four images: Joe Dallet (the Mac-Paps' commissar killed at Fuentes de Ebro), Bob Kerr, Niilo Makela, and Cecil-Smith.[71] The posters were likely constructed by the same artists that Cecil-Smith had worked with in the Progressive Arts Club.

Taylor and Cecil-Smith's conversation was cut short by a report that Nationalist soldiers had been spotted probing the position.[72] Cecil-Smith went out to look and saw a Nationalist patrol nearby. One volunteer remarked, "There come the fascists." Cecil-Smith ordered one of his machine guns to open fire on the patrol. "There WENT the fascists," quipped another.[73] The probe was merely the first of many. The Nationalists had been surprised by the XVth Brigade's attacks, but they were already sending patrols into the area to gather information for their counter-attack. Taylor returned to the XVth Brigade Headquarters.

Copic completed his reconnaissance of the area and ordered Cecil-Smith to attack another hill fort that night. This attack did not go nearly as well as the first, as the Mac-Paps no longer had the element of surprise. The Nationalists knew that the Republicans were in the area, and a Nationalist patrol spotted the Mac-Paps en route to their objective.[74] Cecil-Smith was not able to find a strong position for his firebase, and the assault element was compromised as they were cutting the wire.[75] The clouds broke at an inopportune moment and the assault force was suddenly illuminated under the nearly full moon. The Nationalists fired on the assault force before they were able to breach the barbed wire. Cecil-Smith chose not to press the attack – there was no benefit in reinforcing failure. He still had to preserve enough of his force to be able to defend Atalaya. It was an inauspicious end to an otherwise impressive campaign.

Chapter Eleven

The Retreats

By late February 1938, Cecil-Smith and the Mac-Paps had made valuable contributions to the Republican war effort. They had been instrumental in retaining Teruel against fierce Nationalist counter-attacks, and they had quickly readjusted and launched an effective attack at Segura de Los Baños. It seemed, for the moment, that the Republicans held the initiative. Sadly, this was not the case. The Nationalists were only getting stronger, assisted by increasingly dramatic contributions of men and machines from Germany and Italy. The Nationalists seized Teruel after the Spanish Republican Army abandoned it on 21 February, and worse was yet to come. Franco launched his Aragon Offensive on 7 March, an operation so devastating to the Republic that the soldiers of the International Brigades simply remembered it as "the Retreats."

The XVth Brigade was pulled out of the line following its operations around Segura de Los Baños. Vladimir Copic seemed to expect a period of relative quiet, and much of the XVth Brigade's leadership took advantage of the opportunity for some rest. Copic himself went on thirty-day's furlough to Barcelona. Dave Doran, the XVth Brigade commissar with a penchant for dress uniforms and designs on command of the brigade, went to have his sinus condition treated in Valencia.[1] Robert Merriman, the chief of staff, and possibly the Russian adviser, Nikolaievitch, ran the brigade in their absence. The commander and commissar of the Lincolns similarly went on leave. Cecil-Smith granted leave to twenty of his soldiers, but neither he nor Saul Wellman, his commissar, went themselves.[2] It soon became apparent that this period of relative quiet was merely the calm before the storm.

Cecil-Smith and the other battalion commanders were ordered to report to Merriman at XVth Brigade Headquarters on 6 March. A "minor" Nationalist offensive was expected. Republican forces were already in position to meet the threat, and the 35th Division, the XVth Brigade's higher headquarters, was tasked to move forward to act as a reserve. This meant that the Mac-Paps were not going to be on the line but would be close enough to react to any enemy breakthroughs or to conduct offensive operations if opportunities presented themselves. The Mac-Paps and the 24th Battalion departed their billets in Hijar for the town of Letux. They were sixty kilometres north of Segura de Los Baños, and only six kilometres east of Azuara, the site of Nationalist atrocities in February 1937.[3] The Lincolns were billeted in Belchite, the city they had helped seize prior to Fuentes de Ebro. The British Battalion was billeted in Lecera.[4]

Cecil-Smith appeared to have some idea that the Nationalist offensive would not be "minor." He took the step of employing scouts around the Mac-Paps' billets in Letux. Lawrence Cane, one of these scouts, recalled thinking that this was an unusual decision; they did not normally take such precautions when they were in a rear position.[5] When the Nationalist assault began, it was clear that there was nothing minor about it. Equipped with modern German and Italian tanks and artillery, and employing tactics similar to those the Nazis would use to rout the French Army and British Expeditionary Force in France two years later, the Nationalists launched an offensive for which the Republicans were unprepared.

The Mac-Paps could hear the rumble of shelling and air attacks at the front on the morning of 9 March. The frontline at Fuendetodos crumbled soon afterwards. Along the Letux–Fuendetodos Road, the scouts saw soldiers from the 153rd Brigade retreating as early as 10 a.m. Cane encountered a fleeing group of *Marineros* who had left their rifles behind. They insisted that they had been relieved, an obvious lie.[6] By the early afternoon, the scouts were watching a full retreat. Large groups of mostly unarmed soldiers from the 24th Division were moved east along the Azuara–Letux Road. The artillerymen had abandoned their guns but claimed that they had disabled them before withdrawing.[7] Cecil-Smith and some of his soldiers tried to stop the fleeing troops, first verbally and then at gunpoint.[8] The fleeing soldiers called their bluff or simply went around them.

The Republican front was collapsing. It was clear that the XVth Brigade had to do something, but what? The commanders on the line were not sending back any information. The XVth Brigade was blind: Merriman, the acting commander, had no idea where the enemy was or what they were doing. He sent forward Maurice Constant, one of the XVth Brigade's scouts, to determine the situation at the front.[9] Meanwhile, he directed the battalions to occupy various defensive positions and to conduct reconnaissance. These positions would be tripwires to protect the rest of the brigade.

Merriman first ordered Cecil-Smith to send a company to occupy a defensive line along the Letux–Fuendetodos road, two kilometres northwest of Letux. Cecil-Smith sent No. 1 Company under the command of Jack Thomas.[10] Next, Cecil-Smith was directed to conduct a reconnaissance to determine the situation west of Azuara. A platoon from No. 3 Company went to investigate. Then, in the afternoon, Cecil-Smith and the other commanding officers were called into brigade headquarters for full orders.[11]

Merriman informed the battalion commanders of the situation at the front. Constant reported that the Nationalists had taken large sections of the first- and second-line Republican trenches. Worse yet, Nationalist tanks were massing three kilometres west of Azuara, and more than a hundred trucks full of infantry a further three kilometres west. The Nationalists appeared to be preparing to pour tanks and mobile infantry through this gap in the line. The XVth Brigade was ill equipped to deal with this kind of attack. They did not have enough trucks to quickly reposition their soldiers, nor did they have enough anti-tank weapons. If tanks got into the Republican rear area, chaos would ensue.

No organized forces stood between the XVth Brigade and the Nationalist forces that were preparing for the next phase of their attack. The Republicans still had two Spanish battalions from the 95th Brigade of *Marineros* holding high features along the Fuendetodos–Azuara Road, but their positions were precarious. They were cut off from each other and had limited supplies. Merriman directed the Mac-Paps and the 24th Battalion to "move north from Azuara in the darkness, contact the enemy, counterattack him and drive him back and form a line connecting the two heights held by the 95th Brigade."[12] They would then block the enemy along the Fuendetodos–Azuara Road and prevent any further penetration. This task, advancing at night from east to west, while friendly forces withdrew through them west to east, was an extremely complex task. Fratricide was likely, but it was a risk that Merriman saw as necessary, given the circumstances. Merriman gave the two battalions a company of engineers and an anti-tank gun to help them achieve their mission.[13] Meanwhile, most of the XVth Brigade would establish a main defensive position in Belchite, with the British Battalion securing a high feature nearby.[14]

The XVth Brigade plan for the Mac-Paps and the 24th Battalion changed again. Instead of relieving the soldiers from the 95th Brigade along the Fuentetodos–Azuara Road, the two battalions would form a defensive line with the Mac-Paps north of the town, and the 24th Battalion to the southwest. But then a different set of orders came from Merriman. The 24th Battalion, the engineers, and the anti-tank gun were ordered to move to the XVth Brigade's main defensive position at Belchite.[15] The Mac-Paps, now without any anti-tank weapons or engineers with which to construct anti-tank obstacles, would go to Azuara on their own. Cecil-Smith issued a quick set of orders to his company commanders. He left his kitchen staff in Letux and marched the rest of the battalion six kilometres to Azuara; the two light machine gun teams returned just in time to join the battalion on their march.[16] The battalion, less No. 1 Company, passed through Azuara at about midnight.

Cecil-Smith moved the Mac-Paps to a location where they could safely spend the night. The bulk of the battalion moved into a night hide in a wooded ravine about 1.5 kilometres north and west of Azuara.[17] It was a terribly dark night and no one was yet familiar with the ground, so Cecil-Smith sent out patrols to identify locations for defensive positions and to find the flanks of other units. One such patrol was tasked with finding the Dimitrov Battalion, but the patrol disappeared and its members were presumed captured or killed. Other patrols found some Spanish soldiers to their north, but no one at all to the south.[18] No. 1 Company rejoined the Mac-Paps outside of Azuara, so at east they were now up to a full battalion.[19] The Mac-Paps held their ground through the night. Again, they tried to rally the fleeing Republican soldiers who passed by their position, but most simply went around them.[20]

When the sun rose on the morning of 10 March, the Mac-Paps were in a precarious position. The front had completely collapsed, and Cecil-Smith had no idea where the Nationalists were or what they were doing. Conversely, at first light it became clear that the Nationalists knew exactly where he was. The Mac-Paps took artillery fire and were subjected to air attacks all morning. They held their position, but the Spanish soldiers to their right withdrew. The battalion no longer had any soldiers on their left or right flank, and they were still the only soldiers from the XVth Brigade in their area. Cecil-Smith had not received any further orders from Merriman.

Republican soldiers continued to withdrew past the Mac-Paps' position toward Azuara and Letux. A Spanish battalion commander reported to Cecil-Smith that he had done everything he could to stop the retreat (including shooting four or five of his soldiers) but to no avail. This commander gathered a handful of soldiers who offered to stay behind and assist the Mac-Paps. Their position was made all the more precarious when a group of Republican engineers tried to delay the Nationalist advance by destroying the Azuara Bridge over the Barcalien River – a bridge *behind* the Mackenzie-Papineau Battalion. Fortunately for the Mac-Paps, the demolition was incomplete and they could still cross the bridge on foot.[21]

Reinforcements arrived not long after the failed demolition. The XVth Brigade Machine Gun Company, the same unit that had usefully reinforced the Mac-Paps' right flank at Teruel, arrived to support the battalion. But they came to the front not only without machine guns, but without weapons of any kind![22] These new soldiers were completely useless to Cecil-Smith. He sent them back to the XVth Brigade in Belchite with instructions to request orders from Merriman.[23]

Cecil-Smith tried desperately to get in touch with Merriman, as he had no idea what the Mac-Paps' role was in the plan. Was holding the blocking position north of Azuara critical to what Merriman was planning? Did they need to buy the rest of the XVth Brigade time to prepare the main defensive position at Belchite? How much time? Cecil-Smith had no clue. He could not reach Merriman by radio, but his signallers had managed to cut into the civilian telephone system.[24] They were able to make telephone calls to the battalion kitchen staff in Letux, where Jim Raily, a member of Cecil-Smith's Ward 2 Committee worked. The kitchen staff had no luck getting in touch with Brigade Headquarters in Belchite. They had no way of knowing that Belchite was under heavy attack, that the British Anti-Tank Battery had been destroyed, and that the town would fall to the Nationalists later that day.[25] Cecil-Smith sent a runner, battalion adjutant commissar Joseph Gibbons, an Irish-American CPUSA member from Chicago, to make contact with the brigade.[26] At the end of the day, Cecil-Smith still did not have any new instructions.

The Mac-Paps' position north of Azuara was getting worse. The battalion had already lost ten killed and twenty-nine wounded to the artillery and air attacks before nightfall, and the Nationalists were massing for an attack.[27] Cecil-Smith watched as truckloads of Nationalist soldiers dismounted just beyond the Mac-Paps' machine gun range. He estimated that three full brigades, perhaps ten times his own force, were preparing to advance on Azuara.[28] The Nationalists seized the top of a cliff overlooking his right flank, providing an excellent position for artillery spotters, and, after sunset, Nationalist machine gunners took up positions in the heights behind Azuara. From there, the Nationalists fired into the Mac-Paps' rear area, killing two of the volunteers.[29]

Cecil-Smith was increasingly concerned that his position would be surrounded or bypassed if they remained north of Azuara. But if the Mac-Paps blocked the bridge of the Barcalien River at Azuara, by using the cliffs for elevated machine gun posts and some of the buildings in the town itself, they might be successful in delaying the enemy in crossing their sector and penetrating toward the brigade's position at Belchite. Cecil-Smith decided to move the battalion to Azuara.

The battalion established a new defensive position in and around Azuara. No. 3 Company, temporarily under the command of *Capitan* Raphael Busch Brage, a Spanish American, occupied a position forward and to the left of most of the battalion. Brage, who had come to Spain through the Socialist Party of America, put his command post in a church spire in the village.[30] It was vulnerable to enemy fire but afforded an excellent vantage point overlooking most of the battlefield. The bulk of the battalion was in the ruins of Azuara, supported by machine guns high in the red cliffs on the east side of the river. These machine guns could fire at their maximum range and provide covering fire to the infantry in the village, which would be particularly important should the force have to withdraw across the single bridge. The machine gun crews in the cliffs, under the command of *Teniente* Leo Gordon, took a few days' worth of food and water with them. On the right flank, Cecil-Smith gave one of his four remaining Maxims to the Spanish battalion commander and the half dozen officers remaining from the 95th Brigade.[31] Cecil-Smith also incorporated a few straggling *Marineros* into the position. Every little bit helped. Cecil-Smith issued orders to his company commanders, providing a note in writing lest there be any confusion: "We have no orders except to hold the lines."[32]

Cecil-Smith received instructions later that night. By luck, Gibbons had stumbled upon General Walter, the division commander, as his staff car was driving down the Belchite–Letux road.[33] Gibbons found the battalion kitchen in Letux and passed the message back through the civilian telephone lines: Cecil-Smith was to report to General Walter's headquarters at 4 a.m. to provide a report and receive orders. Cecil-Smith left the Azuara position by car and reported to General Walter. Walter issued him new orders: the Mac-Paps were to withdraw to a reserve position at Kilometre 8 on the Belchite–Lecera Road, behind the XVth Brigade's defensive position at Belchite.[34] Cecil-Smith returned to the Mac-Paps' position by first light.[35]

By the time of Cecil-Smith return to Azuara on 11 March, the Mac-Paps were taking artillery and machine gun fire. The Nationalists were fighting their way into the outskirts of Azuara. The Mac-Paps were down to only three Maxims because the Spanish officers they had incorporated into their position had fled during the night, taking their borrowed Maxim with them and leaving some of the Mac-Paps separated from the rest of the position.[36] Cecil-Smith quickly issued his orders. The wounded were loaded onto trucks, and the rest of the battalion was ready to move within about twenty minutes, except for two Maxim gun crews. Despite Makela and Wellman's best efforts, yelling and firing their pistols into the air, they could not pass on the message that the battalion was withdrawing.[37] Even if they had, it is unlikely that the crews would have made it down safely. The routes from their positions in the cliffs overlooking the town were exposed to the machine gun fire from the Nationalists. The machine gun crews were left behind. They covered the Mac-Paps' withdrawal. Wellman believed that they held their positions for ten to twelve hours before the Nationalists were finally able to put them out of commission.[38]

Incredibly, the Mac-Paps did not take any more casualties during their withdrawal from Azuara. There was a bit of luck involved, and Cecil-Smith also believed that the Nationalists mistook the Mac-Paps for their own troops. The Mac-Paps were marching east, the same direction as the Nationalists, and they were well spread out in order to decrease the risk posed by air and artillery attack. From a distance, the Mac-Paps looked like Nationalist troops.[39] They marched through two groups of Nationalist soldiers without incident, and Nationalist aircraft at one point appeared to be escorting them.[40] The Mac-Paps did not receive any more artillery fire until they were five kilometres away from Azuara.

The Mac-Paps marched nearly twenty kilometres to Lecera. They arrived at 4 p.m., by which time it was clear that they were not going to move into a reserve position. Lecera was under attack, and the battalion was immediately incorporated into its defence.[41] The situation was fluid; Cecil-Smith received three different sets of orders within fifteen minutes.[42] He acted on the last set of orders, and moved the battalion to a position two kilometres south of Lecera. The force adopted a hasty blocking position and fought off some Nationalist tanks and infantry. In the middle of the fight, an angry Republican staff officer confronted Cecil-Smith. That officer explained that the troops that were attacking them were from the XIIIth International Brigade. He presented his map to prove the point. Cecil-Smith was strongly of the opinion that the soldiers attacking his position were not from the XIIIth Brigade, but the staff officer was adamant. He ordered Cecil-Smith to withdraw to a new position three kilometres away. Cecil-Smith begrudgingly followed his orders, and the enemy took the town of Lecera in short order.[43]

Cecil-Smith moved the Mac-Paps to their assigned position, a ravine intersecting the highway. He placed a rifle company in the ravine, supported by his sole remaining Maxim gun and a few light machine guns and automatic rifles. He placed the second rifle company in depth. The third remained in reserve by the highway. When the actual XIIIth Brigade arrived, Cecil-Smith was approached by a Mexican staff officer (it is unclear if the officer was actually from Mexico, or if "Mexican" was being used as a code word for Russian), who requested support for their counter-attack against Lecera. The Mac-Paps provided a company for the XIIIth Brigade's reserve, but ultimately the attack failed.[44] The Mac-Paps remained in their position until 11 p.m., when they received orders to withdraw to Albalate del Arzobispo, almost another twenty kilometres to the east. They were the most westerly element not only of the XVth Brigade, but also of the entire 35th Division, and they provided the rear guard for the division on their night march to Albalate.[45]

The Mac-Paps arrived in Albalate early on March 12. They were exhausted – they had not slept for three days and had marched almost forty kilometres in the preceding twenty-four hours. They were losing their cohesion: some soldiers simply fell behind or got separated from the group, and the battalion was also picking up soldiers from other units as they went.[46]

The Mac-Paps took up a blocking position on the north side of Albalete. By noon, soldiers from the southern blocking positions began to withdraw through the Mac-Paps' lines. Albalate had fallen.[47] Cecil-Smith recorded that they had not heard any shots fired, certainly no artillery or heavy weapons, which indicated that the positions to the south had folded without much of a fight. Cecil-Smith received orders to withdraw to Hijar and then on to Alcaniz.[48] Hijar was ten kilometres away; Alcaniz was a further thirty kilometres beyond that.

The route from Albalete to Hijar was through canalized terrain with hills to the west and a river to the east. The move was disorganized and undisciplined. Vehicles pushed through the soldiers, and units tried to get ahead of other units. Cecil-Smith lost one of his companies as other units crowded between them.[49] The machine gunners put their remaining guns on a truck to lighten their load, only to learn that it was not their unit's truck. When the trucks drove away, the guns were lost, and the Mac-Paps were reduced to their rifles. The Nationalists exploited the chokepoint – and the bedlam. Nationalist cavalry attacked the column and began setting up machine gun positions on the road[50] – it was perhaps on this was occasion that, as he later related to his son, Cecil-Smith was stabbed by a lance.[51] The soldiers scattered, and Cecil-Smith panicked. A commissar with the XVth Brigade staff recalled that several soldiers told him that Cecil-Smith had yelled out, "Direction Alcaniz! Every man for himself!"[52] Cecil-Smith and many of the other soldiers made a run for it and swam across the Martin River to escape.[53]

The XVth Brigade was falling apart. Its leadership was scattered. Copic was still on leave, and Merriman was missing and presumed killed.[54] Doran, returned from medical treatment in Valencia, took command of whatever elements he could find and established a blocking position a few kilometres east of Hijar. Bill Matthews, a Ukrainian Canadian and a former sniper instructor at Pozorubio, recalled that no one knew where Cecil-Smith or Wellman were.[55] Makela had taken temporary command of the Mac-Paps.[56] Cecil-Smith, likely shaken by the cavalry charge and still believing that the XVth Brigade was moving toward Alcaniz, did not find the Mac-Paps until the evening of 12 August. Cecil-Smith received the unenviable task of (again) commanding the XVth Brigade's rear guard. The XVth Brigade would rendezvous at Kilometre Stone 70 on the Alcaniz Road.[57]

The Mac-Paps' task of protecting the XVth Brigade's rear was virtually impossible. The Nationalist tanks, armoured cars, and cavalry moved off-road and harassed the fleeing volunteers as they moved along the highway. The Mac-Paps did not have any effective anti-armour weapons or even machine guns with which to respond. The Nationalist aircraft dropped bombs and tore up the road with their machine guns. The volunteers did as they were trained. They scattered whenever the attacking aircraft neared their position. After each attack, fewer and fewer Mac-Paps returned to their positions. Platoon commanders lost control of their platoons, and company commanders lost control of their companies. Cecil-Smith lost control of his battalion. He commandeered the battalion ambulance in an effort to move up and down the line to put the battalion back together again, but that approach did not work.[58] Panic had set in, and the battalion had been reduced to a mob.

The incessant attacks from the flanks only got worse. Soon there were tanks between the Mac-Paps and their destination of Alcaniz. The bulk of the XVth Brigade had been warned and diverted north toward Caspe. Cecil-Smith and many others did not receive this message. Then, Cecil-Smith and his ambulance ran headlong into a Nationalist roadblock on the road to Alcaniz.[59] The ambulance driver spotted the Nationalists first and got off the highway and onto a cart path, only to find that it was a cul-de-sac. Cecil-Smith and the crew, taking fire from several machine guns and the tank only fifty metres away, abandoned the ambulance and made a run for it.[60] The medic was killed and the group scattered.[61]

Cecil-Smith did not continue toward Alcaniz. It was clear to him that the city had fallen.[62] He travelled cross-country through moon-lit sand dunes toward the town of Maella, about twenty kilometres away. Sometime before sunset, he encountered William Beeching, a Canadian in the Lincoln Battalion, who was also separated from his unit. Beeching recalled that Cecil-Smith was demoralized. Cecil-Smith told him that the Internationals would soon have to fight their way across the Pyrenees to escape to France. After Cecil-Smith taught Beeching how to find north using his pocket watch, the two soldiers parted ways to find their units.[63]

Cecil-Smith found a group of Mac-Paps in Maella. He took command and led them to Batea, a further twenty kilometres away. There were about two hundred soldiers from the XVth Brigade in Batea, but Cecil-Smith did not stay with this group. He learned that a hundred of his soldiers were at a new defensive position at Caspe. Cecil-Smith put the Mac-Paps in Batea under the command of Brage and departed for the front, hitching a ride with an ambulance headed toward the river town of Caspe.[64]

Dave Doran, the XVth Brigade commissar, had decided to make a stand at Caspe, a town along the Ebro River, with a composite group of five hundred soldiers from the Lincoln, British, and Mac-Pap Battalions; the 24th Battalion had been completely wiped out.[65] Doran used French volunteers, separated from the XIVth Brigade, to man checkpoints in the town. The British Battalion, under the command of Sam Wild, fought to keep the Nationalists from entering the town.[66] There was a cutline for the railroad through which they kept infiltrating. Meanwhile, the rest of the forces fought to hold onto Reservoir Hill, a high feature on the west side of the town. That hill dominated the main road into town; whoever held it controlled access to Caspe.[67]

What remained of the Mac-Paps were heavily involved in the fight for Reservoir Hill. Makela arrayed his Machine Gun Company, which had lost its machine guns and was now fighting with scrounged weapons, on the left side of the defensive line.[68] What remained of the Mac-Paps' No. 2 Company, now under the command of Finnish-American volunteer Henry Mack, covered the right.

Makela and Mack fought desperately to hold on to Reservoir Hill. The Nationalists pushed their companies off the hill, only to have Makela and Mack take it back in a counter-attack. At dusk, the Nationalists seized the hill again. In the course of the Mac-Paps' withdrawal, Makela received three serious wounds from tank shrapnel.[69] He was carried off the battlefield and sent to the rear; he died on the hospital train soon afterwards. Gunnar Ebb (real name Paavo Koskinen), a Finnish Communist and carpenter who had been studying at the University of the West in Leningrad when the Spanish Civil War broke out, took over the Machine Gun Company.[70]

Cecil-Smith arrived in Caspe shortly after Makela was wounded. He was briefly involved in defending the town, but Doran soon ordered him to retake Reservoir Hill. The defence of Caspe could not succeed if the hill was in Nationalist hands. Cecil-Smith gathered a mixed force of a hundred Mac-Paps armed only with rifles and one or two light machine guns.[71] Smaller groups from the Lincoln and British Battalions joined the attack, while three companies of infantry from the XIVth Brigade refused to join the attack, and a supporting attack by the Rakosi Battalion did not materialize.[72] The attacking force did not have any fire support from artillery or heavy machine guns, but they did have three tanks. Cecil-Smith launched his attack in the early morning while it was still dark. The force clawed its way up the hill over the course of two hours. The Mac-Paps retook the hill and captured thirty Nationalist prisoners, fifty to sixty rifles, three Italian Fiat-Revelli machine guns, and ten mules.[73]

By first light, Cecil-Smith's force was positioned to defend Reservoir Hill. It was perilously low on ammunition and used captured Nationalist weapons and ammunition.[74] The Nationalist counter-attack came almost immediately, and Cecil-Smith realized that the Nationalists had infiltrated the town and that he was taking fire from behind his position. Most worrisome, the Nationalists had placed a machine gun in a church steeple from which they dominated Cecil-Smith's routes in and out of town. If the Nationalists reinforced this position, the volunteers on Reservoir Hill would be completely cut off and unable to receive reinforcements or much-needed ammunition resupply. Cecil-Smith sent a runner to Doran to get permission to retire. He did not receive a response, and the French soldiers from the XIVth Brigade abandoned their checkpoints in the town.[75]

With little choice, Cecil-Smith made the decision to withdraw. His force was surrounded and running low on ammunition. He advised Sam Wild, the commander of the British volunteers nearby, to withdraw with him. They moved back into the town. Nearly a kilometre from their positions on Reservoir Hill, at the XIIth Brigade's lines, Cecil-Smith encountered a runner with a message from Doran: hold the hill at all costs. Cecil-Smith and Wild had been among the last to leave the position, and most of the volunteers had scattered. At this point, by Cecil-Smith's own admission, "I had lost control of the men."[76] There was no chance of stopping the withdrawal, let alone rallying the fleeing volunteers to retake the hill. The force continued through the town and crossed the bridge to the other side of the Ebro River. They joined the rest of the XVth Brigade at a crossing site downstream.

The XVth Brigade lost the fight for Caspe. Doran sent additional forces into the town to retake several buildings, but they were unable to wrestle Reservoir Hill away from the Nationalists. Doran ordered the XVth Brigade to withdraw from Caspe before dusk.[77] The brigade continued to withdraw to the east until they arrived in Batea. Relieved by the XIIth and XIVth Brigades, the XVth Brigade finally had opportunity to rest.[78]

On 20 March, what remained of the XVth Brigade took stock of their casualties. The Lincolns began the action with 230 soldiers; more than half of them had been killed.[79] The British Battalion was down to a mere 20 volunteers, down from the 600 who had taken to the field at Teruel.[80] Only 250 Mac-Paps were left standing. They had two Maxim guns and one Degtyaryov light machine gun. None of these were part of the Mac-Paps' original arsenal; all of their original guns had been lost, and these had been picked up in the course of the fighting. Only 135 rifles remained among the 250 soldiers.[81] By the end of the battle, almost half of the remaining Mac-Paps were completely unarmed.

Many of the surviving soldiers were evacuated from Batea due to physical and mental exhaustion. The march from Caspe to Batea alone had been forty harrowing kilometres. Sam Wild, the commander of the British Battalion, was pulled out of the field. Wellman was pulled out, replaced by Carl Geiser, a member of the CPUSA from New York who, like Cecil-Smith, had fought in the Washington Battalion at Brunete.[82] Cecil-Smith was also evacuated and Hector Garcia temporarily took command of the Mac-Paps.[83] The remaining Mac-Paps continued to fight for the rest of the Retreats, but Cecil-Smith, "under the strain of command, coupled with physical debilitation," was evacuated to the hospital at Valls.[84] Evacuation probably saved his life, given that the second half of the Retreats was even more disastrous for the XVth Brigade than the first.

Chapter Twelve

Crossing the Ebro

The Aragon Offensive was a stunning victory for the Nationalists, and a crippling disaster for the Republicans. Throughout March and April 1938, the Nationalists swept aside the Republican forces in their path. The Nationalists reached the Mediterranean Sea at the fishing village of Vinaros on 15 April, splitting the Spanish Republic in half. The Republic still held Madrid and Valencia, but this sector was now cut off from Barcelona, now the capital. The XVth Brigade had lost its base at Albacete and was trapped in the eastern half of the Republic on the eastern bank of the Ebro River. The Nationalists and the Republicans were in peace talks, but Republican premier Dr. Juan Negrin wanted a military victory so that he could negotiate from a position of strength. After a few months of reorganization, the Republicans launched their last great offensive of the war: the Ebro Offensive.

After being evacuated from the line mid-way through the Retreats, Cecil-Smith returned to the Mac-Paps in mid-April, and Saul Wellman, previously the battalion's commissar, was reassigned to the XVth Brigade's Machine Gun Company. The two men had had a terrible working relationship, surely a factor in this reassignment. Victor Hoar, who interviewed Wellman extensively and dedicated his book on the Mackenzie-Papineau Battalion to him, described Wellman as, "in many ways, the antithesis of [Cecil-]Smith." Wellman was working class and adamantly dedicated to his ideology. Cecil-Smith, of course, was more of an intellectual.[1] Intellectualism (in the International Brigades as in the Communist Party of Canada) was not viewed as a desirable trait.[2] Cecil-Smith was hardly an ideologue – he had his own opinions about communism and was all too happy to engage in a debate – and saw the commissar's political education sessions for the troops as an unnecessary distraction from military training. There was ample potential for conflict between the two men.

Frank Rogers was assigned as the Mac-Paps' new battalion commissar. A Finnish American from Philadelphia, his knowledge of the native language of many of the Canadian volunteers must have been an asset. He had been part of the Mackenzie-Papineau Battalion during its summer of training under Merriman, and subsequently had served with the Lincoln Battalion during the Retreats. He spent three weeks in the hospital before rejoining the Mac-Paps later in the spring of 1938.[3] Cecil-Smith's relationship with Rogers was not much better than that with Wellman. Cecil-Smith resented the intrusion of ideology into military practicalities; as Rogers viewed it, Cecil-Smith was reluctant to accept "help" from the commissars.[4] Rogers criticized Cecil-Smith for his lack of interest in the "political life of the battalion."

"Political life" in the International Brigades consisted largely of political education run by the commissars. The commissars brought the soldiers together and led them in directed conversations. The soldiers adopted pledges where they swore to do their duty. All of these activities were perturbing to Cecil-Smith's sense of traditional military discipline. Any time out of action should be spent training for the next battle, not discussing a commissar's views on political doctrine. Similarly, Cecil-Smith thought the idea of adopting a pledge was just plain silly.[5] Soldiers should receive orders and act upon them with appropriate discipline. Despite Cecil-Smith's opinions, the commissars ultimately had the authority to run political education that did not immediately interfere with operations, and their co-signature was required on all written orders. Rogers would have essentially had free rein in March and April as the force maintained watch on the Ebro River near Darmos.

The Mac-Paps defence along the Ebro was relatively quiet. They received some limited artillery fire from the Nationalists at Mora d'Ebre, and some rifle and machine gun fire from the troops on the opposing bank, but mostly they traded words.[6] The Nationalists shouted:

> We don't want Spain to be a colony of Russia!
> Russians, we don't want you here!
> We are fighting for a United Spain!
> Don't shoot at us because we won't shoot at you![7]

Rogers, responsible for morale as well as psychological operations, replied with similar taunts delivered by a Spanish soldier. On May Day, the Mac-Paps constructed rafts with Communist slogans and Republican flags to float down the river in an effort to taunt the Nationalists.[8]

Rogers continued to run his classes and meetings for the volunteers when they were off the line and at rest. At one such meeting, the battalion adopted the following pledge:

> Because the security of the Republic and the Independencia of Catalonia depends on an unbreakable line of resistance against the enemy, we the 60th Battalion of the 15th Int. Brigade composed of Canadians, Americans, and Spaniards, pledge to the Battalions on our right and on our left flanks that:
>
> 1. The enemy shall not pass, will not advance one step in the Sector entrusted our Battalion to defend.
>
> 2. We will build unbreakable fortifications so strong that no enemy bombardment, however terrific, will make us leave our positions.
>
> 3. We stand prepared when commanded to launch an offensive to regain lost territory, to take revenge against the fascist criminals, and rid Spain of the foreign fascist envaders [*sic*].
>
> 4. We extend fraternal anti-fascist greeting to you and our firm handshake confident in victory of our cause.[9]

Cecil-Smith remained uninterested in such activities.

Cecil-Smith's political failings in Spain did not appear to have been known or, if known, of much concern back in Canada. Tim Buck was suitably impressed by Cecil-Smith and Niilo Makela's conduct that he wanted them to return to Canada for a propaganda tour. He did not know that Makela had been killed at the Battle of Caspe in March. Buck simply knew that both men had been upstanding members of the party and were among the few Canadians in leadership positions in Spain. He sent a telegraph to Jack Taylor, by then the senior party member in Spain, in May 1938:

> Political buro [*sic*] requests release Cecil Smith Nillo Makella [*sic*] immediately for work here stop See CHEKA [the emergency committee of the Spanish Communist Party] regarding above Buck.[10]

Taylor also did not know that Makela had been killed – he set about looking for him in the International Brigade hospitals. Taylor wrote to Buck to advise him that Makela had been wounded and wrote to Cecil-Smith to inform him of the invitation.

Cecil-Smith received the invitation through Vladimir Copic, the brigade commander, who had returned to the XVth Brigade following the Retreats. Copic approached Cecil-Smith with the opportunity just before the Mac-Paps appeared set to go back into battle. In mid-May, the

Mac-Paps were given orders to assist in an offensive against Lleida. They marched more than a hundred kilometres north over the next five days. It rained the entire time. The Mac-Paps were held in reserve for the attack, close enough forward that Cecil-Smith could hear the battle "quite plainly." He expected orders to support the attack at any moment when Copic informed him that he had received an invitation to return to Canada. "Naturally," Cecil-Smith explained to Taylor, "I told him I could not think of going until after the operation was over."[11]

Cecil-Smith's response to the invitation speaks to his dedication to the war effort. The Retreats must have been an incredibly traumatic experience, and the prospects of overall victory must have seemed slight. The offensive at Lleida did not materialize, and the battalion was soon at rest in Marçà, fifteen kilometres away from the Ebro River, with no planned operations on the horizon. This was arguably an ideal time to return to Canada, but he declined the invitation, adding that "I still feel that I want to see at least one more action, but when this will be I don't know."[12]

Taylor was convinced that Cecil-Smith was avoiding his letters.[13] He was almost certainly correct. Taylor wrote to Cecil-Smith, but Cecil-Smith either did not write back or took an unusual length of time to respond. He waited a full month before responding to Taylor's invitation, a period during which Cecil-Smith had written other letters to Canada, and Taylor and Rogers had maintained regular correspondence.[14] Clearly, the issue was not the mail – it was Cecil-Smith. Taylor admitted defeat in June, writing to Rogers that "I gave up hope of hearing from Smith."[15] Rogers provided Taylor with material for articles in the *Daily Clarion*, but did not appear to have any luck in soliciting Cecil-Smith's involvement.[16]

After the little excitement in May, the rest of June and most of July remained quiet.[17] The battalion did not see any action except for the occasional air raid. Cecil-Smith wrote letters to friends and well-wishers back in Canada, including one to a friend in his Ward 2 Committee that was reproduced in the pages of the *Daily Clarion*:[18]

> Dear Charlie,
> Was glad to get your letter the other day, but as usual am late in answering.
>
> Yes, letters from home certainly help the old morale. Now that we get The Clarion regularly we have a general impression as to what goes on in the country generally – but it's not quite the same thing as getting a letter from some personal friends, even though the letter doesn't contain much news.

I think I'm the only one from ward two with the battalion right now. Of course there are plenty of Canadians in other outfits – the artillery, transport, medical, signals and so forth.

Pardon me – Jim Raily is also with Mac-Paps, just got back the other day from hospital.

Unless we are otherwise busily engaged, we hope to celebrate Dominion Day in a big way here. The new battalion colors are here from Canada and will be officially presented and trooped on that day.

Also, we have a soccer match to play with the only other battalion in these parts which we have not yet soundly trounced. In fact, we have even taken on and beaten teams representing entire brigades.

As for rifle matches, well, we have now to shoot inter-company matches because of lack of real competition.

A lot of boasting in the above, but the fact is that we have a damn fine battalion, even if I do say so myself.

Perhaps we can't perform on a parade ground quite so well as a Guards' battalion, but we are proud of being a fighting outfit in a fighting army.

Spanish beer used to be pretty good stuff but as it takes a good deal of the grain crop to produce beer in quantities, the making of it has been stopped in Spain since last fall, and now there is none left. Worse luck.

And smokes! Boy, is there a famine in these nowadays! We are down to smoking dried bean leaves and so forth. So send millions of smokes ...

Well, retreat has blown and it begins to get dark, so I'll quit. Regards to all the comrades.

Salud y Republica.

E. Cecil-Smith

Dominion Day 1938 was indeed celebrated in a "big way." The Mac-Paps had a parade through a nearby village, a military skills competition, and a special dinner and a night of dancing with local women.[19] In a soccer tournament, the British beat the Mac-Paps 4–2, but the Spaniards in the Mac-Paps trounced a Spanish team 8–0.[20] Yet the day was not without reminders that a war was still on. As a delegation from a Barcelona trade union made a presentation to the Mac-Paps, the air raid siren sounded. The soldiers scattered and German aircraft flew overhead, thankfully without dropping any bombs or strafing.[21]

Cecil-Smith gave a speech that Dominion Day, one of the few that were recorded. He declared that the battalion was rightfully proud of its record, first distinguishing itself at Fuentes de Ebro and then making a "glorious contribution" in the defence of Teruel. Then, at Atalaya, it was the "first and only battalion in the brigade" to capture a fortified hill in a night action. Regarding the Retreats, he explained that "when non-intervention gave the Italian and German invaders enormous superiority in arms and enabled them to make the Aragon offensive, the battalion valiantly did its part in offering resistance." In spite of terrible odds, they were motivated by their loyalty to the Spanish government and its army, and their loyalty as Canadians, "to the democratic traditions of the Fathers of Confederation, Mackenzie and Papineau." He closed with the same vow he had given to Mackenzie King by letter the previous spring: "We will not return until fascism has been smashed."[22]

The International Brigades were increasingly composed of Spaniards as the flow of foreign volunteers turned to a trickle and more and more Spaniards passed through the established training system. Spaniards also began to take over leadership positions that had once been held by foreigners. General Walter, commander of the 35th Division (now consisting of the XVth Brigade, the Thaelmann Brigade, and the XIIIth Brigade, better known as the Dombrowski Brigade), was replaced by Pedro Mateo Merino. Copic, commander of the XVth Brigade, had been recalled to the Soviet Union and handed over command to Spaniard José Valledor.

Many key staff positions continued to be filled by foreigners, such as the XVth Brigade's chief of staff and commissar positions. Both Merriman and Doran had been killed during the Retreats and had to be replaced.[23] Malcolm Dunbar, the Briton who had formerly commanded the British Anti-Tank Battery before it was destroyed, was appointed as Merriman's replacement as the XVth Brigade's chief of staff, the highest position attained by a British subject in the International Brigades. As commissar, Doran was replaced by John Gates (born Israel Ragenstrich). Gates, an American, was only twenty-four-years old but had been a member of the Young Communist League for seven of them.[24] He had been the Lincoln Battalion's commissar and spoke Spanish, which simplified interactions with Valledor.[25] Gates was famous for being a strict disciplinarian – notably sentencing deserting soldiers during the Retreats to the firing squad – and his appointment as commissar likely filled many with a sense of dread.[26]

Within the Mackenzie-Papineau Battalion, those in the junior ranks were increasingly Spanish soldiers with almost no experience. The leadership positions, however, were filled by seasoned veterans. Cecil-Smith was the longest-serving battalion commander in the XVth Brigade. Lionel Edwards, one of the great heroes of Teruel, was now a *teniente* and commanded No. 1 Company. Henry Mack commanded No. 2 Company; he had fought with the Thaelmann Brigade before joining the Mac-Paps just prior to the Retreats, and had been one of the acting battalion commander in Cecil-Smith's absence. Pedro Roca, a Spaniard who had been with the Mac-Paps since August 1937, commanded No. 3 Company. Former medical student Jorge Carbonell (often called George) commanded No. 4 Company, an additional rifle company added to the battalion after the Retreats. Gunnar Ebb, the Finn who took over from Niilo Makela at Caspe, commanded the battalion's Machine Gun Company.[27] This was a team in which Cecil-Smith could have confidence, and potentially could compensate for the mass influx of raw recruits.

Unbeknownst to the Mac-Paps, who were kept in the dark until just before the operation, a plan to strike a blow against the Nationalists was being formulated at the highest levels of the Republic.[28] A special Army of the Ebro, 80,000 strong, was organized for the task of crossing the Ebro, reuniting the divided Republic, and providing a valuable bargaining chip in the ongoing negotiations between the Republicans and the Nationalists.[29] The Ebro Offensive, if successful, stood to turn the tide of the war.

In the 35th Division sector, the plan for the offensive was simple enough. The Thaelmann Brigade would cross the Ebro River first, under the cover of darkness on 25 July. The XVth Brigade would follow in boats manned largely by Mac-Paps – the unit had a fair proportion of soldiers who had made their living on Canada's lakes and rivers – followed by troops crossing on pontoon bridges.[30] The Mac-Paps were to be across the river and secure their objectives, the Nationalist garrisons at Asco and Flix, in time for first light. Once in place on the far bank, they were to link up with the other elements of the XVth Brigade, wheel south and advance toward the town of Corbera where they would meet up with the Thaelmann and Dombrowski Brigades. The whole plan hinged on the element of surprise. They were vulnerable at the crossing sites, but the Nationalists (and indeed the international community as a whole) did not expect the Republicans to go on the offensive.

The crossing was not particularly well organized. Ammunition was distributed at the crossing site, where the force was most vulnerable, instead of in a secure rear area. Fortunately, the XVth Brigade did indeed have the advantage of surprise and the benefit of a dark, moonless night. Cecil-Smith and the Mac-Paps started crossing at 5:40 a.m. without incident. The Mac-Pap companies crossed one by one, first establishing a secure bridgehead within which they could re-organize. No. 1 Company, under the command of Edwards, was the last to cross. The battalion was secure in its position by sunrise.[31] The companies would split up to take their objectives at Asco and Flix simultaneously.

Mack and Edwards took their companies south to attack Asco, accompanied by Cecil-Smith and battalion headquarters.[32] As No. 1 Company left the beachhead toward Asco, Edwards realized that his company had crested a hill, making it visible from a great distance. A Nationalist artillery spotter had seen them, and as Edwards rushed forward to direct his lead troops into a more covered route, the company came under artillery fire. Edwards was badly wounded and knocked unconscious, and most of his company headquarters was killed.[33] His commissar, fellow Albertan and blacksmith Nicholas Myers "ran 100 yards" before he realized his right arm had been cut open by shrapnel.[34] Mack took over No. 1 Company for the attack on Asco, his adjutant presumably taking over No. 2 Company.[35] Asco turned out to be a simple enough objective. It looked abandoned when the companies approached. Before attacking, they sent in patrols to find the enemy, and "barely a shot was fired."[36] As it turned out, the Nationalist soldiers had executed their commander and had no intention of fighting.[37]

Roca and Carbonell moved their companies north to take Flix.[38] That town should have been a difficult objective. Two companies were tasked with attacking a town with a garrison of unknown size – it turned out to be an entire battalion of infantry and a squadron of cavalry – but the Nationalist garrison quickly surrendered.[39] A glance at the map indicates a very practical reason for surrendering. Flix is located on an oxbow; it is practically an island. Once on the west side of the river, even a token force could lay siege to the garrison. Only a well-prepared and highly motivated force could hold out in such conditions, and this did not appear to be the case of the Nationalists in Flix. The town taken, half a dozen Mac-Paps stayed behind to secure the prisoners.[40]

With Flix and Asco secure, Cecil-Smith brought his battalion back together and advanced to the southwest to join the rest of the XVth Brigade at Corbera. The Machine Gun Company, mounted on twenty horses and two mules seized from the Flix garrison, provided the battalion with a screening force. The Mac-Pap "cavalry" conducted reconnaissance of its routes and reported back to Cecil-Smith. The cavalry even smashed a Nationalist roadblock in the path of the main body. Behind the Machine Gun Company's horses, No. 3 and 4 Companies provided the advance guard, with No. 1 and 2 Companies following immediately behind.[41] They marched all day and night, seemingly as fast as they could, and they lost contact with their flanking units.[42]

Most of the Nationalists the Mac-Paps encountered surrendered, a welcome change from their last battle. An entire company of Nationalist infantry surrendered to the battalion without a fight. When the Nationalist commander came forward to formally surrender to Cecil-Smith, it became clear that he assumed Cecil-Smith was a Red Army officer: presumably in an effort to be polite to his captors, he told Cecil-Smith that it was "very nice to meet a Russian."[43]

The Nationalists had initially been taken unawares by the Ebro Offensive and its quick gains.[44] They had not expected the attack and had initially been ill prepared to meet it. Yet resistance stiffened as they reallocated their forces. The sky began to fill with Nationalist aircraft, including Stuka dive-bombers. As usual, the International Brigades did not have enough aircraft to counter these attacks, but the soldiers dispersed as they were trained to reduce the danger. Morale was still high enough that they did not lose cohesion.

The Mac-Paps arrived in Corbera the next day. With a brief respite, they took to scrounging some of the supplies left behind by the Nationalists: canned sardines and octopus, boots, blankets, and clothing. Whatever they did not need, they turned over to the people of Corbera.[45] The XVth Brigade linked up with the Dombrowski Brigade and advanced from Corbera toward Gandesa, the same town through which much of the battalion had passed during the Retreats after Cecil-Smith's evacuation.[46]

Cecil-Smith arrayed all four of his rifle companies side by side, No. 1 on the left and No. 4 on the right. A machine gun section trailed behind each company prepared to support it.[47] The entire 35th Division was now advancing in line against the Nationalists. The Mac-Paps had never fought in an offensive such as this.[48] By dusk, the battalion was within 200 metres of Gandesa and was fighting to seize Hill 481, "the Pimple," which dominated the town.[49] The Mac-Paps held a position to the south of the Corbera–Gandesa road, but there they would stay. They settled in to a defensive posture and dispatched runners to make contact with the Dombrowskis, now on the Mac-Paps' right flank, but would not take the hill in spite of concerted effort.

The Pimple was a heavily fortified defensive position. The British Battalion, so badly mauled at Teruel and during the Retreats, was now more Spanish than British. Its No. 1 Company threw itself against the sheer face of the hill, further hardened by Nationalist fortifications, but to no avail. The British No. 2 Company tried on 30 July, and No. 3 Company the next day, all without success.[50] The Mac-Paps tried next. On 1 August, they were almost successful in taking the hill, with two companies instead of one. No. 2 and 4 Companies led the assault and made it to the crest, but were unable to hold it.[51] The British tried again two days later. Yet, despite their best efforts, neither the Mac-Paps nor

1 Chefoo School class photo in 1909. Edward Cecil-Smith, six years old at the time, is believed to be the third boy from the left in the third row. David Hogg, his childhood friend, and Frances Cecil-Smith, his sister, would have also been present, but have not been identified. Credit: Chefoo Schools Association, held by the Billy Graham Center Archives, Wheaton College.

2 Cecil-Smith (left) interviews labour leader Bob Hunt while working as a newspaperman at the *Worker*, the Communist Party of Canada's newspaper, sometime before 1936. Credit: *Daily Clarion*, 8 March 1938.

3 The final scene of the only performance of *Eight Men Speak*. Cecil-Smith plays Mr. Capitalism, the defence lawyer for the guard who allegedly shot at Tim Buck in his cell in the Kingston Penitentiary. Mr. Capitalism holds a briefcase and cowers behind the guard as they are challenged by a united working class. Oscar Ryan plays the judge, sitting in the middle of the elevated bench. Credit: Toby Gordon Ryan Collection, Archival and Special Collections, University of Guelph Library.

4 Canadian and American volunteers for Spain onboard the *President Roosevelt* sailing from New York City in February 1937. Cecil-Smith is in the front row of those standing, fifth from the right. Credit: Library and Archives Canada, Mackenzie-Papineau Battalion Collection, Victor Hoar Papers.

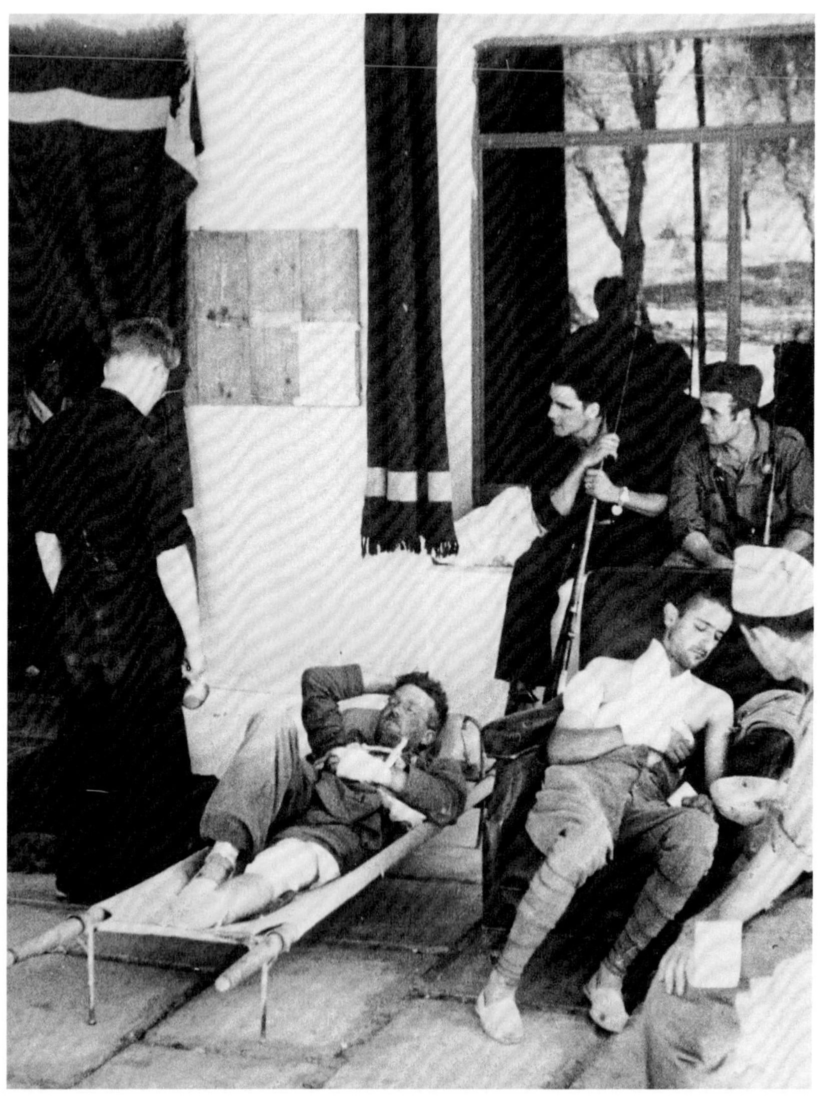

5 Cecil-Smith, following the attack on Villanueva de la Canada, lies at the aid station with bandages on his left hand and knee. According to Cecil-Smith's note on the back of this photo in the family collection, the other soldiers in the photo were captured Nationalist soldiers. Credit: Library and Archives Canada, PA-172401.

6 The Mackenzie-Papineau Battalion in December 1937 at Mas de las Matas. Directly behind the flag, from left to right: Harry Schoenberg, Cecil-Smith, unknown, Niilo Makela. Credit: XVth International Brigade Photographic Unit Photographs Collection, Abraham Brigade Archives, Tamiment Library, New York University.

7 The Friends of the Mackenzie-Papineau Battalion host a rally at Massey Hall on 27 February 1938 in honour of the one-year anniversary of the XVth Brigade. The four faces on the banners are, from left to right, Joe Dallet, Bob Kerr, Niilo Makela, and Edward Cecil-Smith. Credit: *Daily Clarion*, 2 March 1938.

8 The officers of the XVth Brigade gather in Marca in June 1938 on the occasion of the departure of their commander, Vladimir Copic. Copic returned to Moscow and was replaced by Jose Valledor. Cecil-Smith stands to the right of the soldiers sitting in the front row. Behind him to the left stand Copic and Valledor. Credit: XVth International Brigade Photographic Unit Photographs Collection, Abraham Brigade Archives, Tamiment Library, New York University.

9 Cecil-Smith and his headquarters taking a break at Sierra de Pandols. From left to right, Frank Rogers, Harry Schoenberg, Cecil-Smith, and unknown. Credit: XVth International Brigade Photographic Unit Photographs Collection, Abraham Brigade Archives, Tamiment Library, New York University.

10a, 10b Photos sent by Norman Bethune to Lilian Gouge, Cecil-Smith's wife, in 1939. The photo on the left shows Bethune with Mao Zedong; the photo on the right is a portrait of Bethune. The back of the portrait says "To Lil, with Love, from Beth." Credit: Personal collection of Bill Smith.

the British could dislodge the Nationalists from the hill, and therefore could not gain a foothold in the town of Gandesa.

Gandesa was the furthest the XVth Brigade would advance in the Ebro Offensive. The Nationalists had contained the Republican attack; it was now a matter of consolidating what the Republicans had taken and holding it against counter-attacks. On 6 August, the XVth Brigade, along with the rest of the 35th Division, was relieved by the Spanish 27th Division. The Mac-Paps moved to a rear position at Mora d'Ebre for a brief reprieve from the fighting.[52]

According to the *Daily Clarion*, the crossing of the Ebro provided "definite proof" of the Republican government's inherent strength and persistence.[53] It was an astonishing achievement, but the Republicans had advanced as far as they would get for the rest of the war. They now focused on retaining what they had seized while hoping that progress was made at the negotiating table. However, by the time the XVth Brigade had taken position at Gandesa, Franco had already begun to reallocate his forces. The Mac-Paps had encountered Stukas after they crossed the Ebro, and at Gandesa they faced German 88 millimetre howitzers.[54] These guns had a fearsome rate of fire and were highly accurate – they were still considered to be the best in the world in the closing days in the Second World War. The Nationalists poured artillery of all kinds into the sector: eventually 500 artillery pieces were firing 13,500 rounds a day at the Republican forces.[55] In addition, 30,000 Nationalist soldiers would soon arrive for counter-attacks.[56]

After some well-deserved rest at Mora d'Ebre, Cecil-Smith received orders on 14 August to assist in defending the bridgehead. The XVth Brigade was tasked with blocking Nationalist counter-attacks in the mountains south and east of Gandesa, the Sierra de Pandols, nicknamed the Mountains of the Moon.[57] The Mac-Paps marched the twelve kilometres to their new position.

The XVth Brigade occupied three hilltops in the slate-grey Sierra de Pandols. Cecil-Smith and the Mac-Paps were assigned Hill 609, in the middle of the XVth Brigade's position. The Lincolns were to their right, and the 24th Battalion to their left. The British Battalion occupied a depth position.[58] The Pandols were made of jagged, exposed rock; volunteers described the environment as a "virtual hell" and "a nightmare."[59] All of the trees and greenery had been burned away; some fires were still burning when the Mac-Paps moved in to their position.

The soldiers could not dig, either for trenches or to bury the bodies of the Spanish soldiers who had seized the ground just days earlier. Bodies were stacked, and defensive works had to be built up, not dug down. Shrapnel from bombs was piled to form metal barriers, and sandbags were filled with rocks, not sand or soil. In one ravine, the Barranco de Pandols, the Nationalists and the Republicans were almost close enough to engage each other with hand grenades.[60] It is hard to imagine a more hellish landscape.

The XVth Brigade and the Nationalists launched constant attacks and counter-attacks against one another. "Back and forth across the deep ravines and up and down the rocky mountain sides the battle flowed day after day," recalled Cecil-Smith.[61] The Mac-Paps launched attacks by day and by night. Both sides patrolled the ravine at night under the cover of darkness to keep the other side off guard and to gather water to cool their machine guns. On one such patrol in the Barranco de Pandols, the Mac-Paps captured Juan Ruiz Santador, a Nationalist conscript. Santador had been wounded in the leg during one of the Mac-Paps' attacks and subsequently was cut off from his force. He and his comrades took shelter in the Barranco de Pandols and had run out of water after three days. Santador, despite his wounded leg, crawled close to a kilometre to fill the canteens of his even more severely wounded comrades. Cecil-Smith had Santador treated by the battalion doctor and then sent out a patrol to rescue his comrades.

Cecil-Smith was touched by Santador's courage. The pain of crawling so far with a bullet wound in the leg, Cecil-Smith reflected, must have been excruciating, but Santador had done so in the hopes of saving his comrades. Cecil-Smith described him as a hero. Santador was his enemy on the battlefield, but only because he had been drafted by the other side. This was the tragedy of this civil war fuelled by Germany and Italy. "Left to themselves," Cecil-Smith opined, "without foreign intervention, the Spanish people could settle their differences in less than a week."[62]

The Mac-Paps fought to hold the Pandols for eleven days and eleven nights, enduring fierce artillery attacks. They withdrew from their positions on 25 August and had one week of rest. Cecil-Smith received his next set of orders on 4 September. The XVth Brigade was to relieve a Spanish contingent holding on to the hills dominating the Gandesa–Corbera highway. They would leave immediately, marching to the position in order to relieve the Spaniards before dawn.

Upon arriving at the Sierra de Cavalls position under the cover of darkness, Cecil-Smith learned that the relief was not immediately possible.[63] The Spanish battalions on the line had been under attack all night, and they were still under attack when the Mac-Paps arrived.[64] *Capitan* R. Smrcka, the brigade chief of information, took the Mac-Pap leadership as far forward as he could, briefing them on the position and the situation.[65] For the time being, Cecil-Smith kept the battalion to the rear of the position, sheltered in some dead ground along the road.[66] When the sun came up, the Mac-Paps were still to the rear of the Spanish position.

The Nationalist attack ended shortly after dawn. The Mac-Paps were ordered forward to occupy the Spanish position. But Cecil-Smith was no longer among them: overnight, he had been shot in the leg by his own pistol. Gunnar Ebb, the commander of the Machine Gun Company, took command of the battalion as it moved into position. Cecil-Smith was evacuated to the rear.[67]

There was much debate as to whether or not Cecil-Smith's injury was a self-inflicted wound or merely an accident.[68] An anonymous Mac-Pap (an RCMP informer after the war) believed that the discharge was intentional, as did the commissars.[69] But the informer had voiced his personal dislike of CPC members in general, and Cecil-Smith had a bad relationship with the commissars. These people would assume the worst.[70] Additionally, the informer and the commissars inaccurately described the wound itself, casting suspicion on their version of events. The commissars said that Cecil-Smith had "shot himself in the foot," and the informer said that he had shot himself in the "back of the leg about four inches above the knee joint."[71] In fact, Cecil-Smith had been shot in the left calf.[72]

Outside the commissariat, Cecil-Smith's fellow volunteers believed that the injury was merely an accident. Bill Beeching, a Canadian in the Lincoln Battalion, believed the accusations against Cecil-Smith to be unfounded, saying simply, "things like that happened when a man was hungry and exhausted."[73] He refrained from mentioning the incident when he wrote his book about the Canadians in Spain. Gunnar Ebb, who took over for Cecil-Smith after he was wounded, also believed it was an accident.[74]

Either interpretation is possible. Certainly, Cecil-Smith must have been mentally exhausted by this stage of the war; Canadian commissar Harry Rushton returned to Canada in August and reported that Cecil-Smith wanted to go home.[75] The defence at the Sierra Pandols, during which the force endured eleven days of artillery bombardment and close combat, must have been especially taxing; perhaps the idea of another such operation was simply too much for Cecil-Smith. Furthermore, he may have heard the rumours just prior to the incident that the International Brigades were going to be sent home.[76] Perhaps he saw a self-inflicted injury as a means of escaping another battle when the end of the war was in sight.

Yet other facts make a self-inflicted wound seem unlikely. First, Cecil-Smith had been recalled to Canada by the party earlier that year.[77] He had been given an opportunity to go home, and he had refused it.[78] He wanted to stay in Spain in spite of what he had endured at the Brunete offensive, the later days at Fuentes de Ebro, the defence of Teruel, the attack on Atalaya, and even the Retreats. Second, after the incident, Cecil-Smith volunteered to go back into combat twice more, first to defend Barcelona and again during the Second World War. It hardly seems like the behaviour of someone who wanted to avoid combat so much that he would resort to self-harm. Yet, ultimately, it is impossible to know for certain whether the wound was self-inflicted or accidental, as no one actually witnessed the discharge.[79]

PART FOUR

A Dedicated Anti-Fascist (1938–1942)

Chapter Thirteen

Coming Home

The Mac-Paps stayed on the line in Corbera until 23 September 1938, but for Cecil-Smith, the war was over. His wound at Sierra de Caballs put him in the hospital. As he lay recovering, Premier Negrin announced that the International Brigades were to be withdrawn from Spain. Cecil-Smith read the details in the *Volunteer for Liberty* soon after.[1] The Republican leaders hoped that the withdrawal of foreign elements would de-escalate the conflict or at least buy time. The foreigners in the International Brigades were replaced with Spanish soldiers, and the international volunteers converged on Barcelona for a final parade on 29 October. Now there was just the matter of getting home.

Cecil-Smith had not been able to keep abreast of international developments during the war. By the summer of 1938, copies of the *Daily Clarion* were regularly sent over to the Mac-Paps, although he rarely had time to give them much attention.[2] Now, as he lay recuperating in the hospital, he had chance to catch up on the news. He learned that, contrary to the Treaty of Versailles, Hitler had re-armed Germany and created a massive, industrialized military force, aided in no small part by lessons learned in the Spanish Civil War. Germany annexed Austria in March 1938. The international community surrendered the Sudetenland, the largely German-speaking section of Czechoslovakia, that September. This, Cecil-Smith believed, was the greatest betrayal yet. He said that Czechoslovakia lost more in one day of arbitration than Spain had in three years of war. That concession showed how far British Prime Minister Neville Chamberlain would go to avoid a fight with Germany, and it eliminated any hope that a European power would take a stand against Germany and Italy and intervene on the Spanish Republic's behalf. It was clear to Cecil-Smith that a greater war in Europe was on the horizon.[3]

The Mackenzie-Papineau Battalion had always been an amalgam of Canadians and Americans, but it was also filled with Britons, Finns, Spaniards, and Spanish-speaking volunteers from Cuba and Puerto Rico. At the same time, large numbers of Canadians had served elsewhere in the International Brigades – for example, Bill Beeching in the Lincoln Battalion and Ignacy Witczak in the Dombrowski Battalion.[4] Now, in Ripoll, the border town where the International Brigades were sent for demobilization, volunteers were sorted by their country of origin. All of the Canadians became Mac-Paps, and all the Americans became Lincolns. An "all-Canadian" unit finally existed, and Cecil-Smith was its commander. In addition, Cecil-Smith was the senior Communist Party of Canada representative in Spain, following the departure of Bob Kerr in April 1938 and his successor, Jack Taylor, in July. Thus, Cecil-Smith found himself responsible for the Canadian volunteers in Spain.

A League of Nations commission oversaw the repatriation of the foreign volunteers. The commission, led by a Finnish general, a British brigadier, and a French colonel, went to Spain to count the volunteers and send reports back to their countries of origin.[5] Canada sent a representative to help identify and count the Canadian volunteers. Andrew O'Kelly, a Permanent Force colonel posted to Canadian Immigration Services in London, was sent to Ripoll in November.[6] He provided some government oversight of the repatriation effort, identifying who was eligible to re-enter Canada and who was not.[7]

O'Kelly's task was no small matter. The majority of the volunteers had not been born in Canada, and few of them had passports. They had turned in their passports when they arrived at the International Brigade headquarters in Albacete, and most did not get them back. One volunteer, Ignacy Witczak, went to Cecil-Smith personally to see if he could help him retrieve his passport from the Dombrowski Battalion. They were told that the truck it was on had been destroyed. In fact, the passport was on its way to Moscow and would later be used to facilitate the infiltration of a Soviet agent into the United States.[8]

O'Kelly determined eligibility through the rather imprecise process of asking the volunteers questions that he gauged only someone who had spent a certain amount of time in Canada could answer. He did not always like the answers he got. He became annoyed that a frequent response to the request to "name a famous Canadian" was often "Tim Buck."[9] O'Kelly identified at least twenty-one volunteers as being ineligible for return to Canada, but he had not been able to screen everyone.[10] Even as late as the end of November, while 250 Canadians awaited repatriation in Ripoll, an additional 75 were reported to be in hospital and an estimated 100 were trapped in central Spain.[11]

While the League of Nations commission catalogued the volunteers and made assessments of their citizenship, the International Brigade's commissariat made their own assessments of the volunteers. They were assessed with respect to their reliability, discipline, and military proficiency. Commissars made determinations as to whether the volunteers would make for good "cadres" (that is, were potential leaders within the party), were simply good "anti-fascists" (dedicated to fighting fascism but not necessarily to advancing Communism), should be kicked out of or kept from the party in their home country, or required a special degree of supervision. These assessments were presumably sent back to the individuals' home parties. All of them were sent to Moscow as well, where they remain in the Russian State Archive of Socio-Political History.

Cecil-Smith's assessment was harsh. Although his military proficiency was described as "quite good," and elsewhere as "good but poor lately," he was criticized for being cynical, individualistic, and uninvolved with the political life of the battalion. Frank Rogers, Cecil-Smith's last battalion commissar, commented that, "although he understood things intellectually, his nature is so capricious and individualistic that he took an anti-party stand often, feeling that the Party in wishing to help him ... was meddling in his business."[12] Another report noted that he "participated very little in the political life of the battalion ... [and] confined himself solely to his job as a military man."[13]

Cecil-Smith was known to be argumentative, and it comes as little surprise that he would have argued with his commissars. Why should he be beholden to their interpretations of communism? Were his any less valid? Furthermore, why should such matters interfere with military operations? Cecil-Smith understood that fascism was an ideology and that political activity was an important aspect in the fight against it. However, in Spain, he did not believe that political activity should play a role in military operations. His job as a battlefield commander was to physically destroy fascist forces, not to combat their ideas. Every moment spent developing the political life of the battalion was one less spent on training in machine gun drills and tactics.

The commissars recommended restrictions on Cecil-Smith's employment within the CPC. Rogers believed that Cecil-Smith was simply too argumentative for a party leadership role. He described him as a good "anti-fascist" but a bad party member – he simply lacked the discipline. Cecil-Smith's individualistic and capricious behaviour could undermine the confidence others might have in the party's leadership.[14] "My opinion," Rogers wrote, "is that he should be used as a 'Front' by the Party – especially in connection with Spain campaigns. He should also be given some tasks strictly under Party control, to write his experiences in Spain, perhaps for the Party press."[15]

Once they had passed through the processes of the League of Nations commission and the International Brigades, the volunteers were free to depart for their home countries. Although the volunteers had gone to Spain in defiance of their home countries' governments (with the notable exceptions of Russia and Mexico), many countries offered support to get them out of Spain. States that were members of the Non-Intervention Committee, for instance, spent £1.75–2.25 million to repatriate their citizens.[16] Canada, however, would not spend a solitary cent. The volunteers had, after all, left the country of their own volition, paid for by the Communist Party of Canada, its supporters, and, some suspected, Moscow. Furthermore, those who had left Canada after the summer of 1937 had departed in violation of Canada's Foreign Enlistment Act.[17]

Cecil-Smith and the other Canadians in Ripoll watched as volunteers from other countries were sent home. By late November, the French, Belgian, Dutch, and Scandinavian volunteers had been repatriated.[18] The American and British volunteers had at least heard that there was a plan in place to get them home, and the vast majority of them had departed by the beginning of December. Meanwhile, the Canadian volunteers languished with food shortages, cold weather exacerbated by thin blankets and a lack of firewood, and no return date in sight.[19]

The prolonged delay was leading to problems with discipline, as the Canadians became increasingly apprehensive. Soldiers were refusing to perform their guard duties (an officer had to be disciplined when he adopted the habit of striking the shirkers). The Canadians had been organized into companies based on where they were from in Canada, and the British Columbia company was proving to be a problem. Veterans of the BC labour camps, finding their present circumstances to be a bit too familiar, organized grievance committees. A "clique of disrupters," Cecil-Smith wrote, "have sought to create a grievance out of every little inconvenience, finally culminating in attempting to call two meetings on December 13 with the object of organizing some sort of demonstration against the command of this camp and also against the leadership of the International Brigades."[20]

Cecil-Smith was called before the Communist Party of Spain's Central Committee in Ripoll to account for these disciplinary issues.[21] His report outlined various challenges posed by the composition of the Canadian volunteers. He noted that, whereas the American volunteers included a large group of New York members of the Young Communist League who were accustomed to "the discipline of a city industrial unit," the largest group of Canadians came from the BC workers' camps.[22] The veterans of these "slave camps" had never had anything besides the most "casual and transient kind of job," and most had been "on the tramp since leaving school." It was little wonder, he thought, that they were poorly disciplined and prone to rank and fileism.

Cecil-Smith noted that even soldiers who were proven leaders in combat refused to step up and take on leadership roles when they were out of the line. These individuals subscribed to the "theory of spontaneity," a term described by one writer as "a pejorative casting in a negative light the organization's commitment to rank-and-file activism, antiauthoritarianism, and decentralization."[23] For Cecil-Smith, it was the opposite of what a good Communist or a good soldier should be. A good Communist was prepared to lead the vanguard, not reluctant to accept permanent authority. A good soldier was disciplined and accepted orders but did not shy away from responsibility. In a separate letter, written about the same time, Cecil-Smith warned CPC officials in Vancouver that most of the returning men would be an asset but that their background had "in many cases resulted in anarchistic tendencies, lack of discipline and so on."[24]

This culture was exacerbated by the lack of Canadian commissars and officers. In his report, Cecil-Smith noted the insufficient number of Canadian officers. Among the Canadian volunteers in Ripoll, by then totalling 380, Cecil-Smith had only three officers and four commissars, and one officer and two commissars came from units outside the XVth Brigade.[25] Cecil-Smith was the only *mayor* among them. He was dissatisfied with the International Brigades' reluctance to recognize Canadians with appropriate rank or to put them in positions of authority. He admitted that the CPC had sent proportionately fewer party leaders to Spain, compared to the Americans or British, but he did not believe that the Canadian comrades in Spain had been given their due.

Cecil-Smith used the XVth Brigade Scout Platoon as an example of the brigade's failing to properly recognize Canadians. The brigade chief of information, essentially the Scout Platoon commander with some additional staff duties, was the same rank as Cecil-Smith: *mayor*. Canadian volunteer Maurice Constant had served as the brigade chief of information's second in command. By convention, Constant should have been an officer or senior non-commissioned officer. Instead, Constant was going home as a *soldato*, the lowest rank in the army.[26] There were other examples. For instance, there had *never* been a Canadian officer in the XVth Brigade staff; the Canadian battalion had always had an American for its commissar; and, most recently, the Canadians had been given no appointments in running the Ripoll camp. Even after the

British and American battalions had departed, the vacant leadership appointments for the camp were all given to Latin Americans. Beyond promotions, Cecil-Smith explained, there was also a sense among the Canadians that they were the last to receive whatever was being distributed, "from clothings [*sic*] to seats in the train."[27] He might also have included the time preceding the raid on Atalaya, when the Mac-Paps had been the last to receive billets, and Butch Goldstein had felt compelled to tell Dave Doran to "go fuck himself."

In his report, Cecil-Smith accepted responsibility for the failure in discipline within the Mac-Paps and admitted that more could be done to keep the Canadian volunteers occupied. He recognized the effectiveness of the sports program the British had organized and of the political lectures and discussions run by the Americans. The Canadians, he explained, had not done such things in part due to the lack of leadership within the battalion, but also "largely due to the lack of initiative on our part."[28] The solution arrived at was the use of "morale sergeants" instead of a typical military chain of command. Cecil-Smith ended the report by acknowledging his responsibility for the disciplinary issues: "My work as a responsible comrade should be radical[ly] increased and improved."[29]

Cecil-Smith's reports are noteworthy as they appear to be his unvarnished assessment of the Canadian volunteers. His reports, like the commissars' assessments of Cecil-Smith himself, were meant to be private. In public, Cecil-Smith consistently praised the courage of the volunteers. After Teruel and Segura de los Banos, he wrote to Beckie Buhay and specifically praised the courage of Ricardo Diaz and the Spanish soldiers.[30] In a letter home after the Retreats, he praised the courage of a stretcher-bearer who evacuated more than a dozen wounded, as well as two volunteers who had allowed themselves to be captured as a distraction so that their friends could escape.[31] After the crossing of the Ebro, he presented some of the battalion's boatmen to be interviewed by reporters and praised them for their role in the operation.[32] He followed the same pattern after his return to Canada. Publicly, he only praised volunteers for their role in the battalion's successes, never criticized them, and generally minimized his own role in the war effort.

Cecil-Smith and the Mac-Paps were disheartened by the failing Republican war effort. They had been withdrawn from the front in September, and most of them had been in Barcelona and its environs since October. The city was a sad reminder of how devastating the war had been to many Spaniards. The city was teeming with an estimated one million displaced Spaniards.[33] It was also home to the new Republican capital; the government had withdrawn from Valencia because of that city's proximity to the fighting. The Ebro Offensive, which had seemed to be the last great hope of the Republic, was foundering. By mid-November, the bridgehead had become completely untenable, and, on 15 November, the last elements of the Army of the Ebro withdrew to the east side of the river. The casualties did not indicate a clear victor – 6,100 Nationalists and 7,150 Republicans were killed[34] – but the Nationalists could afford these losses and the Republicans could not. The Army of the Ebro would never be rebuilt, and the two sectors of the Spanish Republic would not be united.

For the Canadian volunteers, the disheartening war news was exacerbated by the apparent lack of any kind of plan to get them home. Along with Nicholas Myers, Lionel Edwards's company commissar during the crossing of the Ebro, Cecil-Smith sent a cable to Mackenzie King in early December: "In Geneva last September, Doctor Negrin announced retirement of all foreign volunteers. Since then hundreds of Canadians have waited for reply of your government to return home. We have already passed League of Nations commission. Please act at once."[35]

On 9 December, the *Toronto Star* and the *Globe and Mail* announced that the Canadians would depart Spain shortly, returning in time for Christmas.[36] The source of the information was likely the Friends of the Mackenzie-Papineau Battalion, and, unfortunately, the reports were wrong. The Canadians did not yet have a means to return home. Cecil-Smith received a reply from Mackenzie King's undersecretary of state for external affairs, O.D. Skelton, on 15 December. The cable instructed him to contact the British consul to receive directions for the appropriate arrangements with Canadian immigration authorities.[37] It became clear that the Canadian government would provide only minimal bureaucratic support, and had no intention of dispensing funds from the public purse to repatriate the volunteers.

The repatriation of the Mac-Paps took on greater urgency toward the end of December. Franco launched an offensive on 23 December, pushing toward Barcelona. With the Canadian government refusing to take action, the Canadians in Spain seemed to be in imminent danger, and a plan for getting them home had to be created in a hurry.[38] The day after the offensive began, A.A. MacLeod, the national secretary for the Canadian League for Peace and Democracy (formerly the League Against War and Fascism) sent a letter to Skelton about going to Spain. MacLeod had already been in that country twice, once in the summer of

1936 with Tim Buck and a second time the following summer, when he lobbied for giving the XVth Brigade's new battalion a Canadian name. Since then, the federal government had issued an order-in-council requiring that all Canadian passports bear the stamp "Not Valid in Spain." MacLeod asked Skelton for permission to travel to Spain in an official capacity, stating that he could leave within a week.[39] Skelton gave him permission after MacLeod certified that he would act as a neutral party in the conflict and that he understood that he was acting at his own risk.[40]

MacLeod was in Europe by mid-January. He raised funds and coordinated with government officials and Canadian Pacific Railway (CPR) representatives in London, Paris, and Barcelona to make the necessary arrangements for the Canadians to leave Spain, pass through France and England, and board a ship for Canada. He worked with Colonel O'Kelly from the Canadian High Commission in London and a CPR agent named Coakley.[41]

By the third week of January, almost all of the arrangements had been made for the Canadians to return home. On 20 January, many of the foreign volunteers who had been trapped in Valencia following the Aragon Offensive were moved to Barcelona by sea.[42] Jim Higgins, likely the last Canadian fighting in the Spanish Civil War, rejoined the Mac-Paps soon afterwards.[43] The volunteers had been vetted by a Canadian representative; MacLeod had smoothed over relations with the Spanish, British, French, and Canadian governments; and the CPR had been paid. It was none too soon: on 23 January, the Nationalists had reached the Llobregat River just five kilometres from Barcelona. Republican forces were unable to put up much of a resistance, but fighting could soon be heard in the city.

While many of the volunteers simply wanted to go home, others wanted to stay and defend Barcelona. Cecil-Smith called a meeting to discuss the matter. One volunteer recalled the scene:

> This last meeting of the Canadian combatants on Spanish soil was an eerie affair. In front of the theatre seat stood Smith on a small dais, only discernible by the light of a couple of candles. Behind him, side by side, the sergeants, Ray Henderson and Grenier and McCallum who, since the Ebro, had been appointed commissar; and at Smith's side, Henry Meyer at a table with a sheet of paper. To a few rows of barely visible faces in the pit and the numerous shadows behind, Smith reported in terse staccato on the plight of Barcelona and called for volunteers to go there for a last stand. He stopped as suddenly as he had started, and for a minute or maybe more, there was not a sound. Then, a seat creaked, feet shuffled on

the floor, and out of the dark came the first volunteer and signed in front of Meyer.[44]

Ninety-seven Canadians stepped forward, enough for a rifle company.[45] Cecil-Smith was embarrassed that *only* ninety-seven Canadians had volunteered, although he was confident that the rest of the Canadians would volunteer if the Republic accepted the offer.[46] Cecil-Smith told reporters that enough of the remaining Americans stepped forward to form a field artillery battery, and enough Britons to re-establish their old anti-tank unit lost at Belchite, but it is doubtful that they had the equipment necessary to field such forces. Regardless, the offer was not accepted. An officer from Barcelona simply told the volunteers that the Republican government had promised to repatriate the volunteers and had every intention of keeping its word.[47]

The departing Mac-Paps had replaced their Republican uniforms with civilian clothes, which came from Republican soldiers who had since been killed in the war. Cecil-Smith inherited a green mackinaw coat, which was tight in the shoulders, and a mismatched pair of trousers.[48] As they awaited the train that would take them to France, bombs fell on the city, and Nationalist and Republican soldiers clashed in the suburbs. Finally, they were given a special train to France, departing at 9:15 p.m. on 25 January. A month after the bulk of the volunteers had departed, 292 Canadians (including Cecil-Smith and MacLeod), 95 Americans, and 11 Mexicans boarded a train out of Barcelona to France.[49] Those on the train were most fortunate. Forty British troops were supposed to travel with them, but they seem to have been left behind in the chaos, and an additional 110 Canadians remained with the understanding that they would depart shortly thereafter.

As the train pulled away, the scene must have been one of panic and chaos. Hundreds of thousands of civilians had vacated the city and had begun the long walk to the French border.[50] Bombs were falling on Barcelona and the outskirts – the train had to take shelter in a railway tunnel during a Nationalist bombing raid[51] – and it seemed likely the city would soon fall. If Barcelona fell, the Republic would be reduced to a narrow sliver of land between Madrid and Valencia. Cecil-Smith and the volunteers must have been relieved to be making their way home but apprehensive about the future of the Republic and the comrades they had left behind.

The volunteers were met by consular officials when they arrived in Paris. As the Canadians had already been vetted by Colonel O'Kelly, most of them were already on an approved list. They would ordinarily need passports to enter Canada, but an exception was made, given the unique circumstances and the impossibility of quickly issuing hundreds of passports. The volunteers were instead given special identification cards for one-time use.[52] To ensure that none of the volunteers would abscond during their passage through France, French gendarmes and soldiers guarded them closely in Paris and at each stop along their way.[53]

From Paris, the Mac-Paps took a train to the Dieppe–Newhaven ferry, arriving in England early on a cold winter's morning. They were met by three reporters, one of whom was the *Toronto Star*'s Matthew Halton. Halton rode with them by train as far as London, catching up with Lionel Edwards, an old friend from Pincher Creek, Alberta, and interviewing Cecil-Smith. The Mac-Pap's former commander praised the courage of the volunteers and told Halton that he was apprehensive about how the returning soldiers would be treated. He knew that many Canadians perceived the Communists in general, and perhaps the Mac-Paps in particular, as being dangerous foreigners, but "most of them [have] names as British as my own. I could hardly bear to hear anyone say again that these men are 'adventurers,' 'aliens,' 'dirty reds.' A few of them, no doubt, are soldiers of fortune and aliens, but most are intelligent. Canadians who saw what everyone is beginning to see now, that it is too late; and who had courage to do something about it. Many of them are not even Communist."[54] Cecil-Smith's insistence of the "Britishness" of the volunteers is perplexing, given that the majority of the Canadian volunteers were born neither in Canada nor elsewhere in the British Empire. Clearly, too, he must have known that the majority were members of the Communist Party of Canada.[55] Cecil-Smith may have been attempting to sanitize the Mac-Paps and present them as "Canadian" in a way that would more effectively resonate with the readers of the *Toronto Star.*

Halton watched as the Canadians scarfed down a hearty English breakfast of "porridge, bacon, sausage, kidney, toast" on the train. The volunteers, he noted, were eating as if they had not had a good meal in months. He continued to ask the volunteers questions about their experiences in Spain, eventually asking if the Mac-Paps had had a mascot. The Canadians stopped eating and fell silent. Finally, Cecil-Smith felt compelled to answer: "Yes, we had a mascot. He was a nice dog, named Jim. We haven't got him now. The boys ate him one day."[56] This incident presumably occurred when the Mac-Paps were staying in Ripoll and the food ran short.

The Mac-Paps continued by train to the port of Liverpool. As in France, British bobbies watched the doors at each train stop, an experience Cecil-Smith found to be much like how anthrax-infected cattle were treated.[57] They arrived in Liverpool on the afternoon of 27 January, scheduled to set sail aboard the *Duchess of Richmond* the following day at 3 p.m.[58] Along the way, the Canadians learned the terrible news about events in Barcelona. These 292 Mac-Paps had been on the last train out of the city; the next train to depart had 800 volunteers on board, and all were presumed killed in a Nationalist bombing raid.[59] The Canadians left behind in Barcelona had to leave the city on foot, marching toward France alongside thousands of fleeing refugees.[60] Barcelona had fallen to the Nationalists on 26 January, while the first group of Mac-Paps were in transit, and Republican supporters were soon being tried by courts martial and executed by firing squad.[61] The first group of Mac-Paps had just barely escaped and were understandably very concerned about the Canadian volunteers still in Spain.

Given how closely they had been guarded during their travels, and how eager the British seemed to be to have them immediately depart for Canada, the Canadians seemed to sense that they had a degree of leverage over the British authorities. The Mac-Paps refused to leave the train platform at Liverpool's Riverside Station and demanded assurances that the second group of Mac-Paps would be granted safe passage home. Cecil-Smith may not have organized the strike, but, once it began, he supported it.[62] He reminded the Canadians that another group of volunteers had been turned away at the French border just ten days earlier and subsequently killed by the Nationalists.[63] It is unclear to what event Cecil-Smith was referring, but the point was clear – the safe return of the remaining Canadian and British volunteers was by no means guaranteed. Cecil-Smith reminded the Canadians in Liverpool that, as British subjects, they had every right to remain in Britain for as long as they chose to do so.

Cecil-Smith spoke to reporters to bring some public pressure to bear, telling the journalists, "They [the other Mac-Paps] may have been murdered with no arms in their hands, and before we leave we want to know they are safe."[64] He also took a moment to advocate for the cause of the Spanish Republic more generally, stating, "In time to keep Spain free it won't be very long before my boys will be back in uniform and with earnest willingness too – only this time it will be Canadian uniforms. And the conflagration with be worldwide."[65] When the Liverpool *Evening Express* went to print that night, the Mac-Paps were still refusing to leave the train station.[66]

The next day, Cecil-Smith made telephone calls to the British Foreign Office, insisting that he receive assurances that the next group of Mac-Paps and the thirty volunteers from the British Battalion would be taken care of. Satisfied with the Foreign Office's answers, he gathered the Mac-Paps together alongside the *Duchess of Richmond* and passed along the information. He asked, "With these assurances, will you go aboard?" The Mac-Paps responded, shouting, "Yes!" and "Viva Espagne!" and boarded the ship in an orderly fashion. The *Duchess of Richmond* set sail at 4:30 p.m. instead of 3 p.m., as originally scheduled.[67] It was a joyous occasion but marred by the uncertainty as to the future of the Spanish Republic and a sobering reminder of the strength of fascism beyond Spain – their fellow passengers included Jewish refugees fleeing Germany.[68]

The Mac-Paps had little to entertain themselves with on the six-day steam back to Canada. It was a time for quiet reflection, conversation among comrades in arms, and enjoying three hot meals a day, a luxury most had not known in quite some time. Cecil-Smith posted messages on the ship's bulletin board, much of the information having to do with welcome-home arrangements gleaned from cablegrams sent by the Friends of the Mackenzie-Papineau Battalion.[69] Jim Higgins held on to the last notice that Cecil-Smith pinned to the ship's bulletin board. It read:

> Spain overrun with fascism will present France and Britain with a major problem. If they wish to avoid it they must at once abolish the not only wicked but stupid policy of embargo against the Spanish government.
>
> We, as returning ex-members of the International Brigades, will certainly do all we can to line Canada up with the United States in opposition to the embargo.
>
> The embargo lifted, Spain will be able to better defend world democracy. The next step after that must be to force the withdrawal of all foreign troops from Spain and the terrible threat of world war will disappear, at least for the time being.
>
> E. Cecil Smith[70]

His predictions proved remarkably prescient, although his hopes optimistic: the embargo would not be lifted, the withdrawal of foreign troops would not be forced, and the world war would not be avoided. On 1 February, the *Cortes*, the Spanish Republican Parliament, held its last meeting on Spanish soil in Figueres, inside the very fort where most of the International Brigaders had spent their first night in Spain.

The Mac-Paps made landfall on 3 February. The *Duchess of Richmond* docked in Halifax, and the Mac-Paps disembarked. Reverend Reginald W. Thomas, an Anglican priest and chair of the Friends of the Mackenzie-Papineau Battalion's Rehabilitation Committee, and Jack Taylor, the Friends' former representative in Spain, greeted the volunteers.[71] Thomas and Taylor gave them clean donated clothing to replace the rags that many of them wore, much of which was adequate for Spain but all too thin for the Canadian winter. They also brought boxes of sandwiches made by volunteers for the journey ahead. To add a touch of ceremony to their disembarkation, the ship's captain gave Cecil-Smith a Union Jack so that it could be carried alongside their battalion flag.[72] The Mac-Paps marched off the ship and into the immigration shed, where they sang "O Canada" – not yet the national anthem but a popular patriotic song.[73]

The Mac-Paps were joined in Halifax by Gregory Clark, a *Toronto Star* reporter and veteran of the Great War, who would travel with them as far as Truro, Nova Scotia.[74] Clark was pleased to see Fred Hacket among the Mac-Paps – the two had served in the Great War together. Clark moved about the train, asking the Mac-Paps questions about the supposed anti-Catholicism of the Republicans and the idea that the Canadian volunteers were all Communists. Cecil-Smith told Clark that fewer than half of the Mac-Paps were Communists "or even socialist." He continued: "We have every possible shade of liberal; we have Catholics, devout Catholics, labour unionists, and some who are just indignant farmers and mechanics of no political shade whatever." One of the volunteers told Clark that he was among twelve Catholics who had attended mass onboard the *Duchess of Richmond*. Clark seemed satisfied, remarking that one thing all of the Mac-Paps seemed to have in common was a deep affection for Spain and the Spanish people.[75]

In Montreal, the Mac-Paps were greeted by a large crowd of supporters. The authorities did not let the men off the train, but that did not appear to stifle the jubilance of the occasion.[76] The crowd chanted "Down with [Quebec premier Maurice] Duplessis!" and "Down with Hitler!" Cecil-Smith, when asked if the soldiers were disillusioned, exclaimed, "Fiddlesticks! If we are disillusioned about anything or anybody it is at the terrible things that Premier Chamberlain has done to the Spanish people. As far as going to Spain we Canadians had no illusions in the first place, so we have nothing to be disillusioned at. Much of what happens in the period to come will depend on the role that Britain and France are playing in the international arena. Spain above all else needs arms and food."[77]

The train continued west and stopped briefly in Cornwall, Brockville, Kingston, Belleville, and Oshawa, with cheering crowds at each stop. In Oshawa, the supporters gave the Mac-Paps a case of fruit and cigarettes. Cecil-Smith thanked the gathered crowd and said, "They told us we weren't welcome in Duplessis's Quebec. Well, I bet Montreal has never seen a demonstration like that given us in Windsor Station this afternoon."[78] Finally, at 9:30 p.m., the Mac-Pap train rolled into Toronto.

Cecil-Smith and the other Mac-Paps' return to Toronto was nothing like their departure. When Cecil-Smith left for Spain in 1937, he did so in secret. There was no fanfare, and he had to take precautions to avoid the attention of the RCMP and curious customs officials. No such precautions were taken on his return, on 4 February 1939. The men were greeted by a cheering crowd of 10,000. Supporters filled the platform, the station, Front Street, and the open space around the Royal York Hotel.[79] The throng was held back by fifty police officers and volunteer guards from the Finnish Athletic Club.[80] The Spanish consul to Canada, Fred Rea, was also on hand to formally greet the volunteers. The *Globe and Mail* described it as "the biggest demonstration the Union Station has seen since Canadians left on the Vimy pilgrimage."[81] As the *Toronto Star* put it, "Stealthy Goers-Forth to War Who Come Loudly Home."[82]

Cecil-Smith took command of the Mac-Paps one last time. The men formed up while a brass band played songs from the Great War, the Republican anthem, and "O Canada." Cecil-Smith gave a few commands in Spanish and stood the troops at ease before saluting the crowd with the raised fist of the Spanish Republic. The crowd roared in appreciation. Cecil-Smith ascended to the balcony and addressed the crowd with an optimistic message. "Spain is not licked," he said. "Hitler and Mussolini do not get everything they want, and if there is just one thing we have learned it is this: that if you fight against fascism you can beat it. In two years Spain has not lost as much by war as Czechoslovakia lost in one day of betrayal," a clear reference to the Munich Agreement.[83]

He continued, addressing a concern on the minds of many of the volunteers. "[The Canadian government] is not responsible for you, but I believe there is someone else a great deal stronger than the Canadian government – you have put God in your debt because you went to help a little people, a people left behind, suffering in poverty, in depression. The Lord Jesus said that if you helped the little-people, the down-trodden, the suffering little people, 'I take it as done unto me.'"[84] The crowd continued to clap and cheer.[85] It was a rousing scene, but Cecil-Smith was eager to simply go home. When a reporter asked how he could be reached for further comment, he said, "I'm not sure I've got a telephone. I've been gone so long."[86] If his wife, Lilian Gouge, came to meet him at Union Station, that fact eluded the newspaper reporters who attended that day.

Cecil-Smith was not relieved of his duties just yet. He and the other Mac-Paps had a day to relax with their families, but they were invited to a church parade on the evening of 5 February at St. Mary Magdalene. Reverend Thomas, chair of the Mac-Paps' Rehabilitation Committee and the parish priest at St. Mary Magdalene, raised the flag of the Spanish Republic in the church. He praised the soldiers for their valour. In spite of accusations that they were "atheists and communists" – Cecil-Smith himself had remarked that there were not many religious people among the volunteers – Thomas considered the volunteers to be "true Christians" in light of their sacrifice in service of the Spanish people.[87] The Mac-Paps' official welcome-home ceremony was held at Toronto's Massey Hall the next day. By that time, only a hundred or so veterans remained in Toronto; the rest had stayed in their home provinces in the Maritimes or Quebec, or had continued on to the west.[88]

When the curtain went up, the packed house saw a Canadian Red Ensign on one side and a Spanish Republican flag on the other. In the middle, there was a portrait of Niilo Makela, the designated martyr, with a banner proclaiming "Canada Honors Her Heroes." A memorial alter, resembling the cenotaphs from the Great War now common across the country, had a sign that read "To the Memory of Those Who Died for Democracy in Spain." Honoured guests were already on stage, among them volunteers who had returned months earlier, including Edo Jardas, standing on crutches with a leg missing, or Alec Miller, with his foot wrapped in bandages. Others on stage included Beatrice Colle of the Friends of the Mackenzie-Papineau Battalion; Salem Bland, the *Toronto Star* columnist and Methodist minister; Fred Rea, the Spanish consul to Canada; J.W. Bentley, the secretary of the Toronto Trades and Labor Council (which had banned Communists until 1936); Alderman Stewart Smith; representatives of the Co-operative Commonwealth Federation; and Frank Rogers, the Mac-Pap commissar who had come from Chicago to represent the American volunteers and to give a cheque for $5,000 to the Friends of the Mackenzie-Papineau Battalion for the rehabilitation fund. Reverend Thomas made some introductory remarks, presenting the Mac-Paps as the descendants of the Canadian freedom fighters of 1837, not of Marx and Lenin, after which Rea, Bentley, and Smith laid wreathes at the foot of the monument.[89]

With the wreathes laid, the Mac-Paps marched onto the stage, Cecil-Smith and Thomas McCallum in the front. The applause turned to a five-minute standing ovation, after which Cecil-Smith gave a command in Spanish, the house lights turned off, and a spotlight beamed onto the monument. A bugler played the last post, a moment of silence was observed, and then reveille was played. Cecil-Smith and McCallum saluted with the closed fist of the Spanish Republic.[90]

This was a scene quite unlike anything associated with the Communist Party just years earlier. Here, there were no red stars or hammers and sickles. Speakers did not mention communism or the role of the CPC, or of Russia, in the undertaking. Neither "The Red Flag" nor "The Internationale" was sung. Instead, the hall was decorated with nationalist symbols, the attendees sang "O Canada," and no one booed "God Save the King." The cenotaph, the bugler, and the wreathes embraced the traditions of remembrance adopted throughout the British Empire since the Great War. Even Cecil-Smith, once so critical of that war, now sought to show a connection between its veterans and the volunteers for the Spanish Civil War. He stated that the names of the 300 Canadians buried in Spain "should be added to the 60,000 who were killed in Flanders."[91]

Cecil-Smith was the last of ten speakers on the evening's agenda. Stewart Smith introduced him by quipping that "all bishops were useless except one" – Cecil-Smith's father. Cecil-Smith told the audience that, when he was a child, he had been taught "and still believe[d], that we British people had contributed quite a bit towards establishing democracy in the world." Principal among these accomplishments was Britain's role in defeating "that terrible monster Napoleon," a danger that was averted by Britain's support to Spain. Cecil-Smith described the Peninsular Campaign during the Napoleonic Wars as Spain's first war of independence; the Spanish Civil War was the second. Only a wider war could result if Britain did not again stand with the Spanish people against the spread of fascism:

> I am not saying this in support of British imperialism, I am saying this to point out that Mr. Chamberlain and his government are willing, apparently, to do anything for appeasement, even selling out his own friends ... If a world war comes it will be because we have not been able to prevent the Spanish government from being sold out. It is up to us to act very quickly and definitely, forcing the government of Chamberlain and [French prime minister Édouard] Daladier to change the policy towards the Spanish government and towards the cause of democracy fought for in Spain.

He predicted that war would break out in April. At the end of his speech, Smith led the crowd in giving him three cheers for his service.[92]

The RCMP continued to monitor Cecil-Smith and the returned volunteers. Many of them had active police files before Spain simply due to their membership in the CPC; their status as Mac-Paps led to increased police scrutiny. Former RCMP Commissioner J.H. MacBrien had expressed his concern regarding the Mac-Paps in a letter to O.D. Skelton, undersecretary of state for external affairs on 8 July 1937: "It is felt that these youths are being sent to Spain largely for the sake of gaining experience in practical revolutionary work and will return to this country to form the nucleus of a training corps."[93] Imagine, MacBrien and his successor, Stuart Wood, must have thought, an On-to-Ottawa Trek organized not by the party's labour leaders but by the hardened combat veterans of the Mackenzie-Papineau Battalion! Plainclothes officers awaited the volunteers when they landed in Halifax; an officer sent a telegram to Commissioner Wood informing him that the Mac-Paps had disembarked, and that the Mounties had acquired a copy of the ship's manifest for their records.[94] RCMP detective Robert Irvine, who had been observing Cecil-Smith since 1932, attended the Massey Hall rally and continued to monitor the returned Mac-Paps in Toronto.

Cecil-Smith gave many more speeches and interviews in the coming weeks. On 10 February, he spoke in Hamilton with Lionel Edwards and three other Mac-Paps. They unveiled a cenotaph at the Independent Order of Oddfellows Hall before a crowd of 2,000.[95] The cenotaph was dedicated not to the memory of soldiers who fell in Spain, but to those who had died in the Great War. The fact that Cecil-Smith and the Mac-Paps were viewed as appropriate dedicators for this cenotaph indicates that the Oddfellows believed that the war in Spain was as much "their" war as the Great War had been. Similarly, Cecil-Smith gave a two-hour speech in Niagara Falls, where the RCMP noted that the crowd was "of good class" and there "was no hint of Communism."[96] Cecil-Smith's speeches were well attended and positively received, although the second of his two speeches in Montreal was shut down by the police.[97]

Cecil-Smith toured Quebec and Ontario, and, although his speeches were optimistic in tone, he was growing increasingly despondent behind closed doors. An RCMP plainclothes officer, who appeared to have a pre-existing relationship with him, said that Cecil-Smith was "very far from being cheerful and is non-communicative ... [He] has asked to be relieved of having to travel all over the country to speak at public meetings."[98] A reporter noted that Cecil-Smith's experiences in Spain had aged him, "his face lined and haggard, no longer the genial round face known to many of his former fellow-newspapermen."[99] His experiences in the Spanish Civil War had been traumatic. He had endured combat, been wounded several times, and lost hundreds of soldiers under his command. He was tired and wanted to return to his old life. He had been away from his wife for two years and wanted to spend some time with her but was pulled away for propaganda duties.

The stress and fatigue was no doubt exacerbated by the bad news coming from Spain. He had claimed just weeks earlier that Spain was not licked, but he had been wrong. The Republic was collapsing. The Committee to Aid Spanish Democracy, recognizing the hopelessness of its cause, now focused on aiding the hundreds of thousands of Spanish refugees who had fled the Nationalist advance. The French government opened the border on 27 January 1939, at which point they were completely overwhelmed.[100] The new Canadian Committee to Aid Spanish Refugees, represented in France by Jean Watts, began raising money for humanitarian relief efforts.[101] Meanwhile, Franco was able to focus all of his forces on taking Madrid. The city meant to be the graveyard of fascism finally fell on 1 April 1939.

The Republic for which Cecil-Smith and the Mac-Paps had risked their lives was gone. The international community had stood idly by, justifying their inaction as "neutrality," as the Nationalists, aided by Germany and Italy, crushed Republican Spain. What hope was there for the revolution, for the imposition of the dictatorship of the proletariat, when democracies allowed other democracies to be overthrown by fascist rebels? Cecil-Smith was heartbroken by current events and terribly concerned for the future. He predicted a wider war in Europe by June.[102] Cecil-Smith could do little for Spain, so he would do what he could for the Friends of the Mackenzie-Papineau Battalion to help support the returned volunteers, and would resume his old duties with the party.

The Friends of the Mackenzie-Papineau Battalion reported at the end of April that not all of the Canadian volunteers had returned home. Of the 1,329 known to have gone to Spain, about half of them had been killed, 646 had returned to Canada, and about 100 were being held in refugee camps in France.[103] Others were believed to be in Nationalist prison camps, or worse.[104] Toronto was home to 185 returned volunteers, 39 of whom were disabled. Fundraising efforts in Toronto, including the Massey Hall rally, which had raised $2,600, had generated $6,351 for the Toronto Mac-Paps to date, but more was needed.[105]

Because the records of the Friends of the Mackenzie-Papineau Battalion were seized by the RCMP at the beginning of the Second World War, it is difficult to determine how involved Cecil-Smith was in the fundraising effort.[106] Personal correspondence between Cecil-Smith and Jim Higgins, the commissar on the voyage from Spain back to Canada and then the Friends' secretary for western Canada, shows that Cecil-Smith was using Friends of the Mackenzie-Papineau Battalion Rehabilitation

Committee letterhead. The two wrote back and forth about the whereabouts of different Mac-Paps, their physical health and degree of assistance required, and the nature of their service in Spain. One particularly noteworthy exchange addressed the whereabouts of George Albert Thomas, a volunteer from Saskatchewan who went missing during the Retreats. He was now presumed to have been killed. In the margin, Higgins wrote that he now believed, based on his inquiries in Saskatchewan, that Thomas had been an RCMP informer.[107]

Cecil-Smith was also charged with writing the official history of the Mackenzie-Papineau Battalion. The Communist Party of Canada was eager to produce such a book as it would likely be a popular and commercial success. The project began almost as soon as the volunteers returned from Spain. Maurice Constant, who had served with the XVth Brigade's scouts, was the secretary of the editorial commission. He wrote to the Canadian volunteers in April 1939 and requested that they share their experiences so that they could be compiled.[108] Cecil-Smith was given at least twenty-seven returned forms and letters and began composing his book, titled *The Mac-Paps*, creating a first draft of an introduction.

Cecil-Smith's draft reveals a plan to write a document that would celebrate the service of the volunteers as a group, not elevate his own story. He makes no mention of himself in the draft but, rather, focuses on the individual experiences of the volunteers, which are conveyed largely in their own words. Canada, Cecil-Smith wrote, had sent one thousand of its sons to Spain: "A thousand is a lot. In a small country like Canada it is lot more than in a big country. Especially when a thousand Canucks ignore the warnings of their government, and surmount decrees and difficulties and an ocean and mountains and several thousand miles to say nothing of red tape and hostile officials, and finally land in Spain to fight a war. It doesn't happen often. But when it does, it deserves to be remembered."[109]

Cecil-Smith's book, if completed, likely would have become a seminal work on the history of the Canadians in Spain. Unfortunately, it was never finished. He typed out only a twenty-one-page manuscript over the course of 1939, abandoning the project altogether before the year was through.

The reason for Cecil-Smith's failure to complete the book is hardly clear, but it appears to have been the result of the Communist Party of Canada's meddling in the process. The only clue of this interference is a note written by Jim Higgins. In addition to their communications about the Mac-Paps in western Canada, the two men corresponded about the book project as well. Higgins featured prominently in Cecil-Smith's draft introduction, serving as the main character in nine of the draft's twenty-one pages. At some point in the writing process, Higgins recalled that Cecil-Smith had reached out to him and told him not to send him any more materials "until the problem is resolved ... The writers [Cecil-Smith and likely Maurice Constant] wanted to have the pros as well as the cons incorporated in the book, but the politicals wanted only the good parts written."[110] Whatever the specifics of the disagreement between Cecil-Smith and the party, the book project was never completed.[111]

Outside of his ongoing work with the Friends of the Mackenzie-Papineau Battalion, Cecil-Smith returned to work with the party's Ward 2 Committee. He served as its educational director, developing an educational program about the history of the Communist Party in Russia. He was re-elected to the position of president of the Ward 2 Committee in May.[112] He was also involved in expanding the party's influence in downtown Toronto. The party had grown considerably in recent years, doubling in size since 1935 to its all-time high of 16,000 members in the spring of 1939.[113] The Ward 2 Committee had grown to more than fifty members while Cecil-Smith was in Spain, and this was considered to be too big to be manageable. The Ward 2 Committee created a second committee, charged with expanding the party's influence westward into Ward 3. As part of this work, Cecil-Smith and A.A. MacLeod established a Young Communist League branch and an association for the unemployed in Ward 3.[114]

MacLeod and Cecil-Smith were assisted in their efforts in Ward 3 by an enthusiastic labour leader named Benson, recently returned from party work in Winnipeg.[115] Neither MacLeod nor Cecil-Smith knew Benson from their earlier work in the ward. The Winnipegger had come to Toronto in July 1937 while their attention was focused on Spain, and he had come highly recommended. He was a friend and confidant to Leslie Morris and Beckie Buhay, and had assisted Tim Buck with his campaign in the Toronto municipal election of January 1939. He was a trusted member of the party by the time Cecil-Smith and MacLeod returned from Spain. They would work closely together in establishing the new Ward 3 Committee.[116] Cecil-Smith and MacLeod did not realize, however, that Benson was actually an undercover RCMP officer – Corporal Robert Leaconsfield Trolove.[117] RCMP detective Robert Irvine had given Trolove specific instructions to get close to MacLeod and Cecil-Smith. Trolove was not Irvine's only resource for investigating Cecil-Smith's activities – he also had an informant in Ward 2 on the East Toronto Section Committee and was working to develop others, a matter made easier by the theft of some blank membership cards from the party headquarters.[118]

In addition to his work on the Ward 2 and 3 Committees, Cecil-Smith returned to his work as a newspaperman. He seemed to be eager to begin writing as soon as he returned to Canada; he filed his first story with the *Toronto Star* during his brief stay in Halifax.[119] He wrote a few more stories about his experiences in Spain for the *Star* but did not immediately return to writing for the *Daily Clarion*. On 1 April, it was announced that he had been appointed as the *Clarion*'s associate editor, his transgressions in 1936 seemingly expunged by his conduct in Spain. The announcement noted that he had been part of the editorial staff "since the very beginning" but failed to mention that the paper had fired him.[120] Cecil-Smith did little writing for the *Clarion*, at least not much where he was directly credited. Besides the article announcing that he had joined the staff, and a book review on Marx and Engels's *Revolution in Spain*, the pages of the paper left no clues that he was on staff.[121] He appeared to be active primarily behind the scenes.

Cecil-Smith seemed to be happy to have returned to the *Daily Clarion*. He expressed pride in the accomplishments of the newspaper. He told one audience that the newspaper had shaped the party's policies on housing, not the other way around.[122] The paper had good reporters who produced quality material that the world at large was interested in; he claimed that the *Tattler*, a Toronto-based national tabloid, was reprinting the *Daily Clarion*'s material on fascist groups in Canada "almost word for word," and had seen its distribution jump from 17,000 to 50,000 as a result.[123] There were also other positive secondary effects on the party of maintaining a daily paper, such as giving employment to paper carriers who could then devote themselves full-time to party work. Cecil-Smith claimed that the *Daily Clarion* had paid out $9,000 in wages in the past year.[124] In spite of these benefits and concerted efforts to drive up subscriptions, demand was insufficient to maintain a financially viable national daily paper. Cecil-Smith admitted at a public meeting that, in spite of the claimed distribution of 10,000, the truth was closer to 4,000.[125]

Cecil-Smith believed that well-illustrated regional weekly news magazines were increasingly popular and could be produced by the party on a more cost-effective basis.[126] He announced at a public meeting that the *Daily Clarion* would transition to four weekly titles: the *Advocate* in Vancouver, an existing party paper that would be expanded; the *Mid-West Clarion* for the Prairies; the *Weekly Clarion* (later just the *Clarion*) for Ontario and the Maritimes; and *Clarté* in Quebec.[127] An RCMP observer at the public meeting described Cecil-Smith as "quite enthusiastic about the idea."[128] The last edition of the *Daily Clarion* was published on 19 June 1939.

The RCMP officer's description of Cecil-Smith's conduct at this public meeting provides some insight into why Commissar Frank Rogers did not believe that Cecil-Smith was sufficiently disciplined to take on party leadership roles. Cecil-Smith attended the meeting on behalf of Tim Buck and Tom Ewen, who were unavailable. He was speaking in an official capacity, yet in the course of his speaking he implied that Stewart Smith, a powerful and important member of the party's inner circle, had either been naive or intentionally deceptive about the *Daily Clarion*'s subscription numbers.[129] Similarly, he publicly criticized the way the chair of the meeting ran the event, saying "Here is a comrade who has been in the movement almost twenty years and he still doesn't know how to run a meeting efficiently. Take him away from his Ukes [Ukrainians] and he would be sunk anywhere else." Cecil-Smith also "criticised the dilly-dally, sloppy methods used in conducting the City Committee meetings."[130] Such statements make it clear why the CPC leadership may not have considered him a sufficiently loyal party member.

Cecil-Smith was very involved in the new *Clarion*'s design and was finally credited for his work in the newspaper's masthead. Although he had a credited editorial position in both *Masses* and *Soviet Russia Today*, his editing work for the *Worker* and the *Daily Clarion* had been uncredited since 1931. Eight years later, he was finally a named editor for the party's official newspaper, when the *Weekly Clarion* debuted on Dominion Day 1939. The new publication was handsomely illustrated with more black and white photographs than its predecessor, perhaps inspired by *Life*, a popular magazine created by Cecil-Smith's fellow Chefooite Henry Luce. The *Weekly Clarion* was eighteen pages, to the previous daily's eight, and contained the news, comics, sports, and women's section of its predecessor with the addition of a magazine section. Pat Forkin, a long-time journalist for the CPC who had recently travelled to the Soviet Union for tuberculosis treatment, wrote longer and more colourful reports from Moscow as he explored life in the "Workers' Paradise." Norman Bethune, by that time working with Mao Zedong's Eighth Route Army in China, provided an article for the first edition and a short story for the second.[131] Cecil-Smith began writing more, enjoying the analysis permitted by magazine-length articles to his earlier work as a beat reporter. Retrospectives by Cecil-Smith or the other veterans of the Spanish Civil War were not included in these features, which seems to have been a missed opportunity.

Cecil-Smith's first magazine-length feature in the *Clarion* was an optimistic assessment of China's resistance against Japan.[132] He argued that Japan's industrial, military, and financial resources were taxed to the breaking point. Making reference to the writings of Mao, he explained that the Chinese war was entering the second of three phases. The first phase was characterized by rapid Japanese gains and Chinese withdrawals. The Red Army had avoided confrontation wherever possible in order to preserve its forces. The second phase would see the tide turn as the Japanese became exhausted and the Red Army guerrillas attacked them wherever they were weakest. The Japanese were trying to delay the onset of the second stage by isolating the Red Army from external support, pushing Europeans out of China and elsewhere in Asia, and starving the Chinese people. A third phase would follow when the Japanese were sufficiently weakened and the time was right for a general offensive by the Red Army.[133] Cecil-Smith made similar comments about the situation in China at a public meeting later that month, highlighting the poor treatment of Western missionaries at the hands of the Japanese.[134]

Cecil-Smith's wife, Lilian Gouge, also maintained a strong interest in events in China. She still had contacts within the missionary community, having worked for several years as the secretary at the China Inland Mission's headquarters in Toronto, and her family recalls that she avidly read about events in China even into old age.[135] She was more than a passive observer. In February 1939, she was appointed national director of the Friends of China Society, although we do not know what exactly her responsibilities were. The organization may have been created to support the China Aid Committee, the organization created in New York to send Bethune to China, or may have been completely separate from that mission. The only record of Gouge's involvement in this group is a single entry in Cecil-Smith's RCMP file noting that Gouge had spoken briefly at a meeting for the party's Ward 3 Committee.[136]

The historical record on Gouge herself is vague. We know that she was an early member of the Progressive Arts Club and an actor for the Workers' Theatre, performing for workers during the Stratford Furniture Strike and in *Eight Men Speak*. It is possible that she is the "Lil" who wrote a column for the *Worker* titled "With Our Women, in Sport and Play," but this is merely speculation.[137] The rest of her life remains a mystery. We do not even know if she joined the party, or was simply a quiet supporter of Cecil-Smith's activities. The latter would have been in line with the expectations for the wives of party members at the time.[138] Gouge is similarly absent from the records regarding the Friends of the Mackenzie-Papineau Battalion, which often note the involvement of the volunteers' wives. Thankfully, a notable exception to this dearth of information is found in two letters written by her pen pal in China: Norman Bethune.

By the summer of 1939, Bethune was with Mao's Eighth Route Army in Ho Chia Chung in West Hebei province. Bethune operated on wounded soldiers and helped with preventative medicine initiatives for soldiers and locals alike. At the same time, he was pushing to develop a capability for the Red Army beyond his own two hands. He believed that this was the best way to help the Chinese people. In an update to the party back in Canada, he wrote that "the number of Chinese capable of carrying on by themselves ... is the indication of the worth of foreign units."[139] He wrote a guide on mobile medical units, *The Organization and Technique for Divisional Mobile Units*, and established a medical school. He received supplies from a local Anglican missionary, whose mission house was burned by the Japanese for her trouble, but needed more supplies and money for the school to be a success.[140]

Bethune concluded his letter to the party with a personal appeal. In the postscript, he added a note addressed to Tim Buck:

> P.S. Dear Tim
>
> No letter or word from you in 1 or 1 1/2 years. I sent Lilian a cable in spring this year from Beijing. She could come through there. No reply. I am returning this winter.[141]

The "Lilian" referenced in the letter is not mentioned in any of the other letters reviewed by historian Larry Hannant in his collection of Bethune's writings, nor is she mentioned in Roderick and Sharon Stewart's authoritative biography of Bethune, *Phoenix.* Yet she was clearly important to Bethune. She meant enough to him that he wanted her to join him in China. He also saw it as appropriate to mention this to the party leader himself, and he understood that Buck would know who "Lilian" was, despite not providing her full name or any other context. "Lilian" was Lilian Gouge, Cecil-Smith's wife.

Gouge received a personal letter from Bethune later that summer. He explained that he was returning to Canada to raise the funds he needed to continue his operations. His training school for 200 doctors needed $1000 a month to function, and, although he was aware that money was being raised, "I don't know where the money from Canada and America is going." He enclosed two photographs with his letter (see the photo section of this book). One was a portrait of himself, on the back of which he wrote, "To Lil, with love from Beth. Hong Kong. Feb. 6/38." The second was a photo with him sitting next to Mao. The photo of Bethune and Mao together is the only known copy of this photo, and Bethune saw fit to send it to Gouge.[142]

The content and language of the letter indicates that Gouge and Bethune had a close personal relationship. Bethune addressed the letter to "darling," refers to himself as "your old man," and closes with, "Goodbye, darling Lil."[143] Bethune was writing to Gouge as part of what seems to have been part of a campaign to have her join him in China. He expressed concern that he had not heard from her since he received her last letter in January 1939. He says that he had sent other letters, from Beijing and Yunnan province, but assumed that they did not make it through because he had not received a reply. Bethune wrote that the letters he sent from Beijing had been directing her to join him in Beijing, although he now planned to return to Canada by January 1940, and so he directed that Gouge should instead wait for him in Canada and return to China with him afterwards.[144] Given that she did not have any medical training, language skills, or connections in China that would have made her particularly useful on a medical mission to China, it seems clear that Bethune did not want Gouge to join him for practical reasons. Bethune wanted her companionship.

Bethune and Gouge did not see each other again: Bethune died before he was able to leave for Canada. In November, while performing surgery on a wounded Red Army soldier, not far from the front lines while the fighting with the Japanese raged, Bethune cut his hand with a surgical instrument. The cut became infected and he grew weaker and weaker until he finally expired on 12 November 1939.[145]

As he lay dying, Bethune dictated a will to his translator, Pan Fan.[146] In it, he bade farewell to his family and noted that his two years in China had been the most meaningful of his life. He directed the China Aid Council in New York to take care of his ex-wife, Frances Penney, and set out to whom he wanted to leave some of his personal effects:

> Another Japanese blanket, give to Paracistela
> In a small box there is a bigger silver ring, which Dr. Brown gave me, it should be mailed to Margaret in Canada. Tim Buck knows her address.
> I have two new pairs of straw-made shoes, never worn, they should be given to Phillip Clark.
> The larger Japanese flag, give to Lilian.[147]

Bethune may not have had many items with him at the front, living the Spartan lifestyle of a field surgeon, but what he had he wanted to go to those whom he cared about.

Bethune left items to "Paracistela" – almost certainly Paraskeva Clark, an error attributable to difficulties with transliteration – the artist with whom he had had an affair. Her husband, Phillip, also earned a place in the will. "Dr. Brown" was Dr. Richard Brown, a young Canadian doctor with the Methodist Mission Hospital in Hankow who briefly worked with Bethune. Brown's ring was meant for "Margaret," likely Margaret Day, a young woman whom Bethune had wanted to marry in 1936. She had refused him, although she was pregnant, and she had begged him to perform an abortion. With a heavy heart, he conducted the procedure shortly before departing for Spain.[148] Gouge, therefore, found herself in good company. Although he had little to give away, she had been in Bethune's thoughts in his last days, alongside his ex-wife and two ex-lovers.

Bethune's past behaviour and his letter to Gouge hints at the possibility of a romantic relationship. Judging from what remains of Bethune's letters, she was the only woman he tried to entice to join him in China, and one of the very few he thought about as he lay on his deathbed. She clearly meant a lot to him. Bethune was certainly known for womanizing, and he had not let marriage – either his own or the woman's – stand in his way before. But consider Adrienne Clarkson's comments on Bethune's relationships with women:

> There were many women in Bethune's life – and he loved some of them – but womanizing was not something that preoccupied him. If women threw themselves in his way, he availed himself of them as emergency sexual rations. He loved women, but he didn't attempt to conquer them. His friend Libby Park, who worked with him in the Montreal Group for the Security of People's Health, said that she liked his attitude towards women because he didn't have stereotyped male attitudes about them; to him, a woman was a person with a mind and personality. If he was arguing with a woman, he never made allowances for her sex, and if he disagreed, he didn't do so with a condescending attitude.[149]

This kind of friendship would have been appealing to the feisty Gouge. They were both intelligent people with shared interests in art, literature, and international affairs, not to mention the bond that must have developed between the surgeon and his patient. A romance between the two is possible, but there is no incontrovertible evidence for it. It is just as likely that the two were platonic friends, intrigued by the other's wit and intellect.

Whatever happened between Bethune and Gouge, it does not seem to have affected her marriage to Cecil-Smith. They may have confronted whatever transpired, or they may have simply ignored it. Cecil-Smith knew about the letters and, by the family's account, he and Gouge had a happy marriage in the years after his return from Spain.[150]

While also following the news in Asia, Cecil-Smith was growing increasingly concerned about unfolding events in Europe. He was certain that a wider European war was coming. From his point of view, Germany and Italy had already been at war for years in Spain. When the world watched Germany annex Austria in March 1938, Cecil-Smith was watching German and Italian aircraft and tanks support the Nationalists in the Aragon Offensive. When Chamberlain betrayed Czechoslovakia that September, Cecil-Smith was recovering in the hospital from his leg wound. Then in April 1939, as he concluded his speaking tour, he watched Madrid fall to the Nationalist forces while the international community did nothing. When he returned to Canada in February, he had predicted that a broader war would begin by April or June.[151] In July, he revised his prediction to August.[152] And, indeed, by that month, the Nazis were poised to invade Poland.

How could war be avoided? And how could the Soviet Union be preserved from Nazi aggression – an important question for Cecil-Smith and his peers. The right alliances were critical. Russia's strong diplomatic relationship with France had been essential to Russia's defence in the First World War. The Soviet Union and France again entered into alliance, the Franco-Soviet Treaty of Mutual Assistance, ratified by both parties in 1936, forcing Germany to deal with the risk of fighting a two-front war again. The Soviet Union also sought to forge a new arrangement with the British, a relationship of which Cecil-Smith was very supportive. Years earlier, Cecil-Smith would have likely written an article on the matter for *Soviet Russia Today* and engaged in lobbying efforts through the Friends of the Soviet Union. However, that organization had been moribund since 1938.[153] Cecil-Smith instead wrote articles in the *Clarion* on the matter.

He wrote about the virtues of the Soviet Union, trying to promote the Soviets as an excellent ally for the British Empire. In an article in early August 1939, he wrote about the superiority of the Soviet Navy. He described their proud naval tradition, their growing industrial base, the strength of their ports and fortifications, and the modern character of their ships and sailors. This was all to say that the British Empire would be stronger for uniting with the Soviets in the face of Nazi aggression. Cecil-Smith concluded his article saying, "This great naval strength in the interests of peace and democracy gives another impetus to the demand that the Chamberlain government hesitate no longer, but at once sign this Anglo-French-Soviet treaty against aggression, guaranteeing not only the great powers but also the small Baltic nations from fascism."[154]

This proposed treaty never came to be. A different, and much more unexpected, pact was instituted instead. On 23 August, the Soviet Union signed a non-aggression pact with Germany. This agreement was shocking – the homeland of socialism had entered into an agreement with its ideological antithesis. The agreement was clearly born of self-interest, given that the Soviet Union was not prepared to wage war against Germany. The 3 September edition of the *Clarion* was filled with articles justifying and applauding the agreement. The paper claimed that China applauded the agreement because it weakened the relationship between Germany and Japan.[155] The *Clarion* made the further dubious claim that the Baltic states were thrilled with the development, as it paved the way for their independence.[156] Buck explained that the non-aggression pact was a diplomatic masterstroke. It had split the Axis, he claimed, and had prevented war. Germany had been on the verge of invading Poland prior to the agreement, but would not dare to do so now.[157] Obviously, Buck was wrong. By the time the article went to press, Germany had already invaded Poland.

Chapter Fourteen

A Second Anti-Fascist War

As we have seen, Cecil-Smith had not always been a dutiful adherent to the directives of the Communist Party of Canada. He had picked a fight with Stanley Ryerson in the pages of *Masses*. He had been kicked off the staff of the *Daily Clarion* for some kind of personal conflict. He had not worked well with the commissars in Spain and had been chastised for his individualism. Members had been dismissed for less, but the party seemed to accept Cecil-Smith and his idiosyncrasies, excused, perhaps, because of his military exploits in the Spanish Civil War. But Cecil-Smith again ran afoul the party's leadership during the Second World War, when he publicly disagreed with its policies with respect to the war.[1] He continued to write in support of the Soviet Union and worked with the party-affiliated Canadian Seamen's Union, but this latest disagreement marked the beginning of the end of his relationship with the party.

On 1 September 1939, Cecil-Smith and his wife, Lilian Gouge, were out to see the pictures at the Embassy Theatre on Yonge Street. A newspaper hawker selling the *Globe and Mail* announced the news of the day: Germany had invaded Poland. Neither Britain nor Canada had declared war, but it seemed inevitable. The anti-fascist war that Cecil-Smith believed was coming had finally arrived. Gouge looked at Cecil-Smith and asked, "Are you going to enlist now or wait until after the show?"[2] For Cecil-Smith, the Second World War was part of the same conflict that had played out in Spain. Within days, he had told the *Toronto Star* that he would fight in the Second World War because it was a war against "the same thing we fought in Spain. Certainly Spanish fascism was only second to German nazism and I am 100 percent convinced that we have to get rid of this thing, nazism, once and for all."[3] The party's central leadership in Toronto held the same opinion in the opening days of the war.

Cecil-Smith tried to enlist in the Canadian military on 4 September, the day after Britain declared war. He reported to the Fort York Armouries to join the Royal Regiment of Canada, an infantry regiment, but offered his services "in any capacity whatever."[4] The military was already taking recruits, but there were plenty of volunteers and, despite his experience, Cecil-Smith was not the ideal recruit. He was thirty-six years old (thirty-seven was considered too old), married, and was not in particularly good health: he wore thick glasses and had a variety of war wounds. Perhaps not surprisingly, he was turned away. He then took a different approach to offering his services.

It was obvious to Cecil-Smith that Canada would declare war shortly and begin mobilizing forces for Europe. This mobilization process, however, would be slow, too slow for Canada to get soldiers to Poland in time for it to make a difference. Cecil-Smith thought that the Mac-Paps – as the only body of recent combat veterans in Canada – could be ready to go to Poland almost immediately. He wrote to Defence Minister Ian Mackenzie and offered to lead the battalion once more.[5] He thought that the returned volunteers could muster 1,000 soldiers (a rather optimistic estimate).

Cecil-Smith was not the only one who thought the resurrection of the Mac-Paps was a good idea. Seemingly independent of Cecil-Smith's letter, the *Mid-West Clarion* published a letter from Bill Kardash, a Lenin School graduate and tank crewman at Fuentes de Ebro, requesting that Cecil-Smith "offer our assistance to the military authorities of Canada, stating our readiness to enrol in the expeditionary force and to go overseas to participate actively in smashing fascist aggression and thus save democracy for the peoples of the world."[6]

Not surprisingly, the minister politely declined Cecil-Smith's offer to lead the Mac-Paps into battle. Unlike in the Boer War and the First World War, there would be no privately raised battalions, and certainly none with any attachment to the Communist Party of Canada. Mackenzie simply responded, "Please convey to the members of your battalion my very sincere appreciation of their offer."[7] It was, he explained, simply too early in the war to make such decisions. The RCMP noted that Cecil-Smith had been "severely reprimanded" for making his offer without party approval.[8]

The RCMP were gravely concerned that Cecil-Smith was organizing a quiet infiltration of the Canadian military by members of the CPC. An RCMP report on 9 September 1939 noted that "returned Spanish volunteers in fit condition have been advised to offer their service to the militia. In case of acceptance they are to report to E.C. Smith. Those who are members of the Y.C.L. [Young Communist League] or C.P. [Communist

Party] must first report ... and military units to join will be suggested in order 'to assure a number of progressives in each unit.'"[9] The party's new strategy, the RCMP believed, was to "join [the military] in large numbers and wherever possible ... to create discontent and disorder in the armed forces when an opportune time arrives."[10] Although it does seem likely that the party would have wanted to keep a record of which members had joined which Canadian military units, and Cecil-Smith would have been the natural person to keep track of the volunteers, there is nothing to suggest that the party had any nefarious intentions at this time. In early September 1939, the goals of the Canadian government and the Communist Party of Canada were aligned: the defence of Europe against the advance of Nazi Germany.

Cecil-Smith was adamant that the Western powers had to do something quickly to defend Poland from Nazi aggression. He wrote an article on the subject for the *Clarion* – "Western Front Still All Too Quiet; Poles Bearing Main Brunt" – where he provided a detailed analysis of the situation in Poland.[11] He described Germany's *blitzkrieg* tactics, which he had experienced himself in the Aragon Offensive, although in Poland the German army had achieved greater effects by massing their tanks than distributing them in support of the infantry, as Franco had elected.[12] Cecil-Smith explained that the Polish government might have no choice but to enter into a separate peace with Germany if England and France did not act quickly. The only way to stop Germany was to help Poland by launching a concerted ground offensive against Germany within the next two to three days, a clear impossibility.[13] For Cecil-Smith, the war was about saving Poland and crushing Nazism in its homeland. Nazism was an existential threat to both democracy and communism. The Western powers could not afford to dither any longer.

On 18 September, Cecil-Smith again returned to the Fort York Armouries to try to enlist.[14] Canada had declared war on 10 September and would be sending forces to England. He was rejected for being short-sighted – he commented wryly, "I think they were referring to my eyesight"[15] – but he was undeterred. He memorized the eye chart that night and went to a different recruiting station the next day.[16] He passed the test and found himself back where his Canadian military service had begun. He was again a sapper in the 2nd Field Company of the Royal Canadian Engineers.[17]

Cecil-Smith's unit, like most of the Canadian military, had been ordered to expand at an explosive rate. The 2nd Field Company was only fifty soldiers strong at the beginning of September, but it was ordered to mobilize and grow to a 242-man organization.[18] About half of those soldiers were recruited by the time Cecil-Smith joined, but training was difficult. The company initially had to run its own training, but very few of their soldiers had the specialized skills that a wartime engineer company needed.[19] The company only had one instructor from the Permanent Force.[20] Consequently, Cecil-Smith's recent combat experience and previous training as a sapper proved to be especially valuable. He helped run classes for the soldiers and was often seen coaching the junior soldiers and telling them stories around camp at the Canadian National Exhibition grounds in the evenings after training.

When Cecil-Smith joined the Canadian military, the CPC had been in favour of the war effort against Nazi Germany. The party supported Britain's declaration of war against Germany: "This is our war," Buck told the annual Hungarian picnic in Delhi, Ontario.[21] When Canada declared war a week later, Buck wrote to Prime Minister Mackenzie King and pledged the party's support for the war effort and solidarity with the Polish people.[22] In the 16 September edition of the *Clarion*, Buck declared that the party was aligned with anti-fascist forces everywhere.[23] However, the party quickly changed its position.

On 17 September – the day before Cecil-Smith first tried to enlist – the Soviet Union invaded Poland from the east. The Soviet Union and Germany had carved Eastern Europe into tranches. The Soviet Union's invasion was presented to its devotees as a military imperative – to build a buffer between German and Soviet territory – and also as liberation of oppressed Slavs in eastern Poland. Even the most devout Communists must have had their doubts. Then, on 24 September, the Comintern informed the Communist Party of Canada that its position toward the war had fundamentally changed: the war effort against Germany was now deemed to be an imperialist endeavour, not an anti-fascist crusade. Communists everywhere were directed to oppose their country's march to war.[24] Cecil-Smith rejected the directive, still believing that the Second World War was fundamentally an anti-fascist war.

Cecil-Smith remained a supporter of the CPC and the Soviet Union, but he saw the change in policy as a betrayal of the Polish people. In Spain, the Soviet Union was not directly involved in the conflict but still supported the Spanish people by organizing the International Brigades and sending weapons and supplies. Perhaps the USSR could have done more to support the Spanish people in their war against fascism, but at least it had done *something* while the other Western powers watched the fascists dismantle the Spanish Republic. Now, with the British Empire finally fighting fascism, why would the Soviet Union prohibit support for a war for the liberation of Poland? Why was Poland less important than Spain? Cecil-Smith believed that both the British Empire and the Soviet Union should come to Poland's aid.

Cecil-Smith appeared to be contributing positively to the war effort. His company commander, Major T.F. Howlett, was pleased with his work and had promoted him to lance corporal. There was no indication that Cecil-Smith had been the source of any "trouble" within the company. However, the RCMP and the senior military leadership were concerned about Communists among the volunteers. The commander of the forces destined for England, Major-General Andrew McNaughton, warned Prime Minister King that he had misgivings about the volunteers. He described the soldiers' loyalty as "an unknown quantity" and warned King that they were "largely dissatisfied men with Communistic tendencies."[25] The RCMP shared this concern and believed that Cecil-Smith would play a role in causing trouble.[26] RCMP sources reported rumours of an attempted takeover of the Royal Canadian Engineers. Victor Dunn, a party member and known acquaintance of Cecil-Smith, had been overheard stating in October 1939 that the Engineers were "almost ours [the Party's] already."[27] Cecil-Smith and the No. 2 Field Company therefore attracted the Mounties' particular attention.

The RCMP informed Cecil-Smith's chain of command of his political background. In late September, V.A.M. Kemp, the RCMP officer commanding for Toronto and environs, visited the local military commander to provide a briefing on the matter. Kemp recommended that Cecil-Smith merely be monitored for the time being. If volunteers like Cecil-Smith were immediately discharged, "there is a definite fear that they will enlist under assumed names at other points and continue their activities without our knowledge."[28] The RCMP continued to monitor Cecil-Smith and other party members in the military and maintained contact with their chains of command. In late November, Constable R.J. Smith of the RCMP visited Major Howlett to follow-up on the matter. The constable recorded that Howlett was "aware that Smith is a Communist, [and] was surprised that he has been such a model outstanding Soldier. Between parades, and in the evening, Smith will have a group of green men around him, teaching them his knowledge on the different lines of Army life and work, of which he has a wonderful knowledge. Since being in the Army, he has cultivated a large group of good friends and supporters. Any trouble which has arisen amongst the men, he has taken no part in it."[29]

In spite of Cecil-Smith's "exemplary" record, on 23 November, the intelligence officer for the local military command met with V.A.M. Kamp to inform him that they intended to discharge Cecil-Smith "forthwith."[30] The report does not disclose any particular action by Cecil-Smith that might have necessitated his discharge, beyond this general distrust. A few weeks later, the RCMP identified Cecil-Smith on a list of "known radicals and agitators" who had joined the army. They provided the list to the military and informed them that individuals on the list should not be permitted to proceed overseas or to receive any additional training.[31]

The RCMP recorded on 7 December 1939 that Cecil-Smith had been discharged from the military for "subversive activities"; however, there is no corroborating records in the military's files.[32] In fact, neither the company's war diary nor Cecil-Smith's service file provide any indication that he had been subject to any disciplinary action whatsoever, that he had been involved in subversive activities of any kind, or, indeed, that any such "trouble" had occurred within No. 2 Field Company at all. It seems unlikely that this "subversive activity" actually happened. Furthermore, Cecil-Smith was still in the military on 7 December, and no proceedings, disciplinary or administrative, had been undertaken to remove him.[33] He was discharged from the military, but it was an honourable discharge arising from his poor eyesight. He had a follow-up medical examination on 15 December and failed his eye examination; his eyesight was too poor for overseas service or home defence.[34] It is unclear why the RCMP believed that Cecil-Smith had already been discharged, but it is obvious that the RCMP and the military were not coordinating their activities as closely as one might expect.

Cecil-Smith was not actually discharged from the military until 4 January 1940. In the meantime, he gave an interview to the *Toronto Star* where he condemned a recent statement by the Veterans of the Abraham Lincoln Brigade: the American Spanish Civil War veterans had formally supported the United States' position of neutrality in the Second World War. Cecil-Smith disagreed with their position and condemned the idea of neutrality in any war against a fascist power. He told the *Star* that many of the Mac-Paps had joined the Canadian military, and some were already in England.[35] Cecil-Smith was, in effect, publicly disagreeing with the Comintern and the CPC's position on the Second World War, even as he prepared to leave the military.

The RCMP took steps to ensure that Cecil-Smith did not re-enlist under an assumed name. Superintendent E.D. Bavin, the force's intelligence officer, directed all of the divisional commanding officers to be on the lookout for Cecil-Smith. Bavin provided a physical description and attached a photograph for good measure.[36] Cecil-Smith did not attempt to re-enlist. After he had served in the uniforms of the Shanghai Volunteer Corps, the Canadian Non-Permanent Active Militia, the Spanish Republican Army, and the Canadian Active Service Force, Cecil-Smith's unique military career had come to an end.

Although Cecil-Smith disagreed with the CPC's position on the Second World War, he had not completely severed his relationship from the party, even while he served in the military. In October 1940, the RCMP learned that Cecil-Smith was a district organizer for a union with close ties to the party: the Canadian Seamen's Union (CSU).[37] Although the organization was a legitimate union that strived to improve working conditions for its members, much of its senior leadership were party members, and the RCMP considered it to be a party front and monitored it closely. The CSU's party connection was especially worrisome, given that the union held immense control over a key wartime industry – shipping on the Great Lakes – and the party had taken a position against the Canadian war effort. As the governor of the Canadian Brotherhood of Ships' Employees (a competing union that did not have an affiliation with the party) wrote to the minister of national defence, Ian Mackenzie, "Concentration camps in Canada to-day hold confined many persons who have not and could not create the destructive sabotage action this Canadian Seamen's Union is capable of doing, and promote the efforts against Canada's war interests ... Such persons who make threats of this kind should not have their liberty to execute them and especially as they are not Canadians and under the domination and authority of foreign powers."[38] The writer provided a list of the CSU leadership at the national and branch level. Cecil-Smith was listed as the regional secretary on the union's Lakehead Council, as well as a delegate to the Trades and Labor Council in Toronto.[39] The RCMP concluded that Cecil-Smith's "association with this Union would indicate that he is still a member in good standing of the Communist Party."[40]

The CSU's motto was "Every Seaman an Organizer," but there simply were not enough seamen with the experience or inclination to organize their ships for a successful strike, and it was illegal for a labour organizer to go aboard a ship without permission. The union needed to infiltrate shipping crews with experienced labour organizers – in other words, organizers had to become seamen.[41] The RCMP noted that party members were seeking jobs on Great Lakes steamers during the spring of 1940.[42] One such member – Peter Hunter, the Lenin School graduate and former recruiter for the International Brigades – was directed to get a job as a sailor, join the union, and start organizing for a strike even though he had never worked a day in his life on a ship.[43] Cecil-Smith similarly got a job on the *Renvoyle*, a Midland-registered Canada Steamship Lines ship.[44] Although he was not a career seaman, he was better situated than Hunter, given his experience as a machinist and a recreational sailor. Party members like Cecil-Smith and Hunter were among the 6,000 seamen that struck on 14 April 1940. The CSU brought trade on the Great Lakes to a halt. Two hundred ships rested idle at their docks.

The *Renvoyle,* one of these two hundred ships, sat at its berth in the harbour at the end of Toronto's Bay Street while Cecil-Smith and others organized picketing of the ship and of Canada Steamship Lines' head office.[45] The company was eager to begin the navigation season after the break-up of the winter ice. Five days after the strike began, they started hiring strikebreakers on Friday, 19 April, with the goal of setting sail the next day. Non-union longshoreman loaded the ship on Friday while non-union stokers kept the engine under steam.[46] Canada Steamship Lines had nearly two hundred applicants to work on its ships before noon the next day, and so the *Renvoyle* was able to set sail without Cecil-Smith and its other striking crew members. The ship departed nearly on schedule and reached Hamilton, on its way to the Upper Lakes, before the end of the day.[47]

Although Canada Steamship Lines had managed to crew one ship on the Great Lakes, with two more likely setting sail the next day, the CSU's strike had put significant pressure on the company such that they were willing to concede to some of the union's demands. The CSU voted to return to work the same day the *Renvoyle* set sail. The seamen received a wage increase of $7.50 per month – it was an improvement but only half of their initial demand – and other concessions regarding improved safety equipment.[48] Picketing continued, but onboard the ships so that the sailors could return to work and the companies could continue their operations.[49]

The day after the CSU voted to return to work, the RCMP observed Cecil-Smith attending a union meeting at the Labor Lyceum on Spadina Avenue in Toronto.[50] All of the key players for the CSU were present: Pat Sullivan, the president; Jack Chapman, the secretary-treasurer; Fred Collins, a labour organizer who had also played a key role in the Stratford furniture workers' strike in 1933; and William "Lon" Lawson, Jean Watts's husband and the capitalist judge in *Eight Men Speak*. The RCMP did not know what the meeting was about, but it almost certainly related to the strike and next steps.

The Canadian Seamen's Union strike of 1940 was viewed by many as an attack on the Canadian war effort. The union had legitimate grievances, and its 1938 contract was due to expire in the spring of 1940; it had been preparing for a possible strike since before Germany invaded Poland.[51] However, the role of the CPC in organizing the strike, and the timing and ultimate effect of the action on trade gave the impression that the strike was the "destructive sabotage" about which the governor of the Canadian Brotherhood of Ships' Employees had warned the RCMP. Canada was the breadbasket of the British Empire – it was imperative to the war effort that Canadian wheat and other supplies arrived in the United Kingdom. This chain had almost been cut during the First World War by the German use of unrestricted submarine warfare; now a strike, organized by a union with close ties to the Communist Party of Canada, had cut the chain again by shutting down shipping on the Great Lakes just as Germany invaded Norway and Denmark. Worse yet, an RCMP informant reported that the party saw the strike as a trial for other labour activities to disrupt the war effort.[52] The RCMP also believed that the party would use the ships to smuggle Communist propaganda into Canada and would relay shipping manifests and timetables for purposes of sabotage.[53] None of these allegations were ever confirmed, but they certainly reinforced the RCMP's deeply held suspicion of the party and the CSU.

In spite of the RCMP's view of such organizations, the Canadian government did not suspend their normal civil liberties at the outbreak of the war. The CPC leadership had gone underground in anticipation of such action, but Mackenzie King did not take such steps until the war escalated in June 1940. At the time, Canada's commitment to the war effort had been limited to mobilizing the 1st Canadian Infantry Division – which included Cecil-Smith's No. 2 Field Company – and committing to run the British Commonwealth Air Training Plan. Through May and June, however, it was clear that Canada's contribution would have to grow, commensurate to the crisis in Europe. Germany had invaded France and the Low Countries on 10 May. The German *blitzkrieg,* tested in the Aragon Offensive in Spain, pierced the British and French defences. The British Expeditionary Force had evacuated France through Dunkirk by 3 June, and German forces occupied Paris on the 14th. The Mackenzie King government then took extraordinary steps to mobilize its resources, passing the National Resources Mobilization Act later that month, and restricting civil liberties under the Defence of Canada Regulations.

Less than five years after Mackenzie King repealed section 98 of the Criminal Code, which had outlawed the CPC, the escalation of the war provided the impetus for again banning the party and most of its front organizations. Fifteen organizations were banned by order-in-council PC2363 in June 1940, including the Communist Party of Canada, along with the Young Communist League, the Canadian Labor Defense League, the Canadian League for Peace and Democracy, and a number of left-leaning cultural groups such as the Ukrainian Labor-Farmer Temple Association, the Finnish Organization of Canada, the Russian Workers and Farmers Club, the Croatian Cultural Association, the

Hungarian Workers' Club, the Polish People's Association, and the Canadian Ukrainian Youth Federation.[54] Participating in these outlawed organizations was now an illegal act, but unlike under section 98, violators of the Defence of Canada Regulations were arrested, charged, and interned without a public trial. Prisoners were sent to internment camps run by the military. In total, 133 people were interned for their membership in the CPC.[55]

It is unclear why Cecil-Smith was not arrested and interned. He would seem to have been a likely candidate, given his politics, his military training, the RCMP's belief that he had recently been discharged from the military for subversive activities, and his continuing involvement with a union that the Mounties believed was deliberately undermining the war effort. As recently as early May, Cecil-Smith had told an RCMP informant that he was doing trade union work and was expecting "some orders to come through shortly regarding party activity."[56] Other Mac-Paps were interned, including William Beeching, Bob Kerr, and Alec Miller[57] – yet Cecil-Smith's RCMP file gives no indication that he was ever under any serious consideration for internment. There are a few possible explanations. He may have discontinued his involvement with the party at the appropriate time as a result of his various disagreements with it or because he feared arrest in wartime. Regardless, a note in Cecil-Smith's RCMP file in September 1941 states that he seemed to have stopped his party work, aside from his work with the Canadian Seamen's Union.[58] We can only guess that the RCMP considered Cecil-Smith to be too dangerous to be allowed in the army but not so dangerous that his activities were a threat to Canada and the war effort.

The CSU remained legal, but much of its leadership was interned for their continued involvement with the party. Pat Sullivan, David Sinclair, Charles Murray, Joseph Cline, and Jack Chapman were soon in internment camps, along with the entire editorial staff of the Canadian Seamen's Union newsletter, *Searchlight*.[59] Minister of Justice Ernest Lapointe said that these individuals had not been arrested for their union work but rather for their membership in the CPC.[60] Cecil-Smith was still sailing on the *Renvoyle* during the summer of 1940, but he was brought in to replace the interned editor the following summer and to take charge of the union's educational programs and pamphlets.[61] The RCMP immediately noted Cecil-Smith's appointment. One report noted that "it is assumed that the 'Searchlight' will now take a more Communistic line in its editorials."[62]

The CPC's stance on the Second World War fundamentally changed the same summer that Cecil-Smith began editing *Searchlight*. The 1939

Non-Aggression Pact between Germany and the Soviet Union came to an abrupt end when Hitler invaded Russia in June 1941. The Soviet Union and Canada were now on the same side in the war. Whatever Canadians thought of Marx, Engels, or Lenin, the truth was that Russian cooperation was essential to victory in Europe. Stalin sent a trade delegation to Ottawa within a few weeks, and diplomatic relations commenced one year later, despite concerns that the Soviet Union would use its consular offices as a front for espionage or revolutionary activity.* The Comintern directed the world's Communist Parties to agitate for greater war efforts in their home countries.

The CPC's response to the war changed overnight. It declared that the conflict was no longer imperialist; it was an anti-fascist war. Thus, the party flip-flopped for the second time and became one of the most vocal promoters of the Canadian war effort. Tim Buck and the other party leaders who had been hiding in the United States returned to Canada. They served a token period in the internment camps but were soon released and permitted the re-enter political life under the banner of the Labor-Progressive Party. The Communist Party of Canada remained illegal – Canada was the only country to maintain this ban throughout its wartime alliance with Russia – but this had little practical effect on the party's ability to function as a political party and advocate for the war effort.[63] Party members enlisted in the military in droves. When Mackenzie King called a plebiscite on the introduction of conscription in 1942, the CPC organized "Tim Buck Plebiscite Committees" to advocate for a "yes" vote. It clamoured for the opening of a "second front" against Germany to relieve pressure on the Soviet Union, and pushed unions to agree to "no strike" pledges for the duration of the war. Cecil-Smith was not active with the party at this point, but he still believed in both the workers' struggle and the correctness of the Soviet Union. Shortly after the German invasion, he wrote articles to promote the value of the Soviet Union as an ally.

* Concerns regarding Soviet spying proved to be correct. Igor Gouzenko, a Soviet cipher clerk at the Russian Embassy in Ottawa, defected to Canadian authorities in September 1945 and provided details on a Soviet network in Canada and the United States established over the course of the Second World War. See Honourable Mr. Justice Robert Taschereau and Honourable Mr. Justice R.L. Kellock, Commissioners, *The Report of the Royal Commission to Investigate the Facts relating to and the Circumstances Surrounding the Communication, by Public Officials and Other Persons in Positions of Trust of Secret and Confidential Information to Agents of a Foreign Power* (Ottawa: Printers to the King's Most Excellent Majesty, 27 June 1946).

He wrote a series of articles about the strength of the Red Army, which were carried by the Canadian Press: "Red Officers Know Their Job," "Soviet Fire Power Great," "Long War Basis of Red Tactics," "Russians Favour 'Elastic' Line," and "'Break Through' Is Emphasized as Offensive Defensive Tactic."[64] In doing so, he drew on his experiences with the Red Army advisers in Spain. He tried to show that the Soviet Union was an ally worth supporting, both powerful and reliable. Cecil-Smith's articles on the Red Army were noted by the RCMP, especially by the force in Quebec. Detective Inspector C.W. Harvison, the officer commanding in Quebec, wrote to Commissioner Wood about the articles by an author "well known to you as a member of the C.P. of C ... a sympathizer with extreme left if not Communistic activities." Although Canada and the Soviet Union were now allied in the war, Harvison wrote that the articles were "highly favourable to the RED army," and "it is more than doubtful whether any good is done, particularly in this province, by indiscriminate praise of RUSSIANS as such." Articles such as these were dangerous, the report concluded, because they were most useful as pro-Communist propaganda, or would at least be perceived as such in Quebec, and could have a negative effect on recruiting in Quebec and hamper the war effort.[65]

Concurrent with writing these articles, Cecil-Smith wrote a more detailed book about the Soviet Union: *Red Ally: An Estimate of Soviet Life and Soviet Power*.[66] The book did not mention his experiences with the Red Army advisers in Spain. In fact, he did not mention his service in Spain at all, although book reviews at the time indicate that this was sufficiently common knowledge that it perhaps did not have to be stated outright.[67] Cecil-Smith completed the book in September 1941, noting that he had been disappointed in the media's failure to educate the Canadian public regarding the USSR since they had entered the war. His main objective in writing the book was "to show that Russia is not a great secret land, as most people believe. I refer you to your public library where you will read plenty written from either side. The reader can make up his own mind. The time has surely come when we should try to understand the Soviet Union, even if we do not endorse everything they have done in the past. The war demands this of us."[68] Cecil-Smith's text provided a very positive depiction of the Soviet Union, but he did not offer excuses for its occupation of eastern Poland in 1939 or the Winter War against Finland in 1939–40.

Cecil-Smith wrote that most Canadians knew as little about the Soviet Union as they did about the moon.[69] To counter such ignorance, he provided a brief description of the country's history and geography, highlighting its immense size and wealth in natural resources. Yet much of the book is dedicated to the military might of the Red Army, Air Force, and Navy, including detailed descriptions of their history, equipment, organization, and even badges of rank. Cecil-Smith's love of military history is evident. In describing war on the Eastern Front between Germany and Russia and the Winter War in Finland, he alternatively quotes the military writings of Carl von Clausewitz and Sun Tzu and references events in the Seven Years' War, the American Revolutionary War, the Zulu Wars, the Mahdist War, and the First and Second Boer Wars.[70] As in Cecil-Smith's earlier writings in *Soviet Russia Today*, he described at great length the quality of life enjoyed by Soviet citizens. Food was plentiful, and families had all the comforts they needed: "Perhaps a well-to-do family [in Canada] wouldn't like it, but anyone poorer than that would." He also described a vibrant cultural scene that embraced multiculturalism and equality between the sexes.[71] As for Soviet democracy, he wrote that, since most Canadians did not even understand what "proletariat" meant, they had incorrectly interpreted the term "dictatorship of the proletariat" as simply meaning that the Soviet Union was a dictatorship.[72] Not so, he said. The Soviet Union was remarkably democratic. The single party system was fair because, "In the Soviet Union they claim that there is no need for a second party. Political parties, they say, are only necessary to represent the needs and ambitious [*sic*] of the various class [*sic*] in society. Under socialism, they continue, there can be no class which has anything to express save the working class."[73] As late as September 1941, Cecil-Smith still saw the Soviet Union as the closest thing to an ideal society.

Notably, Cecil-Smith's choice of publisher indicated that he continued to have a positive relationship with the CPC. *Red Ally* was printed on the presses of Eveready Printers, the same presses that had churned out the party leaflets and copies of the *Clarion* even after the party was outlawed. The publisher was managed by Alec Valentine, a former recruiter in Montreal for the International Brigades, and exclusively employed members of the Communist Party of Canada. Although Eveready printed non-Communist materials in order to stay economically viable – including forty-four different titles of "pulp" books and magazines covering sports, adventure, science fiction, true crime, westerns, romance, and pornography – the fact remains that if the party leadership had had a problem with what Cecil-Smith had written on such an important topic, it seems extremely unlikely that this company would have printed it.[74]

By the winter of 1941, fascism seemed to be unstoppable. Germany controlled most of western Europe and was advancing on Moscow. Germany and Italy were consolidating their gains throughout the

Mediterranean. Spain was formally neutral in the war but contributed the Blue Division for service against the Soviet Union. Soon, Japan would launch a massive offensive in Asia. Cecil-Smith continued to receive regular updates from his parents and sister in China as tensions continued to rise. His parents were still in Guizhou, a province that had been relatively quiet since the Long March in 1934. In the intervening years, the British Army had constructed the Burma Road through the province, creating an overland route from Chongqing through the mountain passes to Burma. The province was home to increasing British military traffic and therefore likely targets for Japanese aircraft should war come. Guizhou was no longer safe, and Ida and George made the decision to flee. They would move by foot along the Burma Road, perhaps carrying on to join their son, Sydney, in India.[75] The gruelling march proved impossible for the elderly Cecil-Smiths. George died from natural causes along the route on 11 October 1941.[76] Ida abandoned the plan to escape and decided to hide with converts for as long as necessary.[77] Ida survived the Japanese invasion, although she did not survive the war.

Edward Cecil-Smith learned of his parents' situation from a letter he received from his sister, written on 8 December 1941. Frances had been living in Tientsin with her husband, George Henderson, and son Colin, but had escaped to the relative safety of Shanghai. By the time he received his sister's letter, Cecil-Smith knew that Shanghai was no longer safe. The Japanese had expanded the war, striking European and American possessions at Hong Kong, Singapore, Pearl Harbor, and elsewhere. British citizenship no longer afforded any protection. Frances, George, and Colin were captured and interned in hellish Japanese prison camps for the rest of the war.[78]

Cecil-Smith ended his involvement with the party and the Canadian Seamen's Union in the winter of 1942. Following the CPC's declaration of support for the war effort, the *Searchlight*'s former editor, David Sinclair, was among those released from an internment camp in Petawawa. Sinclair resumed his duties at the CSU newsletter, and Cecil-Smith quietly ended his involvement with the union. Producing his last edition of *Searchlight* in January 1942 appears to have been his final formal act for either the party or the CSU.[79] He did not resume his project of writing a history of the Mac-Paps. He did not write for the Communist press, nor was he observed attending political rallies or involving himself in labour disputes. Instead, he moved on to an "unradical" lifestyle as an editor of mainstream magazines. He began working with Super Publications Ltd. and then Jardine and Young Ltd. in Toronto.[80] This transition was no small feat, considering that his curriculum vitae was riddled with editorial experience with various illegal organizations. He was certainly turned away from a few jobs before he found one that would take him on. He had even applied for a job with the federal government only to be turned away following his RCMP security check.[81]

What caused Cecil-Smith to end his relationship with the CPC? Many prominent members of the party later attributed their departure to events that changed their perception of the Soviet Union, such as the revelation of a wartime Soviet spy-ring in Ottawa, Nikita Khrushchev's "Secret Speech" in 1956 denouncing the actions of Stalin and the cult of personality that had formed around him, or the Soviet invasion of Hungary in 1956. Yet Cecil-Smith left before any of these pivotal events. He did not appear to break from the party – he simply drifted away. He left no record of his reasons, and apparently did not discuss the matter with his family.

Cecil-Smith had devoted himself to the Communist Party of Canada for nearly a decade. He had publicly advocated for the Soviet Union and the requirement and inevitability of revolution, violent or not. He risked imprisonment in Canada and death on the battlefields of Spain. He wrote articles and a play, organized artists and labour groups, and took up arms. And then he simply stopped. Perhaps it was a practical matter. Card-carrying party members were expected to devote themselves wholeheartedly to the cause, and Cecil-Smith may increasingly have been less willing to make such a commitment. Perhaps it was simply because he counted himself lucky to make the transition from the radical press to the mainstream and he wanted to provide for his family and lead a reasonably straightforward life.[82] Perhaps he simply grew tired of the drama in the party, given his years of arguing and taking many steps counter to party policy. His radical views may simply have been tempered by age and economic prosperity. Soon he would have enough income to buy his first house and car, and to support his wife and son, Bill, born in 1942. Ultimately, we can never know why Cecil-Smith so unceremoniously terminated his decade of service with the Communist Party of Canada.

Conclusion

Cecil-Smith was among the Veterans of the Mackenzie-Papineau Battalion when they held a *Fiesta Espagnol* on the evening of 7 February 1947.[1] The Mac-Paps hosted the event in the Ukrainian Labor-Farmer Temple on Bathurst Street in Toronto. It was their first large event since the end of the Second World War, a great victory against Fascist Italy, Nazi Germany, and Imperial Japan. The victory against fascism, however, had not been total. General Francisco Franco still reigned in Spain and would continue to do so until his death in 1975. The evening of comradeship – enjoying a "typically Spanish dinner" while watching Bethune's *Heart of Spain* and another film, *Spain in Exile* – doubled as a fundraiser for the Committee to Aid Spanish Refugees.[2] A.A. MacLeod, a member of the Ontario Parliament under the Labor Progressive Party banner since 1943, gave a speech after the dinner. "Once again," he said, "the Mackenzie Papineau veterans are taking a leading part in the struggle for freedom."[3] The attendees unanimously agreed that the veterans would ensure that their services were of the greatest service to the party. It was an ambiguous resolution, but one that certainly alarmed the RCMP observer in attendance.[4] Cecil-Smith gave no speech, and he played no part in the organization's activities. In fact, it was the last party-affiliated event the RCMP saw him attend.[5]

Cecil-Smith, Lilian Gouge, and their son, Bill, moved to Montreal in 1950. He had secured a job with Holiday Publications, for whom he would edit trade magazines.[6] The RCMP maintained a file on him, checking in periodically but not noting any radical activity. Cecil-Smith lived long enough to see Mao's Red Army overthrow the Chinese Nationalists in 1949 and the Sino-Soviet Split between the two communist powers. This was hardly the solidarity he had hoped for. He followed these developments with interest but he did not resume his political activities. His son recalls that he was visited by cadets from the Mexican military academy (no doubt related to Mexican support for the Spanish Republic during the civil war), and that there were occasionally copies of the *Canadian Tribune*, the descendant of the *Daily Clarion*, around the house. Otherwise, there were few clues attesting to Cecil-Smith's extraordinary life. He rarely told stories of his exploits and was generally content to spend his time reading, cooking Chinese food, and taking his family to nice restaurants, for which he would write reviews in the various magazines he edited.[7]

Cecil-Smith had a stroke in 1960 at the age of fifty-seven.[8] His family returned to Toronto, where he received treatment at the Sunnybrook Veterans' Hospital – he was entitled to this treatment because of his brief time in uniform during the Second World War. Perhaps he had chance to visit his old haunts. The Village, by then generally called Gerrard Street Village, was more bohemian than ever. The crumbling tenements of St. John's Ward had been torn down in the spirit of urban renewal. Chinatown, once on Elizabeth Street, was gone, bulldozed to make room for the new City Hall. Toronto's Chinese population migrated to develop a new Chinatown along Dundas Street and Spadina Avenue, as the Jewish population moved further north. The Standard Theatre, where Cecil-Smith had performed *Eight Men Speak*, still stood, although it was no longer a Yiddish theatre – now it was the Victory Burlesque. Cecil-Smith had opportunities to reunite with some of his old friends, in particular Oscar Ryan (who was then living in Rochester, New York) and David Hogg.[9]

Cecil-Smith died from a second stroke in 1963, five months past his sixtieth birthday.[10] His funeral was a quiet family affair, a standard Anglican ceremony attended by family and friends. There was no formal representation from the Communist Party of Canada or the Mackenzie-Papineau Battalion. Cecil-Smith had left that part of his life behind. His simple tombstone was provided by the Ministry of Veterans' Affairs in recognition of his brief service in the Canadian military in the Second World War. There is nothing on the marker to indicate his service in the Spanish Civil War or his political work during the Depression – no slogans, no rank. But it would seem that Cecil-Smith's beliefs had changed little in his later years. As he was lowered into the ground in the military section of the York Cemetery, his widow smiled and pointed out an ornamental cannon nearby. She told her son that his father would approve of the location; he would probably rise up and put the cannon to good use should the revolution come.[11]

This book began with a question: why would someone go overseas to fight in a war in which his country played no part? There is no single answer, but, from this exploration of Cecil-Smith's life, his decision to go to Spain does not seem either spontaneous or out of character; indeed, it seems like the end result of a natural progression. Cecil-Smith was born British in China. He was deeply religious and influenced by his parents' willingness to take personal risk in order to advance a value system that they believed would serve others, regardless of international boundaries. Cecil-Smith was also raised to believe in British institutions, but he increasingly felt that they had become corrupted and were serving the interests of the few at the expense of the many. The economic realities of the Depression and the loss of traditional rights like those to free speech and assembly disgusted him, as did censorship of the theatre and of open political expression. He saw people being harassed or even beaten by the police for their political affiliation; he saw party leaders arrested and nearly murdered; he ultimately saw a wealthy ruling class riding on waves of privilege generated by the working class. The status quo became unacceptable; to him, communism, made real in the Soviet Union, offered a system that could solve the inequities and injustices of his day, gradually leading him to develop considerable loyalty toward the Soviet Union and the peoples of the world who were similarly working to right such social and economic wrongs.

Cecil-Smith also watched as fascism grew around the world. He saw a Nationalist government in China wage war against the Red Army, Imperial Japan encroach on China, Italy invade Ethiopia, and Nazi Germany seize power and destroy the German Communist Party. He witnessed fascism growing in popularity in Canada. When the Republican government of Spain was threatened by a fascist rebellion and the call went out for volunteers, he felt a moral obligation to act. Previously trained as a soldier, he had a tangible, material opportunity to do more than talk or write or protest. Spain was part a conflict that went beyond national borders, one that spoke to the heart of the revolutionary sensibility that he had spent years developing. For him, the defence of the Spanish Republic was a just war, a meaningful cause, and, he hoped, something that would dig "the grave of fascism" and protect a future for the working class. More than fifty years after his death, the legacy of his contribution to the revolutionary struggle underscores the Canadian, and indeed global, struggle between the extreme right and the extreme left.

Notes

Introduction

1 Jessie E. MacTaggart, "Crowd Hails Canadians from Spain," *Globe and Mail*, 6 February 1939.
2 Michael Petrou, *Renegades: Canadians in the Spanish Civil War* (Vancouver: UBC Press, 2008), 10–25.
3 "Pacifist Toronto Newsman Leads Crack Canadian Unit in Crucial Teruel Defense," *Toronto Telegram*, 8 January 1938.
4 Pierre Berton, *The Great Depression, 1929–1939* (Toronto: McClelland and Stewart, 1990), 483.
5 Arthur Landis, *The Abraham Lincoln Brigade* (New York: Citadel Press, 1967), 173, 354.
6 Victor Hoar, *The Mackenzie-Papineau Battalion: Canadian Participation in the Spanish Civil War* (Toronto: Copp Clark, 1969), 160.
7 Frank Ryan, ed., *The Book of the XV Brigade: Records of British, American, Canadian and Irish Volunteers in the XV International Brigade in Spain, 1936–1938* (Madrid: Commissariat of War, XVth Brigade, 1938), 238–9.
8 Mark Zuehlke, *The Gallant Cause: Canadians in the Spanish Civil War, 1936–1939* (Toronto: Whitecap Books, 1996), 90.
9 See Tim Buck, *Yours in the Struggle: Reminiscences of Tim Buck*, ed. William Beeching and Phyllis Clarke (Toronto: New Canada Publication, 1977), 160. *Yours in the Struggle* was based on a number of interviews with Tim Buck, and this particular statement comes from Mac Reynolds's CBC interview with Buck. Reynolds's taped interviews with Buck and several Canadian and American volunteers in the Spanish Civil War serves as the resource upon which most scholarship regarding Canadians in the Spanish Civil War is based and formed the backbone of Victor Hoar's book, *The Mackenzie-Papineau Battalion*. On the tape, Buck tells Reynolds that Cecil-Smith had previous military and propaganda experience in South

America. Reynolds proceeded to ask his other interviewees if they knew anything about Cecil-Smith's activities in South America. For example, in his interview with Carl Geiser and Lawrence Cane, he explains to the two veterans that he understands that Cecil-Smith was involved in the Chaco War (1932–35) between Bolivia and Paraguay. Neither Geiser, Cane, nor any of the other soldiers indicated any awareness of this fact, but, when Hoar's book was published, the story became that the soldiers of the Mac-Paps understood that Cecil-Smith had experience fighting as a "mercenary soldier" in South America. See CBC Radio Archives, Mac Reynolds interview with Tim Buck (1964) and with Carl Geiser and Lawrence Cane (1964); Hoar, *The Mackenzie-Papineau Battalion*, 160.

10 Allan Levine, "Soldiers of Fortune," *Canadian Encyclopedia* (2007), http://www.thecanadianencyclopedia.ca/en/article/soldiers-of-fortune/, accessed 7 January 2019.

11 Author's interview with Bill Smith, 25 July 2018.

1 An Idyllic Youth

1 This date of birth is corroborated by Chefoo School records, shipping lists, and Library and Archives Canada (hereafter LAC), R112, vol. 30553, Cecil-Smith, Edward Paul, Second World War Service File.

2 Author's interview with Bill Smith, 25 July 2018. See also "In Memoriam: Mr. G. Cecil-Smith," *China's Millions* (November–December 1941), 95.

3 For Ida, see M. Geraldine Guinness, *The Story of the China Inland Mission*, vol. 1 (San Francisco: Chinese Materials, 1977), 469. For George, see "Missionary Journal," *Chinese Recorder* (February 1891), and Guinness, *The Story of the China Inland Mission*, 1: 470.

4 Guinness, *The Story of the China Inland Mission*, 2: 193, and Samuel R. Clarke, *Among the Tribes in South-West China* (London: China Inland Mission, Morgan and Scott, 1911), 1–8.

5 Anping was transliterated as Anp'ing in the Wade-Giles system of transliteration. The spelling of Anshun is the same in both *pinyin* and Wade-Giles.

6 Alvyn Austin, *China's Millions: The China Inland Mission and Late Qing Society, 1832–1905* (Grand Rapids, MI: William B. Eerdmans, 2007), 2–3.

7 Mrs. G. Cecil-Smith, *Three Cries from Chinese Lips* (Toronto: China Inland Mission, 1910), 8.

8 Ibid., 6.

9 Ibid., 4–5.

10 "The Valedictory Meeting," *China's Millions* (November 1921).

11 Clarke, *Among the Tribes*, 155. Ban's name was transliterated as P'an Sheo-shan in Wade-Giles.

12 Ida and George's eldest son, the family recalls, went by Sydney, although his full name as recorded in China Inland Mission documents was John S.[ydney] Aldred Cecil-Smith, born 14 October 1895. Author's interview with Bill Smith; "The Families of the China Inland Mission," *China's Millions* (January 1898).
13 Mrs. Cecil-Smith, "Evangelist Chen: The First Convert in Kweichow," *China's Millions* (May 1916).
14 Author's interview with Bill Smith.
15 Clarke, *Among the Tribes*, 175.
16 "Safety of Missionaries," *Sheffield Independent*, 19 September 1900.
17 See Luella Miner, *China's Book of Martyrs* (Philadelphia: Westminster Press, 1903).
18 "Our Shanghai Letter," *China's Millions* (January 1908).
19 "Our Shanghai Letter," *China's Millions* (January 1933).
20 George Cecil-Smith, "Chinese Music," *Chinese Recorder* (September 1901) and "Characters for 'Sunday'," *Chinese Recorder* (March 1913).
21 See Mrs. G. Cecil-Smith, *Three Cries from Chinese Lips*; George Cecil-Smith, "Standard Mandarin Romanization," *Chinese Recorder* (November 1907); and J.L. Smith, "Women's Conference on the Home Life of Chinese Women," *Chinese Recorder* (January 1901).
22 Austin, *China's Millions*, 5.
23 "Our Shanghai Letter," *China's Millions* (January 1908).
24 Author's interview with Bill Smith.
25 Ibid.
26 Ibid.
27 These quotes come from Cecil-Smith's speech at Massey Hall following his return from the Spanish Civil War. The speech was quoted at length in "Made Stronger Our Fight for Freedom," *Daily Clarion*, 9 February 1939, and paraphrased in LAC, RG146, vol. 4183, CSIS files 95-A-0000-88, Recruiting for Spanish Army File, part 8, box 58, Report by S.O.F. Evans, "Friends of Mackenzie-Papineau Battalion, Toronto, Ont. – Mass Meeting of welcome to returned members 'Mac-Pap' Battn. held in Massey Hall," 7 February 1939.
28 Ibid.
29 Martin Gordon, *Chefoo School: 1881–1951, A History and Memoir* (Braunton, UK: Merlin Books, 1990), 21. See also Sheila Miller, *Pigtails, Petticoats, and the Old School Tie* (London: OMF Books, 1981), 55.
30 Author's interview with Bill Smith.
31 Alan Brinkley, *The Publisher: Henry Luce and His American Century* (New York: Alfred A. Knopf, 2010), 22.
32 Chefoo Schools Association, Chefoo Class Lists, 1900–41.

33 Russian State Archive of Socio-Political History, fond 545, Opis 6, Delo 569, International Brigade Service File of Cecil-Smith, misfiled under Smith.

34 Author's interview with Bill Smith.

35 Marcia Reynders Ristaino, *Port of Last Resort: The Diaspora Communities of Shanghai* (Stanford, CA: University of Stanford Press, 2001), 9–10. See also Robert Bickers, "Shanghailanders: The Formation and Identity of the British Settler Community in Shanghai, 1843–1937," *Past and Present* 159 (1998): 161–211.

36 Unfortunately, no nominal rolls of the Shanghai Volunteer Corps survived the Second World War. Cecil-Smith's membership in the force is confirmed only by the recollections of his son, Bill Smith.

37 See Bickers, "Shanghailanders."

38 Author's interview with Bill Smith.

39 Ibid.

40 Jean Ewen, *China Nurse, 1932–1939: A Young Canadian Witnesses History* (Toronto: McClelland and Stewart, 1981), 13.

41 Ed Cecil-Smith, "Woodsworth 'Discovers' the Orient, but What about the Working Class?" *Worker*, 15 December 1934.

42 LAC, RG76-C, Passenger Lists, 1865–1935.

43 See Ian McKay, *Reasoning Otherwise: Leftists and the People's Enlightenment in Canada, 1890–1920* (Toronto: Between the Lines, 2008).

44 George arrived in Vancouver on 13 September 1920, according to "Announcements," *China's Millions* (October 1920).

45 "North American Notes – Canada, Roll of Members Resident in Toronto," *Chefoo Magazine: The Organ of the Chefoo Schools Association* (hereafter *Chefoo Magazine*) (June 1925).

46 See "Missionary News," *Chinese Recorder* (April 1922).

47 A.J. Kerry and W.A. McDill, *History of the Corps of Royal Canadian Engineers*, vol. 1, *1749–1939* (Ottawa: Military Engineers Association of Canada, 1962), 295.

48 "Pacifist Toronto Newsman Leads Crack Canadian Unit in Crucial Teruel Defense," *Toronto Telegram*, 8 January 1938.

49 "North American Notes – Canada," *Chefoo Magazine* (June 1925).

50 Frances and Edward had attended regular Chefooite reunions in Toronto since 1920, shortly after they arrived in Toronto. See "North American Notes – Canada," *Chefoo Magazine* (June 1920).

51 David Hogg arrived in Vancouver with George Cecil-Smith on 13 September 1920, according to "Announcements," *China's Millions* (October 1920).

52 Cecil-Smith and Hogg were the same age, both born in 1903, and attended Chefoo in 1912–18 and 1913–20, respectively (Chefoo Schools

Association, Chefoo Class Lists, 1900–41). No records remain to show their attendance at Chefoo at the earlier preparatory level, but Cecil-Smith's family confirms that he attended prep school there, and, since David Hogg was the son of Dr. Alfred Hogg, Chefoo's school doctor, it seems likely that he would have as well. If this was the case, they would have known each other from the age of five or six. Author's interview with Bill Smith.

53 Author's interview with Bill Smith.

54 Ibid.

55 Cecil-Smith boarded with a family in 1924. See *City of Toronto Directory*, vol. 3, *Names At–Ea* (Toronto: Might Directories, 1924). Frances continued to stay at the headquarters until 1925. In 1927, the China Inland Mission headquarters moved from its office at 507 Church Street to a new, smaller office at 150 St. George Street. The boarding rooms may have been shut down prior to the office moving, or the Chefooites left in anticipation of the move. See *City of Toronto Directory*, vol. 1, *Streets At–Ea* (Toronto: Might Directories, 1926); *City of Toronto Directory*, vol. 2, *Streets Eb–Z* (Toronto: Might Directories, 1927).

56 Frances was accepted to return to Guizhou as a missionary in the autumn of 1925 and returned to China in early 1926. See "Announcements," *Toronto Bible College Recorder* (September 1925).

57 "Canadian Notes," *Chefoo Magazine* (June 1925).

58 See *City of Toronto Directory*, vol. 3, *Names At–Ea* (Toronto: Might Directories, 1924). See also "North American Notes – Canada, Roll of Members Resident in Toronto," *Chefoo Magazine* (June 1925).

59 "North American Notes – Canada," *Chefoo Magazine* (June 1925).

60 "15 June – Canada," *Chefoo Magazine* (March 1926). Since 1896, 15 June was celebrated as the opening date of the boys' school. The author seized upon the date as an opportunity to consider the broader purposes of a Chefoo education.

61 G.W. Robertson, "A Response to Sir Galahad," *Chefoo Magazine* (November 1926).

62 E. Cecil-Smith, "Response to G.W.R.," *Chefoo Magazine* (November 1927).

63 Hogg was known to be boisterous and argumentative, like Cecil-Smith, and often made references to characters in British folktales and literature. The use of Sir Galahad as a pseudonym would have been in character (author's interview with Bill Smith).

64 Anglican Diocese of Toronto Archives, St. Michael and All Angels Anglican Church, Marriage Register 1922–29.

65 Author's interview with Bill Smith. Cecil-Smith's address is not listed in the City Directory between 1925 and 1929. His 1927 marriage certificate states that he lived at 931 College Street, the address of the West End

YMCA. Cecil-Smith and Lilian Gouge marriage certificate (8 October 1927), personal papers of Bill Smith.

2 Radicalization

1 Library and Archives Canada (hereafter LAC), R112, vol. 30553, Cecil-Smith, Edward Paul, Second World War Service File (hereafter Second World War Service File).
2 Ibid.
3 The date that Cecil-Smith stopped working at the bank is unknown. He began working at the *Mail and Empire* in 1929. He held other kinds of jobs two years prior to beginning work at the newspaper. It is reasonably concluded that his time at the bank ended sometime between 1926 and 1928. "Three Canadians Wounded Fighting with Loyalists," *Toronto Star*, 10 July 1937; "Meet the Worker Staff," *Worker*, 7 March 1935.
4 "Meet the Worker Staff."
5 Russian State Archive of Socio-Political History (hereafter RGASPI), fond 545, Opis 6, Delo 569, International Brigade Service File of Cecil-Smith, misfiled under Smith (hereafter International Brigade Service File), Biografia de Militantes completed by Cecil-Smith, 2 November 1938, 038–041. Buck also worked as a machinist in Toronto and a member of the International Association of Machinists until 1928. See William Rodney, *Soldiers of the International; A History of the Communist Party of Canada, 1919–1929* (Toronto: University of Toronto Press, 1968), 137.
6 James Naylor, *The Fate of Labour Socialism: The Co-operative Commonwealth Federation and the Dream of a Working-Class Future* (Toronto: University of Toronto Press, 2016), 32; Ed Cecil-Smith, "Need We Emulate CCF Politeness When We Mention the Class Enemy? Answering a Questioning Letter from a Subscriber," *Worker*, 3 July 1934.
7 Author's interview with Bill Smith, 25 July 2018.
8 "North American Notes – Canada," *Chefoo Magazine: The Organ of the Chefoo Schools Association* (hereafter *Chefoo Magazine*) (June 1926). It is unclear what exactly the Publications Committee published. They provided reports to the *Chefoo Magazine*, but the existence of a committee would suggest that they did something more than write these brief reports. Unfortunately, there do not appear to be any surviving records of the committee's other work.
9 Author's interview with Bill Smith; "North American Notes – Canada, Roll of Members Resident in Toronto," *Chefoo Magazine* (June 1925).
10 *City of Toronto Directory*, vol. 2, *Names Ca–Ge* (Toronto: Might Directories, 1929). See also LAC, RG146, vol. 1830, CSIS files 95-A-0000-88, Edward

Cecil-Smith, part 1, box 58 (hereafter RCMP File), report by S.O.F. Evans to F.W. Schutz, forwarded to Commissioner Wood, "Re Ed. Cecil SMITH (C.P. of C.) Toronto," 28 August 1939.

11 "Pacifist Toronto Newsman Leads Crack Canadian Unit in Crucial Teruel Defense," *Toronto Telegram*, 8 January 1938.

12 "Shock Leader Once Pacifist," *Globe and Mail*, 7 January 1938.

13 Ibid.

14 "Pacifist Toronto Newsman Leads Crack Canadian Unit."

15 E. Cecil-Smith, "Unemployment," *Masses* (April 1932).

16 Shock Leader Once Pacifist"; "Pacifist Toronto Newsman Leads Crack Canadian Unit."

17 "Shock Leader Once Pacifist."

18 "Pacifist Toronto Newsman Leads Crack Canadian Unit."

19 The words of "The Internationale" were read into the record in the House of Commons by Conservative member of Parliament for Toronto John Ritchie MacNicol during the debates against the Criminal Code provisions that were used to outlaw the party. Canada, *House of Commons Debates* (Ottawa: Queen's Printer, 1933), 16 February 1933, 2193.

20 Jocko Thomas, *From Police Headquarters: True Tales from the Big City Crime Beat* (Toronto: Stoddart, 1990), 33.

21 Buck, *Yours in the Struggle: Reminiscences of Tim Buck*, ed. William Beeching and Phyllis Clarke (Toronto: New Canada Publication, 1977), 159–60.

22 "Police Drive Communists Away from Queen's Park," *Mail and Empire*, 2 August 1929.

23 Ibid.

24 Ibid. See also Buck, *Yours in the Struggle*, 161.

25 "Police Drive Communists Away from Queen's Park."

26 Ibid. See also Jack Scott, *A Communist Life: Jack Scott and the Canadian Workers Movement, 1927–1985*, ed. Bryan Palmer (St. John's: Canadian Committee on Canadian Labour History, 1988), 25.

27 "Police Drive Communists Away from Queen's Park."

28 "Batons and Feet Used Freely as City Police Rout Reds," *Mail and Empire*, 14 August 1929.

29 Ibid.

30 Betcherman, *The Little Band*, 62. See also "Meet the Worker Staff," *Worker*, 9 February 1935.

31 "Batons and Feet Used."

32 Cecil-Smith, "Need We Emulate CCF Politeness."

33 "Draper Says Reds Publicity Seekers," *Mail and Empire*, 14 August 1929.

34 Ibid.

35 "Toronto's 'Red Demonstration' Provides to Be Immediate Fiasco as Watchful Police Arrest Six," *Globe*, 14 August 1929.

36 Stewart Smith, *Comrades and Komsomolkas: My Years in the Communist Party of Canada* (Toronto: Lubus, 1993), 123.
37 "Batons and Feet Used"; see also Betcherman, *The Little Band*, 64–6.
38 Laurel Sefton MacDowell, *Renegade Lawyer: The Life of J.L. Cohen* (Toronto: University of Toronto Press for the Osgoode Society for Canadian Legal History, 2001), 34.
39 Betcherman, *The Little Band*, 36.
40 Under sections 40 and 41 of the Immigration Act, 1910, SC 9-10 Edward VII, c. 27, all public officials were required to report any immigrants who were dependent on relief or had been convicted of a crime. See also Bryan D. Palmer and Gaetan Heroux, "'Cracking the Stone': The Long History of Capitalist Crisis and Toronto's Dispossessed, 1830–1930," *Labour/Le Travail* 69 (2012): 56.
41 Betcherman, *The Little Band*, 43.
42 "Meet the Worker Staff," *Worker*, 9 February 1935.
43 Author's interview with Bill Smith.
44 Oscar Ryan, "A GPU Commune: How the Soviet Union Solves Crime," *Canadian Labor Defender* (September 1930).
45 On the issue of deportation, see Barbara Roberts, *Whence They Came: Deportation from Canada, 1900–1935* (Ottawa: University of Ottawa Press, 1988) and Dennis G. Molinaro, "'A Species of Treason?' Deportation and Nation-Building in the Case of Tomo Cacic, 1931–1934," *Canadian Historical Review* 91 (March 2010): 83.
46 Jaroslav Petryshyn, "A.E. Smith and the Canadian Labour Defense League" (PhD diss., Western University, 1977), 115.
47 *Soviet Russia Today* (November 1933).
48 Petryshyn, "A.E. Smith and the Canadian Labour Defense League," iii–iv.
49 RGASPI, International Brigade Service File, Biografia de Militantes completed by Cecil-Smith, 2 November 1938, 038–041.
50 "Explains How Atheism Is Taught to Children," *Toronto Star*, 10 November 1928; "Communist Chiefs Refuse to Be Sworn, Not Believing in Bible," *Globe*, 30 January 1931.
51 Cecil-Smith and Lilian Gouge marriage certificate, 8 October 1927, personal papers of Bill Smith. Author's interview with Bill Smith. Jessie E. MacTaggart, "Crowd Hails Canadians from Spain," *Globe and Mail*, 6 February 1939. R.F. MacLean, "Ten Thousand Cheers Rise as Army of 120 Canadians Arrives Home from Spain," *Toronto Evening Telegram*, 6 February 1939.
52 Richard Allen, *The Social Passion: Religion and Social Reform in Canada, 1914–1928* (Toronto: University of Toronto Press, 1971), 4.
53 A.E. Smith, *All My Life: An Autobiography* (Toronto: Progress Books, 1949), 43.

54 See Tom Mitchell, "From the Social Gospel to 'the Plain Break of Leninism': A.E. Smith's Journey to the Left in the Epoch of Reaction after World War I," *Labour/Le Travail* 33 (1994).
55 Smith, *All My Life*, 43.
56 Author's interview with Bill Smith.
57 Bryan D. Palmer and Gaetan Heroux, *Toronto's Poor: A Rebellious History* (Toronto: Between the Lines, 2016), 92–3.
58 E. Cecil-Smith, "Unemployment," *Masses* (April 1932).
59 167 Yarmouth Road, *City of Toronto Directory*, vol. 2, *Names Bu–El* (Toronto: Might Directories, 1931); 828 Shaw Street, *City of Toronto Directory*, vol. 1, *Names A–Gil* (Toronto: Might Directories, 1932); and 743 Ossington Avenue, in LAC, RCMP File, report by R.W. Irvine to C.H. King, Commander "O" Division, forwarded to Commissioner J.H. MacBrien Re: E. Cecil Smith: box 212 – Toronto, 15 August 1932.
60 Author's interview with Bill Smith.
61 *City of Toronto Directory*, vol. 2, *Names A–Cl* (Toronto: Might Directories, 1935), and *City of Toronto Directory*, vol. 2, *Names A–Cla* (Toronto: Might Directories, 1936).
62 E. Cecil-Smith, "Unemployment," *Masses* (April 1932).

3 Joining the Party

1 Cecil-Smith may have worked for the *Toronto Star* and the *Mail and Empire* at the same time. For instance, he wrote that he worked for the latter during the Battle of Queen's Park in 1929, and the *City of Toronto Directory* lists him as having worked for that paper as late as 1932. Cecil-Smith's work at *Toronto Star* was described by a fellow reporter in "Canadians in Spain Said 'Best Fighters,'" *Toronto Star*, 7 January 1938, although it does not provide dates. See *City of Toronto Directory*, vol. 2, *Names Bu–El* (Toronto: Might Directories, 1931) and *City of Toronto Directory*, vol. 1, *Names A–Gil* (Toronto: Might Directories, 1932).
2 Ross Harkness, *J.E. Atkinson of the Star* (Toronto: Toronto Star, 1963), 289–309, and Jocko Thomas, *From Police Headquarters: True Tales from the Big City Crime Beat* (Toronto: Stoddart, 1990), 19.
3 "Meet the Worker Staff," *Worker*, 7 March 1935.
4 The establishment of the Progressive Arts Club during the summer of 1931 has been widely accepted in the existing scholarship, but it is possible that informal elements existed even earlier. Cecil-Smith noted in one article that the organization was established in the autumn of 1930. Ed Cecil-Smith, "Growing Workers' Theatre Is Means of Dramatising the Class Struggle," *Worker*, 3 March 1934.

5 See Peter Krawchuk, *Our History: The Ukrainian Labor-Farmer Movement in Canada, 1907–1991* (Toronto: Lugus, 1996), 331–8.
6 See Stephen L. Endicott, *Bienfait: The Saskatchewan Miners' Struggle of '31* (Toronto: University of Toronto Press, 2002), 86–94 and photo insert.
7 M.G., "Proletarian Artists in Toronto Organize Club," *Worker*, 26 December 1931. "M.G." was short for Maurice Granite, Oscar Ryan's pseudonym.
8 See Nancy Butler, "Mother Russia and the Socialist Fatherland: Women and the Communist Party of Canada, 1932–1941, with Specific Reference to the Activism of Dorothy Livesay and Jim Watts" (PhD diss., Queen's University, 2010), 302.
9 Toby Gordon Ryan, *Stage Left: Canadian Theatre in the Thirties, a Memoir* (Toronto: CTR Publications, 1981), 26. Author's interview with Bill Smith, 25 July 2018.
10 See CBC Radio Archives, Mac Reynolds interview with Peter Hunter (1964).
11 Ibid.
12 Author's interview with Bill Smith.
13 "Pacifist Toronto Newsman Leads Crack Canadian Unit in Crucial Teruel Defense," *Toronto Telegram*, 8 January 1938.
14 Butler, "Mother Russia," 222.
15 The Workers' Theatre had originally been named the Worker's Experimental Theatre. The name changed in November 1932. For simplicity, it will be referred to here as the Workers' Theatre.
16 In her memoir, Dorothy Livesay recalls working with Cecil-Smith as the chair in 1932–33. See Dorothy Livesay, *Journey with My Selves: A Memoir, 1909–1963* (Vancouver: Douglas and McIntyre, 1991), 81.
17 William Krehm Personal Papers, letter from William Krehm to Sam Gampel, 30 August 1932.
18 Butler, "Mother Russia," 266, 344.
19 Alan Filewod, *Committing Theatre: Theatre Radicalism and Political Intervention in Canada* (Toronto: Between the Lines, 2011), 116, and Livesay, *Journey with My Selves*, 81. See also Gregory S. Kealey, "Stanley Brehaut Ryerson: Canadian Revolutionary Intellectual," *Studies in Political Economy* 8 (1982): 104.
20 Tim Buck, *Yours in the Struggle: Reminiscences of Tim Buck*, ed. William Beeching and Phyllis Clarke (Toronto: New Canada Publication, 1977), 162.
21 Sam Carr, during a 1949 criminal trial in Ottawa, denied that he had attended the Lenin School. However, given that he was on trial for espionage for the Soviet Union, this claim holds dubious weight, and documents smuggled out of the Soviet Embassy by Igor Gouzenko indicated

that Carr had attended the Lenin School. A.O. Tate, "Carr Denies Ever Helping Soviet to Get Passport," *Toronto Star*, 7 April 1949; Honourable Mr. Justice Robert Taschereau and Honourable Mr. Justice R.L. Kellock, Commissioners, *The Report of the Royal Commission to Investigate the Facts relating to and the Circumstances Surrounding the Communication, by Public Officials and Other Persons in Positions of Trust of Secret and Confidential Information to Agents of a Foreign Power* (Ottawa: Printers to the King's Most Excellent Majesty, 27 June 1946), 97–110.

22 See Dennis G. Molinaro, "'A Species of Treason?' Deportation and Nation-Building in the Case of Tomo Cacic, 1931–1934," *Canadian Historical Review* 91 (March 2010): 83.

23 See Dennis G. Molinaro, "Section 98: The Trial of *Rex v. Buck et al* and the 'State of Exception' in Canada, 1919–1936," in *Canadian State Trials*, vol. 4, *Security, Dissent, and the Limits of State Toleration in War and Peace, 1914–1939*, ed. Barry Wright, Eric Tucker, and Susan Binnie (Toronto: University of Toronto Press for the Osgoode Society for Canadian Legal History, 2015), 324.

24 Criminal Code of Canada, 1927, c. 36, s. 98(1).

25 Ibid., s. 98(8).

26 See Molinaro, "Section 98," 337.

27 Stewart Smith, *Comrades and Komsomolkas: My Years in the Communist Party of Canada* (Toronto: Lubus, 1993), 158.

28 "Meet the Worker Staff," *Worker*, 7 March 1935.

29 According to Cecil-Smith's International Brigade Service File, he joined the party in 1931, although it does not provide the month. Russian State Archive of Socio-Political History (hereafter RGASPI), fond 545, Opis 6, Delo 569, International Brigade Service File of Cecil-Smith, misfiled under Smith (hereafter International Brigade Service File), Biografia de Militantes completed by Cecil-Smith, 2 November 1938, 038–041. It stands to reason, however, that he joined the party *after* the arrests of Tim Buck et al. because Cecil-Smith's name is not present in the extensive documents (which include correspondence and membership lists) seized by the police during the raids. These documents are held in the Archives of Ontario, RG 4-32, A.G.O.: Re Rex vs. Tim Buck, barcode B225262.

30 Cecil-Smith's first date of working at the *Worker* is unknown. Only a small portion of the paper's articles state the name of the author. Although Cecil-Smith is not named as the author of the *Worker*'s coverage of Buck's trial, we know that he was present as a journalist for the paper thanks to subsequent scholarship regarding the authorship of *Eight Men Speak*. See Alan Filewod, "Authorship, Left Modernism, and Communist Power in Eight Men Speak: A Reflection," *Canadian Literature* 209 (Summer 2011): 12. Cecil-Smith is not listed as the author of any articles in the *Worker* until 1934,

and so we do not know what else he may have written. There is a similar problem for determining when he began working as the assistant editor for the *Worker*, as the masthead does not list the names of the editorial staff. According to his International Brigade Service File, he began working for the party's newspaper in 1931 as an assistant editor, although it does not provide the month. RGASPI, International Brigade Service File, Biografia de Militantes completed by Cecil-Smith, 2 November 1938, 038–041.

31 Filewod, "Authorship," 12. Since neither put their names to their articles, it is unclear who wrote which, or if they wrote them collaboratively.

32 "The Communist Party – Leader of Working Class Faces Courts," *Worker*, 7 November 1931.

33 Ibid.

34 Ibid.

35 Library and Archive Canada (hereafter LAC), RG 4-32, file 3188/31, Norman Sommerville, "Re Buck et al, Opening to the Jury," 28L 0137.

36 LAC, RG76-B-1-a 71–5, vol. 738, file 513173, Tim Buck, *Supreme Court of Ontario – Rex v. Tim Buck et al.*, 452–3.

37 Ibid., 429

38 Ibid., 440. See also LAC, RG76-B-1-a 71-5, vol. 738, file 513173, Tom Ewen, *Supreme Court of Ontario – Rex v. Tim Buck et al*, 522.

39 LAC, RG76-B-1-a 71-5, vol. 738, file 513173, Tom Ewen, *Supreme Court of Ontario – Rex v. Tim Buck et al*, 612. Emphasis added.

40 LAC, RG 4-32, file 3188/31, Norman Sommerville, "Closing Address to the Jury," AO, 28L 0147.

41 See chapter 7, "Troublemakers and Communists, 1930–1935" in Roberts, *Whence they Came*, 125–58.

42 "Announcement to Readers of The Worker," *Worker*, 21 November 1931.

43 "The Valedictory Meeting," *China's Millions* (November 1921).

44 E. Cecil-Smith, "Unemployment," *Masses* (April 1932).

45 Ed Cecil-Smith, "Which Is the Road to Socialism in Canada? Answering a Questioning Letter from a Subscriber," *Worker*, 30 June 1934.

46 Ibid.

47 E. Cecil-Smith, "Unemployment."

48 Ed Cecil-Smith, "The Future of Humanity," *New Frontier* (September 1936).

49 Ed Cecil-Smith, "Which Is the Road to Socialism?"

50 Ibid.

51 For more on *New Masses*, see Andrew Hemingway, *Artists on the Left: American Artists and the Communist Movement, 1926–1956* (New Haven, CT: Yale University Press, 2002), 7.

52 Cecil-Smith was known to draw, and it seems likely that he would have applied this skill to ensure that *Masses* was properly illustrated. However,

the drawings in question are signed "Smith," not "Cecil-Smith," which is hardly conclusive of their authorship. However, there was no one else named Smith on the staff of *Masses.* Cecil-Smith often went by Smith, and articles written by Cecil-Smith were alternatingly attributed to Cecil-Smith or just Smith in *Masses'* table of contents. It was certainly easier to carve the abbreviated form of his name into the linoleum blocks. His authorship of the drawings is therefore likely, but not certain.

53 "Our Credentials," *Masses* (April 1932).

54 E.C.S., "Workers' Art," *Canadian Labor Defender* (March 1932). The new magazine was also promoted in the Young Communist League magazine: "Read and Subscribe to 'MASSES'," *Young Worker*, 14 April 1932.

55 E.C.S., "Workers' Art."

56 Oscar Ryan, "The Soviet Theatre Leads the Way," *Soviet Russia Today* (February 1934).

57 Louis Nemzer, "The Soviet Friendship Societies," *Public Opinion Quarterly* (Summer 1949), 271.

58 *Literature of World Revolution*, renamed *International Literature* in 1932, was one of the first English-language periodicals on the subject coming out of the Soviet Union.

59 LAC, RG146, vol. 1830, CSIS files 95-A-0000-88, Edward Cecil-Smith, part 1, box 58 (hereafter RCMP File), "RUSSIAN language [translation of The Cultural Revolution of Soviet Russia]. Reviewed by MHA at R.C.M.P Headquarters," 2 August 1932.

60 LAC, RCMP File, letter from J.H. MacBrien, RCMP Commissioner, to Charles P. Blair, Assistant Commissioner of Customs, 16 July 1932, and letter from Charles P. Blair, Assistant Commissioner of Customs, to J.H. MacBrien, RCMP Commissioner, re: E. Cecil Smith Toronto, 6 July 1932.

61 LAC, RCMP File, Report by R.W. Irvine to C.H. King, Commander "O" Division, forwarded to Commissioner J.H. MacBrien Re: E. Cecil Smith: box 212- Toronto, 15 August 1932.

62 Ed Cecil-Smith, "Need We Emulate CCF Politeness When We Mention the Class Enemy? Answering a Questioning Letter from a Subscriber," *Worker*, 3 July 1934.

4 "Theatre – Our Weapon"

1 Nancy Butler, "Mother Russia and the Socialist Fatherland: Women and the Communist Party of Canada, 1932–1941, with Specific Reference to the Activism of Dorothy Livesay and Jim Watts" (PhD diss., Queen's University, 2010), 251.

2 "Theatre – Our Weapon," *Masses* (December 1932).

3 David Hogg, "Theatre of Actualities," *Masses* (April 1932).

4 "Unity," in *Eight Men Speak and Other Plays from the Canadian Workers' Theatre*, ed. Richard Wright and Robin Endres (Toronto: New Hogtown Press, 1976), 101–2.
5 See Alan Filewod, *Committing Theatre: Theatre Radicalism and Political Intervention in Canada* (Toronto: Between the Lines, 2011), 120.
6 Livesay wrote the story in 1933–34, but it would appear not to have been widely published until it was included in her memoir *Right Hand, Left Hand*. See Livesay, *Right Hand, Left Hand: A True Life of the Thirties – Paris, Toronto, Montreal, the West and Vancouver. Love, Politics, the Depression and Feminism* (Don Mills, ON: Press Porcepic, 1977), 87.
7 "War in the East," in Wright and Endres, *Eight Men Speak*, 117. Ryerson's play was printed in the May–June 1933 edition of *Masses*. See also "Drama in English," in *The Oxford Companion to Canadian Theatre*, ed. Eugene Benson and L.W. Conolly (Toronto: Oxford University Press, 1989), 156.
8 Toby Gordon Ryan, *Stage Left: Canadian Theatre in the Thirties, a Memoir* (Toronto: CTR Publications, 1981), 30–1.
9 Ibid.
10 See Livesay, *Right Hand*, 28.
11 Library and Archives Canada (hereafter LAC), RG146, vol. 1830, CSIS files 95-A-0000-88, Edward Cecil-Smith, part 1, box 58 (hereafter RCMP File), report by C.H. King, "O" Division, to Commissioner J.H. MacBrien re: Strike at the Canadian Canners Ltd. St. Catharines, Ont., 22 June 1933.
12 "Workers' Correspondent," *Worker*, 17 June 1933.
13 Author's interview with Bill Smith, 25 July 2018.
14 William Marchington, "Shots Fired by Guards, Ottawa Is Informed after Prison Outbreak," *Globe*, 18 October 1932.
15 Jack Handleton, "Riots Quelled in Penitentiary," *Globe*, 18 October 1932.
16 "Defense League Struggles for Kingston Inmates," *Worker*, 29 October 1932.
17 Ibid.
18 LAC, RCMP File, Report by C.H. King, Commanding "O" Division, to Commissioner J.H. MacBrien re: E. Cecil-Smith, 7 November 1932.
19 See "Delegation of Communists Arrived in Kingston Today," *Kingston Whig Standard*, 25 October 1932. The author did not appear to be aware that Cecil-Smith had arrived the day before.
20 Note that the RCMP file refers to Fred Hicks, whereas the *Kingston Whig Standard* reports James Hicks. The individual was likely James Hicks, a party member who ran for Toronto city council in Ward 6 the following year.
21 For more on Beckie Buhay, see Anne Frances Toews, "For Liberty, Bread and Love: Annie Buller, Beckie Buhay, and the Forging of Communist

Militant Femininity in Canada, 1918–1939" (MA thesis, Simon Fraser University, 2009).

22 E. Cecil-Smith, "Guthrie on Kingston Penitentiary," *Canadian Labor Defender* (November 1932).

23 Ibid.

24 "Probe into Pen Riots Is to Be Most Complete," *Kingston Whig Standard*, 24 October 1932.

25 Cecil-Smith, "Guthrie on Kingston Penitentiary."

26 Cecil-Smith's article on the trip was published in *Canadian Labor Defender* and the Yiddish-language *Der Kampf*. Cecil-Smith's RCMP file notes its publication in *Canadian Labor Defender* and provides a complete copy and translation of the *Der Kampf* version (LAC, RCMP File, extract from Der Kamp [*sic*] issue for 11 November 1932). This indicates that, although the open source intelligence gathering by the RCMP in Toronto was extensive, it was not comprehensive; the RCMP were not reading and noting every article in every edition of known left-wing publications. Alternatively, it may suggest that the RCMP was sometimes more interested in the ethnic left-wing press than its English equivalents.

27 Ibid.

28 "Legion Wants a Ban Put on Communist Pamphlets," *Kingston Whig Standard*, 26 October 1932.

29 As quoted in P.B. Waite, *In Search of R.B. Bennett* (Montreal and Kingston: McGill-Queen's University Press, 2012), 163.

30 Ed Cecil-Smith, "Bennett's Crocodile Tears Hide Greed of Big Bankers," *Worker*, 9 January 1935.

31 "Sees No Cause Prison Enquiry Be Made Public," *Ottawa Citizen*, 26 October 1932, and "Nothing Yet Indicates Need of Public Prison Inquiry," *Kingston Whig Standard*, 26 October 1932.

32 See Dennis G. Molinaro, "Section 98: The Trial of *Rex v. Buck et al* and the 'State of Exception' in Canada, 1919–1936," in *Canadian State Trials*, vol. 4, *Security, Dissent, and the Limits of State Toleration in War and Peace, 1914–1939*, ed. Barry Wright, Eric Tucker, and Susan Binnie (Toronto: University of Toronto Press for the Osgoode Society for Canadian Legal History, 2015), 327.

33 "Protest Treatment of the Eight in Kingston," *Worker*, 22 October 1932.

34 Cecil-Smith, "Guthrie on Kingston Penitentiary."

35 LAC, RCMP File, Report by R.W. Irvine Re: E.C. Smith, Canadian Labor Defense League – Toronto, Ont., 10 November 1932.

36 Ibid.

37 Ibid.

38 See Buck, *Yours in the Struggle: Reminiscences of Tim Buck,* ed. William Beeching and Phyllis Clarke (Toronto: New Canada Publication, 1977), 114–20.
39 See "Charges Wounded Convict Lay Unaided for 16 Hours," *Toronto Star,* 11 September 1933. See also Dennis Curtis, Andrew Graham, Lou Kelly, and Anthony Patterson, *Kingston Penitentiary: The First Hundred and Fifty Years, 1835–1985* (Ottawa: Canadian Government Publishing Centre Supply and Services Canada, 1985), 123–4.
40 See Buck, *Yours in the Struggle,* 121.
41 "Want 'Frame-Up' upon Tim Buck to Be Stopped," *Kingston Whig Standard,* 20 June 1933.
42 "CLDL Leaders Hounded by Kingston Police," *Worker,* 20 June 1933.
43 Canada, *House of Commons Debates* (Ottawa: Queen's Printer, 1934), 3 July 1934 at 4619.
44 "Defense League Convention Marks a Big Step Forward," *Worker,* 22 July 1933.
45 Ryan, *Stage Left,* 44.
46 Ibid.
47 Elaine Baetz, "The Role of the Working Class in *Eight Men Speak*" (MA thesis, University of Guelph: 1989), 40–1; Alan Filewod, "Authorship, Left Modernism, and Communist Power in Eight Men Speak: A Reflection," *Canadian Literature* 209 (Summer 2011): 19.
48 See "Meet the Worker Staff," *Worker,* 7 March 1935.
49 Program reproduced in Oscar Ryan, Edward Cecil-Smith Mildred Goldberg, and Frank Love. *Eight Men Speak: A Play* (Ottawa: University of Ottawa Press, 2013), 58–62.
50 Ontario Historical Studies oral history project, interview with Oscar Ryan, cited in "Critical Introduction" by Alan Filewod in ibid., xv.
51 Ibid.
52 Lita-Rose Betcherman, *The Little Band: Clashes between the Communists and the Political and Legal Establishment in Canada, 1928–1932* (Ottawa: Deneau, 1982), 23–5.
53 Filewod, "Authorship," 12.
54 Ryan, et al., *Eight Men Speak,* act 1, scene 1.
55 Ibid., act 3, scene 3.
56 Ibid., act 3, scene 4; act 3, scene 5.
57 Ibid., act 3, scene 5.
58 Ibid., act 5.
59 Ibid.
60 Ibid., act 6.
61 Ibid.
62 Baetz, "The Role of the Working Class," 46.

63 "Sing out 'Red Flag,' Hiss and Boo Anthem," *Toronto Star*, 5 December 1933. As other sources state that "The Internationale" was sung in this instance, it is unclear if either the author could not distinguish "The Red Flag" from "The Internationale," or if both songs were sung. Regardless, the other sources consistently report that both "God Save the King" and "The Red Flag" or "The Internationale" were cheered.
64 Filewod, *Committing Theatre*, 121.
65 "Art, Music, and Drama – Standard Theatre," *Varsity*, 5 December 1933.
66 A.C. Cochrane, "Eight Men Speak," *Varsity*, 19 January 1934.
67 "Kingston Play at Standard Theatre: Popular Demand Brings 'Eight Men Speak' for Second Performance," *Worker*, 30 December 1933.
68 Stewart Smith, *Comrades and Komsomolkas: My Years in the Communist Party of Canada* (Toronto: Lubus, 1993), 167.
69 University of New Brunswick Libraries, Archives and Special Collections, R.B. Bennett Papers, MG H96, box 146, file C: Communists, letter from A.E. Miller to R.C. Matthews, 2 January 1934, document #96810–3.
70 E. Cecil-Smith, "Government and Art," *Masses* (March–April 1934).
71 Ibid.
72 Ibid.
73 See Filewod, "Critical Introduction" in *Eight Men Speak*, xv.
74 "The Banning of a Play That Gave Distaste," *Toronto Star*, 15 January 1934.
75 A.E. Smith, *All My Life: An Autobiography* (Toronto: Progress Books, 1949), 166.
76 "One Act of Banned Production Performed at Mass Meeting; Recitation of the Eight Stages as Police Look On," *Varsity*, 18 January 1934.
77 Ibid.
78 "'Eight Men Speak' Is Cancelled Due to Political Interference," *Varsity*, 12 January 1934.
79 E. Cecil-Smith, "Government and Art," *Masses* (March–April 1934).
80 "'Eight Men Speak' Is Cancelled."
81 "Proposed Changes in Detective Force Discussed Today," *Globe*, 24 January 1934.
82 Smith, *All My Life*, 160. See also, A.E. Smith, "How Prisoners Fare Under Socialism," *Soviet Russia Today* (October 1933).
83 Smith, *All My Life*, 165.
84 "One Act of Banned Production Performed."
85 "Resolution on the Freedom of the Stage in Canada," *Masses* (June 1934).
86 A copy of the resolution is reproduced in Livesay, *Right Hand*, 80–2.
87 "One Act of Banned Production Performed."
88 "Winnipeg May Ban Eight Men Speak," *Globe*, 1 May 1934.
89 Cecil-Smith, "Introduction" in Ryan et al., *Eight Men Speak*, 7.

90 Filewod, *Committing Theatre*, 135.
91 Ibid.
92 John Manley, "'Communists Love Canada!' The Communist Party of Canada, 'the People,' and the Popular Front, 1933–1939," *Journal of Canadian Studies* 36 (Winter 2001–2): 62.
93 J. Petryshyn, "Class Conflicts and Civil Liberties: The Origins and Activities of the Canadian Labour Defense League, 1925–1940," *Labour/Le Travail* 10 (Autumn 1982): 39–63.
94 See "Mass Unity Wins" Canadian Labor Defense League Pamphlet (Toronto: April 1934); and Molinaro, "'A Species of Treason?' Deportation and Nation-Building in the Case of Tomo Cacic, 1931–1934," *Canadian Historical Review* 91 (March 2010): 82.

5 Art, Propaganda, and the Popular Front

1 Alan Filewod, "Critical Introduction" in *Eight Men Speak: A Play*, ed. Edward Cecil-Smith Mildred Goldberg, and Frank Love (Ottawa: University of Ottawa Press, 2013), xiv.
2 "Our Credentials," *Masses* (April 1932).
3 E. Cecil-Smith, "Marx Belongs to Us," *Masses* (March–April 1933).
4 See Andrew Hemingway, *Artists on the Left: American Artists and the Communist Movement, 1926–1956* (New Haven, CT: Yale University Press, 2002).
5 T. Richardson, "In Defense of Pure Art," *Masses* (July–August 1932).
6 E. Cecil-Smith, "What Is 'Pure' Art?" *Masses* (July–August 1932).
7 E. Cecil-Smith, "Propaganda and Art," *Masses* (January 1934).
8 Ibid.
9 Ibid.
10 "Working Class Drama 'Eight Men Speak' Is Banned by Authorities! Sergt. Nursey Becomes Dramatic Censor," *Worker*, 20 January 1934.
11 S[tanley] R[yerson], "Out of the Frying Pan," *Masses* (March–April 1934).
12 E. Cecil-Smith, "Let's Have More Discussion," *Masses* (March–April 1934).
13 Ibid.
14 E. Cecil-Smith, "Fascist Tendencies in the Cinema," *Masses* (May–June 1933).
15 Cecil-Smith, "Marx Belongs to Us."
16 Paul Axelrod, "The Student Movement of the 1930s," in *Essays in in the Social History of Higher Education*, ed. Paul Axelrod and John G. Reid (Montreal and Kingston: McGill-Queen's University Press, 1989).
17 "'Eight Men Speak' Is Cancelled," *Varsity*, 12 January 1934; Nancy Butler, "Mother Russia and the Socialist Fatherland: Women and the Communist

Party of Canada, 1932–1941, with Specific Reference to the Activism of Dorothy Livesay and Jim Watts" (PhD diss., Queen's University, 2010), 136–8; Krehm Collection, letter from Jim Watts, Secretary of the Student League, to James Potts, 15 August 1933.

18 E. Cecil-Smith, "The Workers' Theatre in Canada," *Canadian Forum* (October 1933), reproduced in *Canadian Theatre History: Selected Readings*, ed. Don Rubin (Toronto: Copp Clark, 1996).

19 *Masses* (March–April 1934).

20 E. Cecil-Smith, "Growing Workers' Theatre Is Means of Dramatising the Class Struggle," *Worker*, 3 March 1934.

21 Ibid.

22 Library and Archives Canada (hereafter LAC), RG146, vol. 1830, CSIS files 95-A-0000-88, Edward Cecil-Smith, part 1, box 58 (hereafter RCMP File), report by C.H. King, "O" Division, to Commissioner J.H. MacBrien re: Progressive Arts Club, Toronto, Ont., 27 March 1934.

23 Ibid.

24 "'Masses' Will Appear in a New Form," *Worker*, 2 June 1934.

25 Ed Cecil-Smith, "Klig Announces Campaign for Doubling Membership during Next Six Weeks," *Worker*, 13 October 1934.

26 Ed Cecil-Smith, "Strike of Policemen Headed Off," *Worker*, 5 March 1935; Ed Cecil-Smith, "Communist Candidates Take Lead in Fighting Mass Evictions," *Worker*, 22 December 1934.

27 Ed Cecil-Smith, "Strike of Policemen."

28 "Meet the Worker Staff," *Worker*, 7 March 1935.

29 James Naylor, *The Fate of Labour Socialism: The Co-operative Commonwealth Federation and the Dream of a Working-Class Future* (Toronto: University of Toronto Press, 2016), 71–2, 83, 92–3, and 141.

30 J. Cowan, "The N.R.A. and the Five Year Plan," *Soviet Russia Today* (January 1934).

31 G. Pierce, *Socialism and the CCF* (Montreal: Contemporary Publishing, 1934), 160.

32 Ed Cecil-Smith, "Need We Emulate CCF Politeness When We Mention the Class Enemy? Answering a Questioning Letter from a Subscriber," *Worker*, 3 July 1934.

33 Ibid.

34 Ed Cecil-Smith, "Which Is the Road to Socialism in Canada? Answering a Questioning Letter from a Subscriber, June 30, 1934," *Worker*, 30 June 1934.

35 Ibid.

36 E. Cecil-Smith, "Marx Belongs to Us."

37 Ed Cecil-Smith, "Which Is the Road to Socialism?"

38 Pierce, *Socialism and the CCF*, 168.

39 See Naylor, *The Fate of Labour Socialism*, 133–8; Walter D. Young, *Anatomy of a Party: The National CCF, 1932–1961* (Toronto: University of Toronto Press, 1969), 145. See also Stewart Smith, *Comrades and Komsomolkas: My Years in the Communist Party of Canada* (Toronto: Lubus, 1993), 169.
40 Ed Cecil-Smith, "Which Is the Road to Socialism?"
41 Ed Cecil-Smith, "Has Graham Spry Forgotten What He Wrote Last Month?" *Worker*, 30 January 1935.
42 Ed Cecil-Smith, "Manifesto Not Meant to Favor Free Insurance," *Worker*, 7 March 1935.
43 Ed Cecil-Smith, "Woodsworth Discovers the Orient, but Did He Visit Soviet China?" *Worker*, 1 December 1934; "Woodsworth 'Discovers' the Orient, but What about National Minorities?" *Worker*, 8 December 1934; "Woodsworth 'Discovers' the Orient, but What about the Working Class?" *Worker*, 15 December 1934; and "Woodsworth 'Discovers' the Orient, Where Did He Find Wide Democracy?" *Worker*, 26 December 1934.
44 Oscar Ryan, "CCF Leader Refuses to Back Down on Chinese 'Red' Banditry Falsehoods," *Worker*, 5 December 1934.
45 Ibid.
46 Ibid.
47 Ed Cecil-Smith, "Woodsworth Again Offers Support to Bennett," *Worker*, 23 January 1935.
48 E. Cecil-Smith, "Fascist Tendencies in the Cinema," *Masses* (May–June 1933).
49 Ibid.
50 For a description of the rise of fascism in Canada in general, see Lita-Rose Betcherman, *The Swastika and the Maple Leaf: Fascist Movements in Canada in the Thirties* (Toronto: Fitzhenry and Whiteside, 1975), including 45–60 for a specific description of circumstances in Ontario.
51 Cecil-Smith had no known address in 1933. However, his two known addresses in 1932 were both immediately to the west of Christie Pits Park: 828 Shaw Street, *City of Toronto Directory*, vol. 1, Names A–Gil (Toronto: Might Directories, 1932), and 743 Ossington Avenue in LAC, RCMP File, Report by R.W. Irvine to C.H. King, Commander "O" Division, forwarded to Commissioner J.H. MacBrien Re: E. Cecil Smith: box 212 – Toronto, 15 August 1932.
52 See Buck, *Yours in the Struggle: Reminiscences of Tim Buck*, ed. William Beeching and Phyllis Clarke (Toronto: New Canada Publication, 1977), 245–6.
53 "Tim Buck Cheered by 17,000 at Communist Gathering," *Toronto Star*, 3 December 1934.
54 Ibid.

55 Ibid.

56 Ed Cecil-Smith, "Greatest Labor Meeting in History Greets Buck's Return to Struggle," *Worker*, 5 December 1934.

57 Ibid.

58 See John Manley, "Red or Yellow? Canadian Communists and the 'Long' Third Period, 1927–1936," in *In Search of Revolution, International Communist Parties in the Third Period*, ed. Matthew Worley (London: I.B. Taurus, 2004), 220–46.

59 Georgi Dimitrov, "The Fascist Offensive," in *Selected Articles and Speeches* (London: Lawrence and Wishart, 1951), 112.

60 See Buck, *Yours in the Struggle*, 257.

61 J.L. Black, *Canada in the Soviet Mirror: Ideology and Perception in Soviet Foreign Affairs, 1917–1991* (Ottawa: Carleton University Press, 1998), 109.

62 For a description of the conditions in Cabbagetown, see Hugh Garner's novel, *Cabbagetown: A Novel* (Toronto: Ryerson Press, 1968). Garner, who grew up in Cabbagetown, volunteered to fight in Spain.

63 LAC, RCMP File, Report by A.E. Reames, "O" Division, to J.H. MacBrien re Communist Instructional School, 12 November 1935.

64 See chapter 2, "Proletarians and Communists," in Karl Marx and Friedrich Engels, *The Communist Manifesto in Marx/Engels Selected Works*, vol. 1 (Moscow: Progress Publishers, 1969).

65 LAC, RCMP File, Report by A.E. Reames, "O" Division, to J.H. MacBrien re Communist Instructional School.

66 Ibid.

67 "Former Editor Heads MacPaps," *Daily Clarion*, 8 January 1938.

68 Cecil-Smith, "Left Bloc Seen," *Worker*, 11 February 1936.

69 Ibid.

70 Ibid.

71 "Section 98 Wiped Out of Criminal Code," *Daily Clarion*, 22 June 1936; "Sec. 98 Effigy will be Burned by Celebrators," *Daily Clarion*, 24 June 1936.

6 Defend the Soviet Union!

1 Unattributed "O" Division Report stating that Cecil-Smith has been transferred to the Friends of the Soviet Union, 18 January 1933, in Library and Archives Canada (hereafter LAC), RG146, vol. 1830, CSIS files 95-A-0000-88, Edward Cecil-Smith, part 1, box 58 (hereafter RCMP File). In "Former Editor Heads MacPaps," 8 January 1938, the *Daily Clarion* stated that Cecil-Smith had been the national secretary of the Friends of the Soviet Union.

2 "Editor's Note," *Canadian Forum* (October 1933).

3 Canada, *House of Commons Debates* (Ottawa: Queen's Printer, 1935), 12 March 1935, 1653.

4 Frederick Griffin, *Soviet Scene: A Newspaperman's Close-Ups of New Russia* (Toronto: Macmillan, 1932), ix. See also Ross Harkness, *J.E. Atkinson of the Star* (Toronto: Toronto Star, 1963), 291–300, for a description of Griffin's assignment.

5 Griffin, *Soviet Scene*, 183, 270.

6 See Sheila Fitzpatrick, "Foreigners Observed: Moscow Visitors in the 1930s under the Gaze of Their Soviet Guides," *Russian History* 35 (2008): 215–34; Paul Hollander, *Political Pilgrims: Travels of Western Intellectuals to the Soviet Union, China and Cuba* (Oxford: Oxford University Press, 1981); Sylvia R. Margulies, *The Pilgrimage to Russia: The Soviet Union and the Treatment of Foreigners, 1924–1937* (Milwaukee: University of Wisconsin Press, 1968); and Allison Ward, "'I Listened as They Built Up Their Picture of That Terrible Land': Self-Identity and Societal Observations in Traveller's Accounts of the Soviet Union, 1929–1936" (Unpublished MA research paper, Queen's University, 2010).

7 Kirk Niergarth, "'No Sense of Reality': George A. Drew's Anti-Communist Tour of the USSR and the Campaign for Coalition Government in Ontario, 1937," *Ontario History* 107 (Autumn 2015): 215, 222.

8 "Who Is Kapoot?" *Soviet Russia Today* (February 1934).

9 Ed Cecil-Smith, "Democracy in the Soviet Union," *Worker*, 3 November 1934.

10 LAC, RCMP File, unattributed report re: E. Cecil Smith, United Front Election Campaign, 15 December 1932.

11 167 Yarmouth Road, *City of Toronto Directory*, vol. 2, *Names Bu-El* (Toronto: Might Directories, 1931); 828 Shaw Road, *City of Toronto Directory*, vol. 1, Names A–Gil (Toronto: Might Directories, 1932); and 743 Ossington Avenue, LAC, RCMP File, report by R.W. Irvine to C.H. King, Commander "O" Division, forwarded to Commissioner J.H. MacBrien Re: E. Cecil Smith: box 212 – Toronto, 15 August 1932.

12 Ed Cecil-Smith, "Democracy in the Soviet Union," *Worker*, 3 November 1934.

13 See Ed Cecil-Smith, "Two Canadians Describe How Soviet Workers Live," *The Worker*, 2 January 1935. An RCMP officer also attended the meeting and provided a report to Ottawa. See RCMP Security Bulletin No. 739, 9 January 1935, in *RCMP Security Bulletins: The Depression Years, Part II, 1935*, ed. Gregory S. Kealey and Reg Whitaker (St. John's: Canadian Committee on Labour History, 1995), 27.

14 Louis Nemzer, "The Soviet Friendship Societies," *Public Opinion Quarterly* (Summer 1949). See also Albert Inkpin, secretary of the International Committee of the Friends of the Soviet Union (FSA), Amsterdam,

"An International Organization," *Soviet Russia Today* (December 1933). See Tim Buck, *Canada and the Russian Revolution: The Impact of the World's First Socialist Revolution on Labor and Politics in Canada* (Toronto: Progress Books, 1967), 80–2 and "Active Campaign Is now Begun to Build Canadian Section of FSU," *Worker*, 29 July 1932; and W.S. Shainak, "Friends of Soviet Union Laying Basis for Growth," *The Worker*, 3 September 1932.

15 "Former Editor Heads MacPaps," *Daily Clarion*, 8 January 1938.

16 "Who Are the Friends of the Soviet Union?" (Toronto: National Committee of the Friends of the Soviet Union, n.d. [c. 1933]).

17 E. Cecil-Smith, "Canadian Capitalists Foster Intervention," *Soviet Russia Today* (August 1933). J. Cowan, "State Planning in the Soviet Union," *Soviet Russia Today* (August 1933).

18 Menkin, "We Are Master of Our Country: A Letter from a Siberian Collective Farmer to a Canadian Worker," *Soviet Russia Today* (August 1933). Minnie Shelley, "Youth in Canada and in the Soviet Union: A Letter from a Class-Conscious Worker to Her Cousin," *Soviet Russia Today* (August 1933).

19 Shelley, "Youth in Canada."

20 J.F. White, "Canadian Workers 'See for Themselves,' Canadian Workers' Delegates Report What They Have Seen," *Soviet Russia Today* (August 1933); Stan Hood, "The New World," *Soviet Russia Today* (August 1933).

21 White, "Canadian Workers 'See for Themselves.'"

22 J.F. White, "Russian High-lights I," *Canadian Forum* (February 1933); "Russian High-lights II," *Canadian Forum* (March 1933); "Russian High-lights III," *Canadian Forum* (April 1933); "Russian High-lights IV," *Canadian Forum* (May 1933); "Russian High-lights V," *Canadian Forum* (June 1933); "Russian High-lights VI, *Canadian Forum* (July 1933).

23 A.E. Smith, "How Prisoners Fare under Socialism," *Soviet Russia Today* (October 1933).

24 *Soviet Russia Today* (August–September 1935).

25 Robert Lane, "Culture in the Soviet Union," *Soviet Russia Today* (December 1933).

26 "Maxim Gorki on Toys," *Soviet Russia Today* (February 1934); Anna Bell, "Children's Village – A Soviet Museum," *Soviet Russia Today* (August–September 1934).

27 E. Cecil-Smith, "The FSU and Political Parties," *Soviet Russia Today* (October 1933).

28 See Anne Applebaum, *Red Famine: Stalin's War on Ukraine* (Toronto: Signal / McClelland and Stewart, 2017).

29 E. Cecil-Smith, "Who Is Kapoot?" See also E. Cecil-Smith, "$100,000,000 – Will We Take It?" *Soviet Russia Today* (January 1934); "Mr. Cromie

Repents," *Friends of the Soviet Union* (January 1934) and Fred Grance, "An Anti-Soviet Shot Misses Its Mark," *Soviet Russia Today* (December 1934).

30 For more on the media debate regarding the famine, see Peter Krawchuk, *Our History: The Ukrainian Labor-Farmer Movement in Canada, 1907–1991* (Toronto: Lugus, 1996), 248–9.

31 See Dr. Herbert A. Bruce, *Report of the Lieutenant Governor's Committee on Housing Conditions in Toronto* (Toronto: Toronto Board of Control, 1934).

32 Dr. J.M. Stone, "Soviet Medicine," *Soviet Russia Today* (August–September 1934). See also Frederick Banting, "Sir Frederick Banting Tells about Soviet Science," *Soviet Russia Today* (October 1935). Although Banting expressed an interest in communism, even identifying himself as a communist to the lieutenant governor of Ontario, he did not join the party. Michael Bliss, *Banting: A Biography* (Toronto: McClelland and Stewart, 1984), 228.

33 Norman Bethune, "A Plea for Early Compression," *Canadian Medical Association Journal* 27 (July 1932): 36–42.

34 David Lethbridge, ed., *Bethune: The Secret Police File* (Salmon Arm, BC: Undercurrent Press, 2003), documents 1–5.

35 Author's interview with Bill Smith, 25 July 2018.

36 "Who Are the Friends of the Soviet Union?"

37 E. Cecil-Smith, "The FSU and Political Parties," *Soviet Russia Today* (October 1933).

38 "Who Are the Friends of the Soviet Union?"

39 Canada, *House of Commons Debates* (Ottawa: Queen's Printer, 1933), 17 March 1931, Order in Council as read into Hansard by J.S. Woodsworth, 77; A.G. McCallum, "Canadian Exports and Soviet 'Dumping,'" *Soviet Russia Today* (October 1933). See also, "Editorial Comment," *Soviet Russia Today* (December 1933).

40 See RCMP Security Bulletin No. 770, 28 August 1935 in Kealey and Whitaker, *RCMP Security Bulletins: The Depression Years, Part II, 1935*, 458.

41 Louis Kon, "Shall We Trade?" *Soviet Russia Today* (December 1933); W.E. Wiggins, "Wheat and Debts," *Soviet Russia Today* (December 1933); Louis Kon, "A Favorable Balance of Trade," *Soviet Russia Today* (January 1934).

42 E. Cecil-Smith, "Let's Have Soviet Trade," *Soviet Russia Today* (November 1933).

43 E. Cecil-Smith, "$100,000,000 – Will We Take It?"

44 J. Larry Black and Kirk Niergarth, "Revisiting the Canadian-Soviet Barter Proposal of 1932–1933: The Soviet Perspective," *International Journal* 71 (2016): 409–32.

45 Author's interview with Bill Smith.

46 *Soviet Russia Today* and the *Worker* provided their own analysis on the threat posed by Japan against Russia, and also reprinted articles from

the Soviet newspaper *Pravda.* See, for instance, "On the Events in the Far East: Appeal of the International Committee of the F.S.U.," *Soviet Russia Today* (December 1933).

47 See Ed Cecil-Smith, "Woodsworth 'Discovers' the Orient, but What about National Minorities?" *Worker*, 8 December 1934; E. Cecil-Smith, "The Chinese Soviets," *Soviet Russia Today* (December 1933).

48 Ziarong Han, *Red God: Wei Baqun and His Peasant Revolution in Southern China, 1894–1932* (Albany: State University of New York, 2014), 52.

49 E. Cecil-Smith, "The Chinese Soviets," *Soviet Russia Today* (December 1933).

50 Ibid.

51 E. Cecil-Smith, "Woodsworth Discovers the Orient, But Did He Visit Soviet China?" *Worker*, 1 December 1934.

52 "The Bright Side," *China's Millions* (January 1927). The name was transliterated as Chow His-Cheng in Wade-Giles system of transliteration. See also "Our Shanghai Letter," *China's Millions* (April 1928).

53 Transliterated as Szenan in Wade-Giles.

54 "The Bright Side." See also "Our Shanghai Letter."

55 For more on the Red Army's activities in kidnapping and ransoming missionaries, see Arnolis Hayman, *A Foreign Missionary on the Long March: The Memoirs of Arnolis Hayman of the China Inland Mission*, ed. Anne-Marie Brady (Portland, ME: Merwin Asia, 2010), xii.

56 "Editorial Notes," *China's Millions* (May 1933).

57 Ibid.

58 Ibid.

59 Hayman, *A Foreign Missionary*, 5.

60 Ibid., 18.

61 R.A. Bosshardt, *The Restraining Hand* (London: Hodder and Stoughton, 1936), 12.

62 See Otto Braun, *A Comintern Agent in China, 1932–1939* (London: C. Hearst, 1982), 26; Robert G. Colodny, *The Struggle for Madrid: The Central Epic of the Spanish Conflict, 1936–1939* (New York: Paine-Whitman, 1958), 179n101; Boris Volodarsky, *Stalin's Agent: The Life and Death of Alexander Orlov* (Oxford: Oxford University Press, 2015), 228–9.

63 Cecil-Smith, "Woodsworth 'Discovers' the Orient, but What about National Minorities?"

64 Ed Cecil-Smith, "Woodsworth 'Discovers' the Orient, but What about the Working Class?" *Worker*, 15 December 1934.

65 Stephen Endicott, *James G. Endicott: Rebel out of China* (Toronto: University of Toronto Press, 1980), 119–20.

66 Ibid., 124.

67 LAC, RCMP File, Unattributed report re: E.C. Smith, C.L.D.L. meeting (Moss park Branch), 4 June 1935.

68 Ibid.

69 E. Cecil-Smith, "Canadian Capitalists Foster Intervention," *Soviet Russia Today* (August 1933).

70 Ibid.

71 Norman Penner, *Canadian Communism: The Stalin Years and Beyond* (Toronto: Methuen, 1988), 147.

72 E. Cecil-Smith, "Against War, Against Fascism," *Soviet Russia Today* (August–September 1934). Cecil-Smith's statements that the dissenters were Trotskyites is corroborated by their own reporting. See "To All Delegates to the Canadian Youth Congress against War and Fascism: We Are Not Pacifists," *Young Militant* (August 1934).

73 Ibid.

74 "Anti-Fascists and Pro-Soviets," *Soviet Russia Today* (August–September 1934).

75 Thomas P. Socknat, *Witness against War: Pacifism in Canada, 1900–1945* (Toronto: University of Toronto Press, 1987), 164.

76 E. Cecil-Smith, "Against War, Against Fascism."

77 Ibid.

78 William Sydney, "Defenders of the Interests of the Toilers of the World," *Soviet Russia Today* (November 1933).

79 Jack Lind, "Soviet Peace Policy," *Soviet Russia Today* (November 1933).

80 Mark Zuehlke, *The Gallant Cause: Canadians in the Spanish Civil War, 1936–1939* (Toronto: Whitecap Books, 1996), 29.

81 Michael Butt, "Surveillance of Canadian Communists: A Case Study of Toronto RCMP Intelligence Networks, 1920–1939" (PhD diss., Memorial University, 2003), 301.

82 See John Manley, "Audacity, Audacity and Still More Audacity': Tim Buck, the Party and the People, 1932–1939," *Labour/Le Travail* 49 (Spring 2002): 40.

83 Naylor, *The Fate of Labour Socialism*, 212.

84 RCMP Security Bulletin No. 751, 3 April 1935, in Kealey and Whitaker, *RCMP Security Bulletins: The Depression Years, Part II, 1935*, 203. See also Norman Penner, *Canadian Communism: The Stalin Years and Beyond* (Toronto: Methuen, 1988), 147; Naylor, *The Fate of Labour Socialism*, 173–9; and Olenka Melnyk, *No Bankers in Heaven: Remembering the CCF* (Toronto: McGraw-Hill Ryerson, 1989), 171.

85 James Naylor, *The Fate of Labour Socialism: The Co-operative Commonwealth Federation and the Dream of a Working-Class Future* (Toronto: University of Toronto Press, 2016), 213. Regarding MacLeod's devotion to Christianity and the pacifist-socialist alignment, see Socknat, *Witness against War*, 163.

86 Hugh Thomas, *The Spanish Civil War* (London: Eyre and Spottiswoode, 1961), 66–7.

87 Paul Preston, *The Spanish Civil War, 1936–39* (London: Weidenfeld and Nicolson, 1986), 64–5.
88 Ibid., 78–9.
89 "Communist International Calls for United Front of All Workers behind Heroic Struggle of Spanish Masses," *Worker*, 17 October 1934.

7 "No Pasaran!"

1 "Pacifist Toronto Newsman Leads Crack Canadian Unit in Crucial Teruel Defense," *Toronto Telegram*, 8 January 1938.
2 *City of Toronto Directory*, vol. 2, *Names A–Cla* (Toronto: Might Directories, 1936).
3 Library and Archives Canada (hereafter LAC), RG146, vol. 1830, CSIS files 95-A-0000-88, Edward Cecil-Smith, part 1, box 58 (hereafter RCMP File), unattributed report re: E. Cecil Smith, United Front Election Campaign, 15 December 1932.
4 Author's interview with Bill Smith, 25 July 2018; "the Village" has been alternately called Greenwich Village or Gerrard Street Village at various points in its history. See the work in progress by Heather Murray, currently under the title of *Toronto Bohemia: The Early Years (1925–1950) of the Gerrard Street Village*.
5 Author's interview with Bill Smith.
6 Ibid.
7 "Former Editor Heads MacPaps," *Daily Clarion*, 8 January 1938.
8 Hugh Thomas, *The Spanish Civil War* (London: Eyre and Spottiswoode, 1961), 90.
9 Paul Preston, *The Spanish Civil War, 1936–39* (London: Weidenfeld and Nicolson, 1986), 87–9.
10 *Daily Clarion*, 1 May 1936.
11 Russian State Archive of Socio-Political History (hereafter RGASPI), fond 545, Opis 6, Delo 569, International Brigade Service File of Cecil-Smith, misfiled under Smith (hereafter International Brigade Service File), Biografia de Militantes completed by Cecil-Smith, 2 November 1938, 038–041.
12 James Naylor, *The Fate of Labour Socialism: The Co-operative Commonwealth Federation and the Dream of a Working-Class Future* (Toronto: University of Toronto Press, 2016), 198–9; Bryan Palmer and Gaetan Heroux, *Toronto's Poor: A Rebellious History* (Toronto: Between the Lines, 2016), 101.
13 Larry Hannant, "United Front on the Left: The Committee to Aid Spanish Democracy" (unpublished paper presented to the Canadian Historical Association's annual meeting, 23 October 2005), 6–7; Michael Butt, "Surveillance of Canadian Communists: A Case Study of Toronto RCMP

Intelligence Networks, 1920–1939" (PhD diss., Memorial University, 2003), 313.

14 RGASPI, International Brigade Service File, Biografia de Militantes completed by Cecil-Smith, 2 November 1938, 038–041. Although it is known that Cecil-Smith was a member of the initial staff, his firm date of departure is not known, as he is not named in the masthead and did not write any articles under his own name.

15 Tim Buck's memoirs simply state that Cecil-Smith was employed at the time of his departure. Buck, *Yours in the Struggle: Reminiscences of Tim Buck*, ed. William Beeching and Phyllis Clarke (Toronto: New Canada Publication, 1977), p. 267–8. His employment specifically with the *Montreal Star* comes from author's interview with Bill Smith and "Obituary," *Toronto Star*, 24 August 1963.

16 Preston, *The Spanish Civil War*, 93–4.

17 "Loyal Troops Quell Revolt at Madrid," *Montreal Star*, 20 July 1936; "Strategic Points Held by Spanish Rebels," *Montreal Star*, 21 July 1936.

18 See Ross Harkness, *J.E. Atkinson of the Star* (Toronto: Toronto Star, 1963), 301–5.

19 Preston, *The Spanish Civil War*, 117.

20 Ibid., 119.

21 Ibid., 71–84.

22 Speech delivered on 26 September 1936, reprinted in the *Ottawa Journal*, 30 September 1936.

23 "With Our Women, La Passionaria [*sic*], a Call from Spain," *Daily Clarion*, 15 August 1936).

24 Oscar Ryan, "Torquemada and His Fascist Successors," *Daily Clarion*, 19 September 1936.

25 See Edo Jardas, "Djelatnost jugoslavenskih iseljenika," translated and cited in John Peter Kraljic, "The Croatian Community in North America and the Spanish Civil War" (MA thesis, Hunter College, 2002), 62; Michael Petrou, *Renegades: Canadians in the Spanish Civil War* (Vancouver: UBC Press, 2008), 39; Raymond M. Hoff, Christopher T. Brooks, Michael Petrou, and Myron Momryk, "Biographical Dictionary of Volunteers from Canada in the Spanish Civil War" (unpublished manuscript, 2018), 190. Jardas's name was often anglicized as Ed Yardas.

26 "Winnipeg Youth Form Battalion for Spain," *Daily Clarion*, 10 October 1936.

27 See Naylor, *The Fate of Labour Socialism*, 258.

28 "Returns from Spain to Organize Relief Ship For Loyalists," *Toronto Star*, 6 October 1936.

29 See Victor Hoar, *The Mackenzie-Papineau Battalion: Canadian Participation in the Spanish Civil War* (Toronto: Copp Clark, 1969), 8–9. Hoar refers to

MacLeod using the pseudonym Allan Dowd. Regarding the Republican delegation's visit to Toronto, see, "Jewess Gave Wedding Ring to Aid Spanish Loyalists," *Toronto Star*, 22 October 1936. For more on the organization and departure of Bethune's medical mission, see Roderick Stewart and Sharon Stewart, *Phoenix: The Life of Norman Bethune* (Montreal and Kingston: McGill-Queen's University Press, 2011), 138–41. See also Norman Bethune, *The Politics of Passion: Norman Bethune's Writing and Art*, ed. Larry Hannant (Toronto: University of Toronto Press, 1998), 119; "Spanish Hospital and Medical Aid Committee," *New Commonwealth*, 26 September 1936.

30 Naylor, *The Fate of Labour Socialism*, 258–9; Larry Hannant, "United Front on the Left: The Committee to Aid Spanish Democracy" (unpublished paper presented to the Canadian Historical Association's annual meeting, 23 October 2005), 1–3, 15–16.

31 Hannant, "United Front on the Left."

32 See "Canadian Doctor Due in Madrid This Week," *New Commonwealth*, 31 October 1936; Hoar, *The Mackenzie-Papineau Battalion*, 8–10.

33 This is not to say that support for the Spanish Republic was universal. William Randolph Hearst's newspapers depicted the Republican government as "Catholic church burners, killers of priests, rapers of nuns, and looters of small businesses." Mark Zuehlke, *The Gallant Cause: Canadians in the Spanish Civil War, 1936–1939* (Toronto: Whitecap Books, 1996), 27. This view was widely held in Quebec, where the largely anti-clerical and anti-monarchist Republican government had been condemned by Premier Maurice Duplessis and the archbishop of Quebec, Cardinal Jean-Marie-Rodrigue Villeneuve. Pope Pius XI condemned the Republican government for its expropriation of private Catholic schools, the nationalization of church properties, and its generally anticlerical policies. For more on the divided reactions in English and French Canada, see Thor Frohn-Nielsen, "Canada's Foreign Enlistment Act: Mackenzie King's Expedient Response to the Spanish Civil War" (MA thesis, University of British Columbia, 1979); Martin Lobigs, "Canadian Responses to the Mackenzie-Papineau Battalion" (MA thesis, University of New Brunswick, 1992); and Art Cawley, "The Canadian Catholic English-Language Press and the Spanish Civil War," *CCHA Study Sessions* 49 (1982).

34 "Loyalists Hold Madrid in Bloody Fight," *Toronto Star*, 11 November 1936.

35 Preston, *The Spanish Civil War*, 170; Thomas, *The Spanish Civil War*, 324.

36 "Grimmest Battle of War Rages To-Day in Asturias," *Toronto Star*, 28 November 1936; Frederick Griffin, "Valencia's Vivid Skies Hold Threat of Raid as Cortes Is Called," *Toronto Star*, 1 December 1936.

37 CBC Radio Archives, Mac Reynolds interview with Lionel Edwards (1964).
38 "Give the Spanish Workers Arms," *Daily Clarion*, 12 November 1936; "Rebels Burned Tots 'For Fun' – Tim Buck Says," *Toronto Star*, 10 November 1936); William Strange, "World War Already Begun in Spain, Tim Buck Declares," *Toronto Star*, 11 November 1936; "Rouse Canadian Friendship for Loyalists, Buck Urges," *Toronto Star*, 12 November 1936.
39 "Rebels Burned Tots 'For Fun' – Tim Buck Says," *Toronto Star*, 10 November 1936; William Strange, "World War Already Begun in Spain, Tim Buck Declares," *Toronto Star*, 11 November 1936.
40 Buck, *Yours in the Struggle*, 265.
41 Otto Braun, *A Comintern Agent in China, 1932–1939* (London: C. Hearst, 1982), 26; Boris Volodarsky, *Stalin's Agent: The Life and Death of Alexander Orlov* (Oxford: Oxford University Press, 2015), 228–9; Whittaker Chambers, *Witness* (New York: Random House, 1952), 290–300.
42 Michael Alpert, *The Republican Army in the Spanish Civil War, 1936–1939* (Cambridge: Cambridge University Press, 2002), 219; Daniel Kowalsky, "The Soviet Union and the International Brigades, 1936–1939," *Journal of Slavic Military Studies* 19 (September 2006): 687; Arnold Krammer, "Soviet Participation in the International Brigades," *Modern Age* 16 (Fall 1972): 357.
43 Stanley G. Payne, *The Spanish Civil War, the Soviet Union and Communism* (New Haven, CT: Yale University Press, 2004), 148.
44 Tyler Wentzell, "Canada's Foreign Enlistment Act and the Spanish Civil War," *Labour/Le Travail* 80 (Fall 2017).
45 Edward Cecil-Smith, "A Fighting Unit in a Fighting Army," *Daily Clarion*, 30 July 1938; Hoff et al., "Biographical Dictionary," 381.
46 Jessie E. MacTaggart, "Crowd Hails Canadians from Spain," *Globe and Mail*, 6 February 1939.
47 Cecil-Smith's speech was quoted at length in "Made Stronger Our Fight for Freedom," *Daily Clarion*, 9 February 1939, and paraphrased in LAC, RCMP File, Report by S.O.F. Evans, "Friends of Mackenzie-Papineau Battalion, Toronto, Ont. – Mass Meeting of welcome to returned members 'Mac-Pap' Battn. held in Massey Hall," 7 February 1939.
48 R.F. MacLean, "Ten Thousand Cheers Rise as Army of 120 Canadians Arrives Home from Spain," *Toronto Evening Telegram*, 6 February 1939.
49 These were recurring ideas in Soviet propaganda relating to the war effort. See Payne, *The Spanish Civil War*, 148.
50 Toby Gordon Ryan, *Stage Left: Canadian Theatre in the Thirties, a Memoir* (Toronto: CTR Publications, 1981), 47.
51 E.A. Havelock, "The Future of Communism," *Canadian Forum* (August 1936).

52 Ed Cecil-Smith, "The Future of Humanity," *New Frontier* (September 1936), 24.

53 Ibid.

54 See CBC Radio Archives, Mac Reynolds interview with Peter Hunter (1964); Tyler Wentzell, "Canada's Foreign Enlistment Act and the Spanish Civil War," *Labour/Le Travail* 80 (Fall 2017): 233–5.

55 RCMP Security Bulletin No. 838, 6 January 1937, in Kealey and Whitaker, *RCMP Security Bulletins: The Depression Years, Part IV, 1937*, 28.

56 LAC, R112, vol. 30553, Cecil-Smith, Edward Paul, Second World War Service File.

57 Buck, *Yours in the Struggle*, 267.

58 A survey of newspapers and magazines showed that anti-Republican sentiment pervaded Quebec newspapers *La Patrie, Le Devoir,* and the *Montreal Gazette*. Outside of Quebec, *Le Droit* (Ottawa), and the Toronto publications the *Globe and Mail, Maclean's* magazine, and *Saturday Night* were all generally anti-Republican. Conversely, the *Toronto Star,* the *Winnipeg Free Press,* and the *Vancouver Province* were pro-Republican. See Mary Biggar Peck, *Red Moon over Spain: Canadian Media Reaction to the Spanish Civil War, 1936–1939* (Ottawa: Steel Rail, 1988), 10.

59 Preston, *The Spanish Civil War,* 135.

60 Ibid., 125.

61 "Assert Rebels Shoot 1,000; 300 Women Said Abused," *Toronto Star,* 9 February 1937.

62 "Charge Italians, Nazis Shelled Line of Retreat," *Toronto Star*, 9 February 1937.

63 See Roderick Stewart and Jesus Majada, *Bethune in Spain* (Montreal and Kingston: McGill-Queen's University Press, 2014), 68–75 for a description of Norman Bethune's involvement in the relief of the fleeing civilians.

64 R.F. MacLean, "Ten Thousand Cheers Rise."

65 Customs documents show Cecil-Smith crossing the Canada–United States border at Niagara Falls after leaving Toronto by rail on 15 February 1937. See also R.F. MacLean, "Ten Thousand Cheers Rise."

66 See Hoar, *The Mackenzie-Papineau Battalion*, 39.

67 Hoff et al., "Biographical Dictionary," 208; Victor Howard, *We Were the Salt of the Earth! A Narrative of the On to Ottawa Trek and Regina Riot* (Regina: Canadian Plains Research Center, 1985), 56, 76.

68 L.F. Edwards, "Authorship and Canadiana," *Masses* (April 1932); Hoff et al., "Biographical Dictionary," 105.

69 See Howard, *We Were the Salt of the Earth!* 35, 169, 171, 330. Howard refers to Lionel Edwards by his nickname, Ernest.

70 Hoff et al., "Biographical Dictionary," 155.

71 Ibid., 311.

72 See Howard, *We Were the Salt of the Earth!* 61, 64. Note that Victor Howard and Victor Hoar, author of *The Mackenzie-Papineau Battalion,* are the same person. See also Ronald Liversedge, *Recollections of the On-to-Ottawa Trek, 1935* (Vancouver: n.p., n.d. [c. 1961]), 22; Hoff et al., "Biographical Dictionary," 211.

73 RGASPI, International Brigade Service File, Edward Cecil-Smith, "Precis of Statement Made by Myself during a Meeting with Comrade Lewis and Elliott of the Central Committee," c. December 1938, 064–069. Kerr was assigned to the task; he did not volunteer. See RGASPI, fond 545, Opis 6, Delo 569, letter from Jack Taylor to Frank Rogers, 11 June 1938, 064–069.

74 See CBC Radio Archives, Mac Reynolds interview with Lawrence Cane and Carl Geiser (1964) and with Irving Weissman and Larry Ryan (1965).

75 LAC, Edward Cecil-Smith Papers, "History of Mac-Paps – A Draft by Edward Cecil-Smith," (c. 1939), 5.

76 For the climb as described in Ted Allan's fictionalized description of his own experiences, see Ted Allan, *This Time a Better Earth: A Critical Edition,* ed. Bart Vautour (Ottawa: University of Ottawa Press, 2015), 7–11.

8 *Los Norteamericanos*

1 For a description of the conditions in Figueres, see Ted Allan, *This Time a Better Earth: A Critical Edition,* ed. Bart Vautour (Ottawa: University of Ottawa Press, 2015), 12, 24–9.

2 Russian State Archive of Socio-Political History (hereafter RGASPI), fond 545, Opis 6, Delo 569, International Brigade Service File of Cecil-Smith, misfiled under Smith (hereafter International Brigade Service File), questionnaire completed by Cecil-Smith, 31 October 1938, 032.

3 Arnold Krammer, "Soviet Participation in the International Brigades," *Modern Age* 16 (Fall 1972): 363; Myron Momryk, "Ignacy Witczak's Passport, Soviet Espionage and the Origins of the Cold War in Canada," *Polish American Studies* 68 (Autumn 2011): 70.

4 Michael Petrou, *Renegades: Canadians in the Spanish Civil War* (Vancouver: UBC Press, 2008), 14.

5 Petrou's research found only 19 of 815 volunteers who self-identified as journalists. Ibid.

6 Petrou's research identified only 215 Canadian volunteers with previous military experience, or roughly one in eight. Ibid., 21. A Russian document suggests a higher proportion of Canadian volunteers with military experience, showing 351 Canadian volunteers with military experience out of a sample of 705. Of these 351, 35 identified themselves as officers, and 77 claimed to have had combat experience in the First World War or

another conflict. RGASPI, fond 545, Opis 6, Delo 455, 11, General Report on 705 People from Canada, 0081–0093.

7 Petrou, *Renegades*, 13.

8 Ronald Liversedge estimated that 500 of the Canadian volunteers had participated in the On-to-Ottawa Trek. Liversedge was in a reasonable position to make this estimate, as he was himself a veteran of the trek and served in Cadre Services in Spain, where he was responsible for cataloguing the Canadian volunteers regardless of their unit. William Beeching, *Canadian Volunteers: Spain, 1936–1939* (Regina: Canadian Plains Research Center, 1989), 52. Beeching himself was also a veteran of the On-to-Ottawa Trek. Petrou's research identified 52 trekkers (Petrou, *Renegades*, 246 n14).

9 Petrou, *Renegades*, 22–4.

10 Ibid., 23.

11 Ronald Liversedge, *Mac-Pap: Memoir of a Canadian in the Spanish Civil War*, ed. David Yorke (Vancouver: New Star Books, 2013), 110–11, 176.

12 For example, German Canadian Hans Ibing initially went to the XIth Brigade and later the transport organization (Regiment de Tren), and Polish Canadian Ignacy Witczak was sent to the Dombrowski Battalion, which was initially part of the XVth Brigade but then sent to the XIIth Brigade. See Myron Momryk, "Ignacy Witczak's Passport, Soviet Espionage and the Origins of the Cold War in Canada," *Polish American Studies* 68 (Autumn 2011): 67–84; David Goutor, *A Chance to Fight Hitler: A Canadian Volunteer in the Spanish Civil War* (Toronto: Between the Lines, 2018).

13 Ariel Mae Lambe, "Cuban Antifascism and the Spanish Civil War: Transnational Activism, Networks, and Solidarity in the 1930s" (PhD diss., Columbia University, 2015), 109; Antonio Pacheco Padro, *Vengo del Jarama: Glorias y horrores de la guerra (San Juan, PR:* Talleres Tipográficos Baldrich, 1942), 60–1; Emmett O'Connor, "Identity and Self-Representation in Irish Communism: The Connolly Column and the Spanish Civil War," *Socialist History* 34 (2009), 42.

14 Cecil D. Eby, *Comrades and Commissars: The Lincoln Battalion in the Spanish Civil War* (University Park: Pennsylvania State University Press, 2007), 42 n13.

15 James W. Cortada, *Modern Warfare in Spain: American Military Observations on the Spanish Civil War, 1936–1939* (Washington, DC: Potomac Books, 2012), 185; "A Close-Up of Our Chief of Staff," *Volunteer for Liberty*, 13 December 1937; "Robert Hale Merriman," Volunteer Database at the Abraham Lincoln Brigade Archives, http://www.alba-valb.org/volunteers/robert-hale-merriman, accessed 7 January 2019; Marion Merriman and Warren Lerude, *American Commander in Spain: Robert Hale Merriman and the Abraham Lincoln Brigade* (Reno: University of Nevada Press, 1986), 222.

16 Eby, *Comrades and Commissars*, 71–4. For a description of how the attack embittered the Canadian volunteers, but was formally presented as necessary to stabilize the lines, see Ted Allan's articles printed in the *Daily Clarion* following his return to Canada: "Crack Jokes One Day, Tomorrow Are Dead on Field of Battle," 11 November 1937; "Jarama Front Battles First Important Test for Canuck Volunteers," 12 November 1937.
17 Joseph O'Connor, *Even the Olives Are Bleeding: The Life and Times of Charles Donnelly* (Dublin: New Island Books, 1992), 104–5, 107.
18 Eby, *Comrades and Commissars*, 64, 78.
19 RGASPI, International Brigade Service File, Edward Cecil-Smith, "Precis of Statement," 064–069.
20 Raymond M. Hoff, Christopher T. Brooks, Michael Petrou, and Myron Momryk, "Biographical Dictionary of Volunteers from Canada in the Spanish Civil War" (unpublished manuscript, 2018), 155, 288.
21 Ibid., 105, 311.
22 Ibid., 91.
23 Library and Archives Canada (hereafter LAC), MG30 E173, Mackenzie-Papineau Battalion Collection (hereafter Mackenzie-Papineau Battalion Collection), Edward Cecil-Smith Papers, vol. 1, file 15 (hereafter Cecil-Smith Papers), Reminiscences of Gerry Delaney, 27 May 1939.
24 E. Cecil-Smith, "Loyalists Find Bren Gun a Good Weapon," *Toronto Star*, 5 February 1939. See also Victor Hoar, *The Mackenzie-Papineau Battalion: Canadian Participation in the Spanish Civil War* (Toronto: Copp Clark, 1969), 24, where Robert Merriman describes the requirement for twelve different kinds of ammunition to Hazen Sise, a member of Norman Bethune's blood transfusion unit.
25 E. Cecil-Smith, "Loyalists Find Bren Gun a Good Weapon," *Toronto Star*, 5 February 1939.
26 Ibid.
27 Hoar, *The Mackenzie-Papineau Battalion*, 115.
28 Hoff et al., "Biographical Dictionary," 259–60; Ronald Liversedge, *Recollections of the On-to-Ottawa Trek, 1935* (Vancouver: n.p., n.d. [c. 1961]); Liversedge, *Mac-Pap*.
29 Liversedge, *Mac-Pap*, 68.
30 R.F. MacLean, "Ten Thousand Cheers Rise as Army of 120 Canadians Arrives Home from Spain," *Toronto Evening Telegram*, 6 February 1939.
31 LAC, Mackenzie-Papineau Battalion Collection, Victor Hoar Papers, vol. 1, file 3, Correspondence between Victor Hoar and Lawrence Cane, c. 1966–67.
32 Beeching, *Canadian Volunteers*, 58; Hoar, *The Mackenzie-Papineau Battalion*, 116.

33 Robert Merriman, "Merriman Diaries: Exegesis," ed. Raymond Hoff (unpublished manuscript, 2018), 146.

34 John McCannon, "Soviet Intervention in the Spanish Civil War, 1936–39: A Reexamination," *Russian History* 22 (Summer 1995): 161.

35 Ibid., 160; Stanley G. Payne, *The Spanish Civil War, the Soviet Union and Communism* (New Haven, CT: Yale University Press, 2004), 153, 161; Michael Alpert, *The Republican Army in the Spanish Civil War, 1936–1939* (Cambridge: Cambridge University Press, 2002), 225–6.

36 Merriman, "Diaries," 170, 288. "Mexicans" can also refer to individuals coming from Russia, such as political exiles who had taken refuge in Russia, regardless of their country of origin.

37 Cecil-Smith, "Red Officers Know Their Job"; LAC, RG146, vol. 1830, CSIS files 95-A-0000-88, Edward Cecil-Smith, part 1, box 58 (hereafter RCMP File), unattributed "N" Division Report, 4 July 1941.

38 Cecil-Smith, "Red Officers Know Their Job," *Montreal Gazette*, 4 July 1941; Cecil-Smith, "'Break Through' Is Emphasized as Offensive Defensive Tactics," *Montreal Gazette*, 9 July 1941.

39 Cecil-Smith, "Russians Favour 'Elastic' Line," *Montreal Gazette*, 7 July 1941; "Elastic Defence Is Soviet Plan Favored over Immobile System," *Montreal Gazette*, 8 July 1941.

40 Merriman, "Diaries," 146–7, 151; RGASPI, International Brigade Service File, Biografia de Militantes completed by Cecil-Smith, 2 November 1938, 038–041.

41 Danny Duncan, ed., *African Americans in the Spanish Civil War: 'This Ain't Ethiopia, but It'll Do* (New York: G.K. Hall, 1992), 73–4.

42 See diary entries on 29 April and 3 May in Merriman, "Diaries," 202, 214.

43 Gregory Clark, "Mac-Paps Made Bridge of Thread and Roared as Rebels Bombed it," *Toronto Star*, 4 February 1939.

44 Sam Wild, "Defense against Tanks," *Volunteer for Liberty*, 25 May 1938.

45 The British anti-tank guns were destroyed by aircraft, overrun by enemy soldiers, or destroyed in place by their crews to prevent them from falling into enemy hands in their first engagement of "the Retreats" at Belchite. Richard Baxell, *Unlikely Warriors: The British in the Spanish Civil War* (London: Aurum Press, 2012), 308.

46 Cecil-Smith, "Soviet Fire Power Great," *Montreal Gazette*, 5 July 1941.

47 Merriman, "Diaries," 214.

48 John Peter Kraljic, "The Croatian Community in North America and the Spanish Civil War" (MA thesis, Hunter College, 2002), 82.

49 Merriman and Lerude, *American Commander in Spain*, 146–7.

50 Kraljic, "The Croatian Community," 82; "Mirko Markovics," Volunteer Database at the Abraham Lincoln Brigade Archives, http://www.alba-valb.org/volunteers/mirko-markovics, accessed 7 January 2019.

51 Chris Brooks, "The Making of the Washington Battalion," *Volunteer*, 21 March 2014.

52 The phenomenon of rank and fileism arose, in part, due to some fundamental misunderstandings of the nature of a "people's army." The Spanish Republican Army, the volunteers were told, was a "people's army" modelled on the Soviet Red Army. Publications like *Soviet Russia Today* left many of the volunteers with an idealized view of how the Red Army functioned. An editorial by William Sydney claimed that Red Army's discipline "is not the discipline of class division as in capitalist armies, with its humility of the rank and file and the arrogance of the officer. It is the discipline of a workers' army when on duty, when each man has to carry out the tasks allotted to him by the Workers' and Peasants' Government. Outside of duty, each belongs to a classless army, where every man, from the private to the commander, is equal and receives the same treatment. They fraternize and carry on their work in the circles on an absolute basis of equality." William Sydney, "Defenders of the Interests of the Toilers of the World," *Soviet Russia Today* (November 1933). Canadian volunteer Ronald Liversedge explained that this meant "absolute democracy or equality of all ranks when not in action, and full right of debate and criticism after a battle or front-line action." Liversedge, *Mac-Pap*, 72. In reality, the Red Army was as hierarchical as any military organization. Merriman and Cecil-Smith believed that traditional military discipline ("permanent authority") was a requirement for an efficient military force.

53 RGASPI, International Brigade Service File, Edward Cecil-Smith, "Precis of Statement Made by Myself during a Meeting with Comrade Lewis and Elliott of the Central Committee," c. December 1938, 064–069.

54 See Chris Brooks and Lisa Clemmer, "Albin Ragner: An Unpublished Memoir," *Volunteer*, 27 February 2013; Kraljic, "The Croatian Community," 83.

55 See diary entry for 21 May 1937; Merriman, "Diaries," 256.

56 Ibid.

57 Hoar, *The Mackenzie-Papineau Battalion*, 86; RGASPI, International Brigade Service File, Biografia de Militantes completed by Cecil-Smith, 2 November 1938, 038–041.

58 See Ted Allan, "Bombardment at Albacete," *New Frontier* (May 1937).

59 Merriman, "Diaries," 172–4, 210.

60 Lisa A. Kirschenbaum, *International Communism and the Spanish Civil War* (Cambridge: Cambridge University Press, 2015), 138; Fenner Brockway, *The Truth about Barcelona* (London: Independent Labour Party, 1937).

61 George Orwell, *Homage to Catalonia* (1938; reprint, New York: Harvest Books, 1980).

62 Petrou, *Renegades*, 148–57.

63 See diary entries for 9–12 May, Merriman, "Diaries," 226, 230.

64 E. Cecil-Smith, "Loyalists Find Bren Gun a Good Weapon," *Toronto Star*, 8 February 1939.

65 Ibid.

66 Hoff et al., "Biographical Dictionary," 190. Beeching, *Canadian Volunteers*, 56, quotes Bill Brennan's statements that that Cecil-Smith, Bob Kerr, Joseph Kelly, Edo Jardas, and Walter Dent were in attendance. Hoar, *The Mackenzie-Papineau Battalion*, 107 also includes Harry Rushton and Francis [François] Poirier. Although Bill Brennan recalled that Walter Dent had attended this meeting, Dent himself later wrote to Bill Beeching to state that he had not been present. See LAC, Mackenzie-Papineau Battalion Collection, Walter E. Dent Papers, vol. 2, file 9, letter from Walter Dent to Bill Beeching, 19 August 1982. Although Dent was not in attendance, he did sign the letter to Mackenzie King announcing the creation of the battalion. Poirier's party membership is confirmed by his International Brigade Service File. See RGASPI, fond 545, Opis 6, Delo 564, Service File of Francis Poirier, 37. Regarding Rushton, see RCMP Security Bulletin No. 427, 7 October 1936 in Gregory S. Kealey and Reg Whitaker, eds., *RCMP Security Bulletins: The Depression Years, Part III, 1936* (St. John's: Canadian Committee on Labour History, 1995), 422; Petrou, *Renegades*, 18; and RGASPI, fond 545, Opis 6, Delo 567, Service File of Harry Rushton, 26–7. Ron Liversedge recalled that the initial ask had been for giving a new battalion a Canadian name, but, given that he is not listed as having attended the meetings noted above, he may have been referring to a different process altogether or misremembering this small detail. Liversedge, *Mac-Pap*, 69.

67 Hoar, *The Mackenzie-Papineau Battalion*, 102.

68 "Canadians in Spain Ask Full Support," *Toronto Star*, 21 May 1937. The letter was published in full as "In Spain We Fight to Save Democracy and Peace," *Daily Clarion*, 22 May 1937. See also Beeching, *Canadian Volunteers*, 56 and LAC, RCMP File, unattributed RCMP report translating an article in the Croatian newspaper *Sloodna Misao*, 25 May 1937.

69 "Canadians in Spain Ask Full Support"; "In Spain We Fight."

70 CBC Radio Archives, Mac Reynolds interview with Tim Buck (1964); Tim Buck, *Yours in the Struggle: Reminiscences of Tim Buck*, ed. William Beeching and Phyllis Clarke (Toronto: New Canada Publication, 1977), 275–6.

71 For example, when three Canadians, none of whom were supposed to have had passports, were killed in Spain in September, the *Toronto Star* questioned the Friends about any knowledge or involvement they might have had: "Miss Colle said she knew nothing of recruiting activities in Toronto on behalf of the battalion." "Trio Killed in Spain Entry Real Mystery," *Toronto Star*, 27 September 1937.

72 CBC Radio Archives, Mac Reynolds interview with Joseph Salsberg (1965).
73 Hoff et al., "Biographical Dictionary," 440.
74 LAC, MG28-IV11, Canadian Trotskyist Movement Fonds, Ross Dowson Personal Files, vol. 40-9, "President's Report" to the Ontario Executive Committee of the CCF Youth Movement by William Grant, 23 September 1936.
75 See CBC Radio Archives, Mac Reynolds interview with Peter Hunter (1964); D.P. Stephens, *Memoir of the Spanish Civil War: An Armenian-Canadian in the Spanish Civil War*, ed. Rick Rennie (St. John's: Canadian Committee on Labour History, 2000), 24; Hoff et al., "Biographical Dictionary"; Walter Dent, "Would Like to Hear from My Canadian Comrades," *Advance: A Magazine for Youth* (May 1937). See also Bill Dampier's interview with Walter Dent in "The Heroes of a Forgotten War," *Toronto Star*, 26 August 1979. On 28 November 1938, the *Daily Clarion* announced that Dent had been selected to run the Young Communist League in Toronto. For CCF members in the International Brigades, see Petrou, *Renegades*, 24.
76 While two hundred volunteers had come from Quebec, only a small portion of them were French Canadian. Petrou, *Renegades*, 20.
77 CBC Radio Archives, Mac Reynolds interview with Tim Buck (1964); Buck, *Yours in the Struggle*, 275–6.
78 "Canadians in Spain Ask Full Support."
79 Tyler Wentzell, "Canada's Foreign Enlistment Act and the Spanish Civil War," *Labour/Le Travail* 80 (Fall 2017): 234; Liversedge, *Mac-Pap*, 38–9; Hoar, *The Mackenzie-Papineau Battalion*, 40; CBC Radio Archives, Mac Reynolds interview with Peter Hunter (1964).
80 Hoff et al., "Biographical Dictionary," 109–10; RGASPI, International Brigade Service File, Edward Cecil-Smith, "Precis of Statement Made by Myself."
81 LAC, Edward Cecil-Smith Papers, "History of Mac-Paps: A Draft by Edward Cecil-Smith," c. 1939, 2–3.
82 Ed Cecil-Smith, "Revolutionary Tragedy," *Worker*, 7 September 1935. See also, John Manley, "'Communists Love Canada!' The Communist Party of Canada, 'The People,' and the Popular Front, 1933–1939," *Journal of Canadian Studies* 36 (Winter 2001–2): 23.
83 Stanley Ryerson, *1837: The Birth of Canadian Democracy* (Toronto: F. White, 1937), 11.
84 See also Captain Cecil Smith, "Mackenzie and Papineau 100 Years Ago," *Our Combat / Nuestro Combate* (December 1937).
85 Buck, *Yours in the Struggle*, 275; emphasis added.
86 "Canadians in Spain Ask Full Support."

87 Buck, *Yours in the Struggle*, 268.

88 Merriman's diary, written at the time of these events, states that the name Mackenzie-Papineau was arrived at on 28 June. He subsequently mentions the announcement and MacLeod's visit on 1 July, and the creation of a Canadian company within the battalion under the command of Ronald Liversedge a few days later. Liversedge subsequently resigned after disagreements between himself and Merriman as to how an officer should behave. Merriman states that the name was a symbolic gesture and would not result in the reorganization of the forces such that the battalion would become a fully Canadian organization – Canadians in the Lincoln Battalion would stay in the Lincoln Battalion. See Meriman diary entries on 28 June and 1, 2, and 5 July, Merriman, "Diaries," 359, 369–70, 379; Joe Dallet, *Letters from Spain: By Joe Dallet, First Political Commissar (Mackenzie-Papineau Battalion), to His Wife* (Toronto: New Era Publishers, 1938), 52–3; Liversedge, *Mac-Pap*, 74–6; Hoar, *The Mackenzie-Papineau Battalion*, 111–12. For more on MacLeod's visit to Spain and Geneva to protest the bombing of Guernica, see Ted Allan, "Sees Diplomats as Big Poker Players," *Daily Clarion*, 18 November 1937, and "Unionists of Spain Vie in Assistance to Intern'l Brigade," *Daily Clarion*, 30 November 1937.

89 RGASPI, International Brigade Service File, Biografia de Militantes completed by Cecil-Smith, 2 November 1938, 038–041.

90 Chris Brooks, "The Making of the Washington Battalion," *Volunteer*, 21 March 2014.

91 Edwin Rolfe, *The Lincoln Battalion* (New York: Random House, 1939), 86; "Hans Amlie," Volunteer Database at the Abraham Lincoln Brigade Archives, http://www.alba-valb.org/volunteers/hans-amlie, accessed 7 January 2019; James R. Jansen, "The Debs Column and American Socialists in the Spanish Civil War" (MA thesis, University of Nebraska, 2015), 56, 81, 86–90. See also diary entry for 4 May 1937, Merriman, "Diaries," 214.

92 Hoar, *The Mackenzie-Papineau Battalion*, 85; Arthur Landis, *The Abraham Lincoln Brigade* (New York: Citadel Press, 1967), 171; Rolfe, *The Lincoln Battalion*, 86; RGASPI, fond 545, Opis 2, Delo 51, Order du Jour No. 56, 4 June 1937, 105–8.

93 RGASPI, fond 545, Opis 2, Delo 50, 18 May 1937, 109–11.

94 Alpert, *The Republican Army in the Spanish Civil War*, 187.

95 Chris Brooks and Liana Katz, "Blast from the Past (Revisited): The Commissar and the Good Fight," *Volunteer*, 16 December 2015.

96 Alpert, *The Republican Army in the Spanish Civil War*, 174.

97 Ibid., 179–80, 218.

98 LAC, International Brigade Files copied from RGASPI, Reel K-260, Report of Meeting of Political Commissars, 8 June 1937.

99 There is some disagreement in the sources regarding the identity of Cecil-Smith's commissar. Edwin Rolfe, writing only two years after the battle, stated that Bernard Ames (a Washington DC lawyer) was Cecil-Smith's commissar in No. 2 Company, and Morris Wickman was Hans Amlie's commissar in No. 1 Company. See Rolfe, *The Lincoln Battalion*, 86. However, several years later, Arthur Landis stated that Cecil-Smith's commissar was Wickman, and Amlie's commissar was Ames. See Landis, *The Abraham Lincoln Brigade*, 173. Landis's statement was likely a correction to Rolfe's book in consultation with veterans, or it could have been an error resulting from the passage of time. Since Ames and Amlie survived the war (Wickman was killed later in the campaign) and remained active with the American Communist Party, it seems likely that Landis was correcting an error. Since then, documents held in the Russian archives have been released that confirm Wickman as the commissar and David Anderson as the second in command. See RGASPI, fond 545, Opis 2, Delo 51, Order du Jour No. 56, 4 June 1937, 105–8.

100 Markowicz had little time for Mates, an American about whom we know little. Markowicz saw him as a political appointee, lacking in both discipline and military experience. Chris Brooks, "The Making of the Washington Battalion," *Volunteer*, 21 March 2014.

101 Merriman noted on 10 April 1937 that Cecil-Smith was one of three nominees under consideration for the position of base commissar. Merriman, "Diaries," 159.

102 See "Morris Wickman," Volunteer Database at the Abraham Lincoln Brigade Archives, http://www.alba-valb.org/volunteers/morris-henry-wickman, accessed 7 January 2019; Joy Gleason Carew, *Blacks, Reds, and Russians: Sojourners in Search of the Soviet Promise* (New Brunswick, NJ: Rutgers University Press, 2010), 102

103 Jean Watts, "Bravery of Canadian Is Lauded by Buddy," *Daily Clarion*, 6 October 1937.

104 Anderson's rank was listed as second lieutenant on the order of the day prior to Brunete, but, according to Jean Watts, he was a *cabo* (corporal) in October. See RGASPI, fond 545, Opis 2, Delo 51, Order du Jour No. 56, 4 June 1937, 105–8; Watts, "Bravery of Canadian Is Lauded."

105 James K. Hopkins, *Into the Heart of the Fire: The British in the Spanish Civil War* (Stanford, CA: Stanford University Press, 1998), 160. Hopkins later served in the Mackenzie-Papineau Battalion.

106 See Merriman, "Diary," entry for 11 June, at 323.

107 Joe Dallet, *Letters from Spain: By Joe Dallet, First Political Commissar (Mackenzie-Papineau Battalion), to His Wife* (Toronto: New Era Publishers, 1938), 47. See also Liversedge, *Mac-Pap*, 70.

108 Chris Brooks, "The Making of the Washington Battalion," *Volunteer*, 21 March 2014.

109 Ibid.

110 "Copic, Commander of Our 15th Brigade," *Volunteer for Liberty*, 17 November 1937. See also Kraljic, "The Croatian Community," 13; John Kraljic, "From the ALBA Archives: New Material on Vladimir Copic, Commander of the XVth Brigade," *Volunteer* (Fall 1999), 8; Merriman, and Lerude, *American Commander in Spain*, 106.

111 CBC Radio Archives, Mac Reynolds interview with Lawrence Cane and Carl Geiser (1964).

112 Brooks, "The Making of the Washington Battalion."

113 Beeching, *Canadian Volunteers*, 47.

114 Chris Brooks and Lisa Clemmer, "Albin Ragner: An Unpublished Memoir," *Volunteer*, 27 February 2013; Brooks, "The Making of the Washington Battalion."

115 Hugh Thomas, *The Spanish Civil War* (London: Eyre and Spottiswoode, 1961), 460.

116 The initial organization of the XVth Brigade is outlined in RGASPI, fond 545, Opis 3, Delo 426, Orden del Dia, 3 July 1937, 207. See also Chris Brooks, "Jarama Series: The Regiments," *Volunteer*, 13 July 2016.

117 Frank Ryan, ed., *The Book of the XV Brigade: Records of British, American, Canadian and Irish Volunteers in the XV International Brigade in Spain, 1936–1938* (Madrid: Commissariat of War, XVth Brigade, 1938), 129; Eby, *Comrades and Commissars*, 95; Brooks, "Jarama Series: The Regiments."

118 Richard Baxell, "The Malcolm Dunbar Papers," http://www.richardbaxell.info/the-malcolm-dunbar-papers/, accessed 7 January 2019.

119 Ryan, *The Book of the XV Brigade*, 132.

120 Ibid.

121 Herbert L. Matthews, *Two Wars and More to Come* (Rathway, NJ: Quinn and Boden, 1938), 230. Ted Allan, who was present during the Brunete Offensive and visited participants in the hospital, stated that the Spanish brigade had bypassed the town entirely. See Ted Allan, "Honest-to-Goodness Canadian Cigarettes Cause Hospital 'Riot,'" *Daily Clarion*, 2 December 1937. Allan filed his story with the *Daily Clarion* as part of a series of articles following his return to Canada later in the summer of 1937.

122 Petrou, *Renegades*, 97; Beeching, *Canadian Volunteers*, 44.

123 Hoar, *The Mackenzie-Papineau Battalion*, 91.

124 Baxell, *Unlikely Warriors*, p. 225.

125 See Beeching, *Canadian Volunteers*, 46–7. See also LAC, Edward Cecil-Smith Papers, Reminiscences of Bill Brennan, c. 1939.

126 Ryan, *The Book of the XV Brigade*, 132.

127 Landis, *The Abraham Lincoln Brigade*, 190.

128 Szalway had served in the Austro-Hungarian Army during the Great War and later joined the Communist Party of Hungary. Chris Brooks, "Jarama Series: The Regiments." He had taken the name "Chapaieff" or "Chapaiev" as homage to the guerrilla leader in the Russian Civil War, the subject of a popular film from Russia, *Chapieff, the Red Guerilla Fighter.*
129 Duncan, *African Americans in the Spanish Civil War*, 83–4.
130 Landis, *The Abraham Lincoln Brigade*, 190.
131 Brooks and Clemmer, "Albin Ragner."
132 Watts, "Bravery of Canadian Is Lauded by Buddy."
133 "Returned Boys Praise Bravery of Canadians," *Daily Clarion*, 16 September 1938, states that Cecil-Smith was wounded in the knee by tank shrapnel at 10 p.m. that night. However, Ted Allan, in "Honest-to-Goodness Canadian Cigarettes," states that Cecil-Smith's wounds to the knee were the result of an exploding bullet striking his rifle while he was kneeling. A photo taken at the aid station soon after shows that the wound was to his left knee. Given that Allan's source of information was Cecil-Smith himself, and that Cecil-Smith was a right-handed shooter (meaning that, when kneeling, his weight would be on his right knee, protecting it, while his left knee would be up), it seems likely that the knee wound occurred at the same time as the wrist wound. See also Matthews, *Two Wars*, 231, who described Cecil-Smith as being seriously wounded in the attack.
134 Cecil-Smith, "Canadian Volunteers, Home from Spanish War, Lauded by Leader by Valour and Endurance," *Globe and Mail*, 4 February 1939.
135 Matthews, *Two Wars*, 230. Hans Amlie, commanding No. 1 Company, had similarly been wounded in the assault and was pinned down for the rest of the day. See Landis, *The Abraham Lincoln Brigade*, 195.
136 See Hoar, *The Mackenzie-Papineau Battalion*, 93.
137 Ibid., 91, and "Returned Boys Praise Bravery of Canadians," *Daily Clarion*, 16 September 1938.
138 Hoar, *The Mackenzie-Papineau Battalion*, 92.
139 Baxell, *Unlikely Warriors*, 226–8.
140 Hoar, *The Mackenzie-Papineau Battalion*, 93, and Landis, *The Abraham Lincoln Brigade*, 195.
141 "Returned Boys Praise Bravery of Canadians."
142 Mark Zuehlke, *The Gallant Cause: Canadians in the Spanish Civil War, 1936–1939* (Toronto: Whitecap Books, 1996), 150.
143 Rob Stradling, "English-speaking Units of the International Brigades: War, Politics, and Discipline," *Journal of Contemporary History* 45 (2010): 751.
144 Jansen, "The Debs Column," 87.
145 Watts, "Bravery of Canadian Is Lauded."
146 Peter Carroll, *The Odyssey of the Abraham Lincoln Brigade: Americans in the Spanish Civil War* (Stanford. CA: Stanford University Press, 1994), 143–4.

147 Stradling, "English-speaking Units," 751–2.
148 RCMP Report, "Parade and Meeting to Welcome Dr. Norman Bethune to Toronto, June 14, 1937," in *Bethune: The Secret Police File*, ed. David Lethbridge (Salmon Arm, BC: Undercurrent Press, 2003), Document 17. The report was filed by R.W. Irvine.
149 William Strange, "Britain Won't Allow Fascists to Conquer, Dr Bethune Declares," *Toronto Star*, 16 June 1937.
150 Author's interview with Bill Smith.
151 See Roderick Stewart and Sharon Stewart, *Phoenix: The Life of Norman Bethune* (Montreal and Kingston: McGill-Queen's University Press, 2011), 216–17, and Jane Lind, *Perfect Red: The Life of Paraskeva Clark* (Toronto: Cormorant Books, 2009), 102. See also "Youth Will Be Freed – Bethune," *Daily Clarion*, 22 November 1937.
152 Author's interview with Bill Smith.
153 Edgar Snow, *Red Star over China* (London: Victor Gallancz, 1934), 444.
154 Author's interview with Bill Smith.
155 "Lt Lionel Edwards, a Canadian Officer," *Volunteer for Liberty*, 6 October 1938.
156 "Paralyzed Spanish Vet Prays to Fight in China," *Toronto Star*, 6 February 1939.
157 Michael Butt, "Surveillance of Canadian Communists: A Case Study of Toronto RCMP Intelligence Networks, 1920–1939" (PhD diss., Memorial University, 2003), 352.
158 Adrienne Clarkson, in her biography of Norman Bethune, notes that Ted Allan and Sydney Gordon's book *The Scalpel, The Sword* treated Ewen "as if she had never existed." See Clarkson, *Norman Bethune* (Toronto: Penguin Canada, 2009), 154.
159 See Jean Ewen, *China Nurse, 1932–1939* (Toronto: McClelland and Stewart, 1981).

9 The Fighting Canucks

1 Russian State Archive of Socio-Political History (hereafter RGASPI), fond 545, Opis 6, Delo 569, International Brigade Service File of Cecil-Smith, misfiled under Smith (hereafter International Brigade Service File), Biografia de Militantes completed by Cecil-Smith, 2 November 1938, 038–041.
2 Michael Petrou, *Renegades: Canadians in the Spanish Civil War* (Vancouver: UBC Press, 2008), 73; "MacPaps under Fire," *Volunteer for Liberty*, 5 February 1938.
3 "Canadian, British and American Wounded in Spanish War Being Treated in Madrid Hospitals," *Toronto Daily Star*, 9 July 1937; Ted Allan,

"Honest-to-Goodness Canadian Cigarettes Cause Hospital 'Riot,'" *Daily Clarion*, 2 December 1937.

4 Allan, "Honest-to-Goodness Canadian Cigarettes."

5 Jean Watts, "Bravery of Canadian Is Lauded by Buddy," *Daily Clarion*, 6 October 1937.

6 Contemporary photographs also show Cecil-Smith with the Mac-Paps in Tarazona during the summer of 1937, although his specific role in their training remains unknown.

7 For more on the Mac-Paps' training, see Joe Dallet, *Letters from Spain: By Joe Dallet, First Political Commissar (Mackenzie-Papineau Battalion), to His Wife* (Toronto: New Era Publishers, 1938), 44–62.

8 "Rollin Jones Dart," Volunteer Database at the Abraham Lincoln Brigade Archives, http://www.alba-valb.org/volunteers/rollin-jones-dart, accessed 7 January 2019.

9 Victor Hoar, *The Mackenzie-Papineau Battalion: Canadian Participation in the Spanish Civil War* (Toronto: Copp Clark, 1969), 112; Harvey Klehr, *Communist Cadre: The Social Background of the American Communist Party Elite* (Stanford, CA: Hoover Institution Press, 1978), 111–12.

10 Antony Beevor, *The Battle for Spain: The Spanish Civil War, 1936–1939* (London: Penguin Books, 2006), 196–7.

11 Ronald Liversedge, *Mac-Pap: Memoir of a Canadian in the Spanish Civil War*, ed, David Yorke (Vancouver: New Star Books, 2013), 79–81; "Robert George Thompson," Volunteer Database at the Abraham Lincoln Brigade Archives, http://www.alba-valb.org/volunteers/robert-george-thompson, accessed 7 January 2019.

12 See Arthur Landis, *The Abraham Lincoln Brigade* (New York: Citadel Press, 1967), 306. Note that in October 1937, the battalions in the International Brigades were renumbered. The British Battalion became the 57th, the Lincoln Battalion became the 58, the 24th Battalion became the 59th, and the Mackenzie-Papineau Battalion became the 60th. For consistency and simplicity, the 59th Battalion will be referred to by its original name, the 24th Battalion.

13 Steven J. Zaloga, "Soviet Tank Operations in the Spanish Civil War," *Journal of Slavic Military Studies* 12 (September 1999): 145–7; Daniel Kowalsky, "The Soviet Union and the International Brigades, 1936–1939," *Journal of Slavic Military Studies* 19 (September 2006): 695; William Kardash, *I Fought for Canada in Spain* (Toronto: New Era Publishers, 1938); Raymond M. Hoff, Christopher T. Brooks, Michael Petrou, and Myron Momryk, "Biographical Dictionary of Volunteers from Canada in the Spanish Civil War" (unpublished manuscript, 2018), 204.

14 Richard Baxell, *Unlikely Warriors: The British in the Spanish Civil War* (London: Aurum Press, 2012), 271.

15 CBC Radio Archives, Mac Reynolds interview with Lawrence Cane (1964).

16 Petrou, *Renegades*, 77; Hoar, *The Mackenzie-Papineau Battalion*, 148.

17 Cecil D. Eby, *Comrades and Commissars: The Lincoln Battalion in the Spanish Civil War* (University Park: Pennsylvania State University Press, 2007), 255; "William Friedrich Neure," Volunteer Database at the Abraham Lincoln Brigade Archives, http://www.alba-valb.org/volunteers/william-friedrich-neure, accessed 7 January 2019.

18 Eby, *Comrades and Commissars*, 255; Ben Iceland, "A Train Is Bombed," *Volunteer* (June 1983); "Joseph Michael Dougher," Volunteer Database at the Abraham Lincoln Brigade Archives, http://www.alba-valb.org/volunteers/joseph-dougher, accessed 7 January 2019.

19 Hoar, *The Mackenzie-Papineau Battalion*, 147; Landis, *The Abraham Lincoln Brigade*, 320; "Isadore J. Schrenzel," Volunteer Database at the Abraham Lincoln Brigade Archives, http://www.alba-valb.org/volunteers/isadore-schrenzel, accessed 7 January 2019.

20 Hoar, *The Mackenzie-Papineau Battalion*, 112; Hoff et al., "Biographical Dictionary," 273; Sam Suto, "Captain Niila Makela [*sic*]," *Volunteer for Liberty*, 13 August 1938.

21 In his diary on October 19, Merriman notes that Cecil-Smith is joining the Mac-Paps. Robert Merriman, "Merriman Diaries: Exegesis," ed. Raymond Hoff (unpublished manuscript, 2018), 658.

22 Library and Archives Canada (hereafter LAC), International Brigade Files copied from RGASPI, reel K-260, List of Reinforcements to the Mackenzie-Papineau Battalion at Fuentes de Ebro, 20 October 1937. See also Robert Thompson, "The Mac-Paps," *Daily Clarion*, 17 February 1938, where Thompson states expressly that Cecil-Smith was "rushed to the front" after he had healed from his wounds, whereupon Cecil-Smith served as a company commander before Thompson made him his adjutant. This directly contradicts Hoar's account that Cecil-Smith was not at Fuentes de Ebro at all, as well as more contemporary reports found in the *Volunteer for Liberty*, 7 November 1938, and the *Daily Clarion*, 6 October 1938, both of which claimed Cecil-Smith joined the battalion *after* the Battle of Fuentes de Ebro, when the unit had been withdrawn for training at the castle in Pezuela de las Torres. These accounts are likely the result of the fact that Cecil-Smith was not involved with the preparation for and execution of the initial assault. Considering the disorganized nature of the hasty defence, soldiers would have been unaware of the arrival of any individual reinforcements outside their immediate area.

23 LAC, Edward Cecil-Smith Papers, Reminiscences of Bill Boyak, c. 1939; Hoff et al., "Biographical Dictionary," 48.

24 See summary of his service in RGASPI, International Brigade Service File and "Smith Joins Clarion Staff," *Daily Clarion*, 1 April 1939. Liversedge served in No. 1 Company but makes no mention of Cecil-Smith's appearance with the company at Fuentes de Ebro. This is not, however, especially concerning, as Liversedge's memoirs are scattered regarding command appointments at the Battle of Fuentes de Ebro. Liversedge remembers Robert Thompson as the second in command of No. 2 Company (Liversedge, *Mac-Pap*, 94), while it is established that Thompson was actually the battalion commander at the time. Liversedge also recalls a man named Bill Whitehead taking over No. 1 Company after its original commander, Bill Neure (whose name he did not remember), was wounded (ibid., 92). Whitehead was likely Frank Whitfield (Hoff et al., "Biographical Dictionary," 488). Liversedge also states that Niilo Makela, the commander of the Machine Gun Company, took over as the battalion commander toward the end of the Mac-Paps' time on the line (*Mac-Pap*, 97), but this is recorded nowhere else, including Makela's own reminiscences of the battle.

25 Many of the troops had gone into the battle sick, either from pleurisy or dysentery. See Liversedge, *Mac-Pap*, 69, 87.

26 Merriman mentions Thompson's work at Pozorubio on several occasions in his diary.

27 Hoar, *The Mackenzie-Papineau Battalion*, 112.

28 Robert Thompson and Hoar give the date of the relief in place as 23 October, whereas Beeching puts the date at 25 October. See Robert Thompson, "The Mac-Paps," *Daily Clarion*, 17 February 1938; Hoar, *The Mackenzie-Papineau Battalion*, 25; William Beeching, *Canadian Volunteers: Spain, 1936–1939* (Regina: Canadian Plains Research Center, 1989), 78.

29 Merriman, "Diaries," 677.

30 Beeching, *Canadian Volunteers*, 78.

31 It is unclear when Cecil-Smith formally took over command. Thompson was still signing documents in his capacity as battalion commander as late as 14 November. Cecil-Smith was still signing documents as acting battalion commander as late as 17 November.

32 Cecil-Smith made the statement in a speech he delivered upon returning to Canada. See "Made Stronger Our Fight for Freedom," *Daily Clarion*, 9 February 1939), and paraphrased in RCMP File, report by S.O.F. Evans, "Friends of Mackenzie-Papineau Battalion, Toronto, Ont. – Mass Meeting of welcome to returned members 'Mac-Pap' Battn. Held in Massey Hall," 7 February 1939.

33 Hoar, *The Mackenzie-Papineau Battalion*, 209; Hoff et al., "Biographical Dictionary," 79.

34 LAC, International Brigade Files copied from RGASPI, reel K-260, Estado No. 3, October 1937.

35 Cecil-Smith, "Red Officers Know Their Job," *Montreal Gazette*, 4 July 1941.
36 Ibid.
37 Ibid.
38 Ibid.
39 Michael Alpert, *The Republican Army in the Spanish Civil War* (Cambridge: Cambridge University Press, 2002), 225, 255–6.
40 Red Army personnel in Spain normally adopted an innocuous, Western European sounding name. See Arnold Krammer, "Soviet Participation in the International Brigades," *Modern Age* 16 (Fall 1972): 356.
41 Beeching, *Canadian Volunteers*, 57–8.
42 "Ukes and Finns of the Mac-Paps," *Volunteer for Liberty*, 13 August 1938.
43 Alpert, *The Republican Army*, 222.
44 RGASPI, fond 545, Opis 6, Delo 982, Service File of Harry Schoenberg; "Harry Schoenberg," Volunteer Database at the Abraham Lincoln Brigade Archives, http://www.alba-valb.org/volunteers/harry-schoenberg, accessed 7 January 2019; Saul Friedberg, "A Tribute to Harry Schoenberg," *Volunteer*, 12 May 1990.
45 "Ivan John Nahanchuk," Volunteer Database at the Abraham Lincoln Brigade Archives, http://www.alba-valb.org/volunteers/ivan-john-nahanchuk, accessed 7 January 2019.
46 LAC, International Brigade Files copied from RGASPI, reel K-260, Edward Cecil-Smith Report of the Day, 17 November 1937.
47 Hoar, *The Mackenzie-Papineau Battalion*, 147; "Saul Wellman," Volunteer Database at the Abraham Lincoln Brigade Archives, http://www.alba-valb.org/volunteers/saul-wellman, accessed 7 January 2019.
48 Eby, *Comrades and Commissars*, 268.
49 Tim Buck, *Yours in the Struggle: Reminiscences of Tim Buck*, ed. William Beeching and Phyllis Clarke (Toronto: New Canada Publication, 1977), 270.
50 Ibid.
51 LAC, International Brigade Files copied from RGASPI, reel K-260, Guard Report for November 9, 1937.
52 "Notes on the Situation in the International Units in Spain. Report by Colonel Com. Sverchecsky [Walter]," 14 January 1938, cited by Ronald Radosh, Mary M. Habeck and Grigory Sevostianov, eds., *Spain Betrayed: The Soviet Union in the Spanish Civil War* (New Haven, CT: Yale University Press, 2001), 444. Walter was referring to a visit to the British and Canadian battalions "a month earlier." See also Baxell, *Unlikely Warriors*, 279.
53 See Petrou, *Renegades*, 124–37.
54 Landis, *The Abraham Lincoln Brigade*, 345.
55 LAC, International Brigade Files copied from RGASPI, reel K-260, Edward Cecil-Smith, Order of the Day for December 24, 1937.

56 Mark Zuehlke, *The Gallant Cause: Canadians in the Spanish Civil War, 1936–1939* (Toronto: Whitecap Books, 1996), 197.
57 Paul Preston, *The Spanish Civil War, 1936–39* (London: Weidenfeld and Nicolson, 1986), 279.
58 Hugh Thomas, *The Spanish Civil War* (London: Eyre and Spottiswoode, 1961), 504.
59 See "Teruel: City of Victory," *Daily Clarion*, 15 January 1937.
60 "Army of Unity," *Daily Clarion*, 10 February 1937.
61 LAC, International Brigade Files copied from RGASPI, reel K-260, Edward Cecil-Smith, Order of the Day for December 25, 1937.
62 "Canadians get Christmas Wire," *Daily Clarion*, 30 December 1937.
63 LAC, International Brigade Files copied from RGASPI, reel K-260, Guard Report for December 24, 1937.
64 Landis, *The Abraham Lincoln Brigade*, 345.
65 See, for instance, Jean Watts, "Doctor Bethune's Unit Reorganized Covers All Fronts," *Daily Clarion*, 3 March 1937; "Hear 'Salud' as Greeting Every Place," *Daily Clarion*, 11 March 1937; "Bethune Escapes Death, Deadly Fascist Machine-gun Barrage Trained on Canadian Ambulance Unit at Guadalajara," *Daily Clarion*, 12 March 1937; "Daily Clarion Broadcasts from the Madrid Front," *Daily Clarion*, 3 April 1937.
66 Watts, "Bravery of Canadian Is Lauded."
67 Larry Hannant, "'My God, Are They Sending Women?' Three Canadian Women in the Spanish Civil War, 1936–1939," *Journal of the Canadian Historical Association* 15 (2004): 160. See also Nancy Butler, "Mother Russia and the Socialist Fatherland: Women and the Communist Party of Canada, 1932–1941, with Specific Reference to the Activism of Dorothy Livesay and Jim Watts" (PhD diss., Queen's University, 2010), 378; Liversedge, *Mac-Pap*, 195n147.
68 "Jean Watts Returns Via New York," *Daily Clarion*, 8 February 1938.
69 See Liversedge, *Mac-Pap*, 70–1, 109–23, and RGASPI, International Brigade Service File, Edward Cecil-Smith, "Precis of Statement Made by Myself during a Meeting with Comrade Lewis and Elliott of the Central Committee," c. December 1938, 064–069.
70 Emily Murphy, "Case Study Two: Jean Watts, Ted Allan, and the Daily Clarion in Spain," Virtual Research Environment of Canadian Cultural History about the Spanish Civil War, http://spanishcivilwar.ca/case-studies/jean-watts/case-study-two, accessed 7 January 2019. "Frank Rogers," Volunteer Database at the Abraham Lincoln Brigade Archives, http://www.alba-valb.org/volunteers/frank-rodgers, accessed 7 January 2019.
71 Allan's article series, *Salud Nordamericanos*, was published in the *Daily Clarion* between 9 November and 2 December 1937.

72 Allan, "Honest-to-Goodness Canadian Cigarettes."
73 "Toronto Men Hurt in Madrid Fighting," *Toronto Star*, 10 July 1937.
74 "Three Canadians Wounded Fighting with Loyalists," *Toronto Star*, 10 July 1937.
75 "Canadian Troops in Spanish Army Rest on Canadian Holiday," *Ottawa Citizen*, 2 July 1937.
76 Hoar, *The Mackenzie-Papineau Battalion*, 112.
77 "Pacifist Toronto Newsman Leads Crack Canadian Unit in Crucial Teruel Defense," *Toronto Telegram*, 8 January 1938; "Shock Leader Once Pacifist," *Globe and Mail*, 7 January 1938; "Canadians in Spain Said 'Best Fighters,'" *Toronto Star*, 7 January 1938.
78 "Former Editor Heads MacPaps," *Daily Clarion*, 8 January 1938.
79 Ed Cecil-Smith, "Calls on Canadians to Strengthen Rearguard of Fight for Democracy," *Daily Clarion*, 24 May 1937.
80 See, for instance, Cecil-Smith's letters printed in the *Daily Clarion* to Beckie Buhay (11 March 1938); to the East York Workers Association (16 March 1938); to Mr. A.J. Titt, secretary-organizer of Local 132 Journeymen Tailors' Union in Toronto (5 April 1938); to Comrade Berezanski of an unnamed Ukrainian cultural organization (30 May 1938); to the Friends of the Mackenzie-Papineau Battalion (31 May and 8 August 1938); and to "Charlie" of Ward 2 (30 July 1938).
81 Ed Cecil-Smith, "Major Ed Cecil-Smith Describes Heroism of Canadians," a reprinted letter to the Friends of the Mackenzie-Papineau Battalion, *Daily Clarion*, 8 August 1938.
82 CBC Radio Archives, Mac Reynolds interview with Carl Geiser and Lawrence Cane (1964).
83 The first chronicler of the Mac-Paps, Victor Hoar, noted that Cecil-Smith was, "genuinely torn between his aptitude as a military man and his concern for the welfare of the progressive movement." Hoar, *The Mackenzie-Papineau Battalion*, 160–1.
84 See translation of article from *Slobodna Misao* in LAC, RCMP File, translation titled Free Thought, 25 May 1937.
85 Cecil-Smith's appointment as a company commander was first noticed by the RCMP in "Canadian Troops in Spanish Army Rest on Canadian Holiday," *Ottawa Citizen*, 2 July 1937. Regarding Cecil-Smith's appointment as commander of the Mac-Paps, the first mention can be found in an "O" Division Memo on 18 January 1938 and RCMP Security Bulletin No. 881 (19 January 1938) in Gregory S. Kealey and Red Whitaker, eds., *RCMP Security Bulletins: The Depression Years, Part V, 1938–1939* (St. John's: Canadian Committee on Labour History, 1997), 42. His name is redacted in the security bulletin but the bulletin contains the same text as the 18 January report, which leaves Cecil-Smith's name unredacted.

86 Michael Butt, "Surveillance of Canadian Communists: A Case Study of Toronto RCMP Intelligence Networks, 1920–1939" (PhD diss., Memorial University, 2003), 336.

10 The Defence of Teruel

1 Paul Preston, *The Spanish Civil War, 1936–39* (London: Weidenfeld and Nicolson, 1986), 280.
2 Victor Hoar, *The Mackenzie-Papineau Battalion: Canadian Participation in the Spanish Civil War* (Toronto: Copp Clark, 1969), 163.
3 Michael Petrou, *Renegades: Canadians in the Spanish Civil War* (Vancouver: UBC Press, 2008), 80.
4 Ibid.
5 CBC Radio Archives, Carl Geiser and Lawrence Cane interview with Mac Reynolds (1964).
6 Mark Zuehlke, *The Gallant Cause: Canadians in the Spanish Civil War, 1936–1939* (Toronto: Whitecap Books, 1996), 189.
7 La Muela de Teruel is a large and well-known high feature to the west of the town of Teruel. William P. Carney claimed to be standing on it when he was briefed by the Nationalist commander on their plan. See William P. Carney, "Rebels Are Confident," *New York Times*, 20 January 1938. However, this seems unlikely, as the hill was occupied by the XVth Brigade at the time. Landis, *The Abraham Lincoln Brigade*, 377 addresses this discrepancy and accuses Carney of exaggeration. This accords with the reminiscences of other reporters at the time, who accused Carney of sometimes pretending to be "on the scene" when he was in fact safely in a hotel room somewhere. See Paul Preston, *We Saw Spain Die: Foreign Correspondents in the Spanish Civil War* (London: Skyhorse Publishing, 2009), 157–9.
8 Richard Baxell, *Unlikely Warriors: The British in the Spanish Civil War* (London: Aurum Press, 2012), 282.
9 CBC Radio Archives, Mac Reynolds interview with Lionel Edwards (1964). There is confusion in the literature as to who commanded the Machine Gun Company at Teruel. For example, Hoar identifies Jack Thomas as the commander (*The Mackenzie-Papineau Battalion*, 167), while Landis states that it was Leo Gordon (Landis, *The Abraham Lincoln Brigade*, 354).
10 Hoar, *The Mackenzie-Papineau Battalion*, 167, and William Beeching, *Canadian Volunteers: Spain, 1936–1939* (Regina: Canadian Plains Research Center, 1989), 83.
11 There has been considerable confusion as to who held what command appointments at the Battle of Teruel. Victor Hoar and Bill Beeching, for example, stated that Ricardo Diaz was the commander of No. 2

Company, and Lionel Edwards was the commander of No. 3 Company (Hoar, *The Mackenzie-Papineau Battalion*, 167; Beeching, *Canadian Volunteers*, 83). Landis records that the name of the commander of No. 2 Company was lost, and that the No. 3 Company was commanded by Ramon Gonzalez, with Ricardo Diaz as his second in command (Arthur Landis, *The Abraham Lincoln Brigade* (New York: Citadel Press, 1967), 354). However, in a letter written at the time, Cecil-Smith clearly states that Ricardo Diaz was the commander of No. 3 Company during the battle (Cecil-Smith to Beckie Buhay, "Boys Receive Gifts While under Fire," *Daily Clarion*, 11 March 1938), and a biography of Diaz in the *Volunteer for Liberty* on 3 April 1938 identifies him as commanding the company on the Mac-Paps' right flank. Furthermore, Lionel Edwards identifies himself as an *outpost* commander in a 6 October 1938 article in the *Volunteer for Liberty* ("Lt Lionel Edwards, a Canadian Officer") and a machine-gun detachment commander on the right flank in his interview with the CBC in 1964. The confusion arose for multiple reasons: Diaz had commanded No. 2 Company prior to the Battle of Teruel; No. 2 Company was principally made up of Spaniards and was generally commanded by a Spanish-speaking officer; Diaz left the position on the Mac-Paps' right flank in order to rally the *Marineros*, who had withdrawn; and Edwards was a prominent leader along the right flank, who subsequently became a company commander. However, at the beginning of the battle, Edwards was neither a company commander nor a *teniente.*

12 Bob Kerr, "One Year of the Mac-Paps in Spain," *Daily Clarion*, 19 July 1938.

13 Library and Archives Canada (hereafter LAC), Edward Cecil-Smith Papers, Reminiscences of Gerry Delaney, 27 May 1939.

14 Hoar, *The Mackenzie-Papineau Battalion*, 165; Beeching, *Canadian Volunteers*, 80. See also Landis, *The Abraham Lincoln Brigade*, 362; Landis was on the patrol as a battalion scout.

15 Raymond M. Hoff, Christopher T. Brooks, Michael Petrou, and Myron Momryk, "Biographical Dictionary of Volunteers from Canada in the Spanish Civil War" (unpublished manuscript, 2018), 153, states that Haldane lost his leg on or about 10 March, but the available descriptions of the events in which Cecil-Smith was involved suggest that it occurred during patrolling at Teruel. It is possible that Haldane was injured more than once, or that the reporting of the event was misleading and the single incident occurred later.

16 Joseph North, "Canadians on Ebro First into Battle, Write Glowing Page," *Daily Clarion*, 17 August 1937. See also Morris Brier, "Of Comradeship and Courage: Three Friends, Three Volunteers," *Volunteer* (November 1987).

17 Sam Suto, "Captain Niila Makela [*sic*]," *Volunteer for Liberty*, 13 August 1938.
18 William P. Carney, "Rebels Hope Soon to Encircle Teruel," *New York Times*, 22 January 1938.
19 Matthew Halton, *Ten Years to Alamein* (Toronto: S.J. Reginald Saunders, 1944), 56.
20 Landis, *The Abraham Lincoln Brigade*, 372–3; Hoar, *The Mackenzie-Papineau Battalion*, 167–8.
21 Hoar, *The Mackenzie-Papineau Battalion*, 168.
22 Landis, *The Abraham Lincoln Brigade*, 373.
23 See Petrou, *Renegades*, 82.
24 Landis, *The Abraham Lincoln Brigade*, 375.
25 CBC Radio Archives, Mac Reynolds interview with Lawrence Cane (1964).
26 "Boys Receive Gifts While under Fire."
27 Ibid.
28 Beeching, *Canadian Volunteers*, 85.
29 Landis, *The Abraham Lincoln Brigade*, 377–9.
30 "Boys Receive Gifts While Under Fire."
31 Landis, *The Abraham Lincoln Brigade*, 380; Hoar, *The Mackenzie-Papineau Battalion*, 168–9.
32 Chris Brooks and Liana Katz, "Blast from the Past (Revisited): The Commissar and the Good Fight," *Volunteer*, 16 December 2015. See also Saul Friedberg, "A Tribute to Harry Schoenberg," *Volunteer,* 12 (May 1990).
33 Landis, *The Abraham Lincoln Brigade*, 377.
34 Note that while the Mac-Paps' Machine Gun Company was No. 4 Company, the British Battalion tended to number their Machine Gun Company as No. 2 Company. No. 1, 3, and 4 Company were all rifle companies.
35 See Beeching, *Canadian Volunteers*, 88; Baxell, *Unlikely Warriors*, 282–3; and William Rust, *Britons in Spain: The History of the British Battalion of the XVth International Brigade* (London: Lawrence and Wishart, 1939), 110.
36 Landis, *The Abraham Lincoln Brigade*, 381.
37 Beeching, *Canadian Volunteers*, 88.
38 "Lt. Lionel Edwards, a Canadian Officer," *Volunteer for Liberty*, 6 October 1938. See also Halton, *Ten Years to Alamein*, 57.
39 Zuehlke, *The Gallant Cause*, 199, and Beeching, *Canadian Volunteers*, 87. See also Landis, *The Abraham Lincoln Brigade*, 382.
40 Cecil-Smith stated that he had ordered Edwards to retire (see Matthew Halton, "Toronto Commander Tells of His Heroes," *Toronto Star*, 27 January 1939), whereas Edwards recalled that he had made the decision to retreat (CBC Radio Archives, Mac Reynolds interview with Lionel Edwards

(1964)). It is possible that Cecil-Smith issued the order and it never got to Edwards, but he still had no choice but to retreat; alternatively, Cecil-Smith was simply trying to ensure that Edwards was given his due and could not be accused of shirking his responsibility when he retreated.

41 Halton, "Toronto Commander Tells of His Heroes."

42 Halton, *Ten Years to Alamein*, 58.

43 Modesto was in the Teruel sector, bringing a group of British Labour members of Parliament to the front in an effort to encourage them to support the Spanish Republic.

44 There is much confusion in the literature as to when these accolades were bestowed and what, exactly, they were. Modesto visited the Teruel sector on 18 and 19 January, and the commander of the British Battalion recorded in his memoirs that Modesto promoted him to *capitan* on 19 January (see Bill Alexander, *No to Franco: The Struggle Never Stopped, 1939–1975!* (London: author, 1992)). This suggests that the Mac-Paps' citations and promotions occurred in roughly the same timeframe. Indeed, Cecil-Smith's International Brigade Service File notes that he was promoted to *mayor* in January, and the RCMP (relying on secondary sources themselves) also reported Cecil-Smith's rank as *mayor* in January. Yet the secondary source literature says something completely different. Landis, in *The Abraham Lincoln Brigade*, 383, says that the Canadian promotions occurred on 20 January, which fits with the other known facts. However, Beeching (*Canadian Volunteers*, 90) wrote that it occurred after Atalaya in February. Additionally, there is much conflict regarding who was promoted to what rank. Hoar (*The Mackenzie-Papineau Battalion*, 172), for example, cites Landis (*The Abraham Lincoln Brigade*, 383), saying that Diaz and Edwards were promoted to *capitan*. Beeching (*Canadian Volunteers*, 90) wrote that they were both commissioned as *tenientes*. However, contemporary accounts in the *Volunteer for Liberty* show that Diaz was promoted to *capitan*, and Edwards was commissioned as a *teniente*, only being promoted to *capitan* on his departure from Spain. See *Volunteer for Liberty*, 3 April 1938 ("Captain Ricardo Diaz ... promoted to Captain in the field after Teruel") and 7 November 1938 (" On departure ... to Captain: ... Lionel Edwards"). Beeching, Hoar, and Landis agree that Saul Wellman received a citation and that Cecil-Smith was promoted to *mayor*. It is unclear why there is so much confusion regarding a simple matter such as time and nature of promotions, but it certainly highlights the problematic nature of scholarship based principally on interviews conducted decades after the fact.

45 Baxell, *Unlikely Warriors*, 283–4.

46 Zuehlke, *The Gallant Cause*, 200. Note that Beeching, *Canadian Volunteers*, 90 says there were 800, but this is likely a typo, as that figure is well beyond the full-strength size of an infantry battalion.

47 Landis, *The Abraham Lincoln Brigade*, 392, and CBC Radio Archives, Mac Reynolds interview with Lawrence Cane (1964).
48 Zuehlke, *The Gallant Cause*, 162. In Beeching, *Canadian Volunteers*, 92, Bill Matthews recalled that Alec Miller, formerly a company commander in the George Washingtons, commanded No. 2 Company at Atalaya, and that Miller was wounded and replaced for the second hill by Nahanchuk.
49 The *Volunteer for Liberty* stated that Diaz was also a company commander, and No. 3 is the only remaining company. He commanded it before, so it seems reasonable that his command would not change.
50 Beeching, *Canadian Volunteers*, 61. The modern reader will be more familiar with the term "spoiling attack."
51 Hoar, *The Mackenzie-Papineau Battalion*, 116; "Benjamin Goldstein," Volunteer Database at the Abraham Lincoln Brigade Archives, http://www.alba-valb.org/volunteers/benjamin-goldstein, accessed 7 January 2019.
52 "David Doran," Volunteer Database at the Abraham Lincoln Brigade Archives, http://www.alba-valb.org/volunteers/dave-doran, accessed 7 January 2019; John Gates, "Doran – First to Advance, Last to Retreat," *Volunteer for Liberty*, 1 May 1938.
53 Landis, *The Abraham Lincoln Brigade*, 389.
54 Beeching, *Canadian Volunteers*, 90.
55 "Boys Receive Gifts While under Fire."
56 Jack Taylor, "Mac-Paps Win New Laurels, Capture Important Height," *Daily Clarion*, 8 March 1938. Taylor recorded that Makela was the commander of the Machine Gun Company. It is certainly possible that Cecil-Smith employed Makela as both the commander of the Machine Gun Company and as his second in command at the same time.
57 "Boys Receive Gifts While under Fire."
58 Beeching, *Canadian Volunteers*, 91. Note that Rogers was not yet part of the battalion, so his description is based on second-hand information.
59 Bob Kerr, "One Year of the Mac-Paps in Spain," *Daily Clarion*, 19 July 1938.
60 Jack Taylor reported these numbers shortly after the incident, and they are more likely to be true. Lawrence Cane, however, stated in an interview thirty years later that they had captured a hundred soldiers, a number clearly inflated over time. Cane's recollections have been repeated as fact ever since. See Taylor, "Mac-Paps Win New Laurels," and CBC Radio Archives, Mac Reynolds interview with Lawrence Cane (1964).
61 Taylor, "Mac-Paps Win New Laurels."
62 LAC, Mackenzie-Papineau Battalion Collection, Walter D. Dent Papers, vol. 5, file 2 (hereafter Dent Papers), Reminiscences of Bill Matthews, c. 1939.

63 Landis, *The Abraham Lincoln Brigade*, 392 and CBC Radio Archives, Mac Reynolds interview with Lawrence Cane (1964). It is unclear from available English-language sources if these were the same *marineros* that had retreated at Teruel, or an entirely different group.
64 Taylor, "Mac-Paps Win New Laurels."
65 Ibid.
66 Ronald Liversedge, *Recollections of the On-to-Ottawa Trek, 1935* (Vancouver: n.d. [c. 1961]), 53; Victor Howard, *We Were the Salt of the Earth! A Narrative of the On to Ottawa Trek and Regina Riot* (Regina: Canadian Plains Research Center, 1985), 61, 76, 83.
67 Russian State Archive of Socio-Political History, fond 545, Opis 6, Delo 569, Correspondence File of Jack Taylor, letter from Jack Taylor to the Friends of the Mackenzie-Papineau Battalion, 20 February 1938, 082.
68 Taylor, "Mac-Paps Win New Laurels."
69 This information must have come through the Friends of the Mac-Paps, as Cecil-Smith's appointment had not been announced in Canada when Taylor had left for Spain.
70 Taylor, "Mac-Paps Win New Laurels."
71 "Canada Pays Tribute to 15th Brigade," *Volunteer for Liberty*, 9 April 1938.
72 Ibid.
73 Ibid.
74 LAC, Dent Papers, Reminiscences of Bill Matthews, c. 1939. See also Petrou, *Renegades*, 83.
75 Petrou, *Renegades*, 83.

11 The Retreats

1 Edwin Rolfe, *The Lincoln Battalion* (New York: Random House, 1939), 181–2; Cecil D. Eby, *Between the Bullet and the Lie: American Volunteers in the Spanish Civil War* (New York: Holt Rinehart and Winston, 1969), 206, 210; Milt Wolff, "Commissars I've Known (And Admired)," *Volunteer* (November 1985).
2 Arthur Landis, *The Abraham Lincoln Brigade* (New York: Citadel Press, 1967), 405.
3 "Assert Rebels Shoot 1,000; 300 Women Said Abused," *Toronto Star*, 9 February 1937.
4 Hoar, *The Mackenzie-Papineau Battalion: Canadian Participation in the Spanish Civil War* (Toronto: Copp Clark, 1969), 175.
5 CBC Radio Archives, Mac Reynolds interview with Lawrence Cane (1964).
6 Ibid.

7 Cecil-Smith's undated report, believed to have been written while he was recovering in the Valls hospital in late March and early April, LAC, Cecil-Smith Papers, Report of Edward Cecil-Smith (hereafter, Cecil-Smith Report). Beeching's text reproduces a significant portion of this report: William Beeching, *Canadian Volunteers: Spain, 1936–1939* (Regina: Canadian Plains Research Center, 1989), 96.
8 Michael Petrou, *Renegades: Canadians in the Spanish Civil War* (Vancouver: UBC Press, 2008), 84.
9 Beeching, *Canadian Volunteers*, 95.
10 Hoar, *The Mackenzie-Papineau Battalion*, 177.
11 Beeching, *Canadian Volunteers*, 96; Cecil-Smith Report, 1.
12 Ibid. See also Marion Merriman, and Warren Lerude, *American Commander in Spain: Robert Hale Merriman and the Abraham Lincoln Brigade* (Reno: University of Nevada Press, 1986), 222.
13 Beeching, *Canadian Volunteers*, 96; Cecil-Smith Report, 1.
14 Richard Baxell, *Unlikely Warriors: The British in the Spanish Civil War* (London: Aurum Press, 2012), 307.
15 Beeching, *Canadian Volunteers*, 96; Cecil-Smith Report, 1.
16 Jim Higgins Personal Papers, Jim Higgins, "The Softest Rock: A Memoir of the Great Depression and the Spanish Civil War," ch. 9.
17 Ibid; Cecil-Smith Report, 2.
18 Jim Higgins Papers, Letter from Cecil-Smith to Jim Higgins, c. 1939.
19 Beeching, *Canadian Volunteers*, 97; Cecil-Smith Report, 1.
20 Hoar, *The Mackenzie-Papineau Battalion*, 177.
21 Beeching, *Canadian Volunteers*, 98; Cecil-Smith Report, 2.
22 Beeching, *Canadian Volunteers*, 99; Cecil-Smith Report, 2.
23 Beeching, *Canadian Volunteers*, 99; Cecil-Smith Report, 2.
24 Beeching, *Canadian Volunteers*, 99; Cecil-Smith Report, 2.
25 Baxell, *Unlikely Warriors: The British in the Spanish Civil War* (London: Aurum Press, 2012), 308; Thomas, *The Spanish Civil War* (London: Eyre and Spottiswoode, 1961), 519.
26 Landis, *The Abraham Lincoln Brigade*, 423; "Joseph Gibbons," Volunteer Database at the Abraham Lincoln Brigade Archives, http://www.alba-valb.org/volunteers/joseph-gibbons, accessed 7 January 2019.
27 Beeching, *Canadian Volunteers*, 99; Cecil-Smith Report, 2.
28 Ed Cecil-Smith, "Canadian Volunteers, Home from Spanish War, Lauded by Leader by Valour and Endurance," *Globe and Mail*, 4 February 1939.
29 Cecil-Smith Report, 2.
30 Higgins, "The Softest Rock," ch. 9; "Raphael Busch Brage," Volunteer Database at the Abraham Lincoln Brigade Archives, http://www.alba-valb.org/volunteers/raphael-busch-brage, accessed 7 January 2019; see also James R. Jansen, "The Debs Column and American

Socialists in the Spanish Civil War" (MA thesis, University of Nebraska, 2015), 56.

31 Cecil D. Eby, *Comrades and Commissars: The Lincoln Battalion in the Spanish Civil War* (University Park: Pennsylvania State University Press, 2007), 298; Cecil-Smith Report, 2.

32 "The History of the Mackenzie-Papineau Battalion," *Volunteer for Liberty*, 7 November 1938.

33 Landis, *The Abraham Lincoln Brigade*, 423.

34 Beeching, *Canadian Volunteers*, 100; Cecil-Smith Report, 3.

35 Hoar, *The Mackenzie-Papineau Battalion*, 179.

36 Beeching, *Canadian Volunteers*, 100; Cecil-Smith Report, 3.

37 Hoar, *The Mackenzie-Papineau Battalion*, 179.

38 Landis, *The Abraham Lincoln Brigade*, 424; Hoar, *The Mackenzie-Papineau Battalion*, 180; Petrou, *Renegades*, 85.

39 Beeching, *Canadian Volunteers*, 101; Cecil-Smith Report, 3; Author's interview with Bill Smith, 25 July 2018.

40 Cecil-Smith, "Canadian Volunteers, Home from Spanish War."

41 Eby, *Comrades and Commissars*, 299.

42 Beeching, *Canadian Volunteers*, 101; Cecil-Smith Report, 3.

43 Beeching, *Canadian Volunteers*, 101; Cecil-Smith Report, 3.

44 Beeching, *Canadian Volunteers*, 102; Cecil-Smith Report, 3.

45 Eby, *Comrades and Commissars*, 299.

46 Beeching, *Canadian Volunteers*, 103; Cecil-Smith Report, 4.

47 Beeching, *Canadian Volunteers*, 103; Cecil-Smith Report, 4.

48 Beeching, *Canadian Volunteers*, 103; Cecil-Smith Report, 4.

49 Beeching, *Canadian Volunteers*, 103; Cecil-Smith Report, 4.

50 Beeching, *Canadian Volunteers*, 103; Cecil-Smith Report, 4.

51 Author's interview with Bill Smith.

52 See Sandor Voros, *American Commissar* (New York: Chilton, 1961), 394.

53 Beeching, *Canadian Volunteers*, 103; Cecil-Smith Report, 4.

54 Landis, *The Abraham Lincoln Brigade*, 429. Merriman and Lerude, *American Commander in Spain*, 217–22.

55 Beeching, *Canadian Volunteers*, 110; Raymond M. Hoff, Christopher T. Brooks, Michael Petrou, and Myron Momryk, "Biographical Dictionary of Volunteers from Canada in the Spanish Civil War" (unpublished manuscript, 2018), 287.

56 Hoar, *The Mackenzie-Papineau Battalion*, 182.

57 Ibid.

58 Beeching, *Canadian Volunteers*, 104; Cecil-Smith Report, 4; and Hoar, *The Mackenzie-Papineau Battalion*, 183.

59 See Doctor "J.D.," "Field of Bonfires: Story of a Doctor's Escape," *Volunteer for Liberty*, 25 April 1938, for a description of these events from the

point of view of the doctor who was with Cecil-Smith outside Alcaniz. The doctor believed the soldiers were German because they were too blond and tall to be Spanish.

60 Landis, *The Abraham Lincoln Brigade*, 381.

61 Beeching, *Canadian Volunteers*, 104; Cecil-Smith Report, 5.

62 Dr. Degar made his way into Alcaniz, but found that it was occupied by Nationalist soldiers. See Doctor "J.D.," "Field of Bonfires."

63 Mark Zuehlke, *The Gallant Cause: Canadians in the Spanish Civil War, 1936–1939* (Toronto: Whitecap Books, 1996), 214.

64 Beeching, *Canadian Volunteers*, 105; Cecil-Smith Report, 5.

65 Hoar, *The Mackenzie-Papineau Battalion*, 183–4; John Gates, "Doran – First to Advance, Last to Retreat," *Volunteer for Liberty*, 1 May 1938.

66 Baxell, *Unlikely Warriors*, 308.

67 There has been much confusion regarding the name of the hill on which Makela died and that Cecil-Smith subsequently attacked: Cemetery Hill or Reservoir Hill. Based on the available descriptions, the hill on which these two events occurred is referred to as Reservoir Hill (west of Caspe, immediately north of the main east-west road) and the hill on which Dave Doran cited his headquarters east of Caspe as Cemetery Hill. The confusion regarding the names of the hills likely stems from the chaotic nature of the battle and the fact that the hill on which Makela was wounded and that Cecil-Smith subsequently recaptured had both a cemetery and an earth-covered reservoir on it. Cecil-Smith himself described the hill as "the cemetery hill" in his initial report (Beeching, *Canadian Volunteers*, 105), but later corrected himself and called it Reservoir Hill in a subsequent newspaper article (Ed Cecil-Smith, "Canadian Volunteers, Home from Spanish War"). Other sources of confusion include the following: a *Volunteer for Liberty* article on 7 November 1938, stated that Makela was wounded on Cemetery Hill; Paddy McElligott recalled that Makela was killed on a hill with an "earth-covered water reservoir" (Beeching, *Canadian Volunteers*, 113); and Hoar, based on interviews with veterans, referred to Makela's death and Cecil-Smith's attack as both occurring on "the cemetery hill" (Hoar, *The Mackenzie-Papineau Battalion*, 183–4).

68 Sam Suto, "Captain Niila Makela [*sic*]," *Volunteer for Liberty*, 13 August 1938.

69 Ibid.

70 "Mac-Pap Notes," *Volunteer for Liberty*, 6 October 1938); Hoff et al., "Biographical Dictionary," 225.

71 Cecil-Smith's report (Cecil-Smith Report, 5; Beeching, *Canadian Volunteers*, 106) states that the assaulting force had two light machine guns and no grenades. His report after the war stated that they had one light

machine gun and thirty grenades (see Cecil-Smith, "Canadian Volunteers, Home from Spanish War"). In either event, they had fewer grenades and support weapons than they would have wanted to get the job done.

72 Beeching, *Canadian Volunteers*, 105–6; Cecil-Smith Report, 5.

73 Beeching, *Canadian Volunteers*, 106; Cecil-Smith Report, 5; and Hoar, *The Mackenzie-Papineau Battalion*, 184.

74 Beeching, *Canadian Volunteers*, 106; Cecil-Smith Report, 5; and Hoar, *The Mackenzie-Papineau Battalion*, 184. See also Ed Cecil-Smith, "Canadian Volunteers, Home From Spanish War, Lauded by Leader for Valour and Endurance," *Globe and Mail*, 4 February 1939.

75 Beeching, *Canadian Volunteers*, 107; Cecil-Smith Report, 6.

76 Beeching, *Canadian Volunteers*, 107; Cecil-Smith Report, 6. Irving Weissman, a prominent American commissar, later wrote on Cecil-Smith's evaluation, written prior to his departure from Spain, that Cecil-Smith had "attempted desertion at time of retreats," probably referring to this incident. Russian State Archive of Socio-Political History, International Brigade Service File, Report by Irving Weissman on Edward Cecil-Smith, 15 September 1938, 026.

77 Landis, *The Abraham Lincoln Brigade*, 434.

78 Beeching, *Canadian Volunteers*, 107.

79 Eby, *Comrades and Commissars*, 311.

80 Baxell, *Unlikely Warriors*, 312.

81 Beeching, *Canadian Volunteers*, 107; Cecil-Smith Report, 6.

82 Landis, *The Abraham Lincoln Brigade*, 445; "Carl Frederick Geiser," Volunteer Database at the Abraham Lincoln Brigade Archives, http://www.alba-valb.org/volunteers/carl-frederick-geiser, accessed 7 January 2019.

83 Hoar, *The Mackenzie-Papineau Battalion*, 186; Eby, *Comrades and Commissars*, 318.

84 Hoar, *The Mackenzie-Papineau Battalion*, 187; Beeching, *Canadian Volunteers*, 107; Cecil-Smith Report, 6.

12 Crossing the Ebro

1 Hoar, *The Mackenzie-Papineau Battalion: Canadian Participation in the Spanish Civil War* (Toronto: Copp Clark, 1969), 160–1. Note that Wellman had a strong influence on Hoar's writings, whereas Hoar and Cecil-Smith never had the opportunity to speak. Hoar dedicated his book to Wellman and Liversedge for both their service and their assistance.

2 For example, Joe Dallet, the battalion commissar killed at Fuentes de Ebro, had been mortified when he had been caught playing classical piano, lest the soldiers learn and think him to be one "of these bloody bourgeois intellectuals." See Cary Nelson and Jefferson Hendricks, eds.,

Madrid 1937: Letters of the Abraham Lincoln Brigade from the Spanish Civil War (New York: Routledge, 1996), 97.

3 See Cecil D. Eby, *Comrades and Commissars: The Lincoln Battalion in the Spanish Civil War* (University Park: Pennsylvania State University Press, 2007), 296. Robert Merriman, "Merriman Diaries: Exegesis," ed. Raymond Hoff (unpublished manuscript, 2018), 335–3; "Frank Rogers," Volunteer Database at the Abraham Lincoln Brigade Archives, http://www.alba-valb.org/volunteers/frank-rodgers, accessed 7 January 2019.

4 Russian State Archive of Socio-Political History (hereafter RGASPI), International Brigade Service File, Report by Frank Rogers on Edward Cecil-Smith, c. October 1938, 043.

5 Author's interview with Bill Smith, 25 July 2018.

6 Library and Archives Canada (LAC), International Brigade Files copied from RGASPI, reel K-260, Daily Report by Frank Rogers, 14 May 1938.

7 Ibid.

8 Daily Report by Frank Rogers, 5 May 1938, LAC International Brigade Collection holdings from RGASPI, MG10-K260.

9 LAC, International Brigade Files copied from RGASPI, reel K-260, Pledge "They Shall Not Pass," c. 1938.

10 RGASPI, Correspondence File of Jack Taylor, Radiotelegram via Transradio Espanola from Tim Buck to Jack Taylor, c. May 1938, 054.

11 LAC, Mackenzie-Papineau Battalion Collection, Victor Hoar Papers, vol. 1, file 3, correspondence between Victor Hoar and Lawrence Cane, c. 1966–7; RGASPI, International Brigade Service File, letter from Cecil-Smith to Taylor, 15 June 1938, 058.

12 RGASPI, International Brigade Service File, letter from Cecil-Smith to Taylor, 15 June 1938, 058.

13 RGASPI, Correspondence File of Jack Taylor, letter from Jack Taylor to Frank Rogers, 31 March 1938, 013.

14 Cecil-Smith had sent other letters in the same timeframe during which he was not writing to Taylor. See, for instance, "Friends Received a Letter from Cecil-Smith Yesterday," *Daily Clarion*, 31 May 1937.

15 RGASPI, Correspondence File of Jack Taylor, letter from Jack Taylor to Frank Rogers, 2 June 1938, 072.

16 See "The Mac Paps' Commissar Reports," *Daily Clarion*, 30 July 1938.

17 For a detailed synopsis of the events of the summer, see Angela Jackson, *At the Margins of Mayhem: Prologue and Epilogue to the Last Great Battle of the Spanish Civil War* (Pontypool, UK: Warren and Pell, 2008).

18 Edward Cecil-Smith, "A Fighting Unit in a Fighting Army," *Daily Clarion*, 30 July 1938.

19 Jack Taylor, "Mac-Paps Celebrate Dominion Day," *Daily Clarion*, 5 July 1938; and Frank Varia, "Letter from Frank Varia," *Daily Clarion*, 8 August 1938.
20 "How the English Trimmed the Mac-Paps 'Futbal' Whiskers," *Volunteer for Liberty*, 5 September 1938; Varia, "Letter from Frank Varia."
21 Varia, "Letter from Frank Varia." See also George Wheeler, *To Make People Smile Again* (Newcastle upon Tyne, UK: Zymurgy), 59–60.
22 Jack Taylor, "Mac-Paps Celebrate Dominion Day," *Daily Clarion*, 5 July 1938.
23 For a thorough discussion of how Doran and Merriman were killed, see Chris Brooks, "The Death of Robert Hale Merriman," *Volunteer*, 31 March 2016.
24 Bruce Lambert, "John Gates, 78, Former Editor of the Daily Worker, Is Dead," *New York Times*, 25 May 1992.
25 Milt Wolff, "Commissars I've Known (and Admired)," *Volunteer* (November 1985).
26 Eby, *Comrades and Commissars*, 387; Peter Carroll, *The Odyssey of the Abraham Lincoln Brigade: Americans in the Spanish Civil War* (Stanford, CA: Stanford University Press, 1994), 183; Milt Wolff, the commander of the Lincolns during the event in question, did not mention the execution in his reminiscences about Gates, but noted a different incident where Gates met a deserting volunteer, clearly shell-shocked, with compassion. He ensured the volunteer received medical treatment and an assignment to duties in a rear area. Wolff, "Commissars I've Known."
27 William Beeching, *Canadian Volunteers: Spain, 1936–1939* (Regina: Canadian Plains Research Center, 1989), 124; Hoar, *The Mackenzie-Papineau Battalion*, 209. See also "Mac-Pap Notes" and "Gunnar Ebb," *Volunteer for Liberty*, 6 October 1938.
28 Beeching, *Canadian Volunteers*, 126.
29 Preston, *The Spanish Civil War, 1936–39* (London: Weidenfeld and Nicolson, 1986), 288–9.
30 See Joseph North, "Correspondent in Spain," *Daily Clarion*, 17 August 1937.
31 Zuehlke, *The Gallant Cause: Canadians in the Spanish Civil War, 1936–1939* (Toronto: Whitecap Books, 1996), 244; CBC Radio Archives, Mac Reynolds interview with Lionel Edwards (1964).
32 Beeching, *Canadian Volunteers*, 131; Hoar, *The Mackenzie-Papineau Battalion*, 214.
33 CBC Radio Archives, Mac Reynolds interview with Lionel Edwards (1964); Hoar, *The Mackenzie-Papineau Battalion*, 214.
34 "Commissar Nicholas Myer," *Volunteer for Liberty*, 7 November 1938; Raymond M. Hoff, Christopher T. Brooks, Michael Petrou, and Myron

Momryk, "Biographical Dictionary of Volunteers from Canada in the Spanish Civil War" (unpublished manuscript, 2018), 324.

35 Not long after Edwards and the others had been wounded, North reported that Mack was the commander of No. 1 Company. See Joseph North, "Canadians on Ebro First into Battle, Write Glowing Page," *Daily Clarion*, 17 August 1937.

36 Dave Gordon, "With the Mac-Paps," *Volunteer for Liberty*, 5 September 1938.

37 Hoar, *The Mackenzie-Papineau Battalion*, 214.

38 Beeching, *Canadian Volunteers*, 131; Hoar, *The Mackenzie-Papineau Battalion*, 214.

39 Landis, *The Abraham Lincoln Brigade*, 523.

40 Hoar, *The Mackenzie-Papineau Battalion*, 214.

41 CBC Radio Archives, Mac Reynolds interview with Irving Weissman and Larry Ryan (1964); Landis, *The Abraham Lincoln Brigade*, 524–5.

42 Michael Petrou, *Renegades: Canadians in the Spanish Civil War* (Vancouver: UBC Press, 2008), 95.

43 CBC Radio Archives, Mac Reynolds interview with Weissman and Ryan (1964).

44 Preston, *The Spanish Civil War*, 289–90.

45 Manuel Alvarez, *The Tall Soldier: My 40-Year Search for the Man Who Saved My Life* (Toronto: Virgo Press, 1980), 35. Alvarez was a young boy living in Corbera at the time. The day after the Mac-Paps left Corbera, he was swept away by water following a Nationalist bombing raid that destroyed a water tank. Alvarez was saved by Jim Higgins, a Canadian but not a member of the Mackenzie-Papineau Battalion at the time. Alvarez, *The Tall Soldier*, 41–5; Jim Higgins Personal Papers, Jim Higgins, "The Softest Rock," ch. 14.

46 Hoar, *The Mackenzie-Papineau Battalion*, 188.

47 Landis, *The Abraham Lincoln Brigade*, 233.

48 Hoar, *The Mackenzie-Papineau Battalion*, 215.

49 Ibid.

50 Baxell, *Unlikely Warriors: The British in the Spanish Civil War* (London: Aurum Press, 2012), 329–330.

51 Hoar, *The Mackenzie-Papineau Battalion*, 215–16.

52 Landis, *The Abraham Lincoln Brigade*, 544.

53 *Daily Clarion*, 25 August 1938.

54 CBC Radio Archives, Mac Reynolds interview with Lawrence Cane (1964).

55 Preston, *The Spanish Civil War*, 290.

56 Ibid.

57 Hoar, *The Mackenzie-Papineau Battalion*, 217.

58 Ibid., 218; Beeching, *Canadian Volunteers*, 136; Petrou, *Renegades*, 96.
59 Hoar, *The Mackenzie-Papineau Battalion*, 218; Chris Brooks and Lisa Clemmer, "Albin Ragner: An Unpublished Memoir," *Volunteer*, 27 February 2013.
60 Major E. Cecil-Smith, "Wounded Franco Conscripts Hero to Canadian Enemy," *Toronto Star*, 3 February 1939.
61 Ibid.
62 Ibid.
63 Hoar, *The Mackenzie-Papineau Battalion*, 220.
64 Sam Spiller, "Fascist Offensive Crumples before Heroic Resistance of XVth Brigade," *Volunteer for Liberty*, 17 September 1938.
65 Ibid.
66 LAC, Mackenzie-Papineau Battalion Collection, Victor Hoar Papers, vol. 1, file 3, Correspondence between Victor Hoar and Lawrence Cane, c. 1966–67.
67 Hoar, *The Mackenzie-Papineau Battalion*, 220.
68 The debate was well known among the volunteers, but it did not become public knowledge until many years later. Voros appears to have been the first to record it, in his memoir in 1961. It was not mentioned in Canadian scholarship until Zuehlke's book, *The Gallant Cause*, in 1996. See Voros, *American Commissar* (New York: Chilton, 1961), 394, and Zuehlke, *The Gallant Cause*, 241.
69 LAC, RCMP File, Report by R.L. Trolove to V.A.M. Kemp, Commanding "O" Division, forwarded to Commissioner S.T. Wood Re: Major. Ed. Cecil Smith – Ex-Commander of Mac-Paps. – C.P. of C., 18 November 1939. See also RGASPI, International Brigade Service File, Report by XVth Brigade Party Committee on Edward Cecil-Smith, 20 October 1938), 030, and RGASPI, International Brigade Service File, Report by Frank Rogers on Edward Cecil-Smith, c. October 1938, 043.
70 Zuehlke, *The Gallant Cause*, 241.
71 See Voros, *American Commissar*, 394, and LAC, RCMP File, Report by R.L. Trolove to V.A.M. Kemp, Commanding "O" Division, forwarded to Commissioner S.T. Wood Re: Major. Ed. Cecil Smith.
72 The location of the wound is confirmed by the description of Cecil-Smith's scars in his Second World War service file and by the family's recollections. Bill Smith recalls the wound on Cecil-Smith's calf, and his father telling him that once he was shot he had stuck his handkerchief into the wound to stop the bleeding and it had gone all the way through his leg. LAC, Second World War Service File; author's interview with Bill Smith.
73 CBC Radio Archives, Mac Reynolds interview with Bill Beeching (1965).
74 RGASPI, International Brigade Service File, Report on Edward Cecil-Smith by Gunnar Ebb, 26 September 1938, 028.

75 LAC, RCMP File, Untitled report, 17 August 1938.

76 Following the battle of Sierra de Pandols, soldiers had heard the rumour that they would be repatriated in the near future. Several soldiers began openly talking about deserting. See Petrou, *Renegades*, 97.

77 RGASPI, Jack Taylor Correspondence File, Radiotelegram via Transradio Espanola from Tim Buck to Jack Taylor, c. May 1938, 054.

78 RGASPI, Jack Taylor Correspondence File, letter from Cecil-Smith to Jack Taylor, 15 June 1938, 058.

79 See RGASPI, International Brigade Service File, Report by XVth Brigade Party Committee on Edward Cecil-Smith, 20 October 1938, 030, and RGASPI, International Brigade Service File, Report by Frank Rogers on Edward Cecil-Smith, c. October 1938, 043.

13 Coming Home

1 "Special Supplement," *Volunteer for Liberty*, 23 September 1938.

2 See Edward Cecil-Smith, "A Fighting Unit in a Fighting Army," *Daily Clarion*, 30 July 1938.

3 Cecil-Smith's speech was quoted at length in "Made Stronger Our Fight for Freedom," *Daily Clarion*, 9 February 1939.

4 See Myron Momryk, "Ignacy Witczak's Passport, Soviet Espionage and the Origins of the Cold War in Canada," *Polish American Studies* 68 (Autumn 2011): 70.

5 Hugh Thomas, *The Spanish Civil War* (London: Eyre and Spottiswoode, 1961), 559.

6 William Beeching, *Canadian Volunteers: Spain, 1936–1939* (Regina: Canadian Plains Research Center, 1989), 190.

7 See Ninette Kelley and Michael Trebilcock, *The Making of the Mosaic: A History of Canadian Immigration Policy* (Toronto: University of Toronto Press, 2000), 226.

8 Momryk, "Ignacy Witczak's Passport," 71.

9 Ibid. See also John Munro, "Canada and the Civil War in Spain: Repatriation of the Mackenzie-Papineau Battalion," *External Affairs* 23 (February 1971): 52–8.

10 Raymond M. Hoff, Christopher T. Brooks, Michael Petrou, and Myron Momryk, "Biographical Dictionary of Volunteers from Canada in the Spanish Civil War" (unpublished manuscript, 2018).

11 Edwin Rolfe, "Canucks in Spain Returning Home, Rest from Battles," *Daily Clarion*, 28 November 1938.

12 Russian State Archive of Socio-Political History (hereafter RGASPI), International Brigade Service File, Report by Irving Weissman on Edward Cecil-Smith, 15 September 1938, 026.

13 RGASPI, International Brigade Service File, Report by XVth Brigade Party Committee on Edward Cecil-Smith, 20 October 1938, 030.
14 RGASPI, International Brigade Service File, Report by Frank Rogers on Edward Cecil-Smith, c. October 1938, 043.
15 Ibid.
16 Thomas, *The Spanish Civil War* (London: Eyre and Spottiswoode, 1961), 541.
17 For more on the Foreign Enlistment Act, see my articles "Canada's Foreign Enlistment Act and the Spanish Civil War," *Labour/Le Travail* 80 (Fall 2017): 213–46 and "Mercenaries and Adventurers: Canada and Foreign the Foreign Enlistment Act in the Nineteenth Century," *Canadian Military History* 14 (Spring 2014): 57–77.
18 Rolfe, "Canucks in Spain Returning Home."
19 Cecil D. Eby, *Comrades and Commissars: The Lincoln Battalion in the Spanish Civil War* (University Park: Pennsylvania State University Press, 2007), 412; Beeching, *Canadian Volunteers*, 190.
20 RGASPI, International Brigade Service File, Edward Cecil-Smith, "Precis of Statement Made by Myself during a Meeting with Comrade Lewis and Elliott of the Central Committee," c. December 1938, 064–069. See also Michael Petrou, *Renegades: Canadians in the Spanish Civil War* (Vancouver: UBC Press, 2008), 117.
21 RGASPI, International Brigade Service File, Edward Cecil-Smith, "Precis of Statement Made by Myself during a Meeting with Comrade Lewis and Elliott of the Central Committee," c. December 1938, 064–069. Cecil-Smith noted that American political representatives "have found it very difficult to work with these comrades on account of mutual misunderstanding. Especially did comrade Weissmann [*sic*] seem unable to understand them – an unfortunate failing in a fine comrade."
22 Ibid.
23 J. Peter Campbell, "The Cult of Spontaneity: Finnish-Canadian Bushworkers and the Industrial Workers of the World in Northern Ontario, 1919–1934," *Labour/Le Travail* 41 (Spring 1998): 121.
24 RGASPI, International Brigade Service File, Edward Cecil-Smith, "Report by Edward Cecil-Smith to the Vancouver Committee of the Communist Party of Canada," c. December 1938, 070.
25 Ibid.
26 Ibid.
27 Ibid.
28 Ibid.
29 Ibid.
30 "Boys Receive Gifts While under Fire," *Daily Clarion*, 11 March 1938.
31 "Major Ed Cecil-Smith Describes Heroism of Canadians," *Daily Clarion*, 8 August 1938.

32 Joseph North, "Canadians on Ebro First into Battle, Write Glowing Page," *Daily Clarion*, 17 August 1937.
33 Thomas, *The Spanish Civil War*, 572.
34 Preston, *The Spanish Civil War, 1936–39* (London: Weidenfeld and Nicolson, 1986), 291.
35 Edwin Rolfe, "Mac-Paps Urge Premier to Aid Repatriation," *Daily Clarion*, 6 December 1938.
36 "Canadians in Spain Start Home Soon," *Toronto Star*, 9 December 1938; "Canadians Plan to Leave Spain," *Globe and Mail*, 9 December 1938.
37 Beeching, *Canadian Volunteers*, 191. See also "Canadians Keen to Quit Spain," *Montreal Star*, 12 December 1938.
38 By Tim Buck's own admission, the party did not have a plan for repatriating the volunteers: "It certainly never dawned on me that coming home for the boys would be any problem. After the victory, the Republican government would arrange for their transportation home. I suppose that's as much thought as we ever gave it." See Buck, *Yours in the Struggle: Reminiscences of Tim Buck*, ed. William Beeching and Phyllis Clarke (Toronto: New Canada Publication, 1977), 277.
39 Archives of Ontario (hereafter AO), series F-126-1, Alexander Albert MacLeod political and social activities file, box 1, letter from A.A. MacLeod to O.D. Skelton, 24 December 1938; Buck, *Yours in the Struggle*, 277–9.
40 AO, Series F-126-1, Alexander Albert MacLeod political and social activities file, box 1, letter from A.A. MacLeod to O.D. Skelton, 28 December 1938.
41 Hoar, *The Mackenzie-Papineau Battalion: Canadian Participation in the Spanish Civil War* (Toronto: Copp Clark, 1969), 228.
42 Ibid., 232.
43 Jim Higgins Personal Papers, Jim Higgins, "The Softest Rock," ch. 15.
44 Hoar, *The Mackenzie-Papineau Battalion*, 231.
45 Henry Meyer recalled that 125 Canadians had volunteered to defend Barcelona, but his account was given years after the fact, whereas Cecil-Smith's number of 97 was provided very shortly after the event. Hoar, *The Mackenzie-Papineau Battalion*, 231.
46 Matthew Halton, "Toronto Commander Tells of His Heroes," *Toronto Star*, 27 January 1939; "Assured of Comrades' Safety, Canadian Volunteers Set Sail," *Globe and Mail*, 28 January 1939.
47 Halton, "Toronto Commander Tells of His Heroes." Petrou notes that the spirit of volunteerism may have been considerably less. Fred Kostyk told him in an interview that approximately thirty-five Canadians volunteered, enough for a platoon. An RCMP informant in 1948 claimed that the numbers were even less. The informant stated that only Cecil-Smith, the battalion commissar (Nicholas Myers), and two or three other soldiers volunteered. See Petrou, *Renegades*, 101. Petrou also notes that

coercion may have been applied to "encourage" more volunteers; some of the political evaluations in Ripoll indicate that soldiers chose to resign from the party instead of defending Barcelona.

48 "I'd Rather Be Home," *Toronto Star*, 3 February 1939; Greg Clark, "Volunteers Return Garbed in Clothes of Spanish Dead," *Toronto Star*, 6 February 1939.

49 "292 Canadians Quit Barcelona," *Globe and Mail*, 26 January 1939; "Curtain of Fire and Steel," *Globe and Mail*, 26 January 1939. The departure of the Mac-Paps had, incorrectly, been announced a few days earlier. See announcement in the *Daily Clarion* on 21 January 1939.

50 Preston, *The Spanish Civil War*, 294.

51 "292 Canadians Quit Barcelona."

52 RCMP Security Bulletin No. 1 (January–March 1939), in Gregory S. Kealey and Reg Whitaker, eds., *RCMP Security Bulletins: The Depression Years, Part V, 1938–1939* (St. John's: Canadian Committee on Labour History, 1997), 378.

53 Hoar, *The Mackenzie-Papineau Battalion*, 233; "Asserts Veterans Were Segregated," *Ottawa Morning Journal*, 6 February 1939.

54 Halton, "Toronto Commander Tells of His Heroes."

55 See Petrou, *Renegades*, 18, 24. See also Myron Momryk, "Ukrainian Volunteers from Canada in the International Brigades, 1936–1939: A Profile," *Journal of Ukrainian Studies* 16 (Winter 1991): 181–94, and "Hungarian Volunteers from Canada in the Spanish Civil War, 1936–1939," *Hungarian Studies Review* 24 (1997): 83–116.

56 "Hungry Canadians Ate Their Mascot," *Toronto Star*, 27 January 1939.

57 Gregory Clark, "Mac-Paps Made Bridge of Thread and Roared as Rebels Bombed It," *Toronto Star*, 4 February 1939; "Asserts Veterans Were Segregated."

58 The identity of the ship used by the first group has been the cause of much confusion in the secondary literature. Hoar stated that the first group returned to Canada on 3 February 1939 on board the *Duchess of Bedford* (*The Mackenzie-Papineau Battalion*, 233). Shipping lists and contemporary newspaper accounts confirm that this is incorrect. Although a subsequent group of Mac-Paps used the *Duchess of Bedford*, the first load of Mac-Paps travelled onboard the *Duchess of Richmond*. In fact, the second group left Liverpool on 3 February 1939, the same day the first batch of Mac-Paps arrived in Halifax onboard the *Duchess of Richmond*. Beeching's account adds to the confusion, as it correctly states that the first group travelled on the *Duchess of Richmond*, but that they landed at Saint John, New Brunswick, on 4 February 1939 (Beeching, *Canadian Volunteers*, 194). The discrepancy likely arises from the fact that many transatlantic steamers, including the *Duchess of Richmond*, went to Saint John as a second

port following Halifax. Beching himself was onboard the *Duchess of Richmond* and may have continued on the ship to Saint John.

59 "800 Volunteers Killed," *Toronto Star*, 27 January 1939; "Curtain of Fire and Steel"; "Spanish War Veterans Due Here Sunday," *Globe and Mail*, 1 February 1939.

60 See Ron Liversedge's personal experiences with this second group of Mac-Paps at Liversedge, *Mac-Pap*, 147–8.

61 "Courts-Martial and Firing Squad Rule Barcelona," *Toronto Star*, 27 January 1939.

62 Hoar's book describes the strike but states that accounts diverged as to whether it was motivated by a desire to act in solidarity with those left behind or for the opportunity to visit Liverpool. While some of the Mac-Paps may have wanted to visit Liverpool, it seems clear from the newspaper accounts that the Mac-Paps were motivated principally by concern for their fellow volunteers in Spain. Hoar, *The Mackenzie-Papineau Battalion*, 233.

63 "Men Delay Joining Liner for Canada," *Evening Express* (Liverpool), 27 January 1939.

64 "Liner Delayed – Assurance of Their Comrades' Safety Demanded," *Birmingham Gazette*, 28 January 1939.

65 "Assured of Comrades' Safety."

66 "Men Delay Joining Liner for Canada."

67 Ibid.

68 See LAC, RG146, vol. 4183, CSIS files 95-A-0000-88, Recruiting for Spanish Army File (hereafter RSA File), Report re: Return of Spanish Civil War Veterans by H.C. McGuire to F.J. Mead, Officer Commanding "H" Division, forwarded to Commissioner S.T. Wood, 4 February 1939.

69 Jim Higgins Personal Papers, Jim Higgins, "The Softest Rock," ch. 15.

70 Jim Higgins Personal Papers, labelled "Bulletin Board on ship returning to Canada. Original. February 1939."

71 See Jack Taylor in a subsection of Oscar Ryan, "Thousands Jam Railway Depots to Cheer Returning Mac-Paps," *Daily Clarion*, 6 February 1939. See also David Greig, *In The Fullness of Time: A History of the Church of Saint Mary Magdalene, Toronto* (Toronto: Church of Saint Mary Magdalene, 1990), 129.

72 Ryan, "Thousands Jam Railway Depots."

73 Greg Clark, "270 Spanish Gentlemen Now Dons Sing 'O Canada,'" *Toronto Star*, 4 February 1939.

74 "I'd Rather Be Home"; Gregory Clark, "Mac-Paps Made Bridge of Thread"; and Jack Taylor, "Welcome Home, Mac-Paps!" *Daily Clarion*, 4 February 1939.

75 Clark, "270 Spanish Gentlemen."

76 Taylor, "Welcome Home, Mac-Paps!"
77 Ibid.
78 Ibid.
79 R.F. MacLean, "Ten Thousand Cheers Rise as Army of 120 Canadians Arrives Home from Spain," *Toronto Evening Telegram*, 6 February 1939.
80 Oscar Ryan, "Thousands Jam Railway Depots to Cheer Returning Mac-Paps in Montreal, Toronto," *Daily Clarion*, 6 February 1939.
81 Jessie E. MacTaggart, "Crowd Hails Canadians from Spain," and Arthur Suzukl, "Parents Scan Returned Men; Seeking Sons," both in *Globe and Mail*, 6 February 1939. See also R.F. MacLean, "Ten Thousand Cheers Rise as Army of 120 Canadians Arrives Home from Spain," *Toronto Evening Telegram*, 6 February 1939.
82 "Stealthy Goers-Forth to War who Come Loudly Home," *Toronto Star*, 6 February 1939.
83 Ibid.
84 Ibid.
85 See MacLean, "Ten Thousand Cheers Rise."
86 Ibid.
87 David Greig, *In The Fullness of Time: A History of the Church of Saint Mary Magdalene, Toronto* (Toronto: Church of Saint Mary Magdalene, 1990), 129. For Cecil-Smith's comments about the religious beliefs of the volunteers, see MacLean, "Ten Thousand Cheers Rise."
88 "Band Will Welcome Returned Mac-Paps," *Toronto Daily Star*, 4 February 1939.
89 "Made Stronger Our Fight"; "My Life Isn't Enough," *Toronto Star*, 7 February 1939.
90 "Made Stronger Our Fight."
91 Ibid.
92 Cecil-Smith's speech was quoted at length in ibid. and paraphrased in LAC, RCMP File, Report by S.O.F. Evans, "Friends of Mackenzie-Papineau Battalion, Toronto, Ont. – Mass Meeting of welcome to returned members 'Mac-Pap' Battn. held in Massey Hall," 7 February 1939. The RCMP report included the prediction that war in Europe would break out in April, while the *Daily Clarion* article omitted that detail.
93 LAC, RSA File, letter from Commissioner J.H. MacBrien to O.D. Sketon, 8 July 1937.
94 LAC, RSA File, telegram from F.J. Mead, Officer Commanding "H" Division, forwarded to Commissioner S.T. Wood, 3 February 1939.
95 The *Daily Clarion* announced this visit (which would include Cecil-Smith and Hamiltonian Jimmy Southgate) on 7 February. See also "2,000 Welcome Mac-Paps," *Toronto Star*, 11 February 1939.

96 LAC, RCMP File, Report by R.A. Williams (Niagara Falls Detachment) to W. Munday, Commander "O" Division, forwarded to Commissioner S.T. Wood Re: Major Cecil Smith, Commander, MacKenzie [*sic*]-Papineau Battalion Meeting at Niagara Falls, Ont., 14 March 1939.

97 See LAC, RCMP File, unattributed report to H.A.R. Gagnon, Commander "C" Division, forwarded to Commissioner S.T. Wood Re: Friends of the Mackenzie-Papineau Battalion, 17 February 1939, and LAC, RCMP File, Unattributed Report Re: Communist Party of Canada, Montreal, 14 February 1939.

98 LAC, RCMP File, Unattributed Report Re: Communist Party of Canada.

99 MacTaggart, "Crowd Hails Canadians from Spain."

100 Thomas, *The Spanish Civil War*, 575.

101 See Jean Watts, "Information Bulletin No. 1, Report of Miss Jean Watts, our delegate at the recent conference of the Office International pour l'Enfance, on conditions in the refugee camps in France," Canadian Committee to Aid Spanish Refugees, 25 May 1939. See also *Daily Clarion*, 25 May 1939.

102 LAC, RCMP File, Unattributed Report to H.A.R. Gagnon, Commander "C" Division, forwarded to Commissioner S.T. Wood Re: Friends of the Mackenzie-Papineau Battalion, 17 February 1939.

103 Cecil-Smith later wrote an article on the conditions in these camps. See Ed Cecil-Smith, "Spain Volunteers Beaten in French Prison Camp," *Clarion*, 22 July 1939.

104 "Much to Do Yet for Spain Vets," *Daily Clarion*, 2 May 1939; "100 Spain Veterans Not Yet in Canada," *Toronto Star*, 20 April 1939.

105 "100 Spain Veterans Not Yet in Canada."

106 See Buck, *Yours in the Struggle*, 278–9. Numerous access to information requests to Library and Archives in Canada have not yet garnered success in retrieving any surviving seized records.

107 Jim Higgins Papers, letter exchange between Cecil-Smith and Higgins, 1939.

108 Form letter from M[aurice] L. Constant, secretary of the Editorial Commission to "Veteran," 22 April 1939. Copies of this letter can be found in LAC, Edward Cecil-Smith Papers.

109 LAC, Edward Cecil-Smith Papers, "History of Mac-Paps: A Draft by Edward Cecil-Smith" c. 1939.

110 Jim Higgins Papers, letter to self re: 1939, written c. 1977.

111 Moreover, Cecil-Smith refused to hand over his records to the Communist Party of Canada, which continued to demand them years later. Even after Cecil-Smith had passed away and Victor Hoar began the process of writing *The Mackenzie-Papineau Battalion*, published in 1969, the Cecil-Smith family was still concerned that the materials would be used for political

purposes, contrary to Cecil-Smith's wishes. The Communist Party again demanded the papers, with the intention of handing them over to Victor Hoar, but Lilian Cecil-Smith instead chose to donate them to Library and Archives and Canada, where all scholars would have equal access to them. Author's interview with Bill Smith, 25 July 2018.

112 LAC, RCMP File, Unattributed Report Re: C.P. of C. – Toronto, Ont. International Picnic Committee Meeting Held 379 Dundas St. E., 30 May 1939. See also LAC, RCMP File, Report by S.O.F. Evans to F.W. Schutz, for Commander "O" Division, forwarded to Commissioner S.T. Wood Re: C.P. of C. Activities in Ward 2, Toronto, 9 August 1939; LAC, RCMP File, Report by S.O.F. Evans Re: C.P. of C. Activities, Ward 2 Toronto, 25 August 1939.

113 John Manley, "'Communists Love Canada!' The Communist Party of Canada, 'The People,' and the Popular Front, 1933–1939," *Journal of Canadian Studies* 36 (Winter 2001–2): 79.

114 Michael Butt, "Surveillance of Canadian Communists: A Case Study of Toronto RCMP Intelligence Networks, 1920–1939" (PhD diss., Memorial University, 2003), 356.

115 LAC, RCMP File, Report by R.L. Trolove Re: C.P. of C. – Toronto, Ont. International Picnic Committee Meeting Held 379 Dundas St. E., 30 May 1939. Trolove does not sign his name to the report, but it does include his regimental number (9359), confirming his authorship.

116 Butt, "Surveillance of Canadian Communists," 356.

117 Trolove went by Robert, but his actual name was Ronald Leconsfield Trolove; see obituary in the *Globe and Mail*, 22 February 1988.

118 Butt, "Surveillance of Canadian Communists," 353.

119 Major E. Cecil-Smith, "Wounded Franco Conscripts Hero to Canadian Enemy," *Toronto Star*, 3 February 1939.

120 "Smith Joins Clarion Staff," *Daily Clarion*, 1 April 1939.

121 E. Cecil-Smith, "Marx and Engels on Spain Throw Light on Later Happenings," *Daily Clarion*, 12 May 1939.

122 LAC, RCMP File, Report by S.O.F. Evans to W. Munday, Commanding "O" Division, forwarded to Commissioner S.T. Wood Re: Daily Clarion, 12 June 1939.

123 Ibid.

124 Ibid.

125 LAC, RCMP File, report by S.O.F. Evans to W. Munday, Commanding "O" Division, forwarded to Commissioner S.T. Wood Re: Daily Clarion, 16 June 1939.

126 LAC, RCMP File, report by S.O.F. Evans to W. Munday, Commanding "O" Division, forwarded to Commissioner S.T. Wood Re: Daily Clarion, 12 June 1939.

127 The public meeting was held on 16 June 1939. RCMP "Confidential Contact #6" was in attendance. See LAC, RCMP File, report by S.O.F. Evans to W. Munday, Commanding "O" Division, forwarded to Commissioner S.T. Wood Re: Daily Clarion, 16 June 1939.

128 Ibid.

129 Ibid.

130 LAC, RCMP File, report by S.O.F. Evans to W. Munday, Commanding "O" Division, forwarded to Commissioner S.T. Wood Re: Daily Clarion, 12 June 1939.

131 Norman Bethune, "Wounds," *Clarion*, 1 July 1939; and Norman Bethune, "The Dud," *Clarion*, 8 July 1939.

132 Ed Cecil-Smith, "Two Years of War in China Find Japan Near Exhaustion," *Clarion*, 8 July 1939.

133 Ibid.

134 LAC, RCMP File, report by S.O.F. Evans to F.W. Schutz, for Commander "O" Division, forwarded to Commissioner S.T. Wood Re: C.P. of C. Activities – Ward 3, Toronto, 3 July 1939.

135 Author's interview with Bill Smith.

136 LAC, RCMP File, report by S.O.F. Evans Re: C.P. of C. Activities – Ward 3 Branch, Toronto, 23 February 1939.

137 See Lil, "With Our Women, in Sport and Play," *Daily Clarion*, 1 May 1936.

138 Nancy Butler, "Mother Russia and the Socialist Fatherland: Women and the Communist Party of Canada, 1932–1941, with Specific Reference to the Activism of Dorothy Livesay and Jim Watts" (PhD diss., Queen's University, 2010), 23.

139 Norman Bethune, *The Politics of Passion: Norman Bethune's Writing and Art*, ed. Larry Hannant (Toronto: University of Toronto Press, 1998), 351.

140 Ibid.

141 Ibid., 352.

142 The letter was dated 15 August 1939, but it is not known when it arrived in Toronto.

143 Bethune, *The Politics of Passion*, 352.

144 Ibid.

145 See *Selected Works of Mao Tse-Tung*, vol. 2 (Beijing: Foreign Language Press, 1965), 337–8.

146 The document was written in Chinese, translated into English to be sent back to North America, and then subsequently translated back into Chinese when the original was lost. A copy of the Chinese document is held by the Norman Bethune International Peace Hospital in Shijiazhuang, Hebei Province. See Roderick Stewart and Sharon Stewart, *Phoenix: The Life of Norman Bethune* (Montreal and Kingston: McGill-Queen's University Press, 2011), 451–2.

147 Norman Bethune's will, as dictated to Pan Fan and others in November 1939 and turned into Chinese at that time, was held by the Norman Bethune International Peace Hospital in Shijiazhuang, Hebei Province. The few Chinese sentences quoted here were translated into English by Yan Li, associate professor and coordinator, Chinese Language Program, Department of Culture and Language Studies at Renison University College, and director, Confucius Institute in Waterloo, Ontario.
148 See Stewart and Stewart, *Phoenix*, 139.
149 Adrienne Clarkson, *Norman Bethune* (Toronto: Penguin Canada, 2009), 97.
150 Author's interview with Bill Smith.
151 See LAC, RCMP File, unattributed report to H.A.R. Gagnon, Commander "C" Division, forwarded to Commissioner S.T. Wood Re: Friends of the Mackenzie-Papineau Battalion, 17 February 1939.
152 LAC, RCMP File, Report by S.O.F. Evans to F.W. Schutz, for Commander "O" Division, forwarded to Commissioner S.T. Wood Re: C.P. of C. Activities – Ward 3, Toronto, 3 July 1939.
153 Manley, "'Communists Love Canada!'" 66.
154 "Prepared against Aggressors of the Sea," *Clarion*, 5 August 1939.
155 "Non-Aggression Pact Proves Force for Peace," *Clarion*, 2 September 1939.
156 Ibid.
157 See editorial by Tim Buck, *Clarion*, 2 September 1939.

14 A Second Anti-Fascist War

1 Peter Hunter, a Young Communist League organizer, recalled, "To many, it seemed a betrayal. I saw it as a delaying tactic," Hunter, *Which Side Are You on Boys? Canadian Life on the Left* (Toronto: Lugus Publishing, 1988), 119.
2 Author's interview with Bill Smith, 25 July 2018.
3 The story was carried by the Canadian Press and appeared in newspapers across the country. "'Mac-Pap' Commander Hastens to Join Up," *Toronto Star*, 5 September 1939.
4 Ibid.
5 "Mac-Paps Offered to Government," *Montreal Star*, 7 September 1939; "Mackenzie-Papineau Unit Services Offered Canada," *Ottawa Evening Citizen*, 6 September 1939.
6 "Mac-Pap Boys Ready to Help Smash Hitler, Major Smith Advised," *Mid-West Clarion*, 9 September 1939. See also "Offer of Sending the Mac-Paps," *Winnipeg Free Press*, 5 September 1939.
7 "Mac-Paps Offered to Government"; "Mackenzie-Papineau Unit Services Offered Canada."

8 Library and Archives Canada (hereafter LAC), RG146, vol. 1830, CSIS files 95-A-0000-88, Edward Cecil-Smith, part 1, box 58 (hereafter RCMP File), report by M. Black to V.A.M. Kemp, Commanding "O" Division, forwarded to Commissioner S.T. Wood Re: C.P. of C. Activities in Canadian Forces, 29 September 1939. Another RCMP memorandum noted that Cecil-Smith had been "severely rebuked for offering his services ... as he had not consulted the C.P. prior to the issuance of a letter to Hon. Ian Mackenzie." See LAC, RCMP File, report by S.O.F. Evans to V.A.M. Kemp, Commanding "O" Division, forwarded to Commissioner S.T. Wood Re: C.P. of C. Activities in Canadian Forces, 6 September 1939.

9 LAC, RCMP File, report by S.O.F. Evans to V.A.M. Kemp, Commanding "O" Division, forwarded to Commissioner S.T. Wood Re: C.P. of C. Activities in Canadian Forces, 6 September 1939.

10 Ibid. See also RCMP File, report by R.R. Tait, Assistant Commissioner and Director of Criminal Investigation, to RCMP Divisional Officers Commanding Re: Communist Party of Canada – Activities in National Defense Forces, Canada Generally, 9 September 1939.

11 Ed Cecil-Smith, "Western Front Still All Too Quiet; Poles Bearing Main Brunt," *Clarion*, 16 September 1939.

12 Thomas, *The Spanish Civil War* (London: Eyre and Spottiswoode, 1961), 519.

13 Ibid.

14 "Rejected," *Winnipeg Free Press*, 19 September 1939.

15 Ibid.

16 Author's interview with Bill Smith.

17 Ibid. See also LAC, R112, vol. 30555, Cecil-Smith, Edward Paul, Second World War Service File (hereafter Second World War Service File).

18 LAC, RG24, C-3, vol. 14706, War Diary of 2nd Field Company, Royal Canadian Engineers (hereafter War Diary), entry for 1 September 1939.

19 The company's war diary notes that it ran all of its own training until late October, when the different engineer companies began to pool resources to conduct larger scale and increasingly specialized training.

20 Warrant Officer Turner was posted to the company in October. See LAC, War Diary, entry for 4 October 1939. See also A.J. Kerry and W.A. McDill, *History of the Corps of Royal Canadian Engineers*, vol. 2, *1936–1946* (Ottawa: Military Engineers Association of Canada, 1966), 18.

21 Jack Scott, *A Communist Life: Jack Scott and the Canadian Workers Movement, 1927–1985*, ed. Bryan Palmer (St. John's: Canadian Committee on Canadian Labour History, 1988), 54.

22 J.L. Black, *Canada in the Soviet Mirror: Ideology and Perception in Soviet Foreign Affairs, 1917–1991* (Ottawa: Carleton University Press, 1998), 122.

23 *Daily Clarion*, 16 September 1939.

24 Archie Brown, *The Rise and Fall of Communism* (Toronto: Doubleday Canada, 2009), 90–2.

25 LAC, MG 26-J13, Diaries of Prime Minister William Lyon Mackenzie King, entry for 23 November 1939, 1252.

26 LAC, RCMP File, report by R.R. Tait, Assistant Commissioner and Director of Criminal Investigation, to RCMP Divisional Officers Commanding Re: Communist Party of Canada – Activities in National Defense Forces, Canada Generally, 9 September 1939. See also LAC, RCMP File, report by S.O.F. Evans to V.A.M. Kemp, Commanding "O" Division, forwarded to Commissioner S.T. Wood Re: C.P. of C. Activities in Canadian Forces, 6 September 1939.

27 Victor Dunn and Cecil-Smith had worked together at a Communist instructional school in Toronto in 1935. See LAC, RCMP File, unattributed report to A.E. Reames, Commander "O" Division, forwarded to Commissioner J.H. MacBrien, Re: Communist Instructional School, Toronto, 12 November 1935; LAC, RCMP File, unattributed report to V.A.M. Kemp, forwarded to Commissioner S.T. Wood, Re: C.P. of C. Activities in Canadian Forces, 15 October 1939. Another RCMP report, dated 26 October 1939, noted that the 2nd Field Company "should receive special attention, especially Edward CECIL-SMITH who is a member of the R.C.E." See LAC, RCMP File, letter from R.R. Tait, Assistant Commissioner and Director of Criminal Investigations, to Chief Intelligence Officer, 26 October 1939.

28 LAC, RCMP File, report by V.A.M. Kemp, Commanding "O" Division, to Commissioner S.T. Wood Re: Communist Activities in Defence Forces of Canada – Generally, 30 September 1939.

29 Constable R.J. Smith visited the Commanding Officer of the 2nd Field Company specifically to discuss discharging Cecil-Smith. LAC, RCMP File, report by R.J. Smith to F.W. Schutz for Officer Commanding "C" Division, forwarded to Commission S.T. Wood re: C.P. of C Activities in Canadian National Defence Forces, Edward Cecil-Smith Reg. No. B25373 of the 2nd Field Company, R.C.E. C.A.S.F., 7 November 1939. Cecil-Smith was promoted to Lance Corporal on 24 October 1939. LAC, Second World War Service File.

30 LAC, RCMP File, report by V.A.M. Kemp, Commanding "O" Division, to Commissioner S.T. Wood re: Edward Cecil-Smith, Reg. No. B25373 of the 2nd Field Company, R.C.E., C.A.S.F., 24 November 1939.

31 LAC, RCMP File, report by R.R. Tait, Assistant Commissioner and Director of Criminal Investigation, to the office of the Director of Organization, Department of National Defence, re: Edward Cecil-Smith, 14 December 1939.

32 LAC, RCMP File, letter to RCMP Divisional Officers Commanding by E.W. Bavin, Intelligence Officer, Re: Edward Cecil-Smith, 7 December 1939. See also report by R.J. Smith to V.A.M. Kemp, Commanding "O" Division, forwarded to Commissioner S.T. Wood re: C.P. of C. Activities in Canadian National Defence Forces, Edward Cecil-Smith, Reg. No. B25373, of the 2nd Field Engineers, R.C.E. of Canada, 4 December 1939.

33 This confusion continued. On 27 December, the *Toronto Star* published an interview with Cecil-Smith, noting that he was serving in the 2nd Field Company. In the margin, an RCMP officer wrote that he had confirmed with Military District 2 that Cecil-Smith was "discharged some time ago." In fact, Cecil-Smith was not discharged until January, although at the time of the article he knew that he was being discharged for medical reasons. "Commander of Spain MacPaps Now Corporal in Canuck Army," *Toronto Star*, 26 December 1939. LAC, RCMP File, note by V.A.M. Kemp, Officer Commanding "O" Division, to Commissioner S.T. Wood, 27 December 1939.

34 LAC, Second World War Service File.

35 LAC, RCMP File, unattributed newspaper clipping ("Commander of Spain MacPaps now Corporal in Canuck Army," 27 December 1939) with attached report by V.A.M. Kemp, Commanding "O" Division, to Commissioner S.T. Wood, 28 December 1939.

36 LAC, RCMP File, letter to RCMP Divisional Officers Commanding by E.W. Bavin, Intelligence Officer, Re: Edward Cecil-Smith, 7 December 1939.

37 See LAC, RCMP File, letter from H.M. McMaster, Governor of the Canadian Brotherhood of Ships' Employees, to Norman Rogers, Minister of National Defence, 28 October 1939.

38 Ibid.

39 Ibid.

40 LAC, RCMP File, report by E. Drysdale Re: Edward Cecil-Smith, 5 December 1942.

41 *Searchlight* (July 1941).

42 In April 1940, the RCMP noted that, "Well known left wing organizers of the CSU are being posted amongst union locals of the various ports to be effected by the strike should it be called." See RCMP Security Bulletin No. 24, 1 April 1940, in Gregory S. Kealey and Reg Whitaker, eds., *RCMP Security Bulletins: The War Series, 1939–1941* (St. John's: Canadian Committee on Labour History, 1989), 193.

43 See Hunter, *Which Side*, 122.

44 See LAC, RCMP File, report by R.J. Smith to V.A.M. Kemp, Commanding "O" Division, forwarded to Commissioner S.T. Wood re: Edward Cecil-Smith, C.P. of C., 2 May 1940.

45 Introduction, *Searchlight* (July 1941).

46 "Steam Kept up on Two Boats," *Toronto Star*, 19 April 1940; "Shipping on the Lakes," *Toronto Star*, 19 April 1940.

47 "No Accord in Ship Strike," *Toronto Star*, 20 April 1940; "Latest Shipping News," *Toronto Star*, 20 April 1940.

48 Robert Comeau, "La Canadian Seamen's Union (1936–1949): Un chapitre de l'histoire du movement ouvrier canadien," *Revue d'histoire de l'Amerique francaise* 29 (1976): 514.

49 See RCMP Security Bulletin No. 28, 29 April 1940, in Kealey and Whitaker, *RCMP Security Bulletins 1939–1941*, 226.

50 LAC, RCMP File, report by N. Jones Re: C.P. Activity in Canadian Seamen's Union Strike, Toronto, 22 April 1940. The report stated that the meeting was held at the Labor Temple "on Spadina," but this appears to be an error. The Labor Temple, home of the Trades and Labor Council, was located on Church Street, while the Labor Lyceum was on Spadina Avenue. The meeting was most likely held at the Labor Lyceum on Spadina Avenue.

51 See "Build the Strike Fund!" *Searchlight* (August 1939).

52 Kaplan, *Everything That Floats*, 33.

53 Ibid.

54 Order-in-Council 2363, 6 June 1940.

55 See Reg Whitaker, "Official Repression of Communism during World War II," *Labour/Le Travail* 16 (Spring 1986): 146.

56 LAC, RCMP File, report by R.J. Smith to V.A.M. Kemp, Commanding "O" Division, forwarded to Commissioner S.T. Wood re: Edward Cecil-Smith, C.P. of C., 2 May 1940.

57 Ibid.; Peter Krawchuk, *Interned without Cause* (Toronto: Kobzar, 1985), 13.

58 LAC, RCMP File, report by F.W. Schutz to Officer Commanding "O" Division Re Ed Cecil Smith (C.P. of C.) Toronto, 25 September 1941.

59 Other members of the Canadian Seamen's Union, few with any journalism experience, stepped in to replace the arrested editorial staff. The August 1940 issue of *Searchlight* listed the editorial board as Donne, Ferguson, and Sinclair. The September issue listed Donne and Ferguson. The September and October–November issues listed Ferguson and Donne. See also Laurel Sefton MacDowell, *Renegade Lawyer: The Life of J.L. Cohen* (Toronto: University of Toronto Press for the Osgoode Society for Canadian Legal History, 2001), 162.

60 Canada, *House of Commons Debates, 1941* (Ottawa: Queen's Printer, 1942), 27 February 1941, 1073.

61 See *Searchlight* (March–April 1940).

62 LAC, RCMP File, report by C. Batch, Assistant Intelligence Officer, Re: Canadian Seamen's Union, Montreal, 26 July 1941.

63 Whitaker, "Official Repression of Communism," 152.
64 Cecil-Smith, "Red Officers Know Their Job," *Montreal Gazette*, 4 July 1941; Cecil-Smith, "Soviet Fire Power Great," *Montreal Gazette*, 5 July 1941; Cecil-Smith, "Long War Basis of Red Tactics," *Montreal Gazette*, 6 July 1941; Cecil-Smith, "Russians Favour 'Elastic' Line," *Montreal Gazette*, 7 July 1941; "Elastic Defence Is Soviet Plan Favored over Immobile System," *Montreal Gazette*, 8 July 1941; and Cecil-Smith, "'Break Through' Is Emphasized as Offensive Defensive Tactics," *Montreal Gazette*, 9 July 1941.
65 LAC, RCMP File, report written by C.W. Harvison regarding Cecil-Smith's article, 4 July 1941.
66 Major E. Cecil-Smith, *Red Ally: An Estimate of Soviet Life and Soviet Power* (Toronto: Handy Books, 1941).
67 See, for example, "Just Off the Press," *Globe and Mail*, 25 October 1941, which identified Cecil-Smith as "a Toronto newspaper man who fought in Spain."
68 Cecil-Smith, *Red Ally*, 5.
69 Ibid., 8.
70 Ibid., 55, 65, 66.
71 Ibid., 114.
72 Ibid., 83.
73 Ibid., 94.
74 See John Boyd, *A Noble Cause Betrayed ... but Hope Lives On, Pages from a Political Life* (Edmonton: Canadian Institute of Ukrainian Studies Research 1999); David Goutor, *A Chance to Fight Hitler: A Canadian Volunteer in the Spanish Civil War* (Toronto: Between the Lines, 2018), 131–2; LAC, RG25, vol. 1802, file 631-D-Part 1, Statement of Mr. Joseph Robert Berube, Montreal, 19 November 1937; Michelle Smith, "From 'the Offal of the Magazine Trade' to 'Absolutely Priceless': Considering the Canadian Pulp Magazine Collection," *English Studies in Canada* 30 (March 2014): 103. Valentine's role as manager of Eveready, in addition to his other projects, is confirmed in the *Toronto City Directory* (Toronto: Might Directories, 1941), 1457. Eveready would later print materials for the CPC in its legalized wartime form of the Labor-Progressive Party. See, for example, A.E. Smith, "Remove the Ban! The Communists Are Making a Vital Contribution to the War Effort" (Toronto: Eveready Printers, 1942); Tim Buck, "Victory through Unity: Report to the Constituent Convention of the Labor-Progressive Party" (Toronto: Eveready Printers, 1943); Labor-Progressive Party, "Program of the Labor Progressive Party" (Toronto: Eveready Printers, 1944); and Labor-Progressive Party, "A Better Canada to Fight For – to Work For – to Vote For – Electoral Program of the Labor-Progressive Party" (Toronto: Eveready Printers, 1945). After the war,

Eveready was again used for the CPC's activities. It printed, among other things, the *Canadian Tribune*, the party magazine, until the 1990s.

75 Author's interview with Bill Smith.

76 "In Memoriam. Mr. G. Cecil-Smith," *China's Millions* (November–December 1941), 95.

77 Author's interview with Bill Smith.

78 Ibid.

79 LAC, RCMP File, report by N.O. Jones to V.A.M. Kemp, Commander "O" Division, forwarded to Commissioner S.T. Wood Re: Ed Cecil Smith (C.P. of C.) Toronto, 28 January 1942.

80 LAC, RCMP File, RCMP Security Index Work Sheet, 17 April 1951.

81 LAC, RCMP File, Report by A. Drysdale Re: Edward Cecil-Smith, 5 December 1942.

82 Author's interview with Bill Smith.

Conclusion

1 Library and Archives Canada (hereafter LAC), RG146, vol. 1830, CSIS files 95-A-0000-88, Edward Cecil-Smith, part 1, box 58 (hereafter RCMP File), report by J.T. Plyth to T.W. Chard, for Officer Command "O" Division, Re Veterans of the Mackenzie-Papineau Battalion, Toronto, 27 February 1947.

2 Ibid.

3 Ibid.

4 Ibid.

5 Ibid.

6 See LAC, RCMP File, report by J.J Cranney to J.S. Cruikshank, Officer Commanding "C" Division re: Edward Cecil-Smith, Toronto, 17 October 1950.

7 Author's interview with Bill Smith, 25 July 2018.

8 Ibid.

9 Ibid.

10 See obituary, *Globe and Mail*, 24 August 1963. Author's interview with Bill Smith.

11 Author's interview with Bill Smith.

Bibliography

Primary Sources

Archives

ANGLICAN DIOCESE OF TORONTO ARCHIVES

Marriage Register 1922–29, St. Michael and All Angels Anglican Church

ARCHIVES OF ONTARIO

RG 4-32, Attorney General of Ontario, Re – Rex vs. Tim Buck, barcode B225262

Series F-126-1, Alexander Albert MacLeod political and social activities file

CANADIAN BROADCASTING CORPORATION RADIO ARCHIVES, TORONTO

Mac Reynolds interviews with Tim Buck (1964); Lawrence Cane and Carl Geiser (1964); Lionel Edwards (1964); Peter Hunter (1964); Joseph Salsberg (1965); and Irving Weissman and Larry Ryan (1965)

CHEFOO SCHOOLS ASSOCIATION PAPERS

Chefoo Class Lists, 1900–41

JIM HIGGINS PERSONAL PAPERS

Documents in possession of Janette Higgins, notably Jim Higgins, "The Softest Rock: A Memoir of the Great Depression and the Spanish Civil War," edited by Janette Higgins (unpublished manuscript)

WILLIAM KREHM PERSONAL PAPERS

Correspondence among William Krehm, Sam Gampel, James Potts, and Myrtle Eugenia Watts (1932–34)

LIBRARY AND ARCHIVES OF CANADA (LAC), OTTAWA

MG10-K260, International Brigade Files copied from the holdings of the Russian State Archive of Socio-Political History

MG26-J13, Diaries of Prime Minister William Lyon Mackenzie King
MG28-IV11, Canadian Trotskyist Movement Fonds
MG30 E173, Mackenzie-Papineau Battalion Collection
RG76-B-1-a 71-5, vol. 738, file 513173, *Supreme Court of Ontario – Rex v. Tim Buck et al.*
RG76-C, Passenger Lists, 1865–1935
R112, vol. 30553, Cecil-Smith, Edward Paul, Second World War Service File
RG146, vol. 4183, CSIS files 95-A-0000-88, Recruiting for Spanish Army
RG146, vol. 1830, CSIS files 95-A-0000-88, Edward Cecil-Smith

RUSSIAN STATE ARCHIVE OF SOCIO-POLITICAL HISTORY (RGASPI), MOSCOW

Fond 545, Records of the XVth International Brigade

UNIVERSITY OF NEW BRUNSWICK LIBRARIES, ARCHIVES AND SPECIAL COLLECTIONS, FREDERICTON

MG H96, R.B. Bennett Papers, Box 146, file c: Communists

Government Documents

Bruce, Dr. Herbert A. *Report of the Lieutenant Governor's Committee on Housing Conditions in Toronto.* Toronto: Toronto Board of Control, 1934.
Curtis, Dennis, Andrew Graham, Lou Kelly, and Anthony Patterson. *Kingston Penitentiary: The First Hundred and Fifty Years, 1835–1985.* Ottawa: Canadian Government Publishing Centre Supply and Services Canada, 1985.
Taschereau, Honourable Mr. Justice Robert and Honourable Mr. Justice R.L. Kellock, Commissioners. *The Report of the Royal Commission to Investigate the Facts relating to and the Circumstances Surrounding the Communication, by Public Officials and Other Persons in Positions of Trust of Secret and Confidential Information to Agents of a Foreign Power.* Ottawa: Printers to the King's Most Excellent Majesty, 27 June 1946.

Newspapers and Magazines

Canadian Labor Defender
Chefoo Magazine: The Organ of the Chefoo Schools Association
China's Millions
Chinese Recorder
Clarion
Daily Clarion
Globe and Mail
Kingston Whig Standard
Mail and Empire
Masses

Montreal Star
New Commonwealth
New Frontier
Ottawa Citizen
Searchlight
Sheffield Independent
Soviet Russia Today
Toronto Bible College Recorder
Toronto Star
Toronto Telegram
Varsity
Volunteer
Volunteer for Liberty
Worker

Other Published Primary Source Documents

Alexander, Bill. *No to Franco: The Struggle Never Stopped, 1939–1975!* London: Bill Alexander, 1992.

Allan, Ted. *This Time a Better Earth: A Critical Edition*. Edited by Bart Vautour. Ottawa: University of Ottawa Press, 2015.

Alvarez, Manuel. *The Tall Soldier: My 40-Year Search for the Man Who Saved My Life*. Toronto: Virgo Press, 1980.

Bethune, Norman. "A Plea for Early Compression in Pulmonary Tuberculosis." *Canadian Medical Association Journal* 27 (July 1932): 36–42.

– *The Politics of Passion: Norman Bethune's Writing and Art*. Edited by Larry Hannant. Toronto: University of Toronto Press, 1998.

Boyd, John. *A Noble Cause Betrayed ... but Hope Lives On, Pages from a Political Life*. Edmonton: Canadian Institute of Ukrainian Studies Research, 1999.

Braun, Otto. *A Comintern Agent in China, 1932–1939*. London: C. Hearst, 1982.

Brockway, Fenner. *The Truth about Barcelona*. London: Independent Labour Party, 1937.

Buck, Tim. *Canada and the Russian Revolution: The Impact of the World's First Socialist Revolution on Labor and Politics in Canada*. Toronto: Progress Books, 1967.

– *Yours in the Struggle: Reminiscences of Tim Buck*. Edited by William Beeching and Phyllis Clarke. Toronto: New Canada Publication, 1977.

Cecil-Smith, Major E. *Red Ally: An Estimate of Soviet Life and Soviet Power*. Toronto: Handy Books, 1941.

Cecil-Smith, Mrs. G. *Three Cries from Chinese Lips*. Toronto: China Inland Mission, 1910.

Chambers, Whittaker. *Witness*. New York: Random House, 1952.

Clarke, Samuel R. *Among the Tribes in South-West China*. London: China Inland Mission, Morgan and Scott, 1911.

Dallet, Joe. *Letters from Spain: By Joe Dallet, First Political Commissar (Mackenzie-Papineau Battalion), to His Wife*. Toronto: New Era Publishers, 1938.

Ewen, Jean. *China Nurse, 1932–1939*. Toronto: McClelland and Stewart, 1981.

Griffin, Frederick. *Soviet Scene: A Newspaperman's Close-Ups of New Russia*. Toronto: Macmillan, 1932.

Halton, Matthew. *Ten Years to Alamein*. Toronto: S.J. Reginald Saunders and Company, 1944.

Hunter, Peter. *Which Side Are You on Boys? Canadian Life on the Left*. Toronto: Lugus Publishing, 1988.

Kardash, William. *I Fought for Canada in Spain*. Toronto: New Era Publishers, 1938.

Kealey, Gregory S., and Reg Whitaker, eds. *Security Bulletins: The Depression Years, Part II, 1935*. St. John's: Canadian Committee on Labour History, 1995.

–, eds. *RCMP Security Bulletins: The Depression Years, Part III, 1936*. St. John's: Canadian Committee on Labour History, 1995.

–, eds. *RCMP Security Bulletins: The Depression Years, Part IV, 1937*. St. John's: Canadian Committee on Labour History, 1997.

–, eds. *RCMP Security Bulletins: The Depression Years, Part V, 1938–1939*. St. John's: Canadian Committee on Labour History, 1997.

–, eds. *RCMP Security Bulletins: The War Series, 1939–1941*. St. John's: Canadian Committee on Labour History, 1989.

Lethbridge, David, ed. *Bethune: The Secret Police File*. Salmon Arm, BC: Undercurrent Press, 2003.

Liversedge, Ronald. *Mac-Pap: Memoir of a Canadian in the Spanish Civil War*. Edited by David Yorke. Vancouver: New Star Books, 2013.

– *Recollections of the On-to-Ottawa Trek, 1935*. Vancouver: n.d. [c. 1961].

Livesay, Dorothy. *Journey with My Selves: A Memoir, 1909–1963*. Vancouver: Douglas and McIntyre, 1991.

– *Right Hand, Left Hand. A True Life of the Thirties: Paris, Toronto, Montreal, the West and Vancouver. Love, Politics, the Depression and Feminism*. Don Mills, ON: Press Porcepic, 1977.

Mao Tse-Tung. *Selected Works of Mao Tse-Tung*, Volume 2. Beijing: Foreign Language Press, 1965.

Marx, Karl, and Friedrich Engels. *Marx/Engels Selected Works*, Volume 1. Moscow: Progress Publishers, 1969.

Matthews, Herbert L. *Two Wars and More to Come*. Rahway, NJ: Quinn and Boden Company, 1938.

Merriman, Marion, and Warren Lerude. *American Commander in Spain: Robert Hale Merriman and the Abraham Lincoln Brigade*. Reno: University of Nevada Press, 1986.

Merriman, Robert. "Merriman Diaries: Exegesis." Edited by Raymond Hoff. Unpublished manuscript, 2018.

Nelson, Cary, and Jefferson Hendricks, eds. *Madrid 1937: Letters of the Abraham Lincoln Brigade from the Spanish Civil War*. New York: Routledge, 1996.

Orwell, George. *Homage to Catalonia*, 1938. Reprint, New York: Harvest Books, 1980.

Pierce, G. *Socialism and the CCF*. Montreal: Contemporary Publishing, 1934.

Ryan, Frank, ed. *The Book of the XV Brigade: Records of British, American, Canadian and Irish Volunteers in the XV International Brigade in Spain, 1936–1938*. Madrid: Commissariat of War, XVth Brigade, 1938.

Ryan, Oscar, Edward Cecil-Smith, Mildred Goldberg, and Frank Love. *Eight Men Speak: A Play*. Edited and with an introduction by Alan Filewod. Ottawa: University of Ottawa Press, 2013.

Ryan, Toby Gordon. *Stage Left: Canadian Theatre in the Thirties, a Memoir*. Toronto: CTR Publications, 1981.

Ryerson, Stanley. *1837: The Birth of Canadian Democracy*. Toronto: F. White, 1937.

Scott, Jack. *A Communist Life: Jack Scott and the Canadian Workers Movement, 1927–1985*. Edited by Bryan Palmer. St. John's: Canadian Committee on Canadian Labour History, 1988.

Smith, A.E. *All My Life: An Autobiography*. Toronto: Progress Books, 1949.

Smith, Stewart. *Comrades and Komsomolkas: My Years in the Communist Party of Canada*. Toronto: Lubus Publications, 1993.

Snow, Edgar. *Red Star over China*. London: Victor Gallancz, 1934.

Spry, Graham. *Passion and Conviction: The Letters of Graham Spry*. Edited by Rose Potvin. Regina: Canadian Plains Research Center, 1992.

Stephens, D.P. *Memoir of the Spanish Civil War: An Armenian-Canadian in the Spanish Civil War*. Edited by Rick Rennie. St. John's: Canadian Committee on Labour History, 2000.

Thomas, Jocko. *From Police Headquarters: True Tales from the Big City Crime Beat*. Toronto: Stoddart, 1990.

Voros, Sandor. *American Commissar*. New York: Chilton, 1961.

Watts, Jean. "Information Bulletin No. 1, Report of Miss Jean Watts, Our Delegate at the Recent Conference of the Office International pour l'Enfance, on Conditions in the Refugee Camps in France." Canadian Committee to Aid Spanish Refugees. 25 May 1939.

Wright, Richard, and Robin Endres, eds. *Eight Men Speak and Other Plays*. Toronto: New Hogtown Press, 1976.

Secondary Sources

Allen, Richard. *The Social Passion: Religion and Social Reform in Canada, 1914–1928*. Toronto: University of Toronto Press, 1971.

Alpert, Michael. *The Republican Army in the Spanish Civil War, 1936–1939*. Cambridge: Cambridge University Press, 2002.

Applebaum, Anne. *Red Famine: Stalin's War on Ukraine*. Toronto: Signal/ McClelland and Stewart, 2017.

Austin, Alvyn. *China's Millions: The China Inland Mission and Late Qing Society, 1832–1905*. Grand Rapids, MI: William B. Eerdmans, 2007.

Axelrod, Paul, and John G. Reid, eds. *Essays in in the Social History of Higher Education*. Montreal and Kingston: McGill-Queen's University Press, 1989.

Baetz, Elaine. "The Role of the Working Class in *Eight Men Speak*." MA thesis, University of Guelph, 1989.

Baxell, Richard. *Unlikely Warriors: The British in the Spanish Civil War*. London: Aurum Press, 2012.

Beeching, William. *Canadian Volunteers: Spain, 1936–1939*. Regina: Canadian Plains Research Center, 1989.

Benson, Eugene, and L.W. Conolly, eds. *The Oxford Companion to Canadian Theatre*. Toronto: Oxford University Press, 1989.

Berton, Pierre. *The Great Depression, 1929–1939*. Toronto: McClelland and Stewart, 1990.

Betcherman, Lita-Rose. *The Little Band: The Clashes between the Communists and the Canadian Establishment, 1928–1932*. Ottawa: Deneau, 1982.

– *The Swastika and the Maple Leaf: Fascist Movements in Canada in the Thirties*. Toronto: Fitzhenry and Whiteside, 1975.

Bickers, Robert. "Shanghailanders: The Formation and Identity of the British Settler Community in Shanghai, 1843–1937." *Past and Present* 159 (1998): 161–211.

Black, J.L. *Canada in the Soviet mirror: ideology and perception in Soviet foreign affairs, 1917-1991*. Ottawa: Carleton University Press, 1998.

Black, J. Larry, and Kirk Niergarth. "Revisiting the Canadian-Soviet Barter Proposal of 1932–1933: The Soviet Perspective." *International Journal* 71 (2016): 409–32.

Bliss, Michael. *Banting: A Biography*. Toronto: McClelland and Stewart, 1984.

Bosshardt, R.A. *The Restraining Hand*. London: Hodder and Stoughton, 1936.

Brinkley, Alan. *The Publisher: Henry Luce and His American Century*. New York: Alfred A. Knopf, 2010.

Brown, Archie. *The Rise and Fall of Communism*. Toronto: Doubleday Canada, 2009.

Butler, Nancy. "Mother Russia and the Socialist Fatherland: Women and the Communist Party of Canada, 1932–1941, with Specific Reference to the Activism of Dorothy Livesay and Jim Watts." PhD diss., Queen's University, 2010.

Butt, Michael. "Surveillance of Canadian Communists: A Case Study of Toronto RCMP Intelligence Networks, 1920–1939." PhD diss., Memorial University, 2003.

Campbell, J. Peter. "The Cult of Spontaneity: Finnish-Canadian Bushworkers and the Industrial Workers of the World in Northern Ontario, 1919–1934." *Labour/Le Travail* 41 (Spring 1998): 117–46.

Campbell, Peter. *Rose Henderson: A Woman for the People*. Montreal and Kingston: McGill-Queen's University Press, 2010.

Carew, Joy Gleason. *Blacks, Reds, and Russians: Sojourners in Search of the Soviet Promise*. New Brunswick, NJ: Rutgers University Press, 2010.

Carroll, Peter. *The Odyssey of the Abraham Lincoln Brigade: Americans in the Spanish Civil War.* Stanford, CA: Stanford University Press, 1994.

Cawley, Art. "The Canadian Catholic English-Language Press and the Spanish Civil War." *CCHA Study Sessions* 49 (1982): 25–51.

Clarkson, Adrienne. *Norman Bethune*. Toronto: Penguin Canada, 2009.

Colodny, Robert G. *The Struggle for Madrid: The Central Epic of the Spanish Conflict, 1936–1939*. New York: Paine-Whitman, 1958.

Cortada, James W. *Modern Warfare in Spain: American Military Observations on the Spanish Civil War, 1936–1939*. Washington, DC: Potomac Books, 2012.

Coverdale, John F. *Italian Intervention in the Spanish Civil War*. Princeton, NJ: Princeton University Press, 1975.

Duncan, Danny, ed. *African Americans in the Spanish Civil War: "This ain't Ethiopia, but it'll do.* New York: G.K. Hall, 1992.

Eby, Cecil D. *Between the Bullet and the Lie: American Volunteers in the Spanish Civil War*. New York: Holt, Rinehart and Winston, 1969.

– *Comrades and Commissars: The Lincoln Battalion in the Spanish Civil War.* University Park: Pennsylvania State University Press, 2007.

Endicott, Stephen. *Bienfait: The Saskatchewan Miners' Struggle of '31*. Toronto: University of Toronto Press, 2002.

– *James G. Endicott: Rebel out of China*. Toronto: University of Toronto Press, 1980.

Filewod, Alan. "Authorship, Left Modernism, and Communist Power in *Eight Men Speak*: A Reflection."*Canadian Literature* 209 (Summer 2011): 11–30.

– *Committing Theatre: Theatre Radicalism and Political Intervention in Canada.* Toronto: Between the Lines, 2011.

Fitzpatrick, Sheila. "Foreigners Observed: Moscow Visitors in the 1930s under the Gaze of Their Soviet Guides." *Russian History* 35 (2008): 215–34.

Frohn-Nielsen, Thor. "Canada's Foreign Enlistment Act: Mackenzie King's Expedient Response to the Spanish Civil War." MA thesis, University of British Columbia, 1979.

Garner, Hugh. *Cabbagetown: A Novel*. Toronto: Ryerson Press, 1968.

Gordon, Martin. *Chefoo School, 1881–1951: A History and Memoir*. Braunton, UK: Merlin Books, 1990.

Gordon, Sydney, and Ted Allan. *The Scalpel, the Sword: The Story of Dr. Norman Bethune*. Toronto: McClelland and Stewart, 1972.

Goutor, David. *A Chance to Fight Hitler: A Canadian Volunteer in the Spanish Civil War*. Toronto: Between the Lines, 2018.

Greig, David. *In The Fullness of Time: A History of the Church of Saint Mary Magdalene, Toronto*. Toronto: Church of Saint Mary Magdalene, 1990.

Guinness, M. Geraldine. *The Story of the China Inland Mission,* Vol. 1 and 2. San Francisco: Chinese Materials, 1977.

Han, Ziarong. *Red God: Wei Baqun and His Peasant Revolution in Southern China, 1894–1932*. Albany: State University of New York, 2014.

Hannant, Larry. *Infernal Machine: Investigating the Loyalty of Canada's Citizens*. Toronto: University of Toronto Press, 1995.

– "'My God, Are They Sending Women?' Three Canadian Women in the Spanish Civil War, 1936–1939." *Journal of the Canadian Historical Association* 15 (2004): 153–76.

– "United Front on the Left: The Committee to Aid Spanish Democracy." Paper presented to the Canadian Historical Association's annual meeting, 23 October 2005.

Harkness, Ross. *J.E. Atkinson of the Star*. Toronto: Toronto Star, 1963.

Hayman, Arnolis. *A Foreign Missionary on the Long March: The Memoirs of Arnolis Hayman of the China Inland Mission*. Edited by Anne-Marie Brady. Portland, ME: Merwin Asia, 2010.

Hemingway, Andrew. *Artists on the Left: American Artists and the Communist Movement, 1926–1956*. New Haven, CT: Yale University Press, 2002.

Hoar, Victor. *The Mackenzie-Papineau Battalion: Canadian Participation in the Spanish Civil War*. Toronto: Copp Clark, 1969.

Hoff, Raymond M., Christopher T. Brooks, Michael Petrou, and Myron Momryk. "Biographical Dictionary of Volunteers from Canada in the Spanish Civil War." Unpublished manuscript, 2018.

Hollander, Paul. *Political Pilgrims: Travels of Western Intellectuals to the Soviet Union, China and Cuba*. Oxford: Oxford University Press, 1981.

Hopkins, James K. *Into the Heart of the Fire: The British in the Spanish Civil War*. Stanford, CA: Stanford University Press, 1998.

Howard, Victor. *We Were the Salt of the Earth! A Narrative of the On to Ottawa Trek and Regina Riot*. Regina: Canadian Plains Research Center, 1985.

Jackson, Angela. *At the Margins of Mayhem: Prologue and Epilogue to the Last Great Battle of the Spanish Civil War*. Pontypool, UK: Warren and Pell, 2008.

Jansen, James R. "The Debs Column and American Socialists in the Spanish Civil War." MA thesis, University of Nebraska, 2015.

Kaplan, William. *Everything That Floats: Pat Sullivan, Hal Banks, and the Seamen's Unions of Canada*. Toronto: University of Toronto Press, 1987.

Kealey, Gregory S. *Spying on Canadians: The Royal Canadian Mounted Police Security Service and the Origins of the Long Cold War*. Toronto: University of Toronto Press, 2017.

– "Stanley Brehaut Ryerson: Canadian Revolutionary Intellectual." *Studies in Political Economy* 8 (1982): 103–31.

Kelley, Ninette, and Michael Trebilcock. *The Making of the Mosaic: A History of Canadian Immigration Policy*. Toronto: University of Toronto Press, 2000.

Kerry, A.J., and W.A. McDill. *History of the Corps of Royal Canadian Engineers*. Volume 1, *1749–1939*. Ottawa: Military Engineers Association of Canada, 1962.

– *History of the Corps of Royal Canadian Engineers*. Volume 2, *1936–1946*. Ottawa: Military Engineers Association of Canada, 1966.

Kirschenbaum, Lisa A. *International Communism and the Spanish Civil War*. Cambridge: Cambridge University Press, 2015.

Klehr, Harvey. *Communist Cadre: The Social Background of the American Communist Party Elite*. Stanford, CA: Hoover Institution Press, 1978.

Kowalsky, Daniel. "The Soviet Union and the International Brigades, 1936-1939." *Journal of Slavic Military Studies* 19 (September 2006): 681–704.

Kraljic, John Peter. "The Croatian Community in North America and the Spanish Civil War." MA thesis, Hunter College, 2002.

Krammer, Arnold. "Soviet Participation in the International Brigades." *Modern Age* 16 (Fall 1972): 356–67.

Krawchuk, Peter. *Interned without Cause*. Toronto: Kobzar, 1985.

– *Our History: The Ukrainian Labor-Farmer Movement in Canada, 1907–1991*. Toronto: Lugus, 1996.

Mae Lambe, Ariel. "Cuban Antifascism and the Spanish Civil War: Transnational Activism, Networks, and Solidarity in the 1930s." PhD diss., Columbia University, 2015.

Landis, Arthur. *The Abraham Lincoln Brigade*. New York: Citadel Press, 1967.

Lexier, Roberta, Stephanie Bangarth, and Jon Weier, eds, *Party of Conscience: The CCF, the NDP, and Social Democracy in Canada*.Toronto: Between the Lines, 2018.

Lind, Jane. *Perfect Red: The Life of Paraskeva Clark*. Toronto: Cormorant Books, 2009.

Lobigs, Martin. "Canadian Responses to the Mackenzie-Papineau Battalion." MA thesis, University of New Brunswick, 1992.

Lorinc, John, and Michael McClelland, eds, *The Ward: The Life and Loss of Toronto's First Immigrant Neighborhood*. Toronto: Coach House, 2015.

MacDowell, Laurel Sefton. *Renegade Lawyer: The Life of J.L. Cohen*. Toronto: University of Toronto Press for the Osgoode Society for Canadian Legal History, 2001.

MacKenzie, S.P. "The Foreign Enlistment Act and the Spanish Civil War, 1936–1939." *Twentieth Century British History* 10 (1999): 52–66.

Manley, John. "'Audacity, Audacity and Still More Audacity': Tim Buck, the Party and the People, 1932–1939." *Labour/Le Travail* 49 (Spring 2002): 9–41.

– "'Communists Love Canada!' The Communist Party of Canada, "The People,' and the Popular Front, 1933–1939," *Journal of Canadian Studies* 36 (Winter 2001–2): 59–86.

Margulies, Sylvia R. *The Pilgrimage to Russia: The Soviet Union and the Treatment of Foreigners, 1924–1937*. Milwaukee: University of Wisconsin Press, 1968.

McCannon, John. "Soviet Intervention in the Spanish Civil War, 1936–39: A Reexamination." *Russian History* 22 (Summer 1995): 154–80.

McKay, Ian. *Reasoning Otherwise: Leftists and the People's Enlightenment in Canada, 1890–1920*. Toronto: Between the Lines, 2008.

Melnyk, Olenka. *No Bankers in Heaven: Remembering the CCF*. Toronto: McGraw-Hill Ryerson, 1989.

Miller, Sheila. *Pigtails, Petticoats, and the Old School Tie*. London: OMF Books, 1981.

Miner, Luella. *China's Book of Martyrs*. Philadelphia: Westminster Press, 1903.

Mitchell, Tom. "From the Social Gospel to 'the Plain Break of Leninism': A.E. Smith's Journey to the Left in the Epoch of Reaction after World War I." *Labour/Le Travail* 33 (1994): 125–51.

Molinaro, Dennis G. "'A Species of Treason?' Deportation and Nation-Building in the Case of Tomo Cacic, 1931–1934." *Canadian Historical Review* 91 (March 2010): 61–85.

Momryk, Myron. "Hungarian Volunteers from Canada in the Spanish Civil War, 1936–1939." *Hungarian Studies Review* 24 (1997): 83–116.

– "Ignacy Witczak's Passport, Soviet Espionage and the Origins of the Cold War in Canada." *Polish American Studies* 68 (Autumn 2011): 67–84.

– "Jewish Volunteers from Canada in the Spanish Civil War." *Outlook* 34 (July/August 1996): 13–15.

– "Ukrainian Volunteers from Canada in the International Brigades, 1936–1939: A Profile." *Journal of Ukrainian Studies* 16 (Winter 1991): 181–94.

Munro, John. "Canada and the Civil War in Spain: Repatriation of the Mackenzie-Papineau Battalion." *External Affairs* 23 (February 1971): 52–8.

Murphy, Emily. "Case Study Two: Jean Watts, Ted Allan, and the Daily Clarion in Spain." Virtual Research Environment of Canadian Cultural History about the Spanish Civil War, http://spanishcivilwar.ca/case-studies/jean-watts/case-study-two

Naylor, James. *The Fate of Labour Socialism: The Co-operative Commonwealth Federation and the Dream of a Working-Class Future*. Toronto: University of Toronto Press, 2016.

Nemzer, Louis. "The Soviet Friendship Societies." *Public Opinion Quarterly* (Summer 1949): 265–84.

Niergarth, Kirk. "'No Sense of Reality': George A. Drew's Anti-Communist Tour of the USSR and the Campaign for Coalition Government in Ontario, 1937." *Ontario History* 107 (Autumn 2015): 213–39.

O'Connor, Emmett. "Identity and Self-Representation in Irish Communism: The Connolly Column and the Spanish Civil War." *Socialist History* 34 (2009): 36–51.

Othen, Christopher. *Franco's International Brigades: Foreign Volunteers and Fascist Dictators in the Spanish Civil War*. London: Reportage Press, 2008.

Padro, Antonio Pacheco. *Vengo del Jarama: Glorias y Horrores de la Guerra*. San Juan, PR: Talleres Tipográficos Baldrich, 1942.

Palmer, Bryan D., and Gaetan Heroux. "'Cracking the Stone': The Long History of Capitalist Crisis and Toronto's Dispossessed, 1830–1930." *Labour/Le Travail* 69 (2012): 10–62.

– *Toronto's Poor: A Rebellious History*. Toronto: Between the Lines, 2016.

Patterson, Ian. *Guernica and Total War*. London: Profile, 2007.

Payne, Stanley G. *The Spanish Civil War, the Soviet Union and Communism*. New Haven, CT: Yale University Press, 2004.

Peck, Mary Biggar. *Red Moon over Spain: Canadian Media Reaction to the Spanish Civil War, 1936–1939*. Ottawa: Steel Rail, 1988.

Penner, Norman. *Canadian Communism: The Stalin Years and Beyond*. Toronto: Methuen, 1988.

Petrou, Michael. *Renegades: Canadians in the Spanish Civil War*. Vancouver: UBC Press, 2008.

Petryshyn, J. "Class Conflicts and Civil Liberties: The Origins and Activities of the Canadian Labour Defense League, 1925–1940." *Labour/Le Travail* 10 (Autumn 1982): 39–63.

Petryshyn, Jaroslav. "A.E. Smith and the Canadian Labour Defense League." PhD diss., Western University, 1977.

Preston, Paul. *The Spanish Civil War, 1936–39*. London: Weidenfeld and Nicolson, 1986.

– *We Saw Spain Die: Foreign Correspondents in the Spanish Civil War*. London: Skyhorse, 2009.

Proctor, Raymond L. *Hitler's Luftwaffe in the Spanish Civil War*. London: Greenwood Press, 1983.

Radosh, Ronald, Mary M. Habeck, and Grigory Sevostianov, eds. *Spain Betrayed: The Soviet Union in the Spanish Civil War*. New Haven, CT: Yale University Press, 2001.

Ristaino, Marcia Reynders. *Port of Last Resort: The Diaspora Communities of Shanghai*. Stanford, CA: University of Stanford Press, 2001.

Roberts, Barbara. *Whence They Came: Deportation from Canada, 1900–1935*. Ottawa: University of Ottawa Press, 1988.

Rodney, William. *Soldiers of the International: A History of the Communist Party of Canada, 1919–1929*. Toronto: University of Toronto Press, 1968.

Rolfe, Edwin. *The Lincoln Battalion*. New York: Random House, 1939.

Rubin, Don, ed. *Canadian Theatre History: Selected Readings*. Toronto: Copp Clark, 1996.

Rust, William. *Britons in Spain: The History of the British Battalion of the XVth International Brigade*. London: Lawrence and Wishart, 1939.

Smith, Michelle. "From 'the Offal of the Magazine Trade' to 'Absolutely Priceless': Considering the Canadian Pulp Magazine Collection." *English Studies in Canada* 30 (March 2014): 101–16.

Socknat, Thomas P. *Witness against War: Pacifism in Canada 1900–1945*. Toronto: University of Toronto Press, 1987.

Stewart, Roderick, and Jesus Majada. *Bethune in Spain*. Montreal and Kingston: McGill-Queen's University Press, 2014.

Stewart, Roderick, and Sharon Stewart. *Phoenix: The Life of Norman Bethune*. Montreal and Kingston: McGill-Queen's University Press, 2011.

Stradling, Rob. "English-speaking Units of the International Brigades: War, Politics, and Discipline." *Journal of Contemporary History* 45 (2010): 744–67.

Thomas, Hugh. *The Spanish Civil War*. London: Eyre and Spottiswoode, 1961.

Toews, Anne Frances. "For Liberty, Bread and Love: Annie Buller, Beckie Buhay, and the Forging of Communist Militant Femininity in Canada, 1918–1939." MA thesis, Simon Fraser University, 2009.

Volodarsky, Boris. *Stalin's Agent: The Life and Death of Alexander Orlov*. Oxford: Oxford University Press, 2015.

Waite, P.B. *In Search of R.B. Bennett*. Montreal and Kingston: McGill-Queen's University Press, 2012.

Ward, Allison. "'I Listened as They Built Up Their Picture of That Terrible Land': Self-Identity and Societal Observations in Traveller's Accounts of the Soviet Union, 1929–1936." Unpublished MA research paper, Queen's University, 2010.

Wentzell, Tyler. "Canada' Foreign Enlistment Act and the Spanish Civil War." *Labour/Le Travail* 80 (Fall 2017): 213–46.

– "Mercenaries and Adventurers: Canada and Foreign the Foreign Enlistment Act in the Nineteenth Century." *Canadian Military History* 14 (Spring 2014): 57–77.

Whealey, Robert L. *Hitler and Spain: The Nazi Role in the Spanish Civil War, 1936–1939*. Lexington: University Press of Kentucky, 1989.

Wheeler, George. *To Make People Smile Again*. Newcastle upon Tyne, UK: Zymurgy, 2003.

Whitaker, Reg. "Official Repression of Communism During World War II." *Labour/Le Travail* 16 (Spring 1986): 135–66.

Worley, Matthew, ed. *In Search of Revolution: International Communist Parties in the Third Period*. London: I.B. Taurus, 2004.

Wright, Barry, Eric Tucker, and Susan Binnie, eds. *Canadian State Trials*. Volume 4, *Security, Dissent, and the Limits of State Toleration in War and Peace, 1914–1939*. Toronto: University of Toronto Press for the Osgoode Society for Canadian Legal History, 2015.

Young, Walter D. *Anatomy of a Party: The National CCF, 1932–1961*. Toronto: University of Toronto Press, 1969.

Zaloga, Steven J. "Soviet Tank Operations in the Spanish Civil War." *Journal of Slavic Military Studies* 12 (September 1999): 134–62.

Zuehlke, Mark. *The Gallant Cause: Canadians in the Spanish Civil War, 1936–1939*. Toronto: Whitecap Books, 1996.

Index

The letters "pl." before a number denote a plate in the photo section in the book.

Acme Motor and Gear Company, 19
Adler, Lilly, 46
Advocate (newspaper), 203
Albacete, International Brigades base, 108, 110–11, 117, 118, 133, 136, 142, 168
Albalate del Arzobispo (Spain), 163
Alcaniz (Spain), 140, 163, 164, 288n62
Allan, Ted (Alan Herman), 133, 142, 271n121, 272n133, 273n158
All-Union Society for Cultural Relations with Foreign Countries (VOKS), 40
Alvarez, Manuel, 292n45
American Federation of Labor, 19
Ames, Bernard, 270n99
Amlie, Hans, 123, 130, 143, 270n99, 272n135
Anderson, David (Andy), 124, 128–9, 130, 270n99, 270n104
Aragon Offensive (the Retreats), 156–67; attempted attack on Lecera, 162–3; attempted stand and withdrawl from Azuara, 159–62; attempted stand at Caspe, 165–7, 288n67, 288n71; casualties from, 167; Cecil-Smith on, 173; launch of, 156; lull before, 156; preparations for by XVth Brigade, 156–9; victory for Nationalists, 168; withdrawal from Albalate, 163
Arcand, Adrien, 69
Archambault, Joseph: *The Royal Commission Report on Penal Reform in Canada*, 47n
art, role in revolution, 59–63
Axler, Isadore, 55
Azana, Manuel, 98
Azuara (Spain), 105, 157, 158–62

Banting, Frederick, 79, 254n32
Ban Xeo Xiao, 11
Barcelona, 118, 183, 188–9, 190–1, 193, 296n45, 296n47
Bavin, E.D., 216
Baxell, Richard, 127
Beeching, William (Bill): on Battle of Teruel, 280n11, 283n44, 283n46; on Cecil-Smith's injury, 179; encounter with Cecil-Smith in Spain, 164–5; internment during Second World War, 220; in Lincoln Battalion, 184; on Mac-Paps, 138; in On-to-Ottawa Trek, 263n8; on repatriation of Canadian volunteers, 297n58

Belchite (Spain), 134, 157, 158–9, 160, 265n45
Bennett, R.B.: on Cecil-Smith, 47, 86; embargoes against Soviet Union, 80, 81; intervention against *Eight Men Speak*, 55, 56, 64; labour-socialist programs promoted by, 65–6, 68; loss in 1935 federal election, 71
Benson (Robert Leaconsfield Trolove), 202, 301n115, 301n117
Bentley, J.W., 197
Bethune, Norman: articles for *Weekly Clarion*, 204; Canadian Blood Transfusion Service, 98; Cecil-Smith and, 79, 94, 101; in China, 131–2, 206; death and final testament, 207–8; *Heart of Spain* (documentary), 131, 227; Lilian Gouge and, 79, 94, 131–2, 205, 206–7, 208; photographs, pl. 10; relationships with women, 208; on Soviet health care system, 79; Spanish Civil War and, 99, 105, 130–1
Blair, Charles, 40
Bland, Salem, 89, 99, 197
The Book of the XVth Brigade (Ryan), 5
Bosshardt, Alfred and Rose, 83, 84
bourgeoisie, 61–3, 70
Boxer Rebellion, 11–12
Boyak, Bill, 135
Boychuk, John, 34, 58
Brage, Raphael Busch, 161, 165
Braun, Otto, 84
Brennan, Bill, 267n66
Britain, 80, 101, 198
British Anti-Tank Battery, 127, 128, 146, 148, 160, 265n45
British Battalion: in Aragon Offensive, 157, 165, 166, 167; in attack on Fuentes de Ebro, 135; in Brunete Offensive, 128, 129, 130; in capture and defence of Teruel, 146, 150, 151, 154, 283n44; in Ebro Offensive, 176–7; General Walter on, 140; Machine Gun Company in, 282n34; name of, 125; renumbering of, 274n12; repatriation of, 193; in Segura de Los Baños, 152
Brock, Jack, 17
Brown, Richard, 207, 208
Browne, Robert, 25
Bruce, Herbert A., 79
Bruce, Malcolm, 33, 35, 58
Brunete Offensive, 126–30, 142–3, 271n121
Buck, Tim: arrest and trial with CPC leadership, 33, 34, 35–6; Benson (Robert Leaconsfield Trolove) and, 202; Cecil-Smith and, 19, 258n15; on Cecil-Smith in South America, 5, 231n9; on Friends of the Mackenzie-Papineau Battalion, 120, 121; Kingston Penitentiary incident and imprisonment, 45, 48–9, 58; as machinist, 19, 236n5; on Mac-Paps, 122, 140; in 1935 federal election, 70–1; Norman Bethune and, 206; at Queen's Park for International Red Day, 22; release from prison, 69–70; on repatriation of Canadian volunteers, 296n38; request for Cecil-Smith and Niilo Makela to return to Canada, 170; on Second World War, 214, 221; on Soviet-German non-aggression pact, 210; Spanish Civil War and, 98, 99–100, 131; *Yours in the Struggle*, 231n9
Buhay, Beckie, 46, 48, 121, 188, 202
Bukharin, Nikolai, 61
Burma Road, 224

Cacic, Tomo, 34, 58
Canada: bans on CPC and other labour-socialist parties, 36–7, 72–3, 219–20; embargoes against Soviet Union, 80–1; labour-socialist parties in, 65–6; 1935 federal election, 65, 70–1; repatriation of Canadian volunteers and, 184, 189; section 98 of Criminal Code, 34, 36, 37, 49, 57, 71, 72–3; on Spanish Civil War, 101. *See also* Bennett, R.B.; King, Mackenzie
Canada Steamship Lines, 218
Canadian Bank of Commerce, 17, 19, 236n3
Canadian Blood Transfusion Service, 98. *See also* Bethune, Norman
Canadian Brotherhood of Ships' Employees, 217
Canadian Committee to Aid Spanish Refugees, 200, 227
Canadian Encyclopedia, 5
Canadian Forum (magazine), 44, 63, 74, 78, 102
Canadian Labor Defender (magazine), 4, 25, 39, 46
Canadian Labor Defense League (CLDL): ban on, 219; Cecil-Smith in, 26, 34; Chinese immigrants and, 85–6; delegation to Kingston Penitentiary, 45–8; *Eight Men Speak* and section 98 campaign, 49, 56; as front for CPC, 37; membership growth, 58; overview of activities, 25–6; protest against CPC leadership trial, 35
Canadian League Against War and Fascism, 86–7, 88–9, 98, 189, 256n72
Canadian League for Peace and Democracy, 189, 219
Canadian School of Engineering (Halifax), 16
Canadian Seamen's Union (CSU): end of Cecil-Smith's political involvement and, 211, 224; leadership internment, 220; *Searchlight* (newsletter), 220, 224, 307n59; strike by, 217–19, 306n42, 307n50
Canadian Tribune (newspaper), 228, 308n74
Cane, Lawrence, 113, 135, 144, 148, 157, 231n9, 284n60
capitalism, 6n, 28
Carbonell, Jorge, 174, 175
Carney, William P., 280n7
Carr, Sam, 33, 58, 98, 121, 240n21
Caspe (Spain), 140, 164, 165–7, 288n67
Catalonia, 117–18
Cecil-Smith, Edward: attempt to run for office, 76, 93; at Canadian Bank of Commerce, 17, 19, 236n3; Communist involvement (*see* Cecil-Smith, Edward, Communist involvement); death of, 228; early childhood and education at Chefoo, 13–14, pl. 1; Great Depression, 27–8; intellectual background, 18, 32, 43; in journalism, 20, 21, 31, 96, 104, 203, 239n1; lack of scholarship on, 4–6; life after Second World War, 227–8; life and addresses in Toronto, 76, 93–4, 228, 235n65, 250n51; marriage to Lilian Gouge, 17, 18, 208; move to Toronto, 15, 16, 235n55; in Non-Permanent Active Militia, 16–17, 16n, 19, 20; parents of, 9–12; physical description, 40; relations with family in China, 18, 81–2, 224; Second World War and,

183, 209, 211–12, 213–16, 305n29, 306n33; in Shanghai Volunteer Corps, 14–15, 234n36; social life with Chefoo alumni, 17–18, 234n50; in Spanish Civil War (*see* Cecil-Smith, Edward, in Spanish Civil War)
Cecil-Smith, Edward, Communist involvement: advocacy for Soviet Union, 74, 75–6, 78, 209, 221–3; on art's political value, 59–63; *Canadian Forum* and, 63; Canadian League Against War and Fascism, 87–8; and Canadian Seamen's Union, 211, 217–18, 220, 224; on capitalism, 28; on CCF, 66–8; on China, 81–2, 84, 204–5; on Chinese immigrants, 85–6; on communism and revolution, 37–8, 39, 102–3; coverage of Tim Buck's speech upon release from prison, 70; coverage of CPC leadership trial, 34, 35, 241n30; coverage of Queen's Park battles, 21–5; CPC employment, 28; CPC involvement upon return from Spain, 199–200, 202, 299n95; CPC membership and departure, 35, 224–5, 241n29; as CPC Ward 2 president, 95, 202; *Daily Clarion* and, 4, 94, 96, 203–4, 258n14; in delegation to Kingston Penitentiary, 45–6, 47–8; disagreement with CPC position on Second World War, 216; *Eight Men Speak* (play) and, 49–50, 51, 52–3, 54, 55–6, 57–8, pl. 3; on embargoes against Soviet Union, 80–1; on fascism, 68–9, 87; lack of internment during Second World War, 220; *Masses* and, 4, 38–9, 49, 59, 64, 242n52; pacifist beliefs of, 20–1, 86, 93; Progressive Arts Club and, 31–3, 38, 49, 94, 239n4; questions about political loyalty of, 32, 39, 144, 185–6, 204, 211; radicalization of, 15, 19–20, 25, 26–7, 28; on R.B. Bennett, 47; RCMP and, 40–1, 46, 144, 222, 227, 279n85; reconciliation of Christianity with communism, 26–7, 85; *Red Ally*, 222–3; *Soviet Russia Today* and, 76–7, 80; Soviet-style cultural production, 39–40; student engagement by, 63; teaching at Communist School, 71–2; *Weekly Clarion* and, 204–5; *Worker* and, 4, 34–5, 65, 72, 94, 241n30, pl. 2; Workers' Theatre and, 42–5
Cecil-Smith, Edward, in Spanish Civil War: in Aragon Offensive (the Retreats), 156–8, 159–63, 164–5, 166, 167, 288n67, 289n76; in Atalaya battle, 153–4, 155; Barcelona defence and, 190–1, 296n47; basic training, 110–12; in Brunete Offensive, 128–9, 272n133; commissar position and, 124, 270n101; comparison to other volunteers, 108–9; conflict with commissars, 144, 168–9; disciplinary issues while awaiting repatriation, 186–8, 295n21; on discipline, 117, 266n52; Dominion Day speech, 172–3; in Ebro Offensive, 174–7; in Friends of the Mackenzie-Papineau Battalion, 200–1; in Fuentes de Ebro battle, 135–6, 275n22; injuries, 129, 133, 179–80, 183, 293n68, 293n72, pl. 5; invitation to return to Canada, 170–1, 290n14; joining the Mac-Paps, 135, 275n21; journey to

Spain, 105–7, 108, 261n65, pl. 4; on lack of Canadian leaders, 187–8; leadership by, 112–13, 117, 135–7, 139, 184, 276n31; letters home, 171–2; on machine guns, 112; Mac-Paps formation, 119, 267n66; on Mac-Paps' name, 121; Mac-Paps' official history, 201–2, 300n111; at Mac-Paps veterans gathering, 227; motivation for, 93, 101–3, 228–9; news coverage of, 142–3; photographs, pl. 8, pl. 9; political activities and, 143–4, 169, 279n83; predictions for postwar Spain, 194; promotional use of image, 154–5, pl. 7; promotion to *mayor*, 151, 283n44; RCMP file on, 144, 279n85; recruitment process for, 104; on Red Army advisors, 114, 137–8; repatriation back to Canada, 3, 189, 191, 192–4, 195–6, 197–8; security for Albacete governor, 118; in Segura de Los Baños, 152; in Sierra de Cavalls battle, 178–9; in Sierra de Pandols battles, 177–8; support for volunteers, 5, 188, 192; Teruel defence and, 146–51, 282n40; training by, 114–16, 133–4, 139–41, 274n6; in Washington Battalion, 117, 122–3, 124–5, 128–9, 270n99

Cecil-Smith, Frances (sister): childhood, 11, 13, pl. 1; internment by Japanese, 224; move to and life in Toronto, 15, 16, 17, 234n50, 235n55; return to China as missionary, 17, 18, 81, 235n56

Cecil-Smith, George (father): experiences with Chinese communists, 82–4; family background, 9; missionary work in China, 9–10, 11–12, 16; relations with Cecil-Smith, 18, 81; Second World War and death, 224

Cecil-Smith, Ida (mother). *See* Roberts, Ida White

Cecil-Smith, Sydney (brother), 11, 13, 81, 224, 233n12

Chamberlain, Neville, 183

Chapiev (Miklos Szalway), 128, 272n128

Chapman, Jack, 218, 220

Chefoo Magazine, 18, 236n8

Chefoo School, 13–14, 14n, 17–18, 234n50, 235n55, 235n60, 236n8, pl. 1

Chen, Elder, 11

China: Boxer Rebellion, 11–12; Cecil-Smith on, 81–2, 84, 204–5, 227; Japanese fascism and, 69; missionaries in, 9–12, 82–4; Lilian Gouge's interest in, 131–2, 205; Nationalist-Communist conflict, 82–4; Norman Bethune and other foreign volunteers in, 131–2, 206; during Second World War, 224. *See also* Chinese Communist Party

China Inland Mission: Cecil-Smith's parents in, 9–10; Chefoo alumni and Toronto headquarters, 17, 235n55; Chefoo School, 13–14; Lilian Gouge and, 205; Nationalist-Communist conflict and, 82–4; Toronto Bible College, 15. *See also* missionaries, in China

Chinese Communist Party, 68, 82, 83–5, 89, 131–2

Chinese immigrants, 85–6

Chinese Recorder (magazine), 11

Christianity: missionaries in China, 9–12, 82–4; reconciliation with communism, 26–7, 85

Christie Pits Riot, 69

Clark, Gregory, 195

Clark, Paraskeva, 94, 131, 207
Clarkson, Adrienne, 208, 273n157
Clarté (newspaper), 203
Cline, Joseph, 220
Coakley (CPR agent), 190
Cohen, J.L., 25–6
Colle, Beatrice, 121, 197, 267n71
Collins, Fred, 218
Comintern: China and, 84; CPC direction from, 36; international recruitment for Spanish Civil War, 90, 100–1, 103, 109; Popular Front strategy, 70; on Second World War, 214, 216, 221; World Congress Against War and Fascism and, 86. *See also* communism; Soviet Union
commissars, 123–4, 144, 168–9, 185
Committee to Aid Spanish Democracy, 98–9, 130, 200
communism: Cecil-Smith on, 37–8, 39, 102–3; Popular Front strategy, 59, 70–1, 73, 94, 95, 96, 99; reconciliation with Christianity, 26–7, 85; Third Period doctrine, 39, 59, 62, 70, 94; view of world history, 6n. *See also* Cecil-Smith, Edward, Communist involvement; Comintern; *specific parties*
Communist League of America (Opposition), 33
Communist Manifesto (Marx and Engels), 71
Communist Party of Canada (CPC): anti-intellectualism of, 32, 62, 168; arrest and trial of leadership, 33–4, 35–6, 36n, 241n30; bans on, 36–7, 72–3, 219–20; Canadian Labor Defense League and, 26; Canadian Seamen's Union strike and, 217, 218–19; Cecil-Smith as Ward 2 president, 95, 202; Cecil-Smith employment with, 28; Cecil-Smith membership and departure, 35, 224–5, 241n29; Committee to Aid Spanish Democracy and, 98–9; critiques of CCF and pseudo-labour-socialist policies, 66; dissemination of Soviet Union information, 75; on *Eight Men Speak* (play), 55; International Red Day, 21–2; Kingston Penitentiary riots, 45–9; Mac-Paps and, 120–1; Mac-Paps official history and, 201–2, 300n111; May Day parades, 95–6; membership growth, 58; military infiltration concerns by RCMP and military, 212–13, 215, 305n27; Popular Front strategy, 59, 70–1, 73; Queen's Park battles, 22–5; release of party leaders from prison, 58; on Second World War, 211, 214, 220–1; Spanish Civil War and, 103–4, 109, 130–1, 142–3, 296n38
Communist Party of China, 68, 82, 83–5, 89, 131–2
Communist Party of Germany, 57, 69, 70, 89
Communist Party of the United States of America (CPUSA), 60, 61, 106, 116, 120
Communist School, 71–2
Confederation of Autonomous Right-wing Groups (CEDA), 89–90, 95
Connolly Column, 118
Conservative Party, 71. *See also* Bennett, R.B.
Constant, Maurice, 136, 157, 187, 201, 202
Co-operative Commonwealth Federation (CCF): Canadian League Against War and Fascism and, 89; Cecil-Smith and CPC on,

65–8; Committee to Aid Spanish Democracy and, 98–9; infiltration by communists, 71–2; May Day parade and, 96; Popular Front and 1935 federal election, 70–1; Spanish Civil War volunteers and, 120–1
Copic, Vladimir: background, 126; in Brunete Offensive, 127–8, 129, 130; invitation to Cecil-Smith to return to Canada and, 170–1; on leave during Aragon Offensive (the Retreats), 156, 164; Mac-Paps move to Mas de Las Matas and, 140; recall to Soviet Union, 173, pl. 8; in Segura de Los Baños campaign, 152, 153, 154, 155; in Teruel defence, 145, 146, 150; in Zaragoza campaign, 134
Coulthard, Dede, 17
Criminal Code (section 98), 34, 36, 37, 49, 57, 71, 72–3
Cunningham, Jock, 127

Daily Clarion (newspaper): Cecil-Smith at, 4, 94, 96, 203, 258n14; coverage of Soviet Union, 75; coverage of Spanish Civil War, 94–5, 97, 142–3, 143–4, 171–2; on Ebro Offensive, 177; Friends of the Mackenzie-Papineau Battalion and, 120; on Teruel battle, 141; transition to new publications, 203–4; on Walter Dent and Young Communist League, 268n75
Dallet, Joseph, 125, 135, 139, 155, 289n2, pl. 7
Dart, Rollin, 134
Day, Margaret, 207, 208
Degar, Dr., 288n62
Delaney, Gerry, 111
democracy, Westminster vs. Soviet, 75–6
Dent, Walter, 119, 120, 267n66, 268n75
Derry, Joe, 44
Diaz, José, 100
Diaz, Ricardo: in Atalaya battle, 153; Cecil-Smith on, 188; Mac-Paps leadership and promotions, 139, 151, 280n11, 283n44, 284n49; in Teruel defence, 147, 149, 150, 151, 280n11
Dickson-Kenwin, George, 57
Dimitrov, Georgi, 70
Dimitrov Battalion, 125, 126, 127, 128, 134, 159
Dombrowski Battalion, 184, 263n12
Dombrowski Brigade (XIIIth Brigade), 109, 162–3, 173, 174, 176
Donnelly, Charles, 110
Doran, Dave, 152, 156, 164, 165, 166–7, 173, 288n67
Dougher, Joe, 135
Draper, Dennis, 22, 24, 41, 50
Drew, George, 75
Dunbar, Malcolm, 127, 173
Dunn, Victor, 215, 305n27

Ebb, Gunnar (Paavo Koskinen), 165–6, 174, 179
Ebro Offensive, 168, 174–7, 189
Edwards, Lionel: background, 106; basic training in Spain, 110; China plans, 132; in Ebro Offensive, 174–5; journey to Spain, 106; Mac-Paps leadership and promotions, 151, 173–4, 280n11, 283n44; on mobile machine gun posts, 146; on news of Madrid siege, 99; public engagements upon return from Spain, 199; repatriation to Canada, 192; in Teruel defence, 147–8, 149, 150–1, 280n11, 282n40

Eight Men Speak (play), 49–58; attempts to disseminate, 56–8, 63; ban on, 55–6; critical reception, 54–5; debut performance, 51–4, 247n63; impact of, 58; monitoring by Toronto police, 50–1; photograph, pl. 3; political vs. artistic value, 60–1; writing and production process, 4, 49–50
Eisendrath, Maurice, 89
XIth Brigade (Thaelmann Brigade), 109, 118, 134, 146, 147–9, 173, 174, 263n12
Emblem, Grace, 83
Endicott, James G., 85
Engels, Friedrich: *The Communist Manifesto* (with Marx), 71
Estevan (Saskatchewan), 32, 41, 51, 66
Eveready Printers, 223, 308n74
Eviction (play), 44
Ewen, Jean, 132, 273n157
Ewen, Tom, 33, 35, 36, 46, 58, 70–1

fascism, 68–9, 70, 87, 89
Fellowship for a Christian Social Order, 89
XVth Brigade: in Aragon Offensive (the Retreats), 156–67; *The Book of the XVth Brigade* (Ryan), 5; in Brunete Offensive, 126–30, 271n121; composition of, 125; in Ebro Offensive, 174–7; in Fuentes de Ebro battle, 134–6; lack of Canadian leadership, 187–8; leadership of, 126, 134, 173, pl. 8; Mac-Paps formation and, 119, 122; in Segura de Los Baños battles, 152–4, 155; in Sierra de Pandols battles, 177–8; in Teruel defence, 145–51. *See also* British Anti-Tank Battery; British Battalion; Dimitrov Battalion; International Brigades; Lincoln Battalion; Mackenzie-Papineau Battalion; Sixth of February Battalion; 24th Battalion; Washington Battalion
Finnish Athletic Club, 196
First World War. *See* Great War
Fleming, W.S., 11
Forkin, Pat, 204
Fort, Gabriel, 127, 128
XIVth Brigade, 165, 166, 167
Franco, Francisco, 90, 97, 156, 189, 200, 227
French Turn, 72
Friends of China Society, 205
Friends of the Mackenzie-Papineau Battalion: Cecil-Smith and, 200–1; CPC and, 121; establishment and activities, 119–20; gifts and care packages from, 133, 141, 153; information on Spanish events, 142, 285n69; rally by, 155, pl. 7; recruitment of volunteers and, 120, 267n71; repatriation of Canadian volunteers and, 189, 200
Friends of the Soviet Union, 37, 76–7, 79, 80, 94. See also *Soviet Russia Today* (magazine)
Fuentes de Ebro (Spain), 134–6, 275n22

Garcia, Hector, 167
Garland, Walter, 115, 117, 123, 130, 133
Garner, Hugh, 251n62
Gates, John (Israel Ragenstrich), 173, 291n26
Geiser, Carl, 167, 231n9
German Communist Party, 57, 69, 70, 89
Germany, 69, 97, 183, 210
Gibbons, Joseph, 160, 161
Globe (newspaper), 24, 45

Globe and Mail (newspaper), 94, 143, 189, 196
Goldberg, Mildred, 49, 57
Goldstein, Butch, 152, 153, 188
Golinsky, Mike, 34
Gonzalez, Ramon, 139, 280n11
Gordon, Leo, 161, 280n9
Gordon, Sydney, 273n158
Gordon, Toby, 43, 44, 50, 52, 54, 59, 94, 131
Gouge, Lilian (wife): Cecil-Smith departure and return from Spain, 105, 196; death of Cecil-Smith and, 228; *Eight Men Speak* (play) and, 50, 51; Great Depression and, 28; interest in China, 131–2, 205; lack of historical record for, 205; life in Toronto, 93–4; marriage to Cecil-Smith, 17, 18, 208; move to Montreal, 227; Norman Bethune and, 79, 94, 131–2, 205, 206–7, 208; Progressive Arts Club and, 32; Second World War and, 211; tuberculosis, 79; Workers' Theatre and, 43, 45
Gouzenko, Igor, 221n
Grabowski, Peter, 51
Great Depression, 27–8, 34, 65
Great War, 20–1, 86, 93
Greenwold, Cecil, 50
Griffin, Frederick, 74–5
Guizhou province (China), 9–12, 82–3, 224
Guthrie, Hugh, 47–8, 48–9

Hacket, Fred, 195
Haldane, Marcus Aurelius, 147, 281n15
Halliwell, Bill, 106, 110, 117, 143
Halton, Matthew, 192
Hannant, Larry, 206
Harvison, C.W., 222
Havelock, E.A., 102
Hayman, Arnolis and Rhoda, 83
health care, socialized, 79
Hearst, William Randolph, 259n33
Heart of Spain (documentary), 131, 227
Henderson, Colin, 224
Henderson, George, 224
Henderson, Ray, 190
Henderson, Rose, 99
Hicks, James, 46, 244n20
Higgins, Jim, 190, 194, 200–1, 201–2, 292n45
Hijar (Spain), 157, 163
Hill, Tom, 34, 35, 58
Himmelfarb, Lily, 22–3
Hitler, Adolph, 69, 97, 183
Hoar, Victor: on A.A. MacLeod, 258n29; on Caspe battle, 288n67; on Cecil-Smith, 5, 279n83; on command appointments at Teruel, 280n9, 280n11; on Fuentes de Ebro battle, 276n28; *The Mackenzie-Papineau Battalion* (book), 231n9, 289n1, 300n111; on repatriation of Canadian volunteers, 297n58, 298n62; Wellman and, 168, 289n1
Hogg, David: at Chefoo School, 234n52, pl. 1; debate on religious education at Chefoo, 18, 235n63; friendship with Cecil-Smith, 17, 18, 228, 234nn51–2; in journalism, 20; Progressive Arts Club and, 32; Workers' Theatre and, 43
Holiday Publications, 227
Hopkins, James K., 270n105
housing issues, 79
Howlett, T.F., 215
Hunt, Bob, pl. 2
Hunter, Peter, 32, 103–4, 121, 217, 303n1

Ibing, Hans, 263n12
Ibrarruri, Dolores, 100
Immigration Act, 238n40
Infantry Schools, 19
intellectualism, 32, 62, 168, 289n2
International Association of Machinists, 19
International Brigades: arrival in Spain and initial assignments, 108, 109, 110, 263n12; assessment of political potential, 185–6; basic training, 110–12; Canadian volunteers, 99, 108–9, 110, 262n6, 263n8, 268n76; commissars, 123–4, 144, 168–9, 185; composition of, 108, 118; discipline issues, 116–17, 266n52; establishment of, 99; journey to Spain, 105–7, 108; lack of Canadian leadership, 187–8; leadership structure and qualities, 111n, 113, 123; non-field duties, 117–18; numbering of battalions, 274n12; political education, 123–4, 143–4, 168–9; Pozorubio leadership schools, 114–16; recruitment for, 90, 100–1, 103–4; Red Army advisors, 114–15, 137–8, 277n40; repatriation of volunteers, 183, 184, 186, 189–90, 191–6, 294n76, 296n38, 297n49, 297n58, 298n62; shortcomings of, 116, 125; Spaniards in, 139, 173; weapons, 111–12. *See also* XVth Brigade; Spanish Civil War; *other specific brigades and battalions*
"The Internationale" (song), 21, 54, 70, 100, 198, 237n19, 247n63
International Literature. See *Literature of World Revolution* (magazine)
International Red Aid, 26
International Red Day, 21–3
Irvine, Robert W., 40, 46, 48, 88, 199, 202
Italy, 69, 89, 97

Japan, 69, 82, 87, 204–5, 254n46
Jarama Valley (Spain), 110, 116, 125, 126
Jardas, Edo, 98, 119, 123, 130, 143, 197, 267n66
John Brown Battery, 118
Jones, Thomas, 51–2

Kaplansky, Max, 56–7
Kardash, William, 135, 212
Kelly, Joseph, 105–6, 110, 118–19, 267n66
Kemp, V.A.M., 215
Kerr, Robert (Bob): background, 106; as CPC representative in Spain, 120, 142, 143; departure from Spain, 184; fighting in Spain, 110; Friends of the Mackenzie-Papineau Battalion and, 121, 133; internment during Second World War, 220; journey to Spain, 106; Mac-Paps formation and, 119, 139, 267n66; promotional use of image at rally, 155, pl. 7
King, Mackenzie, 72, 81, 97, 119, 189, 219, 221
Kingston Penitentiary, 45–9, 47n
Kleber, Emilio (Manfred Stern), 84, 99, 100
Klig, Meyer, 24–5, 65
Kostyk, Fred, 296n47
Krehm, William, 33, 118

Labor Party of Ontario, 19
Labor-Progressive Party, 221
Labor's Lost Love (play), 43
Landis, Arthur, 5, 270n99, 280n7, 280n9, 280n11, 283n44
Lapointe, Ernest, 101, 220
Latin America, 5–6, 231n9
Law, Oliver, 128, 130
Lawrence, Sam, 89

Lawson, William "Lon," 218
League for Social Reconstruction, 67
League of Nations, 184
Lecera (Spain), 157, 162–3
Letux (Spain), 157, 159, 160, 161
Liberal Party, 71. *See also* King, Mackenzie
Lincoln Battalion: in Brunete Offensive, 128, 129, 130; in Caspe battle, 165, 166, 167; composition of, 109, 184; in XVth Brigade, 134; in Fuentes de Ebro battle, 135; in Jarama Valley, 110, 116; leadership of, 109–10; lull before Aragon Offensive (the Retreats), 156, 157; numbering of, 274n12; in Segura de Los Baños, 152; in Sierra de Pandols, 177; in Teruel defence, 146, 148, 154
Literature of World Revolution (magazine), 40, 243n58
Liversedge, Ronald, 112, 263n8, 266n52, 267n66, 269n88, 276n24, 289n1
Livesay, Dorothy, 33, 44, 102, 240n16, 244n6
Long March, 83, 84
Love, Frank, 49–50, 54, 55
Lovestone, Jay, 61
Luce, Henry, 204
Lunacharsky, Anatoly, 61

MacBrien, James Howden, 40, 199
MacDonald, Jack, 22, 23, 24
machine guns, 112, 146
Mack, Henry, 165, 174, 175, 292n35
Mackenzie, Ian, 212, 217
Mackenzie-Papineau Battalion (Mac-Paps): Albalate retreat, 163; Aragon Offensive (the Retreats) preparations, 156–7, 158–9; in Argente defensive line, 145; assessment post-Aragon Offensive, 167; in Atalaya attack, 152–4, 155, 284n60; Azuara withdrawal during Aragon Offensive, 159–62; banner of, 141; Canadian support for, 119–20; at Caspe attack, 165–6, 288n67, 288n71; Cecil-Smith in, 135–7, 274n6, 275n21, 276n31; Cecil-Smith's support for volunteers, 5, 188, 192; Christmas celebration, 141; commissars, 168–9; composition of, 138–9, 173, 184; CPC and, 120–1; desire to defend Barcelona, 190–1, 296n45, 296n47; disciplinary issues while awaiting repatriation, 186–8; Dominion Day celebration, 172–3; in Ebro Offensive, 169, 174–7; formation of, 118–19, 122, 267n66; in Fuentes de Ebro battle, 134–6, 275n22, 276n28; health issues, 276n25; leadership of, 134, 135–6, 139, 173–4, 269n88, 276n24, 283n44; in Lecera attack, 162–3; in Lleida offensive, 170–1; mascot of, 192; move to Mas de las Matas, 140–1; move to Segura de Los Baños, 151–2; name of, 121–2, 134, 269n88; numbering of, 274n12; official history of, 201–2, 300n111; photograph, pl. 6; political education in, 169, 170; RCMP files on Canadian volunteers, 198–9; rear guard duty during Aragon Offensive, 164; repatriation and welcome back to Canada, 183, 184, 186, 189–90, 191–6, 197–8, 296n38, 297n49, 297n58, 298n62; Second World War and, 212, 304n8; in Sierra de Cavalls battles, 178–9; in Sierra de Pandols battles, 177–8;

in Teruel defence, 146–51, 280n11, 283n44; training and discipline, 139–41; veterans *Fiesta Espagnol* gathering, 227; withdrawal to Barcelona, 188–9. *See also* Friends of the Mackenzie-Papineau Battalion
MacLeod, A.A.: in Canadian League Against War and Fascism (later League for Peace and Democracy), 89, 189; in Committee to Aid Spanish Democracy, 99; at Committee to Aid Spanish Refugees fundraiser, 227; Mac-Paps formation and, 122; repatriation of Canadian volunteers and, 189–90, 191; visits to Spain, 98, 122, 189–90, 258n29, 269n88; Ward 3 communist activity with Cecil-Smith and Benson, 202
MacLeod, Pegi Nicol, 94
MacNicol, John Ritchie, 237n19
Madrid (Spain), 99, 127, 200, 209
Madrigueras, International Brigades base, 116, 117, 118
Mail and Empire (newspaper), 20, 22, 31, 78, 94, 236n3, 239n1
Makela, Niilo: in Aragon Offensive (the Retreats), 161, 164; in Caspe battle, 165; death of, 165, 288n67; friendship with Cecil-Smith, 136; in Fuentes de Ebro battle, 135; invitation to return to Canada, 170; in Mac-Paps leadership, 139, 143, 151, 276n24, 284n56; photograph, pl. 6; promotional use of image, 155, 197, pl. 7; in Segura de Los Baños battles, 153, 154; in Teruel defence, 147, 150
Mann, Dan, 50, 56
Marineros (Spanish naval infantry), 146, 146n, 149, 150, 154, 285n63
Markowicz, Mirko, 116–17, 119, 122, 123, 125, 126, 130, 137, 270n100
Marty, André, 100
Marx, Karl, 26, 62, 63, 67; *The Communist Manifesto* (with Engels), 71
Masses (magazine): Cecil-Smith and, 4, 49, 242n52; content and purpose, 38–9; debate over art's role in, 59–62; *Eight Men Speak* (play) and, 57, 58; end of, 64; on Workers' Theatre festival, 64; *Young Worker* promotion of, 243n54
Mates, David, 124, 270n100
Matthews, Bill, 164, 284n48
May Day parades, 95–6
McCallum, Thomas, 190, 197–8
McElligott, Paddy, 288n67
McNaughton, Andrew, 215
Meerut (mass recitation), 43
Men's Unemployed Council, 50
Merino, Pedro Mateo, 173
Merriman, Robert Hale: in Aragon Offensive (the Retreats), 156, 157, 158, 160, 164; background, 109–10; on Cecil-Smith, 115, 116, 134, 270n101, 275n21; death of, 173; on discipline, 117, 266n52; as XVth Brigade chief of staff, 134; in Jarama Valley battles, 110; on Mac-Paps' name, 122, 269n88; Markowicz and, 116; on non-field duties, 117; as Pozorubio leadership camp commander, 114; on Red Army advisors, 114; on Thompson, 276n26; Washington Battalion and, 117, 125; on weapons, 264n24
Mexicans, 114, 162, 228, 265n36
Meyer, Henry, 190–1, 296n45
Mid-West Clarion (newspaper), 203, 212

military service: confusion about, 5; Non-Permanent Active Militia, Canadian Engineers, 16–17, 16n, 19, 20; Royal Canadian Engineers, 2nd Field Company, 213–14, 215–16, 219, 304n19, 305n27, 305n29; Shanghai Volunteer Corps, 14–15, 234n36. *See also* Cecil-Smith, Edward, in Spanish Civil War
Miller, Alec, 106, 110, 151, 197, 220, 284n48
Miller, Emil, 35
missionaries, in China, 9–12, 82–4
Mitchell, Humphrey, 78
Modesto, Juan, 151, 283nn43–4
Mola, Emilio, 95, 96
Montreal Star, 96, 104, 258n15
Morris, Leslie, 94, 96, 121, 142, 202
Munro, Peter, 76
Murray, Charles, 220
Mussolini, Benito, 69, 97
Myers, Nicholas, 175, 189, 296n47

Nahanchuk, Ivan John, 139, 284n48
Negrin, Juan, 168, 183
Nelson, Steve, 124
Neure, Bill, 135, 276n24
New Commonwealth (newspaper), 67, 68
New Deal, 65
New Frontier (magazine), 102
New York Times, 143
Non-Permanent Active Militia: Canadian Engineers, 16–17, 16n, 19, 20. *See also* 2nd Field Company, Royal Canadian Engineers
North, Joseph, 292n35
Nursey, William, 23, 50, 51, 55, 56

O'Kelly, Andrew, 184, 190
Olsen, Stan, 17
143rd Brigade, 136
120th Brigade, 134
Ormond, D.M., 46, 48
Orr, W.A., 55–6
Orwell, George: *Homage to Catalonia*, 118
Ottawa Citizen, 143

pacifism, 20–1, 86, 93
Park, Libby, 208
Partido Obrero de Unificacion Marxista (POUM), 117–18
Petrou, Michael, 3, 262nn5–6, 296n47
Phillips, Paul, 103–4, 121
Pius XI (pope), 259n33
Poirier, François, 119, 121, 267n66
police courts, 25. *See also* Royal Canadian Mounted Police (RCMP); Toronto police
Popovich, Matthew, 34, 58
Popular Front strategy, 59, 70–1, 73, 94, 95, 96, 99
POUM (*Partido Obrero de Unificacion Marxista*), 117–18
Pozorubio leadership schools, 114–16
Preston, Paul, 104
Price, Herbert, 55
prisons: advocacy by A.E. Smith, 57; Kingston Penitentiary riots, 45–9; *The Royal Commission Report on Penal Reform in Canada*, 47n
Progressive Arts Club: Cecil-Smith and, 38, 49; celebration for Tim Buck's release from prison, 69–70; end of, 94; establishment, membership, and purpose, 31–3, 239n4; as front for CPC, 37; impact of, 59; Kingston Penitentiary riots and, 48; *Masses* (magazine), 38–9; student recruitment by, 63; Workers' Theatre and, 42. See also

Eight Men Speak (play); *Masses* (magazine); Workers' Theatre

Quebec, 69, 222, 259n33, 261n58, 268n76
Queen's Park (Toronto), Battles of, 22–5

Raily, Jim (Ivan Ralloff), 101, 160, 172
Rakosi Battalion, 166
Rea, Fred, 196, 197
Reconstruction Party, 71
Red Ally (Cecil-Smith), 222–3
Red Army (China), 82, 83, 84, 205
Red Army (Soviet Union), 88, 114–15, 137–8, 222, 266n52, 277n40
Red Squad, 23, 50, 51, 56, 57, 64. *See also* Toronto police
Renn, Ludwig, 57
the Retreats. *See* Aragon Offensive
revolution, 37–8
Reynolds, Mac, 231n9
Richardson, T., 60
Roberts, Ida White (mother of Cecil-Smith): background, 9; missionary work in China, 9–10, 11–12, 37; move to Toronto, 15, 16; relations with Cecil-Smith, 18, 81; Second World War and death, 224
Roca, Pedro, 174, 175
Rogers, Frank, 153, 169–70, 171, 185–6, 197, 204, 284n58, pl. 9
Rolfe, Edwin, 270n99
Roosevelt, Franklin Delano, 65
Rossett, Thomas, 76
Royal Canadian Engineers: 2nd Field Company, 5, 213–14, 215–16, 219, 304n19, 305n27, 305n29. *See also* Non-Permanent Active Militia
Royal Canadian Mounted Police (RCMP): at Canadian League Against War and Fascism, 88; Canadian Seamen's Union and, 217, 218–19, 306n42; Cecil-Smith's discharge from army and, 306n33; file on Cecil-Smith, 40–1, 46, 144, 222, 227, 279n85; files on Canadian volunteers, 198–9; at interview of visitors to Soviet Union, 252n13; military infiltration concerns by communists, 212–13, 215, 305n27; monitoring of left-wing publications, 245n26; at Workers' Theatre festival, 64
Royal Commission Report on Penal Reform in Canada (Archambault Report), 47n
Rushton, Harry, 119, 179, 267n66
Ryan, Frank: *The Book of the XVth Brigade*, 5
Ryan, Larry, 119
Ryan, Oscar: on art and politics, 59; Cecil-Smith and, 25, 35, 228; *Eight Men Speak* (play) and, 49–50, 52, 53, 54, 55, 57, pl. 3; on J.S. Woodsworth, 68; Progressive Arts Club and, 31–2; pseudonym of, 44, 240n7; at Queen's Park battle, 23; on religion, 26; on Soviet-style cultural production, 39–40; on Spanish Civil War, 97; student engagement by, 63; Workers' Theatre and, 43; writings by, 44
Ryerson, Stanley, 33, 61–2, 63, 102, 121–2; *1837: The Birth of Canadian Democracy*, 121–2; *War in the East*, 44, 244n7

Salsberg, J.B., 120
Santador, Juan Ruiz, 178
Schoenberg, Harry, 136, 139, 149, pl. 6, pl. 9
Schrenzel, Isadore "Izzie," 135

Searchlight (CSU newsletter), 220, 224, 307n59
2nd Field Company, Royal Canadian Engineers, 5, 213–14, 215–16, 219, 304n19, 305n27, 305n29. *See also* Non-Permanent Active Militia
Second Spanish Republic, 89–90. *See also* Spanish Civil War
Second World War: ban on labour-socialist groups, 219–20; beginning of, 211; Canadian contributions, 219; Canadian Seamen's Union strike, 217–19; Cecil-Smith's enlistment and discharge, 211–12, 213–14, 215–16, 305n29, 306n33; Cecil-Smith's writings on Soviet Union, 221–3; China during, 224; Comintern on, 214, 216, 221; CPC on, 211, 214, 220–1; Mac-Paps proposed for, 212, 304n8; military infiltration by communist concerns, 212–13, 215, 305n27; progression of, 223–4; 2nd Field Company, Royal Canadian Engineers, 213–14, 215–16, 219, 304n19, 305n27
Segura de Los Baños (Spain), 152–4, 155, 284n60
Shanghai, 14–15
Shanghai Volunteer Corps, 14–15, 234n36
Sierra de Cavalls (Spain), 178–9
Sierra de Pandols (Spain), 177–8, 179, 294n76, pl. 9
Sinclair, David, 220, 224, 307n59
Sixth of February Battalion, 125, 127, 128, 134
Skelton, O.D., 189–90, 199
Slobodna Misao (newspaper), 144
Smith, A.E., 22, 26, 27, 57, 58, 67, 70–1, 99
Smith, Bill (son of Cecil-Smith), 225, 227–8, 234n36, 293n72
Smith, R.J., 215, 305n29
Smith, Stewart: *Daily Clarion* and, 96, 204; on *Eight Men Speak* (play), 55; in Friends of the Mackenzie-Papineau Battalion, 121; in Queen's Park battle, 24; at rally for Spanish Civil War, 100; *Socialism and the CCF* (as G. Pierce), 66, 67; at welcome for Canadian returnees, 197, 198; *Worker* and, 34
Smrcka, *Capitan*, 179
Snow, Edgar: *Red Star over China*, 131–2
Social Credit Party, 71, 72
social gospel, 27
Socialist Party of America, 123, 161
Socialist Party of Canada, 89
Sommerville, Gordon K., 35, 36
South America, 5–6, 231n9
Southgate, Jimmy, 299n95
Soviet Russia Today (magazine): Canadian Labor Defense League and, 26; Cecil-Smith and, 4, 76–7; Cecil-Smith on international situation, 86; on embargoes against Soviet Union, 80; on Japan, 254n46; purpose of, 77, 80; on Soviet Union and Red Army, 77–9, 88, 266n52; on working class, 89
Soviet-style cultural production, 39–40. *See also* Workers' Theatre
Soviet Union: building broad support for, 80; Cecil-Smith advocacy for, 74, 75–6, 78, 209, 221–3; Chinese Communist Party and, 84; conflicting information on, 74–5; defence by CPC, 36, 75; embargoes against, 80–1; health care in, 79; non-aggression pact with Germany, 210, 221; Red Army advisors in International Brigades, 114–15, 137–8, 277n40; on Second

World War, 214, 216, 221; Spanish Civil War contributions, 97; spying in North America, 221n; World Congress Against War and Fascism and, 86–7; world peace role, 86–8. *See also* Comintern
Spain: Second Spanish Republic, 89–90
Spanish Civil War: atrocities in, 104–5; author's interest in, 3; beginning of, 94–5, 96–7; Canadian responses, 97–100; CPC and, 103–4, 109, 130–1, 142–3, 296n38; end of, 200; international responses, 97, 259n33; news reports on, 95, 104, 261n58; scholarship on Canadian involvement, 231n9. *See also* Cecil-Smith, Edward, in Spanish Civil War; XVth Brigade; International Brigades; *other specific brigades and battalions*
Spence, Ben, 99
Spry, Graham, 67–8, 89, 99
Stalin, Joseph, 71, 101, 221
Standard Theatre, 51, 55
Stanton, H.J., 48
Starr, J.R.L., 56
Stern, Manfred (Emilio Kleber), 84, 99, 100
Stewart, Douglas, 119, 120
Stewart, Roderick and Sharon: *Phoenix*, 206
Student League, 56–7, 63
Sullivan, Pat, 218, 220
Sun Yat-sen, 14
Sydney, William, 80, 88, 266n52
Szalway, Miklos (Chapiev), 128, 272n128

Tarazona de la Mancha, International Brigades base, 117, 122, 134, 136, 274n6
Tattler (tabloid), 203
Taylor, Jack (Muni Erlick): on Atalaya attack, 284n60; departure from Spain, 184; and invitation for Cecil-Smith and Niilo Makela to return to Canada, 170, 171, 290n14; meeting with Cecil-Smith in Spain, 154, 155; on Niilo Makela, 284n56; roles in Spain, 121, 154; welcome for Canadian returnees, 194–5
Taylor, Marian and Isabel, 17
Teruel (Spain), 141, 145–51, 156, 280n7, 280n9, 280n11
Thaelmann Brigade (XIth Brigade), 109, 118, 134, 146, 147–9, 173, 174, 263n12
theatre, Soviet-style, 39–40. *See also* Workers' Theatre
Theatre of Action, 94, 131
Third Period doctrine, 39, 59, 62, 70, 94
XIIIth Brigade (Dombrowski Brigade), 109, 162–3, 173, 174, 176
35th Division, Spanish Republican Army, 134, 146, 156–7, 173, 174, 176–7
Thomas, George Albert, 201
Thomas, Jack, 151, 158, 280n9
Thomas, Reginald W., 194–5, 197
Thompson, Robert, 134, 136, 137, 275n22, 276n24, 276n26, 276n28, 276n31
Toronto Bible College, 15, 16
Toronto police: *Eight Men Speak* (play) and, 50–1, 55, 56, 57; Queen's Park battle and, 23–4; strike by, 65; at Workers' Theatre festival, 64
Toronto Star: Cecil-Smith at, 31, 203, 239n1; on Cecil-Smith discharge from army, 306n33; on Cecil-Smith

in Spain, 143; on *Eight Men Speak* (play), 54, 56; on repatriation of Canadian volunteers, 189, 192, 196; on Spanish Civil War, 97, 105, 267n71
Trolove, Robert Leaconsfield (Benson), 202, 301n115, 301n117
Trotskyists, 33, 72, 86, 89, 103, 118, 123, 256n72
tuberculosis, 28, 79
XIIth Brigade, 167, 263n12
24th Battalion (*Voluntario 24*): in Aragon Offensive (the Retreats), 157, 158–9, 165; in Brunete Offensive, 128; composition of, 125; in Fuentes de Ebro battle, 134; leadership of, 127; numbering of, 274n12; in Sierra de Pandols, 177; in Teruel defence, 146
27th Division, Spanish Republican Army, 177

Ukrainian Labor News, 35
United States of America, 65, 80, 86, 216
Unity (mass chant), 44

Valentine, Alec, 223, 308n74
Valledor, José, 173, pl. 8
Vapaus (newspaper), 35
Varsity (student newspaper), 54, 55, 56, 60, 63
VOKS (All-Union Society for Cultural Relations with Foreign Countries), 40
Volunteer for Liberty (newsletter), 138–9, 183
Voros, Sandor, 293n68

Walter, General (Karol Swierczewski), 134, 140, 161, 173
War in the East (Ryerson), 44, 244n7
Washington Battalion, 117, 118, 122–3, 124–5, 126, 127, 128–30, 270n99
Watts, Myrtle Eugenia (Jim/Jean): on art and politics, 59; Canadian Committee to Aid Spanish Refugees and, 200; on David Anderson, 270n104; *Eight Men Speak* (play) and, 49, 50, 51; *New Frontier* and, 102; plays by, 94, 131; Progressive Arts Club and, 33; in Spain as reporter, 101, 142; Student League and, 63; Workers' Theatre and, 43
weapons, 111–12
Weekly Clarion (newspaper), 203, 204–5, 210, 213, 214
Weir, Emily, 24
Weissman, Irving, 289n76, 295n21
Wellman, Saul: in Aragon Offensive (the Retreats), 156, 167; Azuara withdrawal and, 161–2; conflict with Cecil-Smith, 168; in Mac-Paps leadership, 139; Taylor's visit and, 154; in Teruel defence, 149–50, 151, 283n44; Victor Hoar and, 168, 289n1
White, J. Francis, 77–8
Whitfield, Frank, 276n24
Wickman, Morris Henry, 124, 130, 270n99
Wild, Sam, 165, 166, 167
Winnipeg General Strike, 15
Winnipeg Workers' Theatre, 57–8
Witczak, Ignacy, 184, 263n12
Wolff, Milt, 291n26
Women's International League for Peace and Freedom, 89
Wood, Stuart, 199, 222
Woodsworth, J.S., 68, 72, 74
Woodsworth, Kenneth, 89

Worker (newspaper): Cecil-Smith at, 4, 34–5, 65, 72, 241n30, pl. 2; on Cecil-Smith blacklisted from newspapers, 31; CPC ban and, 37; end of, 94; on end of *Masses*, 64; on Japan, 254n46; on Kingston Penitentiary, 47; Lilian Gouge and, 205; on Soviet Union, 75; on Tim Buck's speech upon release from prison, 70; on Workers' Theatre festival, 64; on working class, 89
Workers' Sporting Association, 69
Workers' Symphony Orchestra, 63
Workers' Theatre, 33, 42–5, 49, 63–4, 240n15. See also *Eight Men Speak* (play)
Workers' Unity League, 32, 37, 94
World Congress Against War and Fascism, 86. *See also* Canadian League Against War and Fascism
Writers' Group, 33, 43–4, 49, 62

Yanovsky, Avrom, 50
Young Communist League, 109, 186, 202, 219, 268n75
Young Worker (magazine), 60, 243n54

Zaragoza (Spain), 134, 136
Zhou Xizheng, 82
Zuehlke, Mark, 5
Zynchuk, Nick, 44, 51
"Zynchuk's Funeral" (Livesay), 44, 244n6